Rural Financial Markets in Developing Countries

Their Use and Abuse

EDI Series in Economic Development

Rural Financial Markets in Developing Countries

Their Use and Abuse

Edited by
J. D. Von Pischke
Dale W Adams
Gordon Donald

PUBLISHED FOR
THE ECONOMIC DEVELOPMENT INSTITUTE
OF THE WORLD BANK
The Johns Hopkins University Press
Baltimore and London

First printing June 1983

Manufactured in the United States of America.

The Johns Hopkins University Press
Baltimore, Maryland 21218, U.S.A.

The views and interpretations in this book are the authors' and should not be attributed to the World Bank, to its affiliated organizations, or to any individual acting in their behalf, or to the U.S. Agency for International Development, which has funded research in rural finance at the Ohio State University.

Editor Jane H. Carroll
Figures S. A. D. Subasinghe
Book design Brian J. Svikhart
Binding design Joyce C. Eisen

Library of Congress Cataloging in Publication Data

Main entry under title:

Rural financial markets in developing countries.

(EDI series in economic development)
Includes bibliographies.
1. Agricultural credit—Addresses, essays, lectures.
I. Von Pischke, J. D. II. Adams, Dale W III. Donald, Gordon. IV. Series.
HD1439.R87 1983 332.7'1 83-8406
ISBN 0-8018-3074-5

Contents

Contributors

Dale W Adams	*Professor of Agricultural Economics, The Ohio State University, U.S.A.*
R. O. Adegboye	*Professor of Agricultural Economics, University of Ibaden, Nigeria*
D. Brian Argyle	*Credit Adviser, The World Bank*
Chester B. Baker	*Professor of Agricultural Economics, University of Illinois, U.S.A.*
David Bathrick	*Economist, U.S. Agency for International Development*
Vinay K. Bhargava	*Senior Financial Analyst, The World Bank*
V. V. Bhatt	*Senior Lecturer, The Economic Development Institute, The World Bank*
Anthony Bottomley	*Professor of Economics, Bradford University, Bradford, England*
F. J. A. Bouman	*Senior Lecturer, Agricultural University, The Netherlands*
Compton Bourne	*Professor of Economics, University of the West Indies, Trinidad*
Cristina C. David	*Research Fellow, Philippine Institute of Development Studies*
Virginia DeLancey	*Institute of International Studies and Department of Economics, University of South Carolina, U.S.A.*
B. M. Desai	*Associate Professor, Centre for Management in Agriculture, Indian Institute of Management, Ahmedabad*
Robert F. Emery	*Former Staff Member, Board of Governors of the Federal Reserve System, U.S.A.*
G. Gomez Casco	*Consultant, Puerto Rico*
Claudio Gonzalez-Vega	*Professor of Economics, University of Costa Rica and Autonomous University of Central America, both in San José*
Douglas Graham	*Professor of Agricultural Economics, The Ohio State University, U.S.A.*

G. J. B. Green — *General Manager's Assistant, Barclays Bank International, London*

John G. Gurley — *Professor of Economics, Stanford University, U.S.A.*

Barbara Harriss — *Economist, London School of Hygiene and Tropical Medicine*

C. J. Howse — *Field Director for South and Central Africa, OXFAM, Oxford, England*

Hans F. Illy — *Arnold Bergstraesser Institute, Freiburg, Federal Republic of Germany*

Reed J. Irvine — *Former Staff Member, Board of Governors of the Federal Reserve System, U.S.A.*

Omotunde E. G. Johnson — *Senior Economist, International Monetary Fund*

Edward J. Kane — *Professor of Banking and Monetary Economics, The Ohio State University, U.S.A.*

Yuzuru Kato — *Professor of Agricultural Economics, Faculty of Agriculture, University of Tokyo*

Dong Hi Kim — *Director of Planning, Ministry of Agriculture, Republic of Korea*

Jerry R. Ladman — *Professor of Economics and Director, Center for Latin American Studies, Arizona State University, U.S.A.*

Tae Young Lee — *Economist, National Agricultural Economics Research Institute, Seoul, Republic of Korea*

Warren F. Lee — *Professor of Agricultural Economics, The Ohio State University, U.S.A.*

Millard Long — *Operations Adviser, The World Bank*

Arnaldo Mauri — *Director, Institute of Economics, University of Milan, and Adviser, Italian Savings Banks Association and Finafrica*

Richard L. Meyer — *Professor of Agricultural Economics and Director of International Programs, The Ohio State University, U.S.A.*

Marvin P. Miracle — *Consultant, Aptos, California, U.S.A.*

Marcia L. Ong — *Economist, Ontario Ministry of Health, Canada*

Hugh T. Patrick	*Professor of Economics, Yale University, U.S.A.*
David H. Penny	*Professor of Economics, Australian National University, Canberra*
Edward John Ray	*Professor of Economics, The Ohio State University, U.S.A.*
Bruce L. Robert, Jr.	*Research Scholar, Madison, Wisconsin, U.S.A.*
J. Jesus Romero Chavez	*Chief Executive, Comisión del Plan Nacional Hidraulico, Mexico*
Nimal Sanderatne	*Deputy Director of Statistics, Central Bank of Ceylon, Colombo, Sri Lanka*
João Sayad	*Professor of Economics, São Paulo University, Brazil*
Walter Schaefer-Kehnert	*Formerly with The World Bank*
Edward S. Shaw	*Emeritus Professor of Economics, Stanford University, U.S.A.*
Gerardo P. Sicat	*Chairman, Philippine National Bank*
I. J. Singh	*Senior Economist, The World Bank*
Karam Singh	*Professor of Agricultural Economics, Punjab Agricultural University, Ludhiana, India*
Ronald L. Tinnermeier	*Professor of Economics, Colorado State University, U.S.A.*
Robert C. Vogel	*Professor of Economics, Syracuse University, U.S.A.*
J. D. Von Pischke	*Senior Financial Analyst, The World Bank*
Joachim von Stockhausen	*Consultant, Federal Republic of Germany*
R. J. G. Wells	*Lecturer in Economics, University of Malaya, Kuala Lumpur, Malaysia*
Clifton R. Wharton, Jr.	*President, New York State University System, U.S.A.*
Martin W. Wilmington	*Deceased. Former Professor of Social Science, Pace College, New York, U.S.A.*
B. J. Youngjohns	*Deceased. Former Adviser on Co-operatives, British Ministry of Overseas Development*

Foreword

This collection of readings highlights facets of rural financial markets that have often been neglected in discussions of agricultural credit in developing countries. It moves beyond a narrow concern with the simple provision of credit to a broad consideration of the performance of rural financial markets and of ways to improve the quality and range of financial services for low-income farmers. It reflects new thinking on the design, administration, evaluation, and policy framework of rural finance and credit programs in developing countries.

This volume is the first comprehensive collection of readings on rural finance to be published. It is also the first major compendium on rural credit since the U.S. Agency for International Development's *Spring Review of Small Farmer Credit* in 1973. The results of the *Spring Review* were summarized in *Credit for Small Farmers in Developing Countries* (Boulder, Colo.: Westview, 1976) by Gordon Donald, one of the editors of this volume.

This compilation grew out of readings collected since 1976 for the Rural Credit Projects Courses offered by the Economic Development Institute (EDI) at the World Bank under the direction of Walter Schaefer-Kehnert. Both J. D. Von Pischke and Dale W Adams participated in these courses as lecturers. As work progressed, with bibliographic assistance from Mr. Adams's department at Ohio State University, it became apparent that a most interesting body of knowledge had been collected. Much of this literature was not readily available to those working on rural credit problems in developing countries. The director of the EDI at that time, Raymond Frost, felt the readings would be of such widespread interest that he suggested they be edited to form a fully articulated volume.

I know the reader will find these selections as fresh and thought-provoking as have the participants in our courses and the EDI staff.

J. PRICE GITTINGER
Coordinator, Training Materials and Publications
Economic Development Institute

PART I

CHANGING PERCEPTIONS OF RURAL FINANCIAL MARKETS

Until recently the use of agricultural credit as a developmental tool seemed clear and straightforward. Most concerned people believed that increases in the volume of cheap credit were necessary to boost agricultural production, and that the rural poor could be brought into the mainstream of development through supervised credit programs. It seemed that certain ideal types of rural credit institutions offered the promise of meeting farmers' "credit needs," and that experience in the industrialized countries with cooperatives and specialized agricultural finance institutions could be effectively transplanted to low-income countries.

These traditional views—stated in Louis Tardy's *Report on Systems of Agricultural Credit and Insurance* published by the League of Nations in 1938—are still held by many people concerned with rural credit design and operation. These approaches have been applied to developing countries since the early part of this century. India's Cooperative Credit Societies Act of 1904, based on the work of Frederick Nicholson, and British colonial efforts to establish Malays as cash-cropping freeholders are well-documented early examples. The antecedents of these views predate the 1800s. They include British responses to rural indebtedness in India and the use of credit in Spanish efforts to establish tobacco as an export crop in the Philippines.

Those having these traditional views of rural credit had a broad stage for their activities in the evolution of economic development after

World War II. Keynesian economic doctrine provided a justification for a large economic role for governments, and economic planning appeared to be a promising tool. The Marshall Plan's successes were interpreted as evidence that large-scale foreign assistance for investment could bring progress.

Against this general background for modern development assistance, credit programs provide several specifically attractive features. One is their appearance of offering fast relief for complex situations and old and difficult problems: it is much easier to expand the supply of loans than it is to undertake land reform, get agricultural technology adopted, build rural roads, or install new irrigation and drainage systems. Some policy makers believe cheap credit can compensate farmers for the reduction in their income caused by economic policies such as price controls and overvalued exchange rates. Increasing the supply of agricultural credit also appeals to the widespread belief that many farmers are unable to adopt profitable new technologies unless they have loans. Governments interested in increasing agricultural output by promoting the use of fertilizer, improved seeds, and other modern inputs are attracted by the potential of credit to accelerate the adoption of technologies.

Negative views about informal credit extended by traders or moneylenders (or by friends and relatives) underlie the emphasis on developing formal lending institutions. Informal finance is often thought to be antidevelopmental, exploitive, geared to consumption rather than investment behavior, and incapable of expanding to provide an appropriate volume and range of financial services. Many people believe that moneylenders exploit rural households, and that inexpensive formal credit enables farmers to escape their "evil" grasp.

In short, until recently all signs pointed toward supplying rural credit through government institutions to help the poor, increase crop yields, and displace or dilute the financial strength of local rural power structures. There was a possibility of subsidizing this credit to compensate for policies depressing farm incomes and to make it more attractive to the poor, and external financial assistance was often available to support these endeavors and the institutions required for their implementation.

Postwar Initiatives

Early concern for rural credit in modern development was manifested in the All-India Rural Credit Survey begun in 1951 and the recommendations that followed, and at an international conference on agricultural and cooperative credit held in Berkeley, California, in 1952. In the early 1950s a predecessor of the U.S. Agency for International Development (AID) began a series of farm credit projects, much expanded in the 1960s, that marked the start of commitments to this activity by donor agencies and international lending institutions. The Inter-American Development Bank has been active in this field, and the World Bank began adding massively to the flow of external resources for this purpose in the 1970s. These commitments have greatly expanded the supply of loanable funds at the disposal of institutions implementing credit projects, some of which have been established or reoriented as a result of donor participation. The Food and Agriculture Organization (FAO) of the United Nations has promoted rural credit through technical assistance, studies, publications, seminars, and a world conference on agricultural credit in developing countries in 1975. It has also helped establish regional associations of agricultural credit institutions.

The theoretical basis for intervention through the financial system for the sake of development was enhanced by Hugh T. Patrick in a 1966 article describing the advantages and potential of "supply-leading" finance (see chapter 5 below). Patrick suggested the establishment of financial institutions and the provision of loanable funds, in advance of established demand, as a means of stimulating the pace of investment and economic activity. These initiatives were viewed as being relatively low cost and simple to implement. Patrick's work was followed by increased government involvement in rural credit systems and in donor support for these initiatives. In the early 1970s the "world food crisis" and the mounting concern for involving the poor in economic development added to the attractiveness of supplying rural credit through government institutions, to some extent with external assistance.

Questioning of Premises

Criticisms of how rural credit programs were designed and evolved followed shortly. David Penny expressed grave reservations about government credit programs in 1968, on the basis of his observations of small-farmer behavior in Indonesia (see chapter 6 below). Dale Adams ("Agricultural Credit in Latin America: A Critical Review of External Funding Policy," *American Journal of Agricultural Economics*, vol. 53, no. 2, May 1971, pp. 163–72) suggested that the objectives of externally funded rural credit programs in Latin America were frustrated by faulty interest rate policies, and he seriously questioned the basic assumptions about finance on which these projects were based.

Since these first stones were cast, the critical literature on rural credit and finance has rapidly expanded. AID has provided catalytic resources for research and technical assistance, largely with Ohio State University as principal contractor. The work has touched more than forty developing countries and included field research in about fifteen of these countries. AID has also funded conferences over a decade in more than twenty countries. It would be unfair to ascribe all significant intellectual developments in the field to AID's initiatives, but it is probably fair to conclude that AID, through contracts with Ohio State University, set the agenda.

The first burst of assessment and introspection came with the *Spring Review of Small Farmer Credit* (Washington, D.C.: AID, 1972–73). This twenty-volume report containing country studies and academic papers, and its summary by Gordon Donald (*Credit for Small Farmers in Developing Countries*, Boulder, Colo., Westview, 1976) represented the definitive reference work throughout the 1970s, while the World Bank's 1975 policy paper on agricultural credit provided the benchmark for application. During that period many of those studying rural finance found a new perspective in works on the role of finance in development by Gurley, Shaw, Goldsmith, McKinnon (see Part II, Recommendations for Further Reading), and Patrick (chapter 5 below), which was to some extent reflected in the Bank's approach. These writers, who deal hardly at all with rural credit, inspired much of the critical literature that has appeared since the mid-1970s. The nub of the debate is the difference between viewing finance as a process of intermediation rather than as a productive input. Related issues are the desirability of controls and direct intervention in contrast to incentives and indirect regulation, and the role and importance of interest rates.

To present their case, critics of conventional agricultural credit projects, practices, and policies have developed concepts and perspectives that require explanation. One central concept is that of the rural financial market.

What Is a Rural Financial Market?

A rural financial market (RFM) consists of relationships between buyers and sellers of financial assets who are active in rural economies. These relationships are based on transactions that include borrowing, lending, and transfers of ownership of financial assets. Financial assets consist of debt claims and ownership claims. Debt claims are promises to pay. Examples include verbal promises or scraps of paper signed by a thumbprint, as well as more formal evidence of indebtedness by individuals, and deposit accounts that are debt claims on banks. Ownership claims give the holder rights of access, use, or control; cooperative shares are a common example of this type of rural financial asset.

RFMs include informal-sector intermediaries, formal institutions, and private borrowing and lending not involving intermediaries. Financial markets are often characterized by intermediaries between savers and borrowers: banks, government credit institutions, and cooperative savings and loan operations. These organizations are only a part of the market, however. They would not be able to provide their services, linking buyers and sellers of financial assets, unless there was a demand for intermediation from the rural individuals, households, and the farm and nonfarm enterprises that make up the market.

Intermediation occurs when financial claims provided from the savings of individuals or firms are recycled by third parties to others who seek command over resources by borrowing or by selling ownership claims. Intermediation permits the transfer of these claims through time and space, and intermediaries generally pool funds from savers and disaggregate them among borrowers.

This collection of readings does not fully live up to its title as an exposition of all aspects of rural financial markets; it gives too much attention to farm credit. The literature on farm credit is much more extensive than the literature on financing nonfarm rural firms or on rural savings and finance in general. This volume does illustrate, however, new views that stress examination of rural financial transactions within financial markets. Agricultural credit has traditionally been viewed as having more to do with agriculture than with finance, but this perception is changing.

Examination of farm credit programs and institutions has led some development economists to a broader view of rural finance. More attention is being given to financial markets in rural areas, to their performance, structure, institutions, operations, costs, and the nature of their services to rural people. The concept of the RFM has been developed from the bottom up and constitutes a theoretical construct for dealing with issues arising from the performance of farm credit projects.

The Rural Financial Market Perspective

The RFM concept is useful because a large family of problems resides in this corner of finance, often in extreme form. Many rural financial markets have the same sorts of problems, as indicated by the range of countries covered in this book and by the diversity of nationalities of the authors. RFMs have been widely criticized for contributing to income disparities and resource misallocation, for failing to provide medium- and long-term credit, and for being used as political tools.

Despite important differences in the types of institutions active in these markets, the operating assumptions and policies are surprisingly uniform. Specialized farm credit institutions have been created to channel funds from official sources and to address the perceived shortage of credit for development investment. The operations of formal financial institutions in these markets are typically heavily regulated, with controls that keep interest rates low. Partly as a consequence of such interest rate policies, these institutions often reach only small segments of the rural population, such as cattle producers or coffee growers, and provide only a narrow range of financial services.

When RFMS are small and involve relatively few people, it may not appear important to resolve the problems outlined here or to test different theories. With increases in rural production, marketed output, and specialization, however, a greater volume of financial intermediation is required for efficient production and trade; poorly functioning financial markets could act as a serious brake on development. The potential for good performance is seen in the limited number of rural financial market success stories. Success has generally occurred where some emphasis was placed on savings rather than on lending alone, but it has sometimes been found in cases where relatively small amounts have been loaned and social and institutional structures supported good repayment by borrowers.

The Debate This Book Addresses

The purpose of this book is to bring together essays on rural finance written by critics of the conventional views. It also includes important articles by writers who have not been deeply involved in the clash between the critical and the traditional views, but whose observations and analyses have fueled the debate.

Most of the readings are drawn from literature in English that has appeared over the past twenty-five years. Some articles were specifically commissioned for the book to fill gaps in the literature or to provide summaries of unpublished research. Problem identification and issue clarification are the major emphases of this collection. Some analysis is also provided, and the concept of the rural financial market is explored. The thread that runs throughout is that traditional views of rural credit and finance are not very helpful in identifying measures to improve rural finance. Conventional attempts by governments and developers to use rural financial markets often result in abuse when the premises of intervention are false.

Contrasts between the emerging perspective and traditional views can be summarized by a series of statements, given below, pertaining to the nature of finance and financial transactions at the levels of households, nonfarm rural firms, rural financial markets, and national policy.

Issues at the Farm and Local Level

CREDIT AND TECHNOLOGY. A cornerstone of many credit programs is an assumption that farmers need formal credit in order to adopt new technology. The traditional view is that finance is a necessary farm input. Many new agricultural technologies, however, are divisible rather than lumpy, and formal credit is not an essential element in agricultural innovations that are highly divisible. In view of the large strides made by agriculture in developing countries, and the relatively small number of farmers who have received formal credit, it seems reasonable to conclude that most agricultural innovations in these countries have not depended directly on formal credit. The relation between innovation and credit has not been realistically viewed in part because credit tends to support large, lumpy investments in highly visible innovations such as tractors, as opposed to the small, divisible investments in much more numerous and widely spread innovations such as improved seeds.

CREDIT AND PRODUCTION. Government credit programs have traditionally been justified as aiding the adoption of new agricultural technologies and expanding production. This narrow view of credit impact at the farm level is challenged by a broader view that finds the impact reflected in any new activities undertaken by borrowers, not just the activity desired by program sponsors. New activities can include both production and consumption but are not necessarily those for which funds were intended, because credit represents liquidity or a generalized command over resources. Credit support for one of a borrower's activities may alter other aspects of his behavior, so that the impact is not necessarily confined to the activity directly financed by credit.

In the emerging view, evaluating credit projects by estimating their impact on what happens on the farm is generally an impossible exercise. It would be more useful to examine their effects on the vitality of financial systems. It is important to consider the extent to which infusions of funds for developmental purposes are associated with the creation of healthy institutions and with improvement in the overall performance of financial markets.

POVERTY, INDEBTEDNESS, AND SAVINGS. Although it is often maintained that the rural poor are born into, live in, and die in debt, there is considerable evidence that many poor people in rural areas are not net debtors; some are frequently in debt, while others are in debt some of the time, and some are seldom or never in debt. It is also widely held that farmers are poor and cannot save. This conventional wisdom is challenged by the fact that agriculture creates short-run savings capacity, as few other industries can, because of the seasonality of its production. Farm output not consumed at harvesttime constitutes savings that support consumption throughout the year. Considerable circumstantial evidence indicates far more liquidity in rural areas than is generally assumed by decision makers in capital cities.

Issues at the RFM Level

ROLE OF INFORMAL FINANCE. A strongly held belief by traditionalists is that moneylenders are evil and charge exorbitant rates of interest. The emerging view is that moneylenders generally perform a legitimate economic function. Their operations are frequently more cost-effective and useful to the poor than those of the specialized farm credit institutions, cooperatives, and commercial banks that governments use to supplant moneylenders. Such efforts have often been an extremely costly and inefficient means of providing credit.

Informal credit of other types is also believed to be unhealthy and resorted to only because modern financial institutions are not in place or functioning effectively. The emerging perspective is that informal financial arrangements, based on voluntary participation by rural people, are generally robust and socially useful. Widespread use of informal finance suggests that it is well suited to most rural conditions.

CURBING INFORMAL FINANCE. Attempts to replace informal finance with formal credit institutions have followed the traditional assumption that modern, formal lenders are more efficient and socially more desirable. Formal credit projects have been designed specifically to weaken informal lenders. In many respects, however, formal financial institutions appear to serve rural areas poorly because of the high cost of dealing with geographically dispersed small borrowers and savers, the urban orientation of these institutions, and the cultural gaps between lenders and borrowers. Formal credit agencies have been noted for cumbersome and inflexible requirements and procedures and for a reluctance to finance nonfarm rural enterprises. These institutions have not generally been successful in providing services for the rural poor who use informal credit. Small borrowers who do obtain loans from formal lenders are likely to experience delays before receiving their funds, while informal lenders usually provide funds quickly.

CREDIT COSTS AND BORROWERS' CHOICE. A conventional view is that formal sources provide cheaper credit than informal sources. Given a choice, however, poor farmers often prefer to borrow from the informal lender rather than from the formal institution. This preference may be explained by the extent to which formal credit procedures impose substantial transactions or access costs on loan applicants, especially the rural poor. Informal credit is often easily obtained from relatives or friends at a zero rate of interest, at least in financial terms.

UTILITY OF SPECIALIZED LENDING INSTITUTIONS. Conventional approaches to rural financial markets in the name of development have often tried to find simple, one-dimensional solutions to complex problems. One such attempt is the specialized farm credit institution, which delivers credit but few other financial services to the rural community. The usefulness of these institutions is challenged by observations that they generally lose money, fail to become integrated with the rural community, or do not respond in a flexible and efficient manner to investment opportunities.

National Policy Issues

The confrontation between the emerging perspective and traditional views is strongest at the level of national policy making, at least in part because much rural financial policy appears to be based on a peculiar set of assumptions about rural people and the nature of finance.

IMPLICATIONS OF SUPPLY-LEADING FINANCE. It has been widely held that economic activity can be created by supply-leading finance provided in advance of effective demand for rural financial services. Although giving people money obviously enables them to expand their activities, contributors to the emerging perspective note that "easy money" is not likely to inspire borrower commitment to the investment specified in the loan contract, and that borrowers are less willing to repay such loans than in the case of alternative credit for which there is an effective demand. Hence, increases in the supply of loans by governments and development assistance agencies have often not been accompanied by parallel improvements in the market conditions for rural finance. In many developing countries, for example, loan collection problems of agricultural credit agencies are often so serious that they force these lenders to depend on a continuing flow of funds from governments or development assistance agencies.

The supply-leading strategy assumes that credit can stimulate broadly based rural development. This belief disregards certain fundamental aspects of credit: standards of creditworthiness define eligible borrowers; hence, lending is selective. Some people benefit, but others do not. This makes it very difficult for any single credit program or institution to contribute to broadly based rural development unless it ignores creditworthiness and allows defaults to accumulate. In fact, this has often happened. Proponents of supply-leading finance also believe that rural credit programs are an inexpensive development initiative that can be undertaken by a government. Experience has shown, however, that rural credit services are costly to provide through government agencies when the usual low-interest supply-leading approach is followed. In addition, some of the consequences of credit programs are often antidevelopmental.

Another supply-leading tenet is that credit can be successfully directed toward certain crops, technical packages, and husbandry practices and to preferred categories of beneficiaries. The emerging view recognizes that credit is fungible, providing a generalized command over resources. End-use targeting is notoriously difficult to enforce, in many cases impossible, and the effort is always costly—especially where credit is provided for crops or techniques to which credit recipients do not attach high priority or which are inappropriate to local conditions.

IMPLICATIONS OF CHEAP CREDIT. Another very strongly held traditional viewpoint is that low interest rates help rural people, especially the poor. The evidence shows, however, that interest rates kept low by government policy discriminate against the poor. Cheap credit is rationed; the procedures usually are at least in part politically determined and provide opportunities for corruption, cronyism, and favoritism. A select group of relatively wealthy and powerful individuals or families tend to capture the benefits of concessional loans, making it more difficult for the weaker sections of society to obtain credit. While the benefits of agricultural credit programs tend to be concentrated, their costs are diffused and hidden. This creates an excellent opportunity for politicians and others to use credit programs as vehicles of political patronage. Cheap formal farm loans are therefore often concentrated in the hands of a relatively small number of borrowers, some of whom obtain more credit than they can use in a socially desirable manner, while other producers who cannot get formal loans may be kept from pursuing socially advantageous economic opportunities. Cheap credit has been advocated as a convenient means of redistributing wealth in favor of the poor, but experience around the world suggests that it is virtually impossible to redistribute wealth to significant numbers of poor people in that way.

Low interest rates also discourage activities by financial institutions that might otherwise provide services in rural areas; this, in turn, means that rural people do not have easy access to savings facilities. This can lead to circularity in the traditional reasoning: the lack of institutionalized rural financial savings is taken as evidence that rural people cannot save.

NATURE OF SAVINGS BEHAVIOR. The traditional picture of savings capacity is clouded by the assumption of macroeconomic theory that savings are residual funds left over from consumption during any given period. Observation of the behavior of rural people, however, suggests a more appropriate view of savings as funds not immediately spent upon receipt. From this perspective, differences between the flows of receipts and expenditures provide a potential for financial intermediation and create the need for a convenient place and form in which liquidity can be held.

Many policy makers have argued that rural people are insensitive to levels and changes in real interest rates when making decisions on financial savings. Recently collected evidence shows, however, that rural people are sensitive to interest rates. In many countries they have increased their savings when rewarded by remunerative interest rates. When the cost of saving has been decreased by the provision of more convenient financial services, rural people have responded by increasing the volume of funds deposited.

It has been widely held that in rural areas the number of savers is typically smaller than the number of borrowers given access to formal credit. Yet virtually everyone saves in some form in rural areas because of the seasonal nature of agricultural production, whereas formal credit usually reaches less than a quarter of rural households. When access to financial savings and credit facilities is relatively convenient, it is normal to find many savers and considerably fewer borrowers at any given time.

ATTRACTIVENESS OF CREDIT CONTROLS. Many credit projects have been based on the assumption that credit can be force-fed through a financial system, not only by creating new institutions but also by imposing selective credit controls on existing institutions. It is also assumed that funds can be provided through these channels without having any significant impact on other intermediaries or operations in the financial system. The emerging view is that interventions in the form of specialized institutions or selective credit controls have repercussions throughout the financial system, many of which are unfavorable.

Criteria for Satisfactory RFM Performance

The authors of the papers presented in this volume do not all have the same point of view regarding the issues raised. No one of them provides a recipe for making RFMs work perfectly. Taken together, though, the papers contain useful lines of thinking which could lead to policies that cause rural financial markets to perform better.

Better RFM performance cannot be measured by any single criterion. The conventional use of the volume of credit disbursed to farmers as the major measure of success, without regard to borrower repayment or lender viability, must be emphatically discredited. A well-functioning RFM should mobilize rural savings as well as disburse credit; it should grow to meet expanding opportunities without continually requiring subsidized inflows of outside funds; it should have an expanding array of vehicles for attracting savings and offer varied and flexible lending terms and conditions. Market performance of this type requires institutions that are healthy and expanding. There should be active competition among both formal and informal borrowers and lenders. The costs of financial services should fall as a result of financial innovation. The great majority of the economically active rural population should have expanding access to at least some culturally appropriate portion of the market. At the same time, the rural financial market should build up the capability of its participants to take part in larger financial markets at the national level. More effective intermediation to deal with the range and variety of sources and uses of funds is required for integration on this scale.

The route to better RFM performance is not well marked. The importance of the role of government, however, may be inferred from the extent to which intervention has been associated with the failure to produce more effective RFMs. Government's presence should be strong enough to promote and sustain activities that lower costs of financial intermediation and broaden participation, but restrained enough to avoid institutional dependence and to promote socially useful local initiatives by the intermediaries in the market.

Editorial Considerations

The editors have attempted to ensure that the interested layman seeking an overview of the literature will find in this book a succinct, yet wide sample of recent thinking. Many of the articles that constitute the chapters of this book have been greatly shortened to provide concise statements on relevant issues. Footnotes and many mathematical notations and tables have been excluded. Readers having deeper interest should consult the original sources from which these readings (other than the commissioned articles) have been drawn.

The articles that follow are organized into five groups, sudivided by subject or problem. The first group of papers treats the role of finance in development, with special attention to RFMs. The second group deals with farms and rural nonfarm firms, treating the rural family as both a consuming household and a production unit. Of special interest is household saving and borrowing behavior and the ways it relates to farm credit programs and financial market performance. The third and fourth groups of papers discuss the institutions that operate as lenders and savings mobilizers in rural areas. There are two major types: urban-based institutions operating in rural areas and local formal and informal rural financial institutions. Of special interest are the strengths and weaknesses of various institutions providing credit and other financial services to rural people. The fifth group of papers deals with national policies related to rural financial markets, with considerable attention to interest rate regulation and savings mobilization.

An attempt is made throughout to explore general considerations for analysis and policy making; case studies are provided to complement essays in theory. Massive doses of prescription have been avoided, although alternatives are suggested.

PART II

CONTRIBUTIONS OF FINANCE TO DEVELOPMENT

Introduction

The role of financial markets in development has not been explored in detail until recently. There is still much to be learned about this topic and about the relationship between overall economic conditions and the performance of financial markets. Attempts to use these markets to issue cheap credit to offset low agricultural prices and yields, for example, have worked to the detriment of savers and those who cannot get cheap credit, and have vitiated the financial system itself. Other problems caused by insufficient knowledge of how finance interacts with development may be traced to the use of the financial system as a one-way street for moving financial resources to borrowers. This approach provides illusions of control, but is often frustrated because it ignores an essential property of financial instruments, which is fungibility. In addition, the developmental potential of voluntary savings mobilization through financial markets has been neglected, eclipsed by the emphasis on providing cheap loans to special interest groups.

Modern finance may not be very relevant in subsistence economies where trade consists of small amounts of barter. The usefulness of financial instruments increases rapidly, however, as households and firms begin to specialize in production, diversify consumption, and make large investments. Although the use of money as a medium of exchange is taken for granted, the benefits derived increase with the growth of specialization. Farmers, for example, would find it inconvenient to exchange dozens of eggs, flocks of ducks, sacks of rice, stems of bananas, and piles of coconuts for cloth and modern inputs such as chemical fertilizers. Public servants, professors, and editors of books would find it virtually impossible to exchange their services directly for transportation, food, and shelter. Similarly, the benefits of using financial instruments such as loans and property shares increase with the scale of production and trade.

The contributions of financial intermediation to economic development are subtle and complex; secondary effects and indirect relationships abound, often creating very powerful forces that are easily misunderstood. Moneylending, for example, has been looked down on throughout recorded history in many parts of the world. Regulation results, in part, from these qualities of finance. In most countries financial markets are more heavily regulated than other markets.

Until recently, most economists believed that financial markets play largely a passive role in economic development. Those concerned with rural development usually viewed these markets as channels for moving cheap loans, which were regarded as farm inputs. These markets were thought to be a thin veil lightly connecting real economic activities in an economy, and it was believed that this veil could be controlled and its behavior largely regulated by government actions.

In the late 1960s and early 1970s a few economists became uneasy with traditional views about the contribution of financial markets to development. Goldsmith's early work called attention to the rapid expansion of financial activities in developing countries, suggesting unsuspected dynamism. This was followed by Shaw, Gurley, McKinnon, and Patrick, who argued that financial market operations and policies could have substantial effects on the pace as well as the direction of development (see Part II, Recommendations for Further Reading, and chapter 5). Subsequent work in developing countries began to document problems in rural financial markets. These include misallocation of resources, unsatisfactory implications for income distribution, and the poor performance of financial institutions. The income distribution problem is particularly disturbing. Many public policies try to force financial markets to provide services for the poor. Despite this, little of the cheap credit in low-income countries has reached the bulk of the poor. Similarities among these problems in a large number of countries led to searches for common causes.

Recent research has documented that decision makers in financial markets may not always react to policy directives and regulations in the manner desired by regulators. The subtle and geographically dispersed nature of financial activities makes it very difficult to enforce policy directives. Formal lenders and borrowers often end up evading the intent of administrative fiats through financial innovation, the substitution of funds, or their diversion from the purposes specified in regulations. Evading the intent of controls may be necessary if financial institutions are to sustain themselves in certain environments, or if borrowers are to obtain acceptable returns from the liquidity provided by loans. Evasion is increased by policies that fail to reflect realities—financial institutions must generate more revenues than costs if they are to survive without subsidies, and borrowers tend not to invest in unprofitable activities.

Policy directives are often also ineffective in controlling the role of financial markets in allocating resources among regions and economic sectors. Financial markets move substantial amounts of claims on resources from one area or sector to another by lending more or less to a sector or region than is mobilized there. Governments and foreign assistance agencies frequently attempt to direct more funds into agricultural credit, while financial markets often persist in lending to agriculture only a fraction of the deposit balances rural customers voluntarily entrust to banks. Thus claims on resources are moved out of agriculture for use in other activities. While measurement of these flows is frequently difficult, and problems arise from arbitrary classification of depositors and borrowers by region or sector, recent research suggests that the use of selective credit controls to alter these flows in any significant way is often not successful.

Faulty assumptions in research and evaluation have added to the confusion about the contribution of finance to development. There have been many attempts to measure the impact of credit use at the farm level to justify agricultural credit projects. At the same time, relatively little research has been done on lender behavior, on how government policies influence this behavior, and on how credit projects affect the overall performance of rural financial markets. Many researchers have not realized that the primary effect of credit projects is to increase the liquidity of banks and ultimate borrowers, and that the effect of additional liquidity can be measured only by looking at changes in the entire behavior of the unit gaining liquidity. Because of substitution and diversion of loan funds, the purpose stated in the loan application or contract does not necessarily coincide with the borrower's actual use of the additional liquidity. Credit impact cannot be measured merely by tabulating and analyzing the investments listed on loan applications or contracts: some would have occurred without the loans, others may not occur at all. While significant improvements in research have occurred, the full extent of the role of financial services in development is not yet understood.

The essays in this section make several important points. The first is that there has recently been a substantial evolution in thought about the role of financial markets in development. Second, many of the traditional views held about financial markets are suspect. Third, financial markets may play a much larger role in the development process than generally suspected. Fourth, the contribution of financial markets to development is not limited to providing credit; mobilizing savings and facilitating transactions are also important. Fifth, improvements in research are required before the contribution of finance to development can be clearly understood. This includes collecting more information about the impact of overall economic policies on the performance of financial markets.

Functions of Financial Markets

The following sample of new thinking about the role of finance in development makes two major points. First, finance and financial policies matter a great deal in development, but in ways that have often not been well understood. Second, overall economic conditions have a very strong influence on the performance of financial markets. Financial markets cannot overcome major nonfinancial shortcomings in other markets.

Long (chapter 1) summarizes the evolution in modern economic thinking about financial markets and points out four major contributions these markets make to development. Gurley and Shaw (chapter 2) explain how financial markets relate to other mechanisms commonly used to mobilize economic surpluses. Kato (chapter 3) documents how Japan's financial markets have reallocated claims on resources from rural to nonrural uses during that country's rapid transformation to a modern industrial economy. Like Gurley and Shaw, Kato suggests that market-wide measures are required to evaluate performance in financial markets.

By nature, financial markets and intermediaries are innovative, although this feature is often warped by the effects of regulations on individual institutions. Bhatt (chapter 4) discusses some of the reasons for innovativeness and suggests that some innovation responds defensively to regulations. While innovations that reduce the cost of financial intermediation are beneficial to society, it is not clear that innovations arising in response to regulations are of this type.

Patrick (chapter 5) classifies approaches to developing financial services. When increased economic activity expands the demand for financial services, this stimulates expansion of the financial system. Patrick calls this type of financial development "demand-led." He points out, however, that under "supply-leading" strategies financial services may be expanded in advance of significant changes in real economic activities. The assumption behind a supply-leading strategy is that an increase in financial services will induce producers to expand their real activities. Government and donor programs in agricultural credit have clearly been motivated by this possibility. Penny (chapter 6) questions the supply-leading approach. He argues that credit will not significantly stimulate growth unless a number of rather demanding preconditions are present. Borrowers' attitudes are important, and attractive investment alternatives for the liquidity provided by additional loans are essential.

Ray (chapter 7) stresses the relationship between rates of return in real economic activities and the quality of intermediation in financial markets. Overvalued exchange rates, food price ceilings, and export taxes on agricultural products reduce the rates of return that borrowers can expect from their investments in agriculture. This constrains investment and limits farmers' incomes. As a result, farmers are less interested in using and repaying loans, and their loan repayment capacity and ability to save are reduced. Ray concludes that a healthy financial market is heavily dependent on the performance of the economy.

1. *A Note on Financial Theory and Economic Development*

Millard Long

[Over the past twenty years, ideas about the role of money in the development of an economy have undergone profound changes. The simple views that money is irrelevant to real growth and that accumulations of money retard real growth have been replaced by more complex considerations of the role of finance in general, including monetary and nonmonetary financial instruments and functions. This approach has led to the conclusions that finance affects production and that the financial system is a mobilization and allocation mechanism which transforms and distributes risk.]

Over the past fifty years there has been a revolution in thinking about the monetary side of the economy. Prior to the Great Depression of the 1930s, economists felt that monetary changes affected only prices and wages. Output and employment, the real factors in the economy, were considered to be independent of monetary events. The experience of the Depression made economists realize that monetary factors affected not only wages and prices but also changes in output and employment over the business cycle. Today, monetary policy has become the major weapon in the armory of stabilization policies.

The past fifteen years have seen a second major revision in thinking about monetary factors. Finance has been recognized as affecting not only the movement of the economy over the business cycle but also economic growth. Originally this analysis of the effect of finance on growth was highly theoretical, couched in the language of growth models. But in recent years, economists and policy makers have been concerned with the real-world applications of the theory of finance and growth, particularly with regard to the developing countries. This focus on practical questions has forced a substantial revision in the theory. This chapter contains a brief overview of past thinking about the impact of finance on growth, together with suggestions on the direction for further advances. The intention is to provide an intellectual structure for financial policy making in the developing countries.

The chapter starts with a review of the work in the 1960s on money and growth models and ends with a discussion of the four functions of finance: as a medium of exchange, a system for the mobilization and allocation of capital, a system for the transformation and distribution of risk, and a major tool of stabilization policy.

Composition of Money

Thus far, the terms "money" and "finance" have been used almost interchangeably. This has a historic rationale. In the past the financial systems of most countries were dominated by the central bank and the commercial bank, and this is still true in many developing countries. Money has traditionally been defined as consisting of the key liability of the central bank, namely currency, and the key liability of the commercial banks, namely demand deposits. These two assets were the only ones acceptable in transactions, thus they constituted the medium of exchange. But the situation in financial markets has changed, and traditionally defined money—currency plus demand deposits—now constitutes only a fraction of total financial assets. Today other assets such as credit cards are used as a medium of exchange. In addition, economists have increasingly recognized the importance of services supplied by the financial system other than providing the medium of exchange.

One way to deal with the new situation and new concerns is to redefine money to include a broader array of financial assets; the various definitions of money—M1, M2, and M3—include different types of assets. But in this paper the term "money" is given its traditional meaning. Most of the discussion will focus on the broader set of financial assets, institutions, and markets that together constitute the financial system.

Finance and Growth

In a simple Harrod-Domar growth model, the increase in output is a function only of the rate at which physical capital is accumulated and the "efficiency" with which that capital is used. Therefore, the growth in output is a function of the savings rate (which is assumed to represent capital formation) and the output-capital ratio. Thus a country which saved 20 percent of output and had an output-capital ratio of 0.25 would grow at 5 percent a year. To ascertain the impact of money on growth, various writers modified the Harrod-Domar model by assuming that money is part of wealth, and the accumulation of money an alternative for savers to accumulating physical assets. If the overall savings rate remains the same, the accumulation of additional money will reduce the accumulation of physical capital. And if output depends only on physical capital, growth in physical output will slow as money is accumulated instead of physical capital. It follows from this view that if a country wishes to enhance the growth of physical output it must slow the accumulation of money, which it can do by making the holding of money unattractive—say, through inflation.

Many economists found this result both surprising and unacceptable and suggested different reasons this simple approach might be misleading. One suggestion was that income should be more properly defined to include the services rendered by the money stock. Another suggestion was that money should be treated as a factor of production; more money would lead to more production. Either modification of the model is sufficient to render the results ambiguous, because the additional money increases income and, therefore, total savings. As a result, monetary accumulation might or might not reduce the rate of physical capital accumulation and of economic growth.

In the pure growth models, which assume homogeneous output, malleable capital, perfect divisibility, and no risk, it is not at all clear why people hold money balances. Of the various growth models with monetary aspects emerging in the 1960s, the one most clearly addressed to development problems was the attempt by Ronald I. McKinnon (*Money and Capital in Economic Development*, Washington, D.C., Brookings Institution, 1973) to present a modified growth model, with some institutional content descriptive of developing countries, in which there was a reason for holding money. Investment, he assumed, was not perfectly divisible, but lumpy. Furthermore, people could not borrow to finance their investments; before making an investment they had to accumulate purchasing power equal in value to the investment. In an economy without money the accumulation of working balances would be in the form of physical assets. If paper money were available, however, it could be substituted for physical assets, thus freeing resources for more productive purposes. McKinnon called this use of money the "conduit effect" and argued that, to the extent that paper money was used to replace physical goods in working balances, monetary accumulation was a complement to physical capital accumulation, not a substitute. After all the physical working balances had been replaced by paper money, however, further monetary accumulation would, in McKinnon's model, be an alternative to physical capital accumulation, as in the models discussed above. Thus, there is a particular size of the monetary system that maximizes growth.

The basic weakness in McKinnon's approach and, indeed, in similar models of the 1960s is that they are concerned only with currency, as against bank deposits, and so are of little help in understanding the conditions now found in developing countries. McKinnon's model gives insight into only two very particular situations: in the first, paper money replaces commodity money—say, gold or silver—thus freeing these physical resources for use in production. But paper money has been used almost everywhere instead of commodity money for quite some time, except for some gold transactions in international trade. The second case to which McKinnon's analysis may apply is a hyperinflationary environment in which people have chosen not to hold fiat money and have shifted their liquid reserves into physical goods whose price would appreciate with inflation. In this special case, there is a gain to be realized by increasing the use of money and freeing the hoarded real resources for use in productive purposes. McKinnon has made a small change in the neoclassical analysis which can give some insight into the advantages of switching from commodity to fiat money, but he has not presented a general model for understanding how finance affects economic growth.

Edward S. Shaw followed a different path to explain how finance affects growth (*Financial Deepening in Economic Development*, New York, Oxford University Press, 1973). He rather peremptorily dismissed the prior approach by arguing that neither currency nor bank deposits should be considered as wealth. Money is debt; to understand the impact of finance on growth it does not matter that demand deposits are the debt of the commercial banks while currency is a debt of the central bank. Both the central bank and commercial bank debts are parts of the "economic system"; on an aggregated balance sheet for the entire economy, the financial asset "money," like other financial assets, is canceled out against financial liabilities. The only asset remaining on a country's aggregated balance sheet is physical capital. This being so, money—or any other financial asset—is not a component of national wealth, and therefore its accumulation is not a substitute for the accumulation of physical capital.

Shaw then suggested a different approach to the problem. He thought that money should be seen as only one of many financial assets, not singled out for special treatment. Shaw focused on the overall financial system, which he argued should be viewed as a service sector employing inputs to produce outputs. Essentially, Shaw saw the service produced by the financial sector as an intermediate input in the production process. Producing more of that input would enhance the growth of real output. Like McKinnon, he argued that in many developing countries government intervention in the financial system, particularly in the form of interest rate controls in the face of inflation, had "repressed" the size of the financial system. Thus the financial sectors in many developing countries are too small, in the sense that the services provided are less than optimal.

Finance as a Service Sector

For understanding the role of the financial sector, Shaw's approach is more useful than the growth models, however modified. The questions that remain are: What services are provided by the financial sector? Are Shaw and McKinnon correct that in many developing countries the flow of such services is less than it should be? And if so, what retards the growth of the financial sector? What policies should governments pursue to encourage an optimal level and mix of financial sector services?

Here I will lay the groundwork for such an analysis by suggesting some of the more important functions performed by the financial sector. The first is the provision of a medium of exchange; barter is clearly less efficient than monetized exchange. Were this the only contribution of finance, a simple system would be adequate; all that would be required would be a central bank issuing paper money. But the financial system provides other services, not only the mobilization and allocation of capital but also the transformation and distribution of risk. To provide these services, a relatively elaborate financial system is required.

Good investment opportunities in an economy are not distributed among the same places and people as are the capacities to save. Without finance, those who save would do all the investing themselves. Some investments with low yield would be undertaken; some with high yields would not be made. Shaw refers to this failure to allocate capital to the investments with the highest returns as "fragmentation" of the financial markets. A well-functioning financial system mobilizes deposits from those savers with poor investment opportunities, performs the function of search and discrimination, and then allocates the available resources to those with higher-yielding investments. The resulting improvement in resource allocation raises the yield on capital and the level of output. In addition, if savings are responsive to the yield on capital, the overall increase in average yield should raise the economy's savings rate.

How are these functions performed in a well-functioning financial system? The system gathers up the savings of many people, allocates the mobilized funds to a typically smaller number of borrowers who undertake investments, and thus transforms the size of the financial transactions. The financial system also transforms maturities, offering savers the short-term liquid deposits which they prefer, while at the same time providing investors longer-term loans better matched to the cash flows generated by their investments. In addition, it provides professional management, including scale economies in the collection and analysis of information about borrowers.

The transformation and distribution of risk is another key service provided by the financial system. Most investors are risk-averse and must be reimbursed for bearing more risk. But people differ in their tastes for risk; some demand high compensation to bear risk, others less. A well-functioning financial system allocates risk to those who charge the least to bear it. It can also transform risk in many ways. For example, in a project financed by both debt and equity (that is, by loans and by investments in shares of ownership), the debt usually carries less risk, and the equity more, than the project itself. Through finance, people can diversify their risk by holding small participations in many investments, rather than a large stake in just a few.

Some kinds of risks are not only shared but actually reduced by a well-functioning financial system. Financial markets can be made broader and deeper than the markets for physical assets: for example, the risk of loss in liquidating a financial claim is less than that in selling a physical asset. In a financial system that allocates risk poorly, investors will adjust by avoiding the riskier areas of economic activity and by demanding greater compensation in the form of higher prices and profits to compensate for the added risks.

Another major function of a financial system is to help stabilize an economy. All economies, at least in their market-oriented (rather than subsistence) components, experience cyclical changes in output and prices. This affects both the domestic economy and the balance of payments. When disturbances occur, governments employ countermeasures to stabilize economic activity. The policies chosen depend in part on the nature of the disturbance; today, financial policy is a common and usually the key stabilization tool. Through manipulation of the financial system, governments attempt to keep both the domestic economy and the country's foreign position in balance.

Resources are required to provide the financial services mentioned; the costs of the inputs used are reflected in the spread between the lending and borrowing rates of interest. Because there are substantial costs, an optimal financial system in a poor country need not be so large or so complex as in richer ones. Shaw and McKinnon, however, argue that the financial systems in many developing countries are actually below their most advantageous size. One can think of reasons—infant industry problems and externalities—that might in some countries impede the growth of the financial sector. But one of the most important constraints is inappropriate government policy.

As already mentioned, interest rate ceilings, particularly in an inflationary environment, dampen a financial system's growth. Other regulations also constrain particular aspects of financial sector development. For example, specific rules curtailing the allowable degree of maturity transformation by institutions may in part explain the shortage of longer-term finance in developing countries. Such regulation may be justified; maturity transformation is risky, and particularly so in inflationary environments. But there is no economic sector so highly regulated as finance, and one regulation begets another. For example, interest rate ceilings discourage institutions from lending to borrowers, such as small farmers, whose loans carry a greater than average degree of risk and are costly to administer. Countries which apply interest rate ceilings often attempt to offset this bias through selective credit controls that direct financial intermediaries to lend to precisely those small borrowers, new firms, and others to whom banks are discouraged from lending.

Governments must always intervene in the financial system in order to carry out their monetary policy and assure the stability of the financial sector itself. But today intervention in finance has gone well beyond these objectives into credit allocation and selective interest rate regulations. Controls coupled with inflation have repressed the growth of the financial sector in many developing countries. Country experience has shown that a reduction or removal of controls produces growth, both in the financial system and in the economy, but it may be accompanied by a loss of the power some governments would like to exercise over the changing shape of their economies.

Where does thinking now stand on the financial side of the economy? First, no longer is the debate limited to the behavior of banks and their key liability, money. Rather, economists and policy makers are thinking about the role of the whole financial system and the entirety of financial assets. Second, economists no longer consider money merely a variable that affects prices but not output. Rather, they understand that finance affects production, both over the business cycle and in the longer course of economic development. Third, no longer do economists conceive of money as providing only a medium of exchange. Rather, they realize this is only one of four key services, the other three being the mobilization and allocation of funds, the transformation and distribution of risk, and the stabilization of economic activity. Where government policy represses the development of the financial sector, reducing the flow of financial services to a suboptimal level, the pace of development suffers.

2. *Financial Structure and Economic Development*

John G. Gurley and
Edward S. Shaw

[As countries increase their wealth and income, their financial structures usually become increasingly rich in financial assets, institutions, and markets. Differences among countries in financial accumulation persist, however, even after allowance for wealth and income effects. Perhaps the most important reason is that the financial technique is only one way to mobilize economic surpluses, and alternatives are considered more attractive in some countries.]

During economic development, as incomes per capita increase, financial assets usually grow more rapidly than national wealth or national product. This has been true for the United States, where financial assets have grown much faster than gross national product (GNP); the ratio increased from about 1.0 in 1900 to 4.5 by the 1960s. In Japan the ratio of financial assets to real wealth rose from perhaps 10 percent in 1885 to over 150 percent in recent years. In the Soviet Union, this ratio moved from 10 percent in 1928 to 35 percent in the 1960s. Financial growth in excess of real growth is common around the world.

This same picture is revealed by comparing countries at a given time. Countries that are poor in income per capita generally have very low rates of financial to real wealth. The present ratio in Afghanistan and Ethiopia, for instance, is probably little higher than 10 or 15 percent. The ratio is somewhat higher, from 30 to 60 percent, in more prosperous countries such as Argentina, Brazil, Guatemala, Mexico, the Republic of Korea, Venezuela, and Yugoslavia. India, though less developed than most of these countries, has a financial ratio of around 35 percent. In still more highly developed countries, the proportion of financial to real wealth often lies in the range of 80 to 100 percent. Yet

Extracted from *Economic Development and Cultural Change*, vol. 15, no. 3 (April 1967), pp. 257–68, by permission of The University of Chicago Press.

the Soviet Union has a low financial ratio for its income per capita (about 35 percent), while Japan (150 percent), Switzerland (over 200 percent), and the United Kingdom (215 percent) have exceptionally high ones. National stocks of financial assets thus vary from 10 to more than 200 percent of national real wealth, and differences in income per capita go a long way toward explaining this variety of experience.

Reasons for Secularly Rising Financial Ratios

The relationship between growth in financial assets and growth in real wealth and income per capita may be analyzed in various ways. For example, financial development depends on a division of labor that is feasible only with real development—that is, development in other sectors. Financial development depends on conditions of demand for and supply of financial assets that are sensitive to real development.

Finance and self-sufficiency are opposites. Finance is associated with division of labor in three senses:

1. Division of labor in production, when it involves exchanges of factor services and outputs, implies lending and borrowing. In primitive market economies, these transactions are in kind. Subsequently, the diseconomies of finance in kind induce monetization. It seems to be the general rule that the pace of monetization exceeds the pace of real growth in diminishing degree. Once money payments are everywhere, the ratio of money to income, or of money to wealth, hovers near its long-run peak. Data for seventy countries indicate that the money-income ratio starts from approximately 10 percent or less in the poorest countries and moves up to 20 percent in countries with GNP per capita of about $300. The rise in the ratio then slows, though it continues on to 30 percent and a little more.

2. Finance is associated with the division of labor between savers and investors. Where one sector releases factors of production from consumer goods industries and another sector absorbs such factors into accumulation of real capital, financial assets and debt accumulate in both monetary and nonmonetary form. The rate of accumulation depends on the mix of techniques for transferring savings to investment.

This division of labor leads to the issue of primary securities by ultimate borrowers (investors) and to the acquisition of financial assets by ultimate lenders (savers). In between lie the markets in which primary securities are bought and sold. During the growth process, the division of labor between savers and investors becomes more intricate. This institutional evolution implies a more rapid accumulation of primary debt and financial assets than of real wealth, until the evolution approaches its limit. Primary security issues approximate 1 or 2 percent of GNP in the poorer countries; the ratio generally lies in the range of 10 to 15 percent in wealthier countries.

3. Division of labor in a third sense fosters growth in both the quantity and variety of financial assets. Savings and the ownership of primary securities become more specialized: financial intermediaries solicit savings, paying a deposit rate for them, and assume responsibility for savings allocation, charging a primary rate of interest to ultimate borrowers. The spread between the primary rate and the deposit rate compensates for factor costs and risks in intermediation. This spread shrinks during financial development. In combination with shifts in savers' tastes among financial assets, the relative rise in the deposit rate induces layering of indirect debt upon primary debt, and a growth in total financial assets of savers relative to national income and wealth. Stocks of nonmonetary indirect financial assets rise during the development process. They were a negligible fraction of GNP in the United States at the beginning of the nineteenth century, but rose almost continuously from that time, reaching 35 percent by 1900 and 60 percent in the 1960s. Cross-section data have much the same story to tell: time and savings deposits, which make up the bulk of nonmonetary indirect assets, are only 1 or 2 percent of GNP in the poorest countries, 10 percent in countries with national products per capita of about $300 to $400, and 40 or 50 percent in the richer nations.

Reasons for Difference in Financial Ratios

There are differences in national financial systems that cannot be explained by differences in income and wealth. Among countries at any one time, and among phases in the development of one country, financial accumulation is sensitive not only to levels of output but also to growth rates of output. Rapid output growth tends to shrink the financial ratio, while sluggish growth tends to inflate the ratio. The actual turn of events seems to depend on the sectoral distribution of savings and investment that accompanies rapid national growth. We have also observed circumstances in which it was not rates of growth but rather instability in rates of growth that helped explain finance-income ratios.

Financial accumulation is affected by inflation. In some short-run periods or for some low rates of inflation, the value of equities in particular—of amounts issued and of stocks outstanding—may rise relative to income; and inflationary constraint on other forms of financial asset may not have a fully offsetting effect. More often, however, inflation, as a tax on nonescalated securities and as a means of increasing self-finance in investing sectors (see discussion below), compresses the real value of financial assets and reduces the finance-income ratio.

The finance ratio is affected by its history. In some cases, accumulated finance has been dissipated by a prolonged depression that involves debt adjustments, including bankruptcy. In others, debt has been devalued by the state, and foreign claims have been modified by exchange revaluations and expropriations. Finance values are peculiarly vulnerable to major discontinuities that create gaps between finance outstanding and finance that would have been in place if development had been uneventful. Some variations in finance-income ratios, over time or space, have no behavioral importance. Successive loans of the same funds along a chain of government units, for example, can accumulate claims and counterclaims in high proportion to income.

Finance depends on law, the courts, and processes of litigation between debtors and creditors. It depends on forms of land title and on the various aspects of bankruptcy. It requires appropriate accords between governments and financial markets. The institutional paraphernalia of modern finance are accumulated only in long periods of social evolution, and this accumulation proceeds at varying rates in different countries. Direct and indirect inputs of human capital, required by the financial sector, are slow to accumulate anywhere, and their rate of accumulation does not necessarily parallel that of physical capital.

Alternative Techniques for Mobilizing the Economic Surplus

The principal reason for dissimilar financial structures at similar levels of national income and wealth is that there are alternative techniques for mobilizing the economic surplus—for eliciting savings and allocating them to investment. The financial technique, or the debt-asset system, is only one method.

The list of alternative processes for putting savings to the service of selected investment may be compressed into two major classes: internal finance and external finance. In the former, the investing entity draws on its own savings; in the latter, the investor draws on the savings of others. Internal finance comprises self-finance by individuals and firms, and taxation (where government raises the resources and invests them). In self-finance, savings are accumulated by investors as the result of movement in relative prices on commodity and factor markets and on markets for foreign exchange. The taxation technique employs taxes and other nonmarket alternatives to channel savings to the state for either governmental or private investment. Within external finance, the debt-asset system is the technique for mobilizing domestic savings; in addition, savings from abroad may be supplied.

External Finance

The debt-asset system for mobilizing domestic savings depends on and encourages a division of labor between savers and investors, as well as between savers and intermediaries. It belongs in the context of decentralized decision making, market organization, and dependence on relative prices to guide economic behavior. Market rates of interest, as one class of relative prices, bear a heavy responsibility for the rate and direction of investment.

The issue and accumulation of government debt for sale to the public or banks is a component of the debt-asset system. It draws private savings through security markets and intermediaries into both private and governmental uses. The stock of government debt plays a role in portfolio diversification that affects deeply the performance of the debt-asset system.

Internal Finance

The processes of internal finance—both self-finance and taxation—are substitutes for the debt-asset system. Each of them involves more centralization of decision making, less specialization among savers and investors. Each of them leads to a less elaborate financial structure.

The processes of self-finance (as defined here) involve movements in the terms of trade on commodity, factor, and foreign exchange markets that are to the advantage of an investing sector and force involuntary savings on other sectors. These shifts in relative prices could be imposed by government at a stable level or induced through inflation. They may be imposed by private investors with monopoly power on some commodity or factor market. The processes of self-finance can operate not only through socialist central planning, but also through monopolistic or state-directed capitalism, or through inflation.

Socialist centralism forgoes most of the division of labor that we have stressed as one basis for relatively high finance-income ratios. Savings and investment are generated principally within the state sector, so that market transfers of savings at explicit rates of interest are as unnecessary as they are distasteful in socialist doctrine. Demand for financial assets in other sectors is depressed by constraints on personal income and wealth. Other reasons for depressed demand are that the state supplies many services for which people save in capitalist societies, private bequests are minimized, and reduced private risks imply reduced precautionary portfolios. Under these circumstances there is little occasion for markets in either primary or indirect securities.

Socialist centralism reduces dependence on a financial structure;

contacts are made less through financial markets and financial institutions and more through planning bureaus and other central coordinating devices. The order of the day is internal finance and balanced budgets, not external finance and the issue of new securities. The theory and design of a socialist society are incompatible with relatively high ratios of financial assets to income and wealth.

Self-finance arises from several sources. Factor prices are an obvious target for techniques of self-finance. Peasant migration to the city depresses real wage rates and raises real profit rates; urban industry thus has access to flows of new finance for its own capital. Exchange rates are another source. Overvaluation of domestic currency on the foreign exchanges may transfer real income from an exporting sector to an importing sector that is accumulating plant and equipment. Depending on the elasticities of demand and supply, overvaluation can also appropriate foreign savings for domestic use.

Inflation is another source of self-finance because of its impact on relative prices, incomes, and wealth. The prospect of inflation affects anticipated relative yields on financial and real wealth; it reduces real rates of return on assets with inflexible nominal rates and raises real prospective returns on assets with sufficiently flexible nominal rates. The result is to change rates of savings and the channels by which savings flow. Self-finance gains at the expense of debt-asset finance. Foreign aid might gain in importance if inflation reduces domestic saving. The channels that lose are debt-asset finance and also taxation, unless tax rates happen to be progressive to inflation.

Inflation transfers net worth as well as income. It taxes money balances, assessing creditors for the benefit of debtors. If it depresses the wealth of savers and the debt of investors below their preferred levels, a temporary acceleration of savings, investment, and debt-asset finance could ensue. But this result does not follow during a gross inflation that is expected to continue.

Self-finance by large units is centralist. Even in capitalism some changes in the socioeconomic structure involve reversion to self-finance. Degeneration in processes of debt-asset finance reduces savings and investment, but can also divert funds into self-finance. Self-finance may increase if firms combine to avoid "the restraining hand of financial institutions." Cooperative credit among consumers or farmers has reduced their reliance on broader financial markets.

The tax technique is a variant of internal finance, a way of mobilizing the economic surplus that implies centralized decision making. Although some taxes may benefit debt-asset finance, others depress demand for financial assets, displace issues of securities by investors and intermediaries, and even make securities markets superfluous.

Criteria for Choice among Alternative Savings-Investment Technologies

We have discussed four "technologies" or processes of eliciting and allocating savings: self-finance, taxation, debt-asset, and foreign aid. The objective of public policy regarding the savings-investment process, we assume, is to maximize anticipated real consumption. The optimal consumption stream has the qualities of equity and stability that conform to a social welfare function.

The contribution of each savings-investment technology to consumer welfare has a positive (gross yield) component and a negative (factor cost) component. The difference is the net yield of the technology. Additional real resources applied to a savings-investment technology may raise rates of savings and investment, the nation's capital stock, and hence the future flow of consumption. The gross yield of these real resources is the capital value of the economy's anticipated gross additions to its consumption stream. Factor cost is the capital value of the stream of final goods that could have been produced by the real resources if they had not been diverted to a savings-investment technology. The net yield is the difference between these two capital values. We suggest that there is an optimal combination of savings-investment technologies for each economy in each phase of its development.

The optimal combination of technologies is not static over space or time and is not the same in different contexts. Relative yields can vary according to the weights attached in social welfare functions to growth rates of income, equality of income, or income variance over time. They can vary with the response of savings rates to the compulsions of taxation and inflation, or the inducement of deposit rates on financial assets. Relative costs are sensitive to factor prices, factor quality, and technical innovation.

Because of differences and changes in these relative yields and costs, it may be efficient to disperse somewhat the decision making of a centralized society. Some developing countries may do well to focus resources initially on the tax technique and subsequently shift to debt-asset finance as improvements occur in communications, private savings habits, and legal institutions. To ensure stability, relatively mature capitalist societies may prefer to rely more and more on the tax technique.

The four technologies are substitutes. Economic development is marked by repeated probing for the best combination of savings-investment technologies. The search is guided by principle and prejudice, by foreign example, by trial and error, and even by rational analysis. The combinations and permutations of technology are so numerous that no two countries are likely to follow the same probing sequence or to reach the same ratio of financial assets to tangible wealth at any given level of real wealth or income per capita. The probing sequence is most deeply affected by the economy's choice between self-finance with central planning, and technologies that are compatible with decentralized decisions regarding savings and investment. Advocates of either can design imposing proof that it is cheaper in resource inputs, more effective in eliciting and allocating savings, less vulnerable to instability in the consumption stream, and more compatible with the ethics of equity.

As development proceeds, the probing process everywhere seems to lead toward a mixture of self-finance under central planning and decentralized processes. If we dared to suggest a Law of Financial Development, it would be this: each economy begins its development by intensive exploitation of a savings-investment technology that is chosen for historical, political, social, or perhaps economic reasons. Then, as this technology produces a diminishing net yield, it experiments with alternative technologies that are marginally superior in terms of their capitalized returns and costs.

3. *Mechanisms for the Outflow of Funds from Agriculture into Industry in Japan*

Yuzuru Kato

[Since the 1880s funds from Japanese agriculture have flowed to other sectors and made a major contribution to the nation's industrial growth. This article shows how transfers through financial markets came about, and how agriculture was financed.]

Over the years, the principal source of funds for Japanese industrial firms has been loans from financial institutions. The Japanese people have generally deposited their savings in banks, rather than purchase stocks and debentures, and have let the banks supply loans for equipment and operation to the firms. This behavior results from liquidity and safety preferences of the people and is characteristic of the Japanese economy. Today the investment behavior of the Japanese is changing to some extent. Rapid economic growth, the opportunity of receiving premiums because of the frequent issue of new stocks, and the reintroduction of investment trusts in 1951 have made the stock market active. This active market and the growing level of personal incomes enables more average Japanese citizens to purchase stocks and debentures themselves. Nevertheless, indirect finance through financial institutions remains clearly dominant in Japan.

Supply Behavior of Financial Institutions

The supply schedules of banks for providing credit to big industrial firms on the one hand, and to small firms and peasant farmers on the other, are determined by loan costs and risk premiums. If for simplicity we ignore the costs of credit investigations, the costs per unit of capital lent will comprise interest on deposits, on debentures, and on funds borrowed, depreciation of buildings, furniture, and the like, the salaries of bank employees, and normal profit. All of these are independent of the amount of the individual loans, which gives the supply a

Extracted from *Rural Economic Problems*, vol. 3, no. 2 (December 1966), pp. 1–20.

downward sloping curve. With regard to risk premiums, the final insurance against an inability to repay is the equity capital of the borrower; and since this is constant in the short term, risk premiums will rise progressively in proportion to the volume of loans. As a result, the supply schedule curve first declines and then turns upward. Its elasticity depends principally on risk premiums. The risk premiums are greater on agricultural loans than on industrial loans because of the smallness of peasant capital and the uncertainty of harvests and agricultural prices. The loans to peasants are much smaller in volume than those to industrial firms.

A ceiling on interest exists in the organized financial market, whether it is externally given or self-imposed. The Agricultural Cooperative Credit Associations, the main supplier of private credit to peasants, are not subject to interest regulation. Since one objective of these associations is to lend money to farmers at as low a rate as possible, however, they usually charge less than merchants and moneylenders. If they cannot earn a profit at a low rate of interest, they usually do not make loans. The surplus funds brought about by their conservative lending policy are deposited with larger affiliated financial institutions or used to purchase government bonds or debentures. The larger affiliated agricultural cooperative credit institutions have close contacts with the money market and put their surplus funds into call loans, agribusiness loans, and securities. The other financial institutions such as commercial banks usually lend only a negligible part of their funds to peasants, even when they accept a large amount of deposits from peasants. The share of agricultural loans in total loan balances was only 0.3 percent in 1956–58 for all banks, excluding government credit institutions, mutual savings institutions, and agricultural credit cooperatives.

Peasants borrow money from Mujin or Tanomoshiko mutual savings and loan associations in rural areas, and also from pawnshops, merchants, moneylenders, or others at a higher rate of interest. The supply schedule of noninstitutional lenders does not have an interest ceiling. Since 1912 many surveys have indicated that peasants' access to loans has been limited by the credit rationing of the lenders in the organized market. The share of the informal lenders in the borrowing of farm households has decreased steadily, however, from 69 percent in 1912 to 32 percent in 1960.

Banks prefer to lend to industrial firms because they expect a considerably larger profit from such loans than from the same amount loaned to farmers. The rate of interest charged industries is usually lower than that to farmers, but banks still prefer industrial loans because of their lower costs. This preference is strengthened by the trade-position motive, with each bank trying to keep large, rapidly growing businesses as its own exclusive customers. Banks usually charge large industries the prime rate. Their supply of funds to big business is perfectly elastic with respect to interest rate, and the demand of big business has grown continuously and dramatically because of continuous technical innovation and market growth. Thus the largest portion of bank funds is allocated mainly to industry or big business.

Loan and Deposit Behavior of Peasants

The outflow of capital funds from agriculture through financial institutions reflects the bankers' distaste for lending to peasants and their preference for making loans and investments in the nonagricultural sector. But it is also due to the preferences of the peasants. As a group, although they deposit their savings with the financial institutions, they borrow a very much smaller sum from these institutions than they deposit. The difference represents a flow of funds out of the agricultural sector. The loan-deposit ratio—that is, the ratio of the balance of loans to the balance of deposit liabilities—of the Agricultural Cooperative Credit Associations is much less than 1. These balances are a large portion of total farmer participation in the organized market. Since all the borrowers served by the Agricultural Cooperative Credit Associations and all their depositors are peasants, it is clear that the peasants are borrowing from these associations a much smaller sum than they deposit.

Why do they deposit money at low rates of interest and contract loans at higher rates? There are several reasons. The depositing and borrowing strata of the peasantry are differentiated. Landlords and bigger farmers, who make many of the deposits, have little desire to borrow even if the financial institutions would lend to them; in contrast, small-scale owner-operators and tenants, who are bad loan risks, desire to borrow. Attempts to buy additional land and enlarge the size of one's holding meet with great resistance in Japan today, where there is a large surplus population, and purchases are not easily effected. But the marginal efficiency of supplementary investment in a holding of a given size declines rapidly after a certain level. Any attempt to avoid this by enlarging the size of the holding may result in a financial loss, however, because the price of land is so high (driven up largely by nonagricultural demand). The uncertainty of harvests and agricultural prices increases the risk. As a result, peasants who possess funds will not invest them in their holdings, but prefer to deposit them safely. Rich peasants restrain their agricultural investments to avoid risk. The peasants who do want to borrow are those with the smallest holdings, and loans to them are risky. Consequently, agriculturalists as a whole obtain loans which amount to only a small part of their deposits.

Most peasants have both deposits and borrowings. Although the rate of interest on deposits is nominally low, deposits may be withdrawn whenever necessary. This liquidity is an important advantage because peasants must always be ready for contingencies such as poor crops and disease. In addition, total available funds may be larger if a peasant borrows as well as saves. There are two ways to obtain purchasing power from a deposit: one is by withdrawing the deposit, and the other is by borrowing money on the pledge of the deposit. It may often be advantageous for a farmer to borrow at a rather low rate of interest on the pledge of a time deposit, rather than to liquidate the deposit to meet a short-term need for funds.

These factors explain the behavior of the demander of funds. When the behavior of the demander and the supplier are considered together, it is easy to understand the tendency of funds to flow out of the agricultural sector and into the nonagricultural sector. This tendency contributes to the structural difference between the growth rates of the two sectors.

It is difficult to quantify the intersectoral flow of funds, for data concerning the sectoral origin of the funds financial institutions acquire by accepting deposits and by issuing debentures are not generally available. Ichioka estimated the flow of funds out of agriculture into nonagriculture for specific years (see table 3-1), and similar estimates have been made by Nakayama [in Tobata and Kawano, eds., *Nihon no Keizai to Nogyokozo Bunseki*] and the Economic Planning Agency [*Keizai Seicho to Nogyo, Noka Keizai*, 1956].

Brief History of Agricultural Credit Institutions

Special credit institutions for agriculture were established in the 1890s. The Hypothec Bank of Japan (HBJ) was established in 1896

Table 3-1. *Estimated Net Outflows from Agriculture*
(million yen)

Year	*Cash surplus of farm household (A)*	*Outflow from agriculture (B)*	*Percentage transferred (B/A)*
1935	270	189	70
1936	378	200	53
1937	719	499	69
1951	80,718	38,538	48
1952	72,785	51,161	70

Notes: Figures are net increase of balance during the year.

Source: Estimated by K. Ichioka in S. Tobata and S. Kawano, eds., *Nihon no Keizai to Nogyokozo Bunseki* [Structural change of agriculture in the expanding economy], 1956, p. 250.

mainly to supply long-term credit on the mortgage of paddy fields, upland fields, and forests. Prefectural Agricultural and Industrial Banks were established from 1896 to 1900, and the Hokkaido Colonial Bank (HCB) was established in 1899. To supply operating loans on personal credit to small peasants without mortgageable land, Industrial Cooperative Associations (IAS, the predecessors of the present Agricultural Cooperative Credit Associations) were established from 1900 on. All these financial institutions received some form of government aid, such as subscription, subsidy, or tax exemption. HBJ and the IAS were the main long-term and short-term credit institutions respectively up to World War II.

The IA credit system operates at the city, town, and village level, and there are Prefectural IA Credit Federations plus the Central Cooperative Bank for Agriculture and Forestry in Tokyo. City, town, and village IAS accept deposits from peasants, lend money to them, redeposit to and borrow from the Prefectural IA Credit Federations. Their loan-deposit ratio (L/D), calculated from the consolidated balance sheet of total IAS, has tended to decline sharply. It was well above unity before 1917, when deposits received by IAS did not cover the demand for funds by peasants. But after the rural boom during World War I, L/D decreased to around 0.7 in the 1930s and 0.2 in the early 1940s. The L/D values of IAS in industrial districts have always been less than that of IAS in agricultural districts, because the former group has been closer to money markets and has found more opportunities to invest funds outside agriculture.

The tendency for credit institutions established especially for agriculture to shift from agricultural to industrial and commercial finance was especially marked during World War II, when agricultural inputs were in short supply and peasants' demand for funds was extremely low. The surplus funds of peasants in the agricultural credit institutions were utilized for purchasing government bonds and for making loans to the munitions industry; agricultural credit institutions at that time were called "pumping-up" institutions.

Since 1945, the agricultural cooperative credit system has been the main supplier of short-term and intermediate credit to peasants. HBJ and HCB, which had lent to peasants with land as security in the prewar period, were transformed into commercial banks because land became illiquid as a result of the postwar land reform. To promote food production, the government made large-scale investments in land reclamation and improvement. Long-term agricultural credit for that purpose was supplied through the Special Account for Agriculture, Forestry and Fisheries Finance which was established to succeed the earlier long-term agricultural credit institutions; this special account was transformed into the present Agriculture, Forestry and Fisheries Finance Corporation (AFFFC) in 1953.

The agricultural cooperative credit system supplied peasants' production credit for staple foods by borrowing from the Bank of Japan at favorable terms during 1948–58. At that time, after the cessation of investment during the war, the rate of investment by peasants was extraordinarily high. The loan-deposit ratio increased to 0.54, returning to the 1937–38 level by 1954, but it has decreased since then. The agricultural cooperative credit system now functions again as a pump which absorbs funds from agriculture and pours them into nonagriculture. The Central Cooperative Bank for Agriculture and Forestry gathers the surplus funds from affiliated members and lends to agribusiness, to other banks, and the call market. Funds for agricultural loans to cooperative members come partly from the government, and the share of government funds has increased year by year. Funds for the long-term loans of AFFFC come from the national budget and are also borrowed from the Trust Fund Bureau Special Account, the Post Office Life Insurance, and the Postal Annuity Special Account. Thus private funds for agricultural finance are now being replaced by government funds.

Summary

In the process of Japan's economic growth, nonagricultural sectors have grown much faster than agriculture. One factor producing this discrepancy has been the continuously greater allocation of capital to the nonagricultural sector, and an important element producing this allocation of capital has been the flow of funds through financial institutions. To alleviate the shortage of capital in agriculture as a result of profit-seeking on the part of financial institutions, special credit institutions for agriculture have been set up. But insofar as these institutions are also run on a profit-making basis, they have not halted the outflow of funds from the sector. Credit provision for agriculture has gradually shifted from private capital to government capital. This tendency has existed in Japan ever since the Meiji period (1868–1912) but has become more conspicuous since World War II as a result of three major factors. The first two stem from land reform. This reform liquidated landlords, who had greater access to bank credit than did the small owner-operators who replaced them. The reform also made land illiquid, and therefore less attractive as collateral. The third factor has been the extraordinary high rate of growth of the nonagricultural sector.

4. *Financial Innovations and Development*

V. V. Bhatt

[Financial innovations tend to reduce transaction costs and risk, both subjective and objective, and as a result bring about the widening, deepening, and integration of capital markets. Such financial development accelerates the pace of economic development through its favorable impact on savings, investment, and output.]

Finance and Development

The pace and pattern of economic development are a function, as Adam Smith perceptively observed two centuries ago, of the sequential and circular relationship between the growth of the division of labor and the extent of the market for real goods and services. The innovations of money and finance tend to increase the size and extent of exchange relationships, or markets, and thus promote the division of labor and lead to increasing returns to scale and technical change.

Money as a unit of account and a medium of exchange reduces the transaction and search costs of barter transactions. Money as a store of value provides greater flexibility in the timing of purchase decisions and thus reduces risks. By reducing transaction costs and risk, money tends to enlarge the size of the market for real goods and services and hence the possibility for division of labor—two interacting, mutually reinforcing processes that account for sustained economic development.

Just as money reduces transaction costs and risk for exchanges across space, credit or financial instruments reduce costs of transactions and risk for intertemporal exchanges of goods and services. In this way, the existence of a credit or capital market enlarges the market for real goods and services. The impact of money and capital markets on the market for real goods and services is similar to that of a reduction of transport costs on trade or exchanges across space.

Unlike most markets for goods and services, credit or capital markets are inherently imperfect in that there is less initial certainty about the completion of a credit transaction. A credit transaction is completed only when the borrower repays the amount borrowed, and there is uncertainty about this repayment.

First, there is a borrower's risk: the expected excess income required for repayment may or may not materialize. In addition, there is the lender's risk, which has two elements. One relates to the same risk the borrower faces—inability to repay—but the lender may have a different perception of it. The other element relates to the borrower's willingness to repay; even if able to repay, he may not actually do so. Both the lender's and the borrower's expectations—their perceptions of the riskiness of their ventures—are of necessity subjective, based, of course, on whatever data and information are available and the individual's ability to interpret them.

There is double counting of one part of the risk. A borrower has a certain perception of the risk he faces with regard to, say, his investment project. The lender takes account of the same risk, but he may have a different perception of expectation of it. The borrower's subjective risk is r_1; the lender's risk is ar_1 (a being more than one, as the lender is likely to be more conservative in his expectations than the borrower) plus r_2, his subjective risk with regard to the borrower's willingness to repay. The total risk premium thus would be $r_1 + ar_1 + r_2$, and the borrower's expected rate of return on his investment should exceed the pure interest cost by this magnitude—that is, $r_1 (a + 1) + r_2 + t$ (the pure transaction costs). No credit transaction can take place so long as this magnitude exceeds the expected return to the borrower or the expected probability of repayment as seen by the lender.

Credit or capital markets come into being and evolve as a result of financial innovations that tend to reduce the total value of r (representing $r_1 [a + 1] + r_2 + t$) to a level that is mutually acceptable to both lenders and borrowers. The evolving nature and characteristics of these markets, the dealers and the other market participants, and the credit or financial instruments are crucially shaped by the nature of financial innovations that are feasible in a given socioeconomic context.

Financial innovations tend to reduce the lender's subjective risk much more than they increase transaction costs of lending and borrowing. Risk, of course, can be reduced with better and more accurate information, but this would involve an increase in transaction costs to the lender or the borrower, or to both. Hence, to be effective an innovation should have a risk-reducing effect much greater than its cost-increasing effect.

Nature and Characteristics of Financial Innovations

The evolution and integration of capital markets through the introduction and diffusion of financial innovations are not possible without some occupational specialization in the field of credit and finance.

Hence the significance of dealers and intermediaries. Isolated and individualized financial transactions (lending and borrowing) among households and firms have been and are quite important in sectors such as agriculture and small enterprises. But for capital markets to evolve, it is essential to have dealers who specialize in financial transactions—that is, who deal in financial claims or instruments. A dealer need not be an intermediary; he need not borrow in order to lend. For a financial intermediary, however, lending activity is crucial because his ability to borrow depends on the quality of his lending. The lender's subjective risk and the innovations that reduce this risk assume critical significance.

What, then, are the nature and characteristics of such innovations? The degree of subjective risk depends on how well a lender knows the prospective borrower and his ability and willingness to repay. Of course, the lender can demand information from the borrower and appraise it; but such information can be costly to collect and may not be reliable. The following innovations have been significant.

1. A *personal guarantee* reduces risk without at the same time increasing transaction costs. Such a guarantee generally has to be by a well-known person or firm with a reputation for financial integrity, considerable assets, and a business which enables the guarantor to judge the character and nature of the prospective borrower. For example, a well-established trader might give a personal guarantee for another trader not known to the lender. It is thus that a dealer's market expands. Of course, this device becomes feasible only when the market participants accept and adhere to a common code of business ethics; violation of this code leads to moral reprobation and excommunication from the market. Such code and sanctions also provide the logic for all types of cooperative credit arrangements among relatively homogeneous groups, which may not be considered individually creditworthy by other dealers and intermediaries. Lending by a dealer to individuals forming a homogeneous and cohesive group and offering *collective guarantees* belongs to this class of innovation. [See chapter 18 on guarantee mechanisms.]

2. *Short-term credit that is renewed or rolled over*, provided repayments are made regularly and on time, is a very economical and effective device for selecting reliable and dependable borrowers. Short-term loans for working capital or liquidity requirements have this rationale: a regular borrower, who repays on time and borrows at regular intervals for a known remunerative purpose, poses much less risk than a new borrower without previous history. The loan size in these cases is a function of the degree of the lender's knowledge of the borrower; what might appear as credit rationing is merely a device for reducing risk to acceptable levels.

3. Short-term lending against personal or collective guarantees,

and/or to dependable and reliable regular borrowers, is possible only when the dealers or lenders have a fairly intimate and personal knowledge and information about the borrowers and their occupations and assets. But the market for loans based on such personal contacts and on moral or social sanctions would doubtless be limited. For enlarging and expanding the market, some objective substitute for personal guarantees (formal or informal) becomes essential—a substitute that can have a legal sanction. This is the logic of the innovation of *collateral* or *security*, made up of real or financial assets.

If the borrower deals in or possesses goods or assets that are easily marketable without much risk of capital loss, the loan size could be made a function of the value of such assets. The risk of capital loss can be reduced by making the loan smaller than the market value of such assets; thus the borrower is forced to use his own money to finance this margin. This *security-cum-equity* type of innovation reduces the lender's subjective risk in two ways: risk arising from the possible unwillingness of the borrower to repay virtually disappears, and at the same time the risk relating to the borrower's ability to pay is reduced because the borrower is motivated by his equity stake to manage his business as efficiently as he can.

4. It is somewhat difficult for one type of dealer to finance the acquisition of, and take as security, assets with which he is not familiar. Each class of dealer tends to specialize in one type of asset and thus to deal with one class of borrower; their technology for transactions and risk appraisal is in tune with this type of asset and borrower. It would increase both transaction costs and risk for a dealer with a technology suited for one type of transaction to undertake a different type. For example, if a commercial bank has acquired over time a technology for financing medium-large firms in industry and trade, it would not be viable for such a bank to finance agriculture or small enterprises without first acquiring a new type of technology suited to these transactions. Informal market dealers have a technology for financing small enterprises of all types; and if a commercial bank wants to expand its business in this type of transaction, it may be more economical and effective for it to lend to informal market dealers than to lend directly to the primary borrowers. Innovations that expand and deepen the scope of capital markets are generally introduced by new entrepreneurs with technology and expertise as well as financial instruments that are different from those of existing dealers. It is thus that new markets evolve.

5. Since financial innovations lead to a variety of specialized dealers and markets, they create a diversity of financial instruments, each with unique characteristics and features. This diversity of financial products

enables both primary savers and borrowers to choose among instruments better suited to their special requirements, and it thus stimulates saving in the form of financial assets as well as borrowing that promotes a more efficient allocation and use of investable resources. Further, the competition among this array of specialized dealers in mobilizing financial resources from the primary savers tends to integrate the various financial markets.

What are the preconditions for the emergence of such financial innovations, whose nature and characteristics are broadly indicated above?

Obviously, no such innovations are possible without a general climate of trust and confidence among the market participants. This needs to be reinforced by the stability and predictability of an effective, enforceable legal framework. But if lenders or borrowers have to resort to legal safeguards for the greater part of their dealings, transaction costs would become prohibitive; hence the significance of the general state of trust and confidence.

In addition, there has to be some degree of monetary stability. Without that, the subjective evaluation of risk by market participants would be extremely difficult.

Finally, there should be no legal or customary obstacles to experimentation and innovation, particularly with regard to the so-called informal credit markets. The established large formal dealers are reluctant to change from one type of technology or expertise to another; the subjective risk as well as transaction costs for an untried technology appear to them to be much higher than those relating to their existing technology. Since informal market dealers operate largely on the basis of personal information and knowledge, they are in a much better position to identify new opportunities for financial transactions—new markets requiring new products and processes. At the same time, their transaction costs and risks for such experimentation are, for obvious reasons, unlikely to be high. Further, as formal markets expand with economic evolution, informal dealers have a certain compulsion to innovate and thus, quite often, create and nurture new markets with innovative products. Once these new markets grow to a certain size, the formal institutions with their scale economies are in a position to introduce the new products and compete effectively with the informal markets. This vital role of the informal market in identifying new opportunities for financial transactions, in introducing new financial instruments and processes or new technology for appraising risk and soundness of purpose, and in creating and nurturing new markets is little appreciated in the literature or by policy makers.

Role of Public Policy

Innovations are generally spontaneous, but they can also be induced by two types of policy intervention. One is cost- and risk-reducing; the other relates to overcoming and offsetting the negative impacts of government policies and is cost- and risk-increasing.

Cost- and Risk-increasing Intervention

Interest rate ceilings and credit allocation quotas prescribed for commercial banks by central bank or government authorities with a view to enlarging the flow of credit to, say, small enterprises of all types (including those in the agricultural sector) are self-defeating and in fact raise the cost of credit to the very sector the government intends to support. Since the transaction costs and risk are higher for deals with small enterprises than for those with medium-large enterprises in trade and industry, either the banks do not lend to the small sector or they forestall the government directive by passing on a greater part of their costs and risk to the small sector through noninterest charges of various types. If the banks were to implement government directives literally, their financial viability would be adversely affected; this would endanger the health of the financial system and have undesirable consequences for economic development generally and the development of the small sector in particular. In any case it is meaningless to fix the price as well as the quota, for this leads to credit rationing and gives considerable scope for corruption. Arbitrary interest rate ceilings on bank lending lead to low interest rates on deposits, and this diverts private savings into commodities or private lending.

Another instance of such negative policy intervention is the variety of restrictions on the functioning of the informal credit market. This market actually mobilizes resources from and purveys credit to sectors generally outside the formal market. Restriction of its activity, therefore, raises the cost or reduces the availability of credit to these sectors.

Cost- and Risk-reducing Intervention

Other types of government intervention have an impact similar to financial innovations or may induce such innovations. For example, deposit insurance would reduce subjective risk of primary savers and thus may increase the rate of financial saving. Viable credit guarantee schemes for small enterprises may reduce the subjective risk of dealers and may induce them to lend to these borrowers. Effective and self-supporting crop insurance schemes may reduce the risk of lending to the farm sector and may at the same time result in resource mobilization greater than would otherwise occur. Improving the access of farmers and small enterprises to financial and technical consultancy services can raise their productivity and thus reduce the risk of lending. Exempting saving in the form of financial assets from taxable income can raise the real rates of return on financial saving and thus increase the rate of financial saving. A fixed-sum subsidy to, say, a commercial bank to cover the initial cost of acquiring the financial technology necessary for effective and economical lending to small enterprises, or to open a branch in an unbanked area, can make it possible for the bank to introduce financial instruments suited to the potential depositors and borrowers.

The impact of policy intervention on the capital market should be judged on the basis of this simple criterion: does it reduce transaction costs and risk associated with financial transactions? If it does not have this cost- and risk-reducing effect, it would harm rather than help the evolution and integration of capital markets.

5. *Financial Development and Economic Growth in Developing Countries*

Hugh T. Patrick

[Supply-leading finance is the creation of financial institutions and instruments in advance of demand for them in an effort to stimulate economic growth. This strategy seeks to make the allocation of capital more efficient and to provide incentives for growth through the financial system. The success of supply-leading finance appears to require government support, cautious experimentation, public confidence, and relatively stable prices.]

Demand-Following and Supply-Leading Phenomena

Generally, where enterprise leads, finance follows. The same impulses within an economy which set enterprise on foot make owners of wealth venturesome, and when a strong impulse to invest is fettered by lack of finance, devices are invented to release it. Habits and institutions are then developed. Such an approach emphasizes the demand side; as the economy grows it generates demand for financial services, which bring about a supply response in the growth of the financial system. In this view, the lack of financial institutions in developing countries indicates the lack of demand for their services. The term "demand-following" refers to the creation of modern financial institutions, their financial assets and liabilities, and related financial services in response to the demand for these services by investors and savers in the real economy. In this case, the evolution of the financial system is a consequence of economic development.

The nature of the demand for financial services depends on the growth of total output and on the commercialization and monetization of agriculture and other traditional sectors. The more rapid the growth rate of real national income, the greater will be the demand of

Extracted from *Economic Development and Cultural Change*, vol. 14, no. 2 (January 1966), pp. 174–89, by permission of The University of Chicago Press.

enterprises for external funds (the savings of others) and, therefore, financial intermediation. The greater the variance in growth rates among different sectors or industries, the greater will be the need for financial intermediation to transfer savings to fast-growing industries from elsewhere in the economy.

The supply response of the financial system is presumed to come about automatically. It is assumed that the supply of entrepreneurship in the financial sector is highly elastic, so that the number and types of financial institutions expand sufficiently; and a favorable legal, institutional, and economic environment is also assumed. The government's attitudes, goals, and policies, as well as the government debt, are of course important influences on the economic environment.

The demand-following approach implies that finance is essentially passive. In fact, the increased supply of financial services in response to demand may not be at all automatic, flexible, or inexpensive in developing countries. Restrictive banking legislation, religious barriers against interest charges, and imperfections in the operation of the market mechanism may dictate an inadequate demand-following response by the financial system. Lack of financial services then inhibits effective growth patterns and processes.

Less emphasis has been given to the supply-leading phenomenon: the creation of financial institutions and the supply of their financial assets, liabilities, and related financial services in advance of demand for them, especially the demand of entrepreneurs in the modern or growth-inducing sectors. Supply-leading finance has two functions: to transfer resources from traditional or nongrowth sectors to modern sectors and to promote and stimulate entrepreneurial responses. Access to supply-leading funds opens new horizons, enabling the entrepreneur to "think big." Moreover, the top management of financial institutions may also serve as entrepreneurs. They assist in the establishment of firms in new industries or in the merger of firms by underwriting a substantial portion of the capital and by assuming entrepreneurial initiative.

A supply-leading financial institution may initially be unable to operate profitably by lending to the nascent modern sectors. There are, however, several ways in which new financial institutions can be made viable. First, they may be government institutions, using government capital and supplied with direct subsidies. Second, private financial institutions may receive direct or indirect government subsidies, usually the latter. Commercial banks may have the right to create deposit money with low (theoretically, even negative) reserve requirements and with central bank rediscount of commercial bank loans at interest rates effectively below those on the loans. Third, new financial institutions may lend most of their funds profitably to traditional commercial sectors and then gradually shift their loan portfolio into modern activities as these begin to emerge. This more closely resembles the demand-following phenomena; whether such a financial institution is supply-leading depends mainly on its attitude in searching out and encouraging new ventures of a modern nature.

It cannot be said that supply-leading finance is a necessary condition or precondition for self-sustained economic development; rather, it presents an opportunity to induce real growth by financial means. In practice, there is likely to be an interaction of supply-leading and demand-following phenomena. The following sequence may be postulated. Before sustained modern industrial growth gets under way, supply-leading finance may be able to induce real innovation. As the process of real growth occurs, the supply-leading impetus becomes less important, and the demand-following financial response becomes dominant. This shift is also likely to occur within and among specific industries or sectors at different phases of their growth.

Finance and the Real Capital Stock

The financial system can influence the capital stock for growth purposes in three major ways. First, financial institutions can encourage efficient allocation of the stock of tangible wealth by bringing about changes in its ownership and composition through intermediation among various types of asset holders. Second, financial institutions can encourage efficient allocation of new investment by intermediation between savers and entrepreneurial investors. Third, they can activate an increase in the rate of accumulation of capital by providing increased incentives to save, invest, and work.

Allocation of a Given Amount of Tangible Wealth

The flow characteristics of savings provide some indication of the stock characteristics of wealth in developing countries. For example, in a sample of Asian countries between one-half and two-thirds of gross saving is done by households, and one-half to three-fourths of household net saving is in the form of increases in tangible assets—findings that probably reflect the structure of ownership and composition of wealth for these countries. Most of the assets held by savers are under their direct control. Individual real wealth in the poorer developing countries typically consists mainly of land and land improvements, houses, simple agricultural and handicraft tools, livestock, inventories (notably foodstuffs), and durable consumer goods including precious metals and jewelry. In part, this composition of wealth results from a lack of productive investment opportunities or ignorance of their existence. As the economy changes and brings out investment opportunities, pressures develop to diversify and improve the composition of wealth. Creating and making available additional types of financial assets gives savers the opportunity to select more efficient portfolios.

A considerable portion of tangible wealth in developing countries is held in forms unproductive of sustained growth. Some can readily be transformed into productive capital goods. This is especially true of precious metals, excess holdings of inventories, and the depreciating portion of the capital stock. The amounts involved could be significant. It is not unreasonable to think of ratios of tangible wealth to GNP, even excluding land, of 2 or 3. A reallocation of as much as 10 percent of this wealth to more productive forms would be equivalent to 20 or 30 percent of GNP and could increase output by about 10 percent. Changes in composition of a given stock of wealth to more productive forms are a once-and-for-all adjustment; output is raised but continued growth does not result.

In many developing countries inventories of foodstuffs, other primary products, and in some cases finished manufactured goods are held in amounts considerably in excess of normal consumption or production requirements. In the absence of suitable alternative financial assets, inventories are the only assets that are relatively liquid and divisible and that offer some protection against inflation. Storage and spoilage costs can be high, however, and for individual commodities risks of price fluctuation or other losses are also high. I conjecture that in the early stages of development individuals shift their holdings from inventories in excess of their normal production or consumption requirements to newly created financial assets which have more attractive terms. These inventories are freed to be transformed into productive fixed capital goods.

How does the development of new types or additional quantities of financial assets assist in transforming a given amount of tangible assets into more productive form? Individuals who hold tangible assets capable of being transformed are not necessarily those who are willing to hold productive fixed assets. The productive uses of fixed assets in developing countries usually entail entrepreneurial and managerial functions as well as ownership, and not all wealth holders want to engage in these functions. The opportunity to hold alternative assets enables the holders of tangible assets to give them up for financial assets that are superior to inventories and specie as a store of wealth; other people can then transform the freed, tangible assets into a more productive form. What is crucial is, on the one hand, substituting financial assets for real assets in the portfolios of certain individuals and, on the other, permitting entrepreneurs to incur financial liabilities so that they can obtain a larger amount of productive assets than they could otherwise. The important gain is this substitution between real assets and financial claims; substitutions among various kinds of financial assets in individual portfolios are useful but less important.

More Efficient Allocation of Investment

The foregoing discussion is essentially an extension of the Gurley-Shaw analysis of the role of financial intermediation in improving the efficiency of investment (see chapter 2 above). The Gurley-Shaw theory rests on two assumptions: individual savers are not all the most efficient investors, and savers are not willing to make the full amount of their savings directly available to the most efficient investors. Saving depends primarily on income levels, while efficient investment depends on entrepreneurial talents, knowledge, and willingness to take risk. Savers in developing countries tend to invest in real assets, often of relatively low social productivity. By contrast, efficient entrepreneurial investors are unable to invest as much as they would like.

Under these circumstances, financial intermediaries provide an important mechanism for transferring claims on real resources from savers to the most efficient investors. The more perfect are the financial markets, the more nearly is an optimum allocation of investment achieved. In this way, the financial system accommodates economic growth. To the extent that the financial system is underdeveloped or inefficient, it restricts growth. Financial institutions effect this transfer by issuing their liabilities (selling indirect securities) to savers, and by providing the assets so accumulated to investors by purchasing their primary securities.

An important function of the financial system is to change relatively safe, liquid, short-term financial claims into riskier, less liquid, longer-term real assets. When examining specific projects, we must distinguish between the degree of risk for individuals and for society as a whole and between two types of risk—insolvency and illiquidity. For both types the degree of risk is less for society than for individuals. The risk of unprofitability of a specific investment project is pooled with risks of other projects for society, but not for individuals, unless this is done by financial intermediaries. Financial intermediation reallocates and spreads the risks among individuals.

As a developing country grows, the composition of its tangible wealth is altered to a more growth-productive mix, both by the once-and-for-all shifts and by the differential composition of the gross additions to wealth. With the growth of financial intermediation, funds are channeled mainly to finance productive industrial and infrastructural investment. Accordingly, the proportion of producer durables and business structures in total wealth rises, while land and consumer durable assets decline.

Provision of Incentives to Growth

The development of a financial system and the associated provision of financial claims and services offer positive incentives for growth. The standard approach has been to point out that financial intermediation narrows the difference between the interest rate savers receive and that which investors have to pay.

Financial institutions also stimulate savings by offering a wide array of financial assets. With increased availability of assets having higher yield, lower risk, and other desirable characteristics, the return on savings is higher than it was before. With the tradeoff between saving and present consumption becoming more favorable to the former, individuals save more.

Financial intermediation also provides incentives to investors. For many entrepreneurs, increased availability of funds as a result of financial intermediation may be considerably more significant than reduction in costs. This is probably particularly true in developing countries, where most markets are much less perfect than in developed countries. Availability of funds from financial institutions enables the efficient entrepreneur to assume greater debt than he could otherwise and to engage in a larger amount of productive investment. Moreover, access to funds on reasonable terms from financial institutions can encourage entrepreneurs to expand their horizon of conceivable opportunities. Not simply access to funds, but the entire financial milieu and the rationalism it implies trigger creative entrepreneurial responses.

Financial Policy and Financial Institutions

The basic objectives of financial policy for economic growth are to encourage savers to hold their savings in the form of financial rather than unproductive tangible assets; to ensure that investment is allocated efficiently to the socially most productive uses; and to provide incentives to increase saving, investment, and production. To achieve these objectives, policy makers must encourage the foundation and expansion of financial institutions.

The monetary authorities have an important institution-building role: they encourage the establishment of a wide array of financial markets, and institutions operating in these markets, to allocate savings more competitively to the most productive investors. One approach is to encourage the private development of the financial system, in response to the demand for its services, by clearing away legal, institutional, or customary obstacles. The financial authorities can create an environment which is conducive to the growth of both the real economy and the financial system. In this situation, reliance is placed on private market incentives to achieve an efficient allocation of resources.

Private entrepreneurial response in the financial sector may not be adequate, however, or external economies may be possible. For example, financial markets may develop on a compartmentalized basis with little integration. Deliberate creation of a supply of financial services could be expected to have favorable allocative and incentive effects. Under these circumstances, it may be desirable for the government to establish state-owned financial institutions or to subsidize private financial institutions. Nonetheless, political pressures, bureaucratic inefficiency, and corruption can divert the flow of funds under government programs away from optimal allocation patterns. A supply-leading approach should be handled cautiously, with emphasis placed primarily on eliminating bottlenecks in the provision of financial services.

I have emphasized the efficiency of financial intermediation through the private market mechanism in allocating scarce capital to its most productive uses. Under some conditions, however, the private optimal allocation diverges from the social optimum. In the financial sphere, institutions may conceive of their function only narrowly, or they may avoid risk more than is socially desirable. The monetary authorities should encourage financial institutions to allocate their funds to investment activities where the social marginal productivity is relatively high. Which sectors deserve most encouragement depends on the country. In many developing countries both private industrial investment and productive agricultural investment are starved in relation to commerce and government; there is a need for long-term funds to finance productive fixed investment. If there is an effective long-term capital market in which individual and institutional savers are able and willing to purchase long-term securities, most of the problem is solved. However, since private individual participation in capital markets is extremely unlikely early in the development process, financial intermediation is even more important in developing countries to carry out the functions of the capital market.

The central bank can make investment activities more attractive by open market purchases or by accepting as collateral for loans to financial institutions their holdings of industrial bonds, long-term loans or even equities, or loans for productive purposes in agriculture. It can indirectly aid by assisting in the development of financial institutions with special functions—such as long-term credit development banks, agricultural and industrial credit cooperatives, and savings institutions, as well as regular commercial banks—to ensure a full spectrum of financial services. The monetary authorities could also take steps to make financial assets attractive to individual savers by developing and maintaining public confidence in the financial system and its institutions. Means include legal sanctions on and regular inspection of financial institutions, and government insurance of deposits, savings and loan shares, or other assets. The competitive appeal of financial assets in relation to real assets depends on their safety, liquidity, and yield. Some developing countries today misguidedly pursue low interest rate policies, which effectively inhibit financial assets from competing with real assets, and thus stunt the growth of the financial system as well as encourage unduly capital-intensive techniques of production.

In developing countries, a considerable portion of the savings used relatively unproductively are probably hoarded by large numbers of relatively poor people. To reallocate such savings more productively requires financial assets in very small units, simple and convenient to use, and readily available in rural areas. Bank offices may be too expensive to operate in rural areas or small towns until agricultural incomes rise substantially. Postal savings programs, utilizing the network of post offices, may be the cheapest and most practical way to channel small rural wealth and savings into financial assets.

To encourage financial intermediation as a means of obtaining resources for growth and of allocating those resources efficiently, the monetary authorities have to pursue broad economic policies which not only directly promote growth, but also enhance public confidence in the financial system. Relatively stable prices are important for this purpose. Deflation will generally slow down the growth rate, but it does not follow that inflation speeds up the rate of growth. The relationship between inflation and growth evidently depends on individual behavior patterns and structural and institutional rigidities within the particular economy. Mild inflation probably increases entrepreneurial demand for real investment, initially at least. It conceivably may also increase the saving rates of individuals, though more often increases in the aggregate saving ratio are deemed to come from a redistribution of income and wealth from spenders to savers. Inflation, however, changes the effective yields on various assets, tending to raise yields on relatively unproductive investment, such as the holding of inventories. Since most financial assets are predicated on a reasonable degree of price stability, inflation discourages the holding of financial assets and encourages a return to the holding of socially unproductive real assets. Therefore, if an inflationary policy is to be adopted, the financial authorities should develop financial assets whose yield and value will not be hurt by price rises.

6. *Farm Credit Policy in the Early Stages of Agricultural Development*

David H. Penny

[In the early stages of development, peasant attitudes toward debt are such that cheap credit is unlikely to be a useful growth stimulus. The effectiveness of credit depends on the ability and willingness of peasants to devote such additional funds to productive uses. The poor performance of many government rural credit programs in low-income countries is discussed, and criteria for a successful program are presented.]

There is a growing literature on how to turn a static agriculture into a developing one. Unfortunately, the literature grows more rapidly than the incomes of the peasants. This chapter will discuss only one aspect of development, the farm credit policies pursued by governments in low-income countries. The thesis is that what most governments do to overcome the so-called rural debt problem wastes resources and fails to spur development.

The majority view on the debt problem is summed up in the following excerpts. M. Harsoadi of Indonesia [in E. K. Bauer, ed., *Proceedings of the International Conference on Agricultural and Cooperative Credit*, vol. 2, Berkeley: University of California, 1952] expresses a typical view when he writes: "Since the vast majority of farmers are smallholders . . . the raising of the economic level should be attained by developing and organizing the credit to the smallholders." The conclusions of the well-known development economists, W. A. Lewis [*The Theory of Economic Growth*, Homewood, Ill., Irwin, 1955], B. H. Higgins [*Economic Development*, New York, Norton, 1959], and H. Leibenstein [*Economic Backwardness and Economic Growth*, New York, Wiley, 1957], are: "Farmers need much more capital than they can afford to save"; "Credit may be necessary for expansion in some areas, especially small agriculture

Extracted from *Australian Journal of Agricultural Economics*, vol. 12, no. 1 (June 1968), pp. 32–45.

and small industry"; and "If capital, labor, entrepreneurial facilities, technical knowledge, *and credit facilities available* [emphasis added] increase, the income per head will rise." Governments in most low-income countries have vigorously followed the advice given in these and similar writings, but their programs of more and more cheaper credit for farmers have done little to encourage agricultural development. The reason for their lack of success will be made clear below.

This introduction would be incomplete, however, without noting some minority views. Writing in 1952, J. K. Galbraith [in Bauer, *Proceedings*, vol. 1] said that credit systems "can be an instrument of progress, and of stagnation and repression." He also noted that credit can become an instrument for progress only after there has been some development. C.-M. Li [in Bauer, *Proceedings*, vol. 1] has argued that farmers should be on the road to becoming commercial farmers before governments start their credit programs. J. W. Mellor [*The Economics of Agricultural Development*, Ithaca, N.Y., Cornell University Press, 1966] has said that "cooperative credit programs might better accompany or follow programs of technical change, not precede them, as has been general in development programs." The weight of both expert and political opinion is against Galbraith and the few who share his views. But Galbraith, Li, and Mellor are right, and government rural credit programs will remain ineffective until governments come to a better understanding of the role of credit in peasant economies, and the attitudes of peasant farmers toward savings, investment, and debt.

Peasants and Debt

> Neither a borrower, nor a lender be;
> For loan oft loses both itself and friend,
> And borrowing dulls the edge of husbandry.
>
> —Polonius's advice to his son, Laertes,
> in Shakespeare's *Hamlet*, I, iii.

Are farmers in debt because they want to be, or because they have to be? For commercial farmers this question is not easy to answer since there are always some farmer-borrowers in both categories. For peasant farmers who operate in static, low-income agriculture, the answer is unequivocal: they have felt compelled to borrow. Most writers on the subject would agree, and they ascribe this compulsion to the risky and uncertain nature of agricultural production and the social framework in rural areas. Recurrent themes from studies of the debt problem are "farmers too poor to save," "many in debt," "moneylenders," and "interest rates too high," and the authors then conclude that the solution to these problems is more and cheaper credit. But they

Table 6-1. *Farmer Borrowing and Expenditure on Production Requisites in Eight North Sumatran Villages*
(average per farm, 1961–62 crop year)

Village and rank on index of economic-mindedness[a]	*Percentage of farmers in debt*	*Debt per farm (rupiahs)*	*Use of borrowed money*		*Expenditure on production requisites (rupiahs)*	*Expenditure on production requisites as percentage of gross farm receipts*
			Main use	*Secondary use*		
I. Tiga Nderket	24	2,100	Production requisites	—	15,300	10.0
II. Nagasaribu	50	1,000	Production requisites	Housebuilding	15,200	20.1
III. Namumbelin	0	none	—	—	800	1.5
IV. Sumbul	57	2,400	Production requisites	Consumption and education	3,200	7.1
V. "Tamiang"	5	—[b]	—	—	30	< 0.1
VI. Pematang Djohar	0	none	—	—	80	0.1
VII. Lintong ni Huta	57	14,800	Consumption	Ceremonies and education	2,300	3.4
VIII. Lubuk Tjemara	38	700	Consumption	Ceremonies and petty trade	20	< 0.1

Note: Farmers in all villages face approximately the same set of economic opportunities: there is equal access to markets, and where land is in short supply within the confines of the village (villages I and VII), it is cheaply and freely available elsewhere.

a. For explanation, see text.

b. The one farmer interviewed in this village who borrowed was a net creditor.

Source: D. H. Penny, "The Transition from Subsistence to Commercial Family Farming in North Sumatra," Ph.D. dissertation, Cornell University, 1964.

have rarely given adequate consideration to peasant attitudes toward lending and borrowing, to how these attitudes arose, or to the implications of these attitudes in the success or failure of credit programs.

The hypothesis to be examined here is that peasant attitudes toward debt and credit in the early stages of development are such that cheap credit is unlikely to be a useful growth stimulus. Most of the data used to test this hypothesis are from the Indonesian province of North Sumatra. In 1962 I studied eight villages in different parts of the province and found that the farmers differed widely from village to village in their attitudes toward economic development and, as will be shown, toward debt. In two of the villages many farmers were already economic-minded; that is, they were aware of the economic opportunities that existed and had proved they were both able and willing to use them. In three villages the farmers remained subsistence-minded; that is, they were unaware, for the most part, of the opportunities for development and lacked both the will and the ability to exploit them. The farmers in the three remaining villages were in an intermediate position. There is a direct relationship between the degree of economic-mindedness attained by a farmer and his willingness and ability to use credit productively for development (see table 6-1).

Only in villages I, II, and IV do farmers borrow to finance the purchase of production requisites. Borrowing for consumption and ceremonies is characteristic of villages IV, VII, and VIII. The farmers in villages III, V, and VI are in debt and provide the most interesting insights into peasant attitudes toward debt. These three villages are comparatively new settlements from the 1940s and early 1950s. The villagers are either former plantation laborers of peasant stock or Sumatrans who were forced by population pressure in their home villages to seek new land. Farmer committees allocated land to the newcomers on the basis of need. There are no landlords or moneylenders. In short, these villagers were able to create an economy in which they could achieve the peasant ideal of being independent freeholders.

When it comes to borrowing and lending, these farmers have the same philosophy as Polonius, and they adhere to it. But they are subsistence-minded, and their ideal peasant economy is therefore inherently unstable. The time is coming when some of these men will be forced to borrow to finance consumption by their growing families. Those most likely to lend to them are the relatively more successful farmers. The end result of this evolutionary process will be that the most successful among the new settlers will become both landlords and creditors, and the villages will be saddled with the "problem of debt." This is the inevitable result of the economic dynamics of peasant communities if the debt-free and landlord-free farmers do not decide to use the economic potential at their command for development.

Village VIII, Lubuk Tjemara, clearly demonstrates what happens in the longer period if the farmers remain subsistence-minded. Lubuk Tjemara was a new village in 1910; by now the landlordism and debt that characterized the villages from which the migrants came have reappeared on a fairly wide scale. In some cases, however, new settlers from peasant backgrounds seriously exploit the economic potential of their resources, as the farmers in village III have begun to do.

The data in table 6-2 illustrate how the economics of new settlements may evolve. The subsistence-minded farmers would prefer to stay out of debt, and new settlers are able to do so for several years. From a debtless position, peasants can move toward the creative use of credit or into the toils of debt. Which path they follow depends on their willingness and ability to exploit the resources at their disposal. Family incomes are most nearly equal in Pematang Djohar, a new settlement and a village with quite a low ranking on the index of economic-mindedness. The question then becomes whether the trend toward greater inequality that will occur over time will be a consequence of economic retrogression or advancement. For example, will village VI, Pematang Djohar, move in the direction of village VIII or in the direction of villages I and III, where development is taking place?

The farmers in these new settlements earn incomes that are ample to finance the purchase of fertilizer, new tools, improved seeds, or other modern inputs *if they want to*. Clearly, there is no need to provide these farmers with credit merely to get development under way. But where new settlements have undergone economic retrogression, as in Lubuk Tjemara, the mere provision of credit is even less likely to make

Table 6-2. *Family Income of Farmers in Four North Sumatran Villages, 1961–62*

Village and rank on index of economic-mindedness	*Average income (rupiahs)*		*Incomes earned by lower half as percentage of those earned by top half*
	Top half in sample	*Lower half in sample*[a]	
I. Tiga Nderket	159,600	45,300	28
III. Namumbelin	74,800	30,000	40
VI. Pematang Djohar[b]	52,300	33,000	63
VIII. Lubuk Tjemara	58,100	29,400	51

a. All farmers in these four villages earned more than enough in 1961–62 to finance their basic consumption: none would be regarded as poor by local standards.

b. Javanese farmers only.

farmers development-minded than it would in Pematang Djohar: a debtor's first thought is to pay off his old debts and to achieve the peasant ideal of being "free and clear." Such a situation no doubt makes the former debtor very happy, but it will still take time before he is ready to assume the risks and burdens of economic change. Only after formerly subsistence-minded farmers have proved their willingness to innovate, to sacrifice present income for future, and to learn new techniques and methods do they become creditworthy.

Let there be no mistake—profitable economic opportunities abound in both Lubuk Tjemara and Pematang Djohar, but the will to develop is absent. As long as it is absent, farmers will not wish to borrow to finance productive investment; and although governments often coerce farmers, for their own supposed good, into borrowing, farmers will not ensure that any such borrowings are used in a developmental way.

This conclusion is supported by farmer responses to the following questions: "How would you use cash gifts of Rp1,000, Rp10,000, and Rp50,000?" A condition of the gift was that it be used for productive investment. Farmers accustomed to using cash capital in their farm operations would be expected to give economically rational answers to this question. If they are basically subsistence-minded, however, they will not know how to use cash capital in a profitable way because they have never, or rarely, considered the possibility of using their resources for productive investment (see table 6-3).

Farmer responses to the question differ greatly from village to village, but the response pattern should not be surprising given what has already been said about differences in farmer attitudes toward economic development. If government credit were made available to farmers in villages I or II, they would be willing to use it for production and would know how to use it profitably. In villages III, IV, and V, some farmers would use credit in a profitable way, while in villages VI, VII, and VIII, few would do so. One can only conclude that many writers who advocate easier credit have not fully analyzed the likely effects of their recommendations: they appear to take for granted that farmers already possess the right mental attitude for development.

Most peasants in the early stages of development are like those in villages VI, VII, and VIII. P. G. K. Panikar ["Rural Savings in India," *Economic Development and Cultural Change,* vol. 10, no. 1, 1961] has noted that the actual net savings of Indian farmers are far more than most people think—at least 8 percent of their income—but the bulk of these savings go into unproductive uses. He cites the result of a study made in Hyderabad in 1949–50: 25 percent of savings were used to repay debts, 48 percent for consumer durables and ceremonies, 9 percent for land purchase, and only 18 percent for agricultural production. For India as a whole, farmer spending on life-crisis cere-

Table 6-3. *Farmer Response to a Hypothetical Question on Uses for a Cash Gift of Rp50,000 in Agriculture*
(percent)

Village and rank on index of economic-mindedness	*Uses assisting development*		*Uses not assisting development*	
	Modern production requisites	*Commercial perennial crops or livestock production*	*Land purchase*	*Other, not profitable*[a]
I. Tiga Nderket	41	56	3	—
II. Nagasaribu	38	62	—	—
III. Namumbelin[b]	—	45	43	12
VI. Sumbul[b]	17	8	75	—
V. "Tamiang"	—	62	29	9
VI. Pematang Djohar[c]	—	—	83	17
VII. Lintong ni Huta[d]	—	—	60	40
VIII. Lubuk Tjemara[b]	5	—	75	20

Note: The questions about "gifts" of Rp1,000 and Rp10,000 produced the same general pattern of response. If farmers suggested, say, two possible uses for each amount of gift capital, both possibilities were recorded in the appropriate category and given an equal weight of 0.5. Single answers were given a weight of 1.

a. Unprofitable uses would include the purchase of additional traditional tools of low productivity and investment in livestock where there is already overgrazing.

b. Most farmers own more land than they are currently using.

c. Double cropping of current holdings would be highly profitable.

d. Farms are small, but no land is locally available.

monies equals their total annual borrowings. It is not lack of capital access in agriculture that inhibits development, but lack of farmer motivation to use for development the capital sources they already have.

To sum up: the peasant ideal is to be an independent freeholder. "Ideal" peasant societies, like those in the new settlements described above, evolve in time into rural economies characterized by debt and landlordism. In an earlier era this decay did not matter so long as new land was readily available, for when the situation became too difficult, farmers could migrate to other areas and set up new farms. Where new land is no longer freely available—in India and Java, for example—debt and landlordism become more intractable. The peasants' ideal, however, remains unchanged, and if peasants have the chance, as the Javanese plantation workers did in 1942, they will establish new settlements which allow each man to become economically independent—for a time at least. It is not capital or credit they lack, but the motivation to use resources for development. Until governments realize this point, and act accordingly, money will continue to be lent to farmers without a corresponding increase in production.

Implications for Government Credit Programs

Most governments in low-income countries have tried to improve their agricultural credit systems. They feel that development is inhibited because farmers are too poor, lack capital, and must pay high interest rates when they borrow. Their goal is more and cheaper credit for farmers; but the resources used in credit programs rarely give a satisfactory profit compared with the returns from investments in agricultural research and extension or in social capital (such as roads and harbors).

It is not difficult to discover whether farmers need additional (borrowed) capital from outside in order to undertake profitable investments: simply ascertain whether farmers can afford fertilizer, new tools, and so on, and whether they have begun to buy them. Governments often do not need to provide credit, since many peasant farmers can afford to finance some investments from their own resources. Once peasants have shown themselves willing to do this and have also shown an ability to invest wisely, even if only on a small scale, credit may then serve a useful purpose. If governments are unwilling to wait, they will surely misallocate scarce capital resources through their credit programs.

Government credit programs have some elements in common: costs exceed returns and require subsidy; interest rates are below market rates, and real rates are often negative, partly because of inflation and partly because governments are lenient creditors. Frequently the repayment of loans is very poor. And frequently these credit programs add to inflationary pressures.

Why are credit programs advocated and pursued so vigorously, when it should be clear from the experience of many countries that they are an expensive and wasteful way of encouraging agricultural development? There appear to be at least four reasons. The first and most important is that governments, and apparently many economists, are unaware of the attitudes of peasants toward debt and credit and the unwillingness of many farmers to use credit developmentally at the time it is offered. Second, governments see credit programs as an easy way to increase the flow of capital to the rural sector, but they forget that credit does not necessarily represent capital. Capital is not created merely by increasing the supply of money, nor can capital be used developmentally if farmers are permitted to use their borrowings for consumption. Third, governments in many low-income countries seem to feel that modern financial institutions to serve farmers can be created by a stroke of a pen; they fail to realize that the growth of such institutions is as much a result as a cause of development.

Fourth, governments do not recognize the powerful economic reasons for the high nominal rates of interest charged in the so-called unorganized money markets. Loanable funds are in short supply in low-income countries, and, at first glance, it is not surprising that market interest rates are higher than in high-income countries. It is rarely realized, however, that the men who control this scarce capital—moneylenders of all sorts—do not earn by any means as much as the nominal interest charges suggest. Data in the All-India Rural Credit Survey indicated that village moneylenders grossed only an average of 11 percent on their lendings. [*All-India Rural Credit Survey*, vol. 1, *The Survey Report*, pt. 2, Bombay, Reserve Bank of India, 1957, pp. 490–91.] High rates on short-term loans do not necessarily mean high annual rates of return on capital, because much of the moneylenders' funds may be idle for six months or more.

Most farmers do not have to be bribed with cheap credit to adopt profitable innovations if there is a satisfactory market for the additional output. If extension workers try, they can often induce farmers to finance the purchase of new inputs or tools from their own resources, without offering credit. After a number of years, if lack of capital is indeed determined to be the main factor preventing adoption, then, and only then, a government and the economy may benefit from the establishment of special credit facilities.

Should policy makers feel it is politically essential to have a credit program, no doubt they will have one. If so, perhaps all an economist can advise is that it be kept small, even smaller than extension, road-building, and similar programs.

7. *Impact of General Economic Policies on the Performance of Rural Financial Markets*

Edward John Ray

[Policies that discriminate against the rural sector in favor of import-substitution industries or other activities in which a developing country has no competitive advantage are likely to repress agricultural production and rural incomes, encourage rural-to-urban migration, and lead to inflation and balance of payments problems. Such policies hinder the development of rural financial markets capable of equitable and efficient resource allocation.]

Widely prevalent in developing countries are attempts to promote economic growth by industrial import substitution. Such policies have so distorted the economies of a number of these countries that it has become difficult to develop their rural areas.

During the 1950s and early 1960s, the focal point for development planning was the industrial sector. The general prescription for rapid economic progress was to strive for economic characteristics of the industrial West. Each developing country was urged to develop its own textile manufactures, steel mills, auto industry, and the like, with little regard for the domestic resources that were available. With the economic stagnation that often followed, academicians and planners began to rethink their prescription. During the latter half of the 1960s and the decade of the 1970s, they shifted toward a more export-oriented expansion in areas in which countries had traditionally exhibited strength and had demonstrated a comparative advantage in production and trade. For many countries this policy approach was a dramatic reversal.

The earlier strategy implied that the agricultural surplus should be heavily taxed and the revenue used to subsidize the creation of a modern industrial sector. All too often that strategy produced industries that grew rapidly under the artificial stimulus of government subsidies and import restrictions but were incapable of competing effectively internationally, and an agricultural sector that failed to modernize and was hard pressed to provide enough food to meet domestic needs.

The more recent strategy planning—for rapid expansion in areas of traditional economic strength, which is certainly appropriate—suggests a paradox. According to neoclassical economics, resources flow to their most productive uses, and both in the short run and over time, markets allocate resources efficiently. If so, why is government intervention needed to encourage resources to flow to their most productive uses? The explanation is that few markets are perfectly competitive, lacking in distortions, externalities, or rigidities; therefore, they often fail to allocate resources optimally. Attempts of governments to intervene in markets to speed up growth have, however, produced their own distortions and competitive shortcomings. Other chapters in this book deal with the results of distortions in financial markets. This essay looks at economic policies in broader terms and endeavors to show the powerful impact of general policy orientation on rural development and rural financial markets.

The impact that distortions in *nonfinancial* markets can have on the ability of financial markets to facilitate rapid growth in agriculture is not well understood. Some have argued, for example, that many of the problems found in rural financial markets would disappear if they were deregulated—that is, if there were free entry into and out of the banking industry with no restrictions on lending or borrowing rates. The presumption that deregulation of financial markets alone will result in an efficient allocation of investment within a country ignores the lesson of the 1950s and 1960s, when a strategy of growth through industrialization caused extensive and systematic market distortions which continue to misdirect investible funds.

Specifically, government programs for growth through industrialization have included low-cost credit (at below free-market interest rates) for capital formation in the industrial sector; direct government investment in housing, transportation, and sanitation projects in urban areas; high tariffs and other trade restrictions to promote import substitution in manufacturing; and domestic price ceilings on food and other essential items. Deficient rural infrastructure, lack of new technology, and low rates of return on investment in the rural sector have resulted from these urban-oriented programs.

Low-cost loans for capital improvements in the industrial sector have hurt developing countries in two important ways. First, such loans bias investment in the direction of manufacturing and away from agriculture, regardless of the country's true comparative advantage. Second, such loans promote the use of capital-intensive techniques of manufacturing in countries that often have a relative abundance of low-skilled labor and a scarcity of capital. Thus, such loans create a bias toward investment in the wrong sectors of the economy and the use of inappropriate techniques of production.

Heavy government investment in housing, transportation, and sanitation in urban areas has reduced the profitability of the agricultural sector in at least three ways. By underwriting many of the costs of living in the urban sector through subsidized public investment, the government encourages labor migration from rural to urban areas at higher rates than would otherwise prevail; this migration adds to the pools of unemployed or underemployed workers in the cities. At the same time, the lack of social investment in rural communities makes it difficult to provide enough off-peak employment in light manufacturing and service industries in the rural areas to ensure the local supply of manpower needed during seasonal peaks in farming cycles. In effect, government-induced labor migration to the cities raises the labor component of production costs in the agricultural sector. Further, the disproportionate use of government revenues to finance the construction of overhead capital in the cities means that social overhead capital must lag in the rural areas. Government capital is less available for research and development activities to modernize agricultural production, or for financing rural electrification, roads, irrigation, and other projects which directly affect unit costs.

If tariffs and other trade restrictions succeed in promoting domestic production of importable manufactures in developing countries, it is because they give domestic producers an artificial competitive advantage. Such trade restrictions divert private investment flows away from agriculture, where a country may have a current comparative advantage, toward manufacturing industries in which the country does not have and may never have a comparative advantage. In addition, import restrictions tend to raise artificially the international price of domestic currency, which in effect raises the foreign currency price of the country's exports. As a consequence, foreign demand for exports is depressed; in addition, import tariffs have an effect equivalent to export taxes. For many developing countries, the agricultural sector is the principal victim of lost export opportunities and of the consequent depressed domestic prices and profits that accompany industrial import-substitution schemes.

While central planners often have a strong desire to pump money into housing, transportation, and social services in urban areas, they frequently lack the political will (or technical ability) to collect sufficient taxes to fund such projects without budget deficits. Monetary expansion is then used to finance public investment in urban overhead capital. Rapid monetary expansion puts upward pressure on the domestic prices of food and other essentials and downward pressure on the exchange rate. To minimize the political hostility among the urban poor, governments often impose price ceilings on food and other essential imported commodities. In the more perverse cases, the government actually subsidizes imports of food and other consumer products at the same time that its price ceilings are holding down domestic farmers' incomes.

If rapid monetary expansion and price inflation continue for a long time, there will be unavoidable pressure to depreciate the currency. But such an exchange rate adjustment would put upward pressure on the domestic prices of food and other consumer goods. To avoid that adjustment, countries often turn to agencies such as the World Bank for loans. Whatever the earmarked purpose of such loans, they are used mainly to help finance current account deficits and postpone exchange rate depreciation. The currency remains overvalued. Implicitly these international loans are used to subsidize imports of consumer goods for the urban population and to tax exportables, including rural products.

I began the discussion with a review of the evolution of economic development planning in the postwar period, because many of the typical market distortions and misguided policy objectives observed in developing countries today are the remnants of that early strategy of growth through rapid industrialization and import substitution. Of course, the extent to which one can attribute the disincentives to investment in the rural sector to the market distortions and government policies outlined above will vary from country to country. The more these policies have prevailed, the greater the negative results for agriculture. Financial reforms are a critical component of any sound economic development plan; but in many countries financial reform needs to be accompanied by substantial changes in other government policies affecting the rural sector. The value of having financial flows respond quickly and strongly to nonfinancial market signals is substantially reduced if those signals are artificial and distorted.

The changes that ought to accompany financial reforms in many developing countries would include: (1) less emphasis on industrial capital formation and more attention to human capital development; (2) more emphasis on financing of highways, dams, bridges, communications networks, and research and development activities in the rural sector; (3) less emphasis on import substitution and more emphasis on export promotion; (4) less reliance on price controls, trade controls, deficit financing, and inflation; and (5) more reliance on market forces to promote efficient production of food at home, in a setting of balanced budgets and monetary stability.

A greater emphasis on human capital development through general and vocational education would benefit the industrial sector by redressing the current inappropriate bias toward capital-intensive techniques of production in countries that are relatively labor abundant and capital poor. Raising the general level of literacy should reduce production costs in agriculture by improving the quality of management, organization, and investment planning in the rural sector. Individual farmers are in the best position to judge which new techniques of production or innovations are most promising in reducing their unit costs. They are more likely to make intelligent choices if they can read and understand descriptions of the available alternatives.

The best efforts of farmers to reduce costs and increase yields will count for very little if bridges and roads are inadequate for getting crops to market. Development of communication and transportation systems in rural areas are essential to bring down delivered prices of agricultural products. In addition, a redress of the disproportionate social investment in the urban areas by shifting government investment in sanitation, communication, transportation, and housing projects to the rural sector will help reduce the number of migrants to the urban areas and encourage the development of small-scale nonagricultural production in the rural sector. Those changes could reduce the rapidly rising political and social pressures associated with underemployment of labor in the urban areas, and in some cases may alleviate the highly seasonal shifts of employment opportunities in the rural sector. The potential benefits to the rural sector of dams, electrification, irrigation projects, and agricultural research and development are obvious.

The beneficial effects of freer trade are considerable. It will remove the artificial stimulus to invest in inefficient import-substitution projects and encourage a redistribution of resources toward agriculture and other areas which have a comparative advantage. The politics of trade liberalization, however, are complex. A commitment to balanced budgets and monetary stability is also important, but no less politically difficult for policy makers to embrace.

Conclusions

A vigorous and healthy economic environment in rural areas is necessary to ensure numerous agriculturalists high and reasonably stable incomes and to hold out good prospects for rural financial institutions. Large numbers of individuals cannot profitably use loans, repay their debts promptly, and also make extensive use of financial savings facilities unless farming is a relatively good business. And even the best-run financial intermediary cannot make large numbers of good loans if most farmers receive low and unstable incomes. General economic policies, therefore, can strongly influence the economic vitality of rural areas and the rural financial markets that serve them.

Evaluating the Contribution of Finance

Governments and donor agencies have evaluated the performance of many agricultural credit projects. In most cases the evaluations focus on the impact of the project on yields, on use of inputs, on borrower income, or possibly on employment. This approach is consistent with the way in which the objectives of credit projects are commonly stated. Relatively few studies have been conducted on the performance of an entire financial sector or of particular rural financial markets. Credit studies seldom examine what happens to the overall supply of agricultural credit, to the term structure of loans, to the liquidity mobilized by rural financial markets, and the lenders' costs of providing various types of financial services. Insufficient attention is given to the vitality of the financial system and to what financial markets are doing to, or with, voluntary savings. The political economy of agricultural credit has also received little attention.

The essay by Von Pischke and Adams (chapter 8) points out the problems that fungibility causes for analysis of specific financial market activities. Fungibility makes it very difficult and costly to measure incremental sources and uses of liquidity at the farm household, lender, or national level. David and Meyer (chapter 9) reinforce these points by examining specific credit impact studies. Problems of fungibility arise when one tries to track down what farmers and lenders do with their liquidity and what governments do with their budgets. Evaluation of the impact of a loan at any level requires that "additionality" be documented—that is, the change in activity that occurred because of the loan. The diversion and substitution of funds must be netted out to do this. David and Meyer stress that most farm level studies of credit impact fail to deal with the fungibility problem and suffer from other attribution problems. It is very difficult to set up an experiment that isolates the effects of additional credit.

Harriss, elsewhere in this volume (chapter 26), also points out the interlocked nature of markets in rural areas, which makes evaluation even more difficult. For example, an informal loan may not carry explicit interest charges, but it may require borrowers to sell their product to the lender at below-market prices. Loans may also entail labor exchanges and assurances of credit reserves for use in times of emergency.

The two essays in this section outline the problems of research and evaluation in rural financial markets. They analyze the overall performance of financial markets and conclude that research should acknowledge fungibility. They also imply that less emphasis should be placed on trying to measure the impact of credit at the farm level.

8. *Fungibility and the Design and Evaluation of Agricultural Credit Projects*

J. D. Von Pischke and Dale W Adams

[Fungibility is the interchangeability of units of money. Agricultural loan funds are essentially fungible. In project evaluation, measurement of the effects of a credit program should focus on "additionality," which is the difference between what happened under a project and what would have happened without it. At the farm level additionality is very difficult to measure; at the lending agency and national levels, it can take forms entirely unrelated to project objectives. More attention should be accorded to measurable aspects of rural financial market performance.]

Agricultural credit is an important element in development efforts in most low-income countries. Many of these projects have been formally evaluated, although only a few evaluations have been published. To determine whether the project's purposes have been fulfilled, donor agencies rely on such measures as the disbursement of project funds and recovery rates on loans to farmers. Most evaluations also attempt to measure the impact of loans on farm activities; impact is usually expressed in terms of increases in crop area or yields or by the quantity of animals, fertilizer, or tractors bought with loans.

Although project evaluations may show slow loan disbursement or repayment problems, they often indicate that the projects achieved many of their objectives and that the goals for production, input use, investment levels, and target group participation were largely met. Nevertheless, a number of observers are increasingly concerned about the quality and quantity of financial services provided in low-income countries by rural credit institutions and by the rural financial markets (RFMS) of which they are a part. Critics charge that although donor funding for agricultural credit has increased substantially, the real

Extracted from *American Journal of Agricultural Economics*, vol. 62, no. 4 (November 1980), pp. 719–26.

value of total agricultural loans has decreased in many countries; that concessionary loans often end up in the hands of the well-to-do; that loans for agricultural purposes are diverted to nonagricultural uses; that policies in many RFMs encourage consumption and discourage saving; that the term structure of agricultural loans often contracts or fails to expand; and that the RFMs are adopting few cost-decreasing technologies in the provision of financial services. It is disconcerting that rural financial markets could perform poorly while projects within these markets are judged to be doing well. An attempt is made in the following discussion to resolve this paradox by showing how design and evaluation procedures which ignore fungibility lead to faulty conclusions about agricultural credit project results.

Fungibility, Additionality, Substitution, and Diversion

Fungibility is a prime characteristic of modern currency. *Webster's New Collegiate Dictionary* defines fungible as being "of such a kind or nature that one specimen or part may be used in place of another specimen or equal part . . . interchangeable." The fungibility of loan funds makes credit activities hard to evaluate. The reasons given to justify a loan may have little relation to the activities actually stimulated at the margin by the additional liquidity provided. At the farm level, for example, many credit projects treat loans as if they were production inputs, ignoring the fact that a unit of borrowed money is identical to other units of money held by the borrower. Even if a loan is given in kind, such as bags of fertilizer, the goods provided can generally be sold and converted into cash if the borrower desires. For all practical purposes, loans in kind or in cash can be used to buy any good or service available to the borrower in the market.

Additionality, substitution, and diversion are terms that define some of the problems fungibility poses for credit projects. Additionality refers to the question of whether a project really added something that would not otherwise have occurred; it is the difference between the with- and the without-project situations. It is generally assumed, for example, that a credit project funded by a foreign donor should induce the borrowing country to increase its total loans to farmers by an amount at least equal to the donor's contribution. At the lender level, credit for a target group or purpose should expand by an amount at least equal to the project funds provided. Similarly, it is expected that individual farmers will increase their input purchases and investments by amounts comparable to the loans they receive from a project.

To measure additionality is difficult, however, because it is impossible to know exactly what governments, lenders, and farmer-borrowers would have done in the absence of a credit project. To what extent would the government have allocated more funds to agricultural credit without the donor's assistance? Would local credit institutions have channeled funds away from other activities to serve project objectives in the absence of the project? Would borrowers have used cash from their own reserves or informal credit sources, or reduced their consumption, to fund a project-supported activity without the project in question? In other words, to what degree do project funds simply substitute for other resources that would have been used for project purposes in any event, rather than supply an additional element?

Diversion is a more extreme form of substitution. Diversion occurs, for example, when a farmer obtains a cattle loan but does not buy any cattle and uses the money for a purpose not authorized by the loan contract. Although donors may be lax in supervising projects, or the management information systems used by project agencies may be faulty, diversion occurs even in well-administered programs. The close supervision of thousands of rural borrowers is very costly. Changes in the purchasing power of money can further complicate the analysis of additionality. Even when the nominal amounts of loans and farmer expenditures expand in the desired direction, the real value of these expenditures may remain constant or decline when inflation erodes the purchasing power of the currency.

The hypothetical case studies that follow illustrate the difficulties of measuring the impact of credit projects. The cases were made up from elements commonly found in experience, but are not actual examples.

A Farm Household in Africa

Mrs. Kariuki is an African farmer who recently received a loan for the purchase of three milk cows and other materials needed to establish a dairy operation. The amount of the loan was $1,200, divided as follows on the loan contract: three milk cows, $800; fencing, $200; a water tank, $100; and a milking shed, $100. She went into debt because of the easy terms offered (80 percent financing, five years to repay, interest at 10 percent) and the range of attractive investment opportunities available in her locality. Many of her neighbors were expanding their dairy and tea enterprises, and several had entered the transport business. Land prices were increasing, and many families were improving their homes.

Mrs. Kariuki is an attractive credit risk because her family's farm is productive and well maintained. In addition to the ten-acre farm owned by her husband, she owns an urban lot which she used as loan collateral. She had $600 in her post office savings account, which was not disclosed on her loan application—in conformity with local tradition.

Mrs. Kariuki used the funds borrowed to obtain the goods specified in her loan agreement. Her loan was disbursed by the lender, out of funds supplied by a donor agency, against invoices submitted directly by the suppliers from whom Mrs. Kariuki obtained the dairy cows and materials. But the $100 worth of iron sheets and lumber for the milking shed were not used to build a shed, which in the local community would be considered ostentatious. Rather, they were used to extend and reroof the family's house. In addition to the loan proceeds, Mrs. Kariuki invested $300 of her own funds in the dairy project to help purchase the cattle and pay for labor to install the fencing and water tank.

Mrs. Kariuki's first investment priority was to establish a dairy enterprise because of its expected profitability and steady labor demands, and the family's preference for fresh milk. Just before the loan was approved, she sold her entire herd of five inferior dairy animals for $800 in cash. She had borrowed to purchase the new stock and materials, even though she could have financed most of the project out of the sale of the five cows and the $600 in her savings account.

Her other priorities included acquiring more land, planting more tea, which requires hired labor, and joining her husband and some friends in purchasing a taxi to link their community more dependably with a market town twelve miles away. Accordingly, Mrs. Kariuki spent $250 for tea planting and $300 to purchase a half acre from an elderly neighbor after receiving the dairy loan. In addition, Mrs. Kariuki's family decided to spend an additional $100 to buy a new coat for her husband and two new school uniforms for her children, and to finance a visit to relatives. Of her $1,400 in cash and in the post office savings bank, $450 remained after these expenditures. She wanted to keep $200 on hand for a rainy day and leave $250 for investment in a share of a taxi.

The conventional project interpretation assumes that Mrs. Kariuki's loan financed a dairy enterprise establishment. Therefore, the impact of the loan is assumed equal to changes in Mrs. Kariuki's dairy enterprise. This approach ignores the changes in consumption and adjustments in all other uses and sources of household liquidity that were associated with the loan.

In contrast to the conventional project evaluation, a financial view of Mrs. Kariuki's activities would take a broader perspective; the loan gave her liquidity—an increase in her general command over resources. Because of fungibility, a financial view does not attempt to relate the loan to just one use of liquidity. The impact of the loan can be found in the marginal changes in *all* sources and uses of household funds which resulted from the additional liquidity provided by the loan. Obviously, the type of information needed to document all these liquidity flows for a representative sample of farm households is very time-consuming and costly to collect.

A Credit Agency in Asia

The effects of fungibility are also found among lending agencies. The institutions in the following hypothetical example from an Asian country are a diversified local lender called the Farmers' Small Enterprise Bank (FSEB), a central rediscounting agency (CRA) which lends donor and government funds to local lenders such as FSEB, and a foreign donor agency which helped design the project. The main objective of the project was to increase the volume of loans to a target group of farmers with less than two hectares of land. CRA advanced $0.80 for every $1.00 which lenders extended to the target group. The interest rate on CRA loans to lenders was 4 percent, while the lenders charged farmer-borrowers 10 percent a year. CRA, in turn, claimed from the donor agency 75 percent of its advances under the project and obtained the other 25 percent from the national treasury. The project reflected the national priority given to farm credit, as did central bank regulations favoring agriculture (rural banks such as FSEB must devote 40 percent of their loan portfolios to agriculture).

The effect of the project on lender behavior is illustrated by FSEB's plans and actions before and after the project. Before the project in 1980, FSEB directors had developed a budget for 1981. As shown in table 8-1, the major source of funds in the original budget was loan repayments from borrowers, which provide funds for further lending. The allocation of new loans was budgeted to ensure compliance with the requirement that 40 percent of total loan balances on the books be farm loans, and the FSEB directors expected that new loans of $750,000 to these borrowers would meet this target. The directors also expected an increase in deposits because annual interest rates on savings had recently risen from 5 to 6 percent. They allocated a portion of this expected increase in deposits to non-interest-bearing statutory reserves held with the central bank, and to liquidity reserves in the form of government bonds and cash required to support the expanded level of deposits.

Shortly after FSEB directors approved the 1981 budget, the general manager was visited by representatives of the donor agency and CRA, who informed him that the FSEB could participate in a small-farmer credit project. The general manager later presented to his board a revised budget assuming FSEB participation in the project (table 8-1). In presenting the revised budget, the manager noted that about $300,000 of the $750,000 in planned loans to farmers in the original budget met the credit project's lending criteria. FSEB could discount with CRA 80 percent of the $300,000 and gain $240,000 in loanable funds. The manager proposed to his board that $15,000 of these additional funds be used to buy more high-yielding government securities (9 percent a

Table 8-1. *Farmers' Small Enterprise Bank: Plans for Sources and Uses of Funds in 1981*
(thousands of dollars)

FSEB *funds*	*Original budget*	*Revised budget*
Sources of funds		
Loan repayments	1,500	1,500
Increase in deposits	300	200
CRA rediscount of project loans	—	240
Net profit	50	55
Total	1,850	1,995
Uses of funds		
Increase in statutory reserves (25 percent of deposits)	75	50
Increase in cash and government securities	25	40
New loans		
To farmers	750	755
To others	1,000	1,150
Total	1,850	1,995

— Not applicable.

year), and that $150,000 be used for loans to landlords and businessmen in the area, who could offer substantial collateral for their loans. He recommended that FSEB roll back interest rates paid on savings from 6 to 5 percent in order to reduce projected increases in deposit liabilities from $300,000 to $200,000; otherwise, the addition of project resources to the previous deposit target would cause FSEB to fall below the minimum capital-to-assets ratio required by the central bank. Because the revised budget would increase FSEB net profits by 10 percent, it was approved by the board. Late in 1981 the manager reported to the board that budget targets were substantially achieved.

The net results of FSEB participation in the new loan program were: a decrease in local deposit mobilization, lower rates of return to all depositors, an increase in government securities held by the bank, and an increase in the amount of money loaned to borrowers other than the project's target group. Only a small amount ($5,000) of additional lending to the target group resulted from the project. Substitution removed almost all of the intended effects of the $240,000 project in this particular lender's activities.

A Latin American Country

From 1960 to 1978 a Latin American country received $80 million in ten loans or grants from foreign aid agencies for agricultural credit projects. All ten projects have been evaluated. Several had loan recovery problems which undermined at least one of the new lending institutions. Yet the analysis of loan applications and interviews with both loan officers and borrowers indicated that project objectives related to type of borrower, enterprise, inputs, and loan term structure were largely met. Overall, these evaluations suggest that the projects did a surprisingly good job of achieving their specified goals. One donor was sufficiently satisfied with its projects to give the country an additional loan of $15 million to expand medium- and long-term lending to small farmers. During 1979 the loan was disbursed for the purposes intended. An evaluation gave a glowing report of the results.

Despite these projects, farmers, and especially small farmers, continued to complain about the shortage of loans. As a result, one of the donors engaged consultants to prepare another sizable agricultural credit loan proposal, and a financial analyst on the consulting team was asked to assess the performance of the country's financial markets. He did not take a conventional project focus in his analysis, but examined imports, the government budget, and overall financial market performance. He reasoned that changes in activities associated with the most recent loan would be the best indicator of what might be expected from the next loan.

The analyst collected information on imports and budget allocations. He found that imports of agricultural investment goods had increased by $15 million in 1979. Because of inflation in world prices, however, the total real value of these imports in 1978 prices had declined from $200 million in 1978 to $195 million in 1979. At the same time, the real value of imports of nonagricultural investment goods and government and defense goods had increased. Military hardware and supplies to furnish new tourist hotels accounted for most of the real increases in imports. From these figures the analyst concluded that the 1979 agricultural loan had made more foreign exchange available, and that arms for the military and bathtubs and toilets for new hotels were the main result.

The analyst then reviewed the 1979 government budget. The nominal amount allocated for agricultural programs increased from $250 million in 1978 to $265 million in 1979. The government had met the conditions of the agricultural loan agreement by adding to the agricultural bank's loan portfolio the $15 million generated by sales of goods imported under the loan. But because of domestic inflation the real value in 1978 prices of the sum going to agriculture had decreased from $250 million in 1978 to $241 million in 1979, despite the donor's loan. Real increases in planned 1979 spending for defense, nonagricultural development, and general expenses had occurred, however;

this shift reflected government priorities. From these data the analyst concluded that the government budget was not influenced in the desired direction by the agricultural credit project.

The analyst next looked at activities in rural financial markets in the country. The nominal amount of new agricultural loans made each year by formal lending institutions had increased from $50 million to $144 million between 1960 and 1980. In real terms, however, the amount of purchasing power represented by this agricultural loan portfolio peaked in 1975 and declined by about 5 percent through 1980. The $94 million increase in the nominal amount of new agricultural loans made annually from 1960 to 1980 corresponded closely to the $95 million in foreign grants and loans received in these years for agricultural credit, since the average loan duration was approximately one year. The analyst concluded that foreign funds had substituted for at least some local funds which would have been allocated to agricultural credit in the absence of external assistance.

The analyst was disappointed to see that the ratio of agricultural credit to total credit had declined from 0.12 in 1970 to 0.08 in 1980, and the ratio of agricultural credit to GNP from agriculture had declined from 0.27 to 0.21. In spite of heavy emphasis by donors on expanding agricultural credit during the 1970s, it appears they were unable to effect structural changes in credit allocation in favor of agriculture. Furthermore, the decline in the deposit-to-loan ratio from 0.18 in 1970 to 0.16 in 1980 shows that some rural financial markets were becoming more, rather than less, dependent on outside resources. The analyst also found a decrease after 1970 in the proportion of farmers who received formal credit: in 1970 about 17 percent of the farmers obtained bank loans, compared with only 12 percent in 1980. Most of the increase in agricultural credit had apparently gone into larger loans to previous borrowers. Because agricultural lenders' records did not include details on borrowers' economic characteristics, the analyst could not document loan allocation by economic class: small loans do not necessarily go to low-income borrowers, and a wealthy borrower may have multiple loans. He did find, however, that those agencies serving mainly the rural poor had very modest real increases in their loan portfolios from 1970 to 1980, while agencies lending mainly to high-income borrowers had expanded substantially.

Finally, the analyst concluded that the credit projects of the 1970s were associated with a trend toward shorter terms for agricultural loans. Although in 1970 the average loan matured in fifteen months, in 1980 the corresponding term was only eleven months. Between 1978 and 1979 this average dropped from thirteen to eleven months, despite the addition of two- to five-year loans under the $15 million 1979 project. This happened because funds from medium- and long-term loans which matured outside that project were re-lent at shorter maturities.

In his report the financial analyst argued that fungibility and substitution had substantially diluted the intended impact of the eleven credit projects, especially the 1979 project. Although the 1979 loan did relax the foreign exchange limitations, it was associated with additional imports of military and tourist hotel hardware. It was not accompanied by a net increase in real imports of agricultural investment goods, and it did not reverse the trend toward shorter average terms for formal agricultural loans. Because of inflation and concessionary interest rates to farmers, the flow of external resources for agricultural credit failed to maintain, let alone increase, the purchasing power of the formal agriculture portfolio. There is little evidence that the rural poor received much additional funding, despite the donors' emphasis in various credit projects on expanding financial services for this target group. It appeared that donor funds accounted for virtually the entire nominal increase in agricultural credit.

Recommendations

At the farm level it is very costly, if not impossible, to determine the impact of credit. At the national and lender levels, many countries provide an environment in which substitution and diversion can flourish. This enviroment is created by distorted exchange rates, balance of payments problems, rigid interest rate policies, and substantial inflation that leads to negative real rates of interest. Because of these facts, we feel it is necessary to alter the traditional design of credit projects and to modify substantially the way they are evaluated. Several different approaches might diminish the extent to which performance varies from project objectives.

At the project level it is vital to view loans as additional liquidity rather than as farm inputs. This would force project designers to be more sensitive to the alternatives available to those who will gain access to additional liquidity from project loans. Only after it is shown that the targeted activities are among the more profitable or satisfying uses of additional liquidity for the borrowers in question can it be concluded that a major part of the liquidity provided by the loan will be used as projected.

Farm activities receive primary emphasis in traditional credit projects. The strategy we propose would be centered on the performance of the institutions responsible for project implementation, on the assumption that target groups are most effectively benefited when institutions serving them are efficient and financially strong. Projects which undermine the vitality and financial integrity of a credit agency should not be termed successes.

Specific additionality requirements, stated in real terms, might be written into a project; but any such targets should apply to an entire financial market. For example, if an objective of a new supervised credit program is to lend to 5,000 *new* small borrowers, the 4,000 borrowers transferred to this agency from another agricultural bank should not be counted as "new." Progress toward additionality targets should be measured at the national as well as the credit agency level, although this requirement could raise problems of data reliability and create incentives for evasion unless it was carefully defined.

Because of fungibility, project design and evaluation should consider the general performance of the rural financial market. For example, if an agricultural credit project is to supply more medium- and long-term credit, project design should include an assessment of why the pertinent RFM is not adequately providing this financial service. Once this deficiency is explained, the designers of the project should try to show how the project will cause the RFM to offer a service it is currently unable or unwilling to provide.

At the national level, credit projects usually bring about more direct government participation in RFMs, typically through various schemes for rationing or allocating credit. But because of fungibility, finance is difficult to control. Direct attempts to gain control often fail to achieve stated objectives and generally have unexpected secondary effects. We feel that the best intervention is often indirect. Various experiences suggest that many RFMs might respond favorably to flexible interest rate policies, especially when supported by other measures designed to increase competition in the provision of finance. This approach accommodates fungibility and encourages resource reallocation by enabling financial markets to function more efficiently.

In sum, we feel that because of fungibility the focus of project design and evaluation should shift from the traditional emphasis on the demand side of farm credit and move toward the supply side. Less emphasis should be given to trying to evaluate the impact of credit use at the farm level, which is virtually impossible to measure, and more emphasis placed on how intervention in RFMs affects lender behavior, lender vitality, and the overall operations of RFMs.

9. *Measuring the Farm Level Impact of Agricultural Loans*

Cristina C. David and Richard L. Meyer

[A variety of quantitative analytical techniques commonly used in studies of the impact of agricultural credit programs have serious methodological shortcomings. Credit impact appears very hard to isolate with the use of common social science research tools; studies ignoring certain factors easily overestimate the value of credit as a tool for agricultural development. Research methods should be sensitive to the problems of fungibility, attribution, and the interdependence of farm and household decision making.]

Expansion of formal agricultural credit has become a major policy in many low-income countries. The current amount in all low-income countries could range from $30 thousand million to $40 thousand million a year, and concessionary interest rates, high administrative costs, and low repayment rates require substantial subsidies. There is growing concern that this credit has not produced the desired improvements in farm income, output, and income distribution.

Role of Credit in Resource Allocation

The lack of a sound theoretical framework has led to errors in the specification of credit research models and misinterpretation of results. Two issues are particularly troublesome. First, farm households are complex units simultaneously making production and consumption decisions. Second, given fungibility (that is, the ability to shift money from one use to another) in the cash flow management of farm households, it is difficult to identify a loan's effect on the farm as opposed to its effect on the household. Since government credit is usually intended to increase production, not consumption, many researchers assume that loans extended for productive purposes are actually used for production.

The empirical measurement of the total benefits of borrowing by a

Extracted from *Borrowers & Lenders*, edited by John Howell (London: Overseas Development Institute, 1980), pp. 201–34.

farm household is much more complex than is implied by simplified farm models that ignore possible changes in consumption and nonfarm activities. The effect of borrowing with which we are most concerned is the increase in farm inputs and output, but because of fungibility, loans may simply substitute for a household's savings or other sources of liquidity (cash or loan). Accounting for substitution may improve the measurement of the impact of loans on the farm, but documenting the impact on other farm household activities remains difficult. Complete evaluation requires information on all the household's sources and uses of additional liquidity, not merely on the impact of the direct expenditure of loan funds. But such information is extremely difficult to collect through typical cross-sectional farm surveys.

Even with more comprehensive data, the attribution problem remains. It consists of trying to isolate the effect of loans by observing differences between borrowers and nonborrowers, or by observing borrowers before and after the loans. At least four factors other than credit can explain differences between borrowing and nonborrowing farm households:

- Differences in technology, technical information, irrigation, weather, and other variables not easily quantified in production models
- Differences in yield, price uncertainty, and management ability
- Differences in product and input prices
- Differences in household financial constraints or savings.

Multipurpose agricultural credit programs also contribute to the attribution problem, since they frequently provide intensive extension services and input subsidies in addition to credit. Many researchers assume that extension explains little of the differences between borrowers and nonborrowers, but this is not well documented. The effect of input subsidies on input use and production may be significant and needs to be separated from the impact of credit.

Concessionary low interest rates further complicate research. They create excess demand for loans, which forces lenders into nonprice rationing (that is, lender selection of borrowers). This typically favors loans to farmers with large factor endowments, access to the best technical information, and better managers. Therefore, borrowers may be systematically different from nonborrowers, with borrowing the result rather than the cause of differences in performance.

Review of Empirical Literature

Surprisingly little research has measured the impact of the vast sums spent on agricultural credit programs. For example, the 1973 *Spring*

Table 9-1. *Percentage Differences in Selected Measures between Borrowers and Nonborrowers, Selected Areas*

				Percentage differences per hectare			
Area	*Year*	*Number of observations*	*Farm size*	*Operating expenses*	*Investment*	*Production*	*Net farm income*
Brazil	1965	132	78	112	n.a.	30[a]	2
Southern Brazil	1965	954	94	127	80	62[a]	n.a.
	1969	732	68	281	338	133[a]	n.a.
Colombia	1968	52	74	104	n.a.	6	n.a.
	1968–65[b]	25	30	56	n.a.	35	n.a.
Guatemala	1975	1,600	5	39	n.a.	−3	0[c]
Korea, Rep. of	1970	438	3	5	5	n.a.	−1
Philippines	1975–77[d]	577	16	15	n.a.	n.a.	4
	1975–77[e]	497	2	−15	n.a.	n.a.	0
Taiwan	1965, 1970, 1975	1,373	16	21	n.a.	8	−2

n.a. Not available.

a. Gross farm income per hectare.

b. Comparison of borrowers before (1965) and after (1968) the credit program.

c. Based on lower 76 percent of farms by size.

d. Nonborrowers include those who borrowed from nonformal institutions.

e. Comparison of borrowers from nonformal sources and nonborrowers.

Sources: *Brazil*: P. F. de Araujo, "An Economic Study of Factors Affecting the Demand for Agricultural Credit at the Farm Level," M.A. thesis, Ohio State University, 1967. *Southern Brazil*: G. Singh, "Farm Level Determinants of Credit Allocation and Use in Southern Brazil, 1965–69," Ph.D. thesis, Ohio State University, 1974. *Colombia*: D. Colyer and G. Jimenez, "Supervised Credit as a Tool in Agricultural Development," *American Journal of Agricultural Economics*, vol. 53, no. 4 (November 1971), pp. 639–42. *Guatemala*: S. R. Daines, "Guatemalan Farm Policy Analysis: The Impact of Small Farm Credit on Income, Employment and Food Production," Analytical Working Document no. 10 (Washington, D.C.: U.S. Agency for International Development, Bureau for Latin America, 1975), pp. 1–106. *Korea, Rep. of*: O. Nyanin, "Credit and Farmers in South Korea," M.S. thesis, Ohio State University, 1978. *Philippines*: V. Cordova, P. Masicat, and R. W. Herdt, "Use of Institutional Credit in Three Locations in the Philippines, 1975–77" (Laguna: International Rice Research Institute, 1978), pp. 1–8. *Taiwan*: Farm household record-keeping data available to the Department of Agricultural Economics and Rural Sociology, Ohio State University.

Review of the U.S. Agency for International Development contained about sixty papers describing various credit programs, but none systematically assessed the farm level impact of loans. Some studies reported trends in aggregate output, use of inputs, or adoption of new varieties, while lamenting the scarcity of data for more detailed analysis. We review briefly the following types of study on the farm-level impact of borrowing: descriptive studies, econometric studies—of the production function, the input demand function, and the efficiency gap function—and programming studies.

Descriptive Studies

The most common analysis of credit programs is the comparison of farm inputs, production, and productivity before and after borrowing, or between borrowers and nonborrowers. Most descriptive studies are unpublished reports or graduate theses. Table 9-1 summarizes the results of studies from six countries to illustrate the variables examined and the impact usually attributed to borrowing. Except in the case of Colombia, these studies were cross-sectional analyses of borrowers and nonborrowers. Before-and-after comparisons are few because evaluation is generally initiated after the program begins. Quantification of the "before" situation is based on questionable farmer recall.

The Latin American studies cover relatively large farms producing multiple crops, and programs including both short- and medium-term loans. Asian studies refer to small monoculture rice farms receiving only short-term credit. Despite these differences, several common patterns emerge. Borrowers had considerably larger farms than nonborrowers in Brazil and Colombia, whereas farm size differences in Asian countries were only 2 to 16 percent; Guatemalan farms were of similar size because of the sampling procedure. Operating expenses and investment were higher for borrowers, but production differences per hectare were less marked. Moreover, reported differences in net farm income per hectare were clearly small.

Inferences about loan impact must be treated with caution because of attribution problems. Small differences in production and net farm income do not necessarily imply that borrowing leads to misallocation or that loans have been diverted. In the Guatemala study, Daines used a sampling procedure designed to control for potential effects of farm size and region-related factors. Differences in value of production between borrowers and nonborrowers were decomposed to reveal the effect of price, yield, crop mix, and crop area. Daines concluded that expansion in cropped area, which explains most of the production differences, was largely due to credit.

A decomposition technique was also used in a 1976 World Bank evaluation of projects providing medium- and long-term credit to crop farms in the Philippines, Pakistan, and Morocco and to livestock farms in Uruguay and Mexico. Crop production changes were accounted for by changes in cultivated area, cropping intensity, and yields, and changes in livestock production by changes in breeding cattle, feeders, reproduction rates, and beef yields. Judgments were made about the probable effects of the project on each source of growth; adjustments were also made for the possible effect of other loan sources. The study concluded that the projects raised crop production by 67 percent, compared with the observed unadjusted 82 percent.

This World Bank study also dealt with substitution. First, borrowers were asked to estimate the investment they would have made without the program, and the probable source of finance. Second, investments of borrowers and nonborrowers were compared. Third, assets financed by the project were related to the borrowers' total assets. On the basis of these data, a crude substitution factor of 40 percent was assumed; after making this second adjustment, the credit projects explained approximately 28 percent of the net production increase rather than 67 percent.

Econometric Studies

Several recent studies have used econometric techniques to analyze the impact of borrowing. Three different models have been used: a production function, an input demand function, and an efficiency gap function.

PRODUCTION FUNCTION. Colombian, Brazilian, and Ghanaian studies hypothesized that loans influence the farm production relationship, with the credit variable specified in several ways (table 9-2). The Colombian studies treated credit as a separate unit; one study further hypothesized that borrowers have a different production technology, so separate production functions were estimated for borrowers, nonborrowers, and borrowers prior to the supervised credit program. In the Brazilian model credit was assumed to shift production coefficients for operating expenses, modern inputs, and machinery but not for land, labor, or animal power. The Ghanaian study assumed all production parameters were affected by credit. It used time series aggregate data, while the other studies used cross-section farm level data.

Production function studies have some major weaknesses. First, specifying credit as a separate production input presents a conceptual problem, because loans are claims on resources and do not directly generate output; double counting of inputs occurs when credit is treated as a separate variable. Second, attributing to borrowing the differences in production functions between borrowers and nonborrowers implicitly assumes a relationship between the source of liquidity and the production function. The unclear picture of loan impact in these results is not surprising. Short-term credit programs attempt to encourage adoption of new seed-fertilizer technology, but there is little reason to expect a shift in a production function to be conditional on such borrowing. Modern varieties of seed frequently imply greater operating expenses for the optimal use of fertilizer and chemicals than do traditional seeds. But seed costs are similar, modern varieties are usually more responsive to all levels of fertilization, and fertilizer is highly divisible. Therefore, farmers with varying financial constraints should simply be located at different points on the same modern production function. Medium- and long-term credit, however, may be more likely to change the production relationship because these loans could finance "lumpy," or large, indivisible inputs more difficult to fund internally.

Apparent differences in production coefficients between borrowers and nonborrowers may be due to the omission of other inputs, such as technical information or irrigation, associated with loans. Short-term loans would not be expected to have a major impact on these variables, but progressive farmers with irrigation and better technical information would probably borrow more. Thus, causality is as likely to run from higher inputs, outputs, and income to loans, as it is from loans to these changes.

INPUT DEMAND FUNCTION. Input demand studies do not directly test loan impact on production and thus avoid the problem of relating loans to the production function. In a comprehensive analysis of the impact of uncertainty on resource allocation, for example, Schluter estimated input demand functions for labor, modern varieties, fertilizer, crop area, and animal and machine power (see table 9-3). The explanatory variables included financial constraints represented by credit availability and income, nonfarm assets and farm size, technology and knowledge.

Table 9-3 presents Schluter's results for modern seed varieties and fertilizer, the main targets of supervised credit programs. Access to loans, dairying income, area cropped, and assets were significant explanatory variables for fertilizer use. Schluter regarded assets and farm size as indices of farmers' ability to bear risk: farmers more able to cope with uncertainty and with better access to institutional loans were significantly more likely to adopt modern rice varieties. Interestingly, these variables did not explain adoption of new wheat varieties. Access to loans and land planted with modern rice varieties were the most significant factors explaining fertilizer use. Access to loans appeared to be less important, however, in explaining demand for inputs (not reported in table 9-3) other than rice and fertilizer.

Table 9-2. *Estimates of Effect of Borrowing on the Cobb-Douglas Production Function, Selected Countries*

Item	Brazil (1971–72)	Colombia (1960)	Colombia: Borrower[a] 1965	Colombia: Borrower[a] 1968	Colombia: Nonborrower (1968)	Ghana 1962–74
Log *a*	1.514		1.174	2.899	0.740	0.006
Land	0.293*	0.303*	0.379*	0.777*	0.418*	−2.127
	(4.42)	(1.620)[b]	(1.560)	(3.964)	(1.742)	(1.217)
Labor	0.009	n.a.	0.396*	0.049	0.456*	4.248*
	(0.88)		(1.472)	(0.383)	(2.505)	(1.977)
Farm equipment	0.045*	−0.103*	0.144	0.048	0.034	n.a.
	(1.34)	(−1.873)	(1.043)	(0.533)	(0.354)	
Livestock	0.009*	n.a.	n.a.	n.a.	n.a.	n.a.
	(1.83)					
Operating expense	0.246*	0.115[c]*	0.314*	0.279*	0.405*	0.336
	(4.30)	(1.885)	(1.377)	(1.898)	(3.092)	(0.269)
Modern varieties	0.356*	n.a.	n.a.	n.a.	n.a.	n.a.
	(5.02)					
Credit	n.a.	0.641*	0.064	−0.084	0.104*	n.a.
		(3.705)	(0.877)	(−1.000)	(1.825)	

Credit × land	n.a.	n.a.	n.a.	n.a.	n.a.	1.559
						(1.505)
Credit × labor	n.a.	n.a.	n.a.	n.a.	n.a.	−1.941
						(−1.691)
Credit × operating expense	0.0001*	n.a.	n.a.	n.a.	n.a.	−0.395
	(1.97)					(−0.297)
Credit × modern inputs	−0.00003	n.a.	n.a.	n.a.	n.a.	n.a.
	(−0.37)					
R^2	0.96	0.89	0.57	0.90	0.80	0.85
Number of observations	129	17	27	27	25	13

n.a. Not available.

a. Borrowers are participants in supervised credit programs. Nonborrowers are nonparticipants, including farmers borrowing from nonformal sources.

b. Figures in parentheses are *t*-values. Asterisk indicates statistical significance at 10 percent or better confidence interval.

c. Includes fertilizer only.

Sources: *Brazil*: P. B. Rao, *The Economics of Agricultural Credit Use in Southern Brazil* (Waltair, Andhra Pradesh, India: Andhra University Press, 1973). *Colombia*: D. Colyer and G. Jimenez, "Supervised Credit as a Tool in Agricultural Development," *American Journal of Agricultural Economics*, vol. 53, no. 4 (November 1971), pp. 639–42; and W. S. Becker, "Agricultural Credit and Colombia's Economic Development," Ph.D. thesis, Louisiana State University, 1970. *Ghana*: A. B. Gyeke, E. T. Acqah, and C. D. Whyte, "An Evaluation of Institutional Credit in Ghana" (Petersburg, Va.: Virginia State College, Bureau of Economic Research, 1977).

Table 9-3. *Linear Regression of Factors Affecting Use of Modern Rice and Wheat Varieties and Fertilizer in Surat District, India, 1971–72*

	Modern varieties		
Variable[a]	*Rice*	*Wheat*	*Fertilizer*
Credit[b]	0.182*	−0.114	82.676*
	(2.02)[c]	(−1.57)	(4.28)
Assets	0.020*	−0.005	−0.585
	(2.52)	(−0.89)	(−0.3)
Nonagricultural income	0.089	−0.016	8.575
	(1.38)	(−1.28)	(1.18)
Dairying income	0.100	0.073	25.656*
	(1.54)	(1.53)	(2.49)
Area under crop[c]	0.661*	0.541*	66.998*
	(6.59)	(3.84)	(4.78)
Gross cropped area	−0.056*	0.006	—
	(−2.17)	(0.29)	
Area under improved rice	—	—	54.359
			(2.48)*
Area under traditional rice	—	—	18.513*
			(2.50)
Area under unirrigated crops	—	—	−8.991
			(−0.89)
Education	−0.005	0.076*	−5.129
	(−0.12)	(3.23)	(0.97)
R^2	0.76	0.74	0.63
Number of observations	59	56	25

— Not applicable.

Note: Figures in parentheses are *t*-values. Asterisk indicates significance at 1 percent level.

a. Two other variables, number of family workers and home consumption requirements, were included in these equations but were not statistically significant.

b. Refers to maximum amount the cooperative would be willing to lend the farmer for various inputs based on area, cropping pattern, assets, and character of the farmer.

c. For fertilizer, this represents area under high-yielding rice varieties.

Source: M. G. Schluter, "The Interaction of Credit and Uncertainty in Determining Resource Allocation and Incomes on Small Farms, Surat District, India," Occasional Paper no. 68 (Ithaca, N.Y.: Cornell University, Department of Agricultural Economics, February 1974).

EFFICIENCY GAP FUNCTION. The third econometric approach relates credit not directly to input or output levels but to the farmer's ability to allocate resources efficiently. These studies attempt to determine whether loans explain differences in ability to use optimal levels of inputs. Some studies simply compare whether borrowers and nonborrowers equate marginal value products to prices of inputs frequently financed by loans. Separate production functions are estimated for borrowers and nonborrowers, but the differences in initial level of savings, managerial ability, and perception of risk are usually not considered. An exception is a Malaysian study which classified farmers by capital availability rather than as borrower and nonborrower.

A study of Philippine rice farms by A. M. Mandac and R. W. Herdt ["Economic Inefficiency as a Constraint to High Rice Yields in Nueva Ecija, Philippines," paper presented at International Rice Research Institute, Laguna, Philippines, 1978] supplies an alternative way of measuring loan impact. They compared data on normal farming operations with data from experimental trials conducted on the farmers' same fields to determine efficiency. Measures of technical as opposed to allocative inefficiencies were identified for each farm: it was expected that levels of technical knowledge and environmental factors such as irrigation and soil fertility would influence technical efficiency, while managerial ability, perception of risk, financial constraints, and credit availability would affect allocative efficiency.

Efficiency gap models are conceptually appealing, and future analysis might be extended to estimate loan impact on farm production or income. However, the use of experimental data to establish a frontier production function and thus to distinguish physical from price efficiency is rarely possible. In many cases farm practices of the "best" farmers may have to be used, as in other empirical studies of technical efficiency.

Programing Studies

Several studies of loan impact and demand have used mathematical programing. These studies provide estimates of normative behavior and simulate the impacts of alternative policy changes. Single period linear models are commonly used. Typically, a representative model is developed for reasonably homogeneous farms with respect to size, technology, resource endowment, and other characteristics. Profit maximization is normally assumed, subject to maximum and minimum farm or household constraints. The activities included can represent what exists or explore what is expected under alternative scenarios.

Multiperiod models, with and without discounted future cash flows, provide important advantages for the study of the impact of loans on investment, growth of enterprises, and liquidity management. Various issues have been studied with multiperiod models. For example, Michael D. Boehlje and T. Kelly White ["A Production-Investment Decision Model of Farm-Firm Growth," *American Journal of Agricultural Economics*, vol. 51, no. 1, February 1969, pp. 546–63] compared results of maximization of income versus net worth. Baker and Bhargava (chapter 12) and S. S. Hadiwigeno ["Potential Effects of Modification in the Credit Program for Small Farms in East Java, Indonesia," Ph.D.

dissertation, University of Illinois, 1974] tested how the value of unused cash and credit could influence liquidity management.

Recursive models of both representative farms and agricultural regions have been used. Unlike other multiperiod models, the objective function is solved each year with the result for one period linked to previous periods by feedback constraints. These constraints are specified to reflect farmer behavior—for example, accounting for risk aversion by safety-first objectives. Another feature of regional models is decomposition by farm size to test competition for resources—as in the case of a fixed regional credit constraint—among different size farms.

Several similar results emerge from these programing studies. Technological change, adoption of new varieties and cropping systems, mechanization, and farm income are frequently found to be constrained by the lack of formal loans. It has also been shown that certain productive alternatives would allow farmers to pay substantially higher interest rates with only a limited reduction in their borrowing. Small farmers appear particularly insensitive to interest rate levels.

Results and Methodological Problems

Virtually all these econometric studies—whether of production function, input demand function, or efficiency gap function—or programing exercises show positive contributions of credit to farm production, many of them statistically significant. The interpretation of several methodological issues, however, requires caution. The actual or expected impact of borrowing or demand for loans may be substantially under- or overestimated in a particular study for at least six reasons.

• Few studies capture the complexity of farm household behavior. Model activities are largely limited to the farm, with few efforts to include household resources allocated to off-farm activities. Since loan funds are fungible, the true impact of loans is hard to determine without an integrated household model and extensive data on the household's sources and uses of liquidity.

• Many studies focus on working capital. But in many countries where long-term credit is scarce, there is an excessive use of short-term loans to help finance investment. The impact of short-term loans must be considered in relation to investment, not to production alone.

• True costs and benefits of borrowing may not be adequately captured by interest rates and borrowing limits. Borrowing costs, especially for small farmers, may far exceed interest charges. Also, the reliability of the credit source, expectations about the need to repay, and noncredit services influence the extent to which a borrower will switch from an informal to a formal source, or borrow rather than use savings.

- In spite of various elaborate methods, it is not clear that research has adequately dealt with risk and uncertainty. If credit were priced at equilibrium rates, with repayment expectations and farmer attitudes toward risk adequately captured, optimal borrowing might be significantly less than many studies have estimated.
- Compared with some other methodologies, mathematical programing models offer fewer possibilities for statistical tests of goodness of fit. It is not clear whether farmer behavior has really been captured by the models, and if not, their projections are dubious.
- The applicability of these models to many low-income countries is questionable. Many sophisticated models have been developed, but few low-income countries have sufficient data to justify their use.

Research on rural finance will improve as researchers develop greater appreciation for the major issues raised here: interdependence of farm and household decision making, fungibility, and attribution. The immediate priority is to develop a data base sufficient for more detailed analysis of agricultural finance. Fungibility and farm household decision making indicate the need for collecting comprehensive data on sources and uses of farm household liquidity. All sources of liquidity need to be quantified and related to the various farm and household uses. Careful monitoring of production expenses, investment, consumption, and nonfarm activities is necessary to describe accurately when and where additional liquidity is allocated. Once this is described, more rigorous analysis can identify factors explaining the allocation and impact of loans. The massive cross-section surveys currently undertaken in many countries are not suitable for this purpose. Much more careful collection of data over time from the same households is required, even if it means a smaller sample size.

Finally, the ultimate objective of agricultural credit policies and programs should be to improve rural welfare. Although the benefits and shortcomings of credit are frequently enumerated, they have not been systematically compared with the benefits and costs of other policy instruments, such as input or product price policy, that could be used to meet the same objectives. We suspect such an analysis would reveal that agricultural credit programs are less cost-effective, but are preferred because they are easy to administer and because rich, politically powerful farmers can manipulate them to their advantage.

Recommendations for Further Reading

Goldsmith, Raymond W. *Financial Structure and Development.* New Haven, Conn.: Yale University Press, 1969.

Gurley, John G., and Edward S. Shaw. *Money in a Theory of Finance.* Washington, D.C.: Brookings Institution, 1960.

Gurley, John G., and Edward S. Shaw. "Financial Aspects of Economic Development." *American Economic Review*, vol. 45, no. 4 (September 1955), pp. 515–38.

McKinnon, Ronald I. *Money and Capital in Economic Development.* Washington, D.C.: Brookings Institution, 1973.

Nelson, Benjamin N. *The Idea of Usury: From Tribal Brotherhood to Universal Otherhood.* Princeton, N.J.: Princeton University Press, 1942; 2d ed., enlarged, Chicago: University of Chicago Press, 1969.

Shaw, Edward S. *Financial Deepening in Economic Development.* New York: Oxford University Press, 1973.

Issues for Discussion

1. How can rural financial markets affect the distribution of income and of asset ownership? What policies could cause rural financial markets to have a *neutral* effect on income and wealth distribution?
2. How does financial intermediation assist in overcoming the disadvantages of barter?
3. How does financial intermediation affect the efficiency of resource allocation?
4. What types of change in financial markets can be expected as an economy develops?
5. What are the differences between a supply-leading and a demand-following strategy of finance in development?
6. How important are formal agricultural loans in early stages of development? Does their importance decrease or increase as development progresses?
7. What are the effects of trying to control fungibility by tightening up the administration of agricultural credit programs?
8. What measures could a donor use to document the extent to which additionality was achieved in a small-farmer credit project?
9. If a group of borrowers have crop yields substantially higher than a group of nonborrowers, can one conclude that all the difference in yields was due to credit use?
10. Is it desirable for rural financial markets to mobilize funds through savings deposits in rural areas and recycle them as loans to nonagricultural activities?
11. How do prices and yields in agriculture affect the ability of financial markets to serve rural areas?

PART III

CREDIT AND FINANCE IN FARM HOUSEHOLDS AND RURAL FIRMS

Introduction

Rural credit programs are intended to help farm households make changes in their economic activities. Some credit programs attempt to stimulate a specific type of production, such as corn or dairy farming, while other programs promote the purchase of modern farm inputs, such as chemical fertilizer and hybrid seed, or of improved breeds of cattle. Still other credit is directed toward investment in capital goods, such as irrigation pumps, farm machinery, or land improvements. Credit programs are usually intended to alter production decisions in the borrowing farm household by providing funds for production purposes. Their real impact, however, may emerge as changes in household consumption or nonfarm activities. This is because in low-income countries the farm and the farm household are in effect a single financial unit, jointly using and supplying, in a variety of interchangeable ways, the funds, labor, and tangible inputs employed on the farm. It is difficult, if not impossible, to predict the ultimate impact of a loan under such conditions, even with detailed information and strict regulation of loan use.

Extensive information about the operation of farm households is required for fruitful administration of agricultural credit programs. Because of the intertwined activities of farm and household, the debt capacity of the household may be overestimated by lenders if they consider only its agricultural activities. The extension of too much credit can overburden borrowers and defeat credit program objectives. Farmers' reasons for borrowing are complex; not only do they want to increase production, but they also have to cope with the seasonal variations in cash flow typical of rural households. They may use financial markets because of risk; maintaining an unutilized "credit reserve"—a source that could supply a loan if needed—may be very important when a household is faced with an illness or emergency. Some farmers use loans to mobilize sufficient liquidity for large, "lumpy" investments such as a tractor. Still other farmers rely on credit to help finance expansion of their operations, including the purchase of land. Many households also use loans to offset unpredictable shortfalls in income or to maintain consumption when their food supply runs low.

Some farm households go into debt only occasionally, while others make regular use of loans. Not all farm households want or can effectively use credit all the time. Often an apparent clamor for loans by farmers is chiefly a desire for easy money—a result of the very low interest rates charged on formal loans or of the belief that lenders are unwilling or unable to enforce repayment. Where realistic interest rates are charged on loans and repayment requirements are enforced, the demand for credit is deflated.

Many discussions of rural finance are limited to credit activities and ignore the savings side. Under normal circumstances many households in even the poorest areas have significant surpluses beyond what is needed for short-term consumption. Rural people would choose to hold a portion in financial form if given opportunities and incentives to do so. Attractive financial assets can help rural households manage their cash and liquidity flows. The heavy emphasis in much of the literature on the alleged "need" for agricultural credit has obscured the fact that most investments in rural areas are financed by internal household savings rather than loans. Arguments for increasing the credit supply to meet "needs" usually ignore the fact that many inputs used in the production activities of the farm household are contributed in kind, and that seasonal labor surpluses permit much capital accumulation.

Several chapters in this part are linked by the theme of liquidity and liquidity management. Lee (chapter 10) emphasizes that the nature of agricultural production and the heterogeneity of rural households create opportunities for financial intermediation. These opportunities do not depend on the existence of financial assets, but arise from the nature of the rural economy. Lee points out that convenient access to financial assets in appropriate form can lower the costs of liquidity management. He strongly implies that efforts to mobilize savings have more potential than credit programs for increasing participation in rural financial markets.

Meyer (chapter 11) takes income flows as his starting point for discussing the importance of nonfarm activities in the economy of rural households and communities. These rural units seem to be particularly uncreditworthy from the standpoint of formal financial intermediaries, although Meyer suggests why small-scale rural entrepreneurs may not be interested in formal credit.

Baker and Bhargava (chapter 12) construct a model of farmer behavior in a district in India. Their model uses liquidity—and includes unutilized debt capacity as a source of liquidity—as a basis for predicting the adoption of a credit-supported on-farm innovation.

Ong, Adams, and Singh (chapter 13) examine farm household data from Taiwan in the 1960s, when rural savings were rapidly accumulating and mobilized in financial form. The authors attribute Taiwan's rural savings performance to appropriate policies and to the presence of effective rural financial institutions. They conclude that stimulation of voluntary savings should be a rural development priority.

Howse (chapter 14) suggests that credit projects can easily produce antidevelopmental consequences, and argues that programs to help mobilize rural savings are more constructive. He points out that savings programs can be run with relatively low overhead in even very poor rural areas. Furthermore, their operations can be simple and open and contribute to social cohesiveness. Savings programs may also serve as vehicles for agricultural innovations.

DeLancey (chapter 15) documents the savings behavior of women employed as plantation workers and of non-wage-earning women in an area in Cameroon. She concludes that both groups save, as shown by the accumulation of consumer durables and financial assets, payment of school expenses for children, and other activities of a provident or productive nature.

10. *The Role of Financial Intermediation in the Activities of Rural Firms and Households*

Warren F. Lee

[All rural families need to save some of the time and may borrow at other times. Financial institutions can help potential savers and borrowers by adjusting to their different behavior, and this process will increase the community's investments and productivity. This chapter reviews the rural activities that require financial services and the ways in which such services are provided.]

Since incomes and expenditures are rarely, if ever, perfectly synchronized, all firms and households, urban or rural, must carry some reserves of liquidity. If financial markets are undeveloped and cannot provide usable services at reasonable cost, as is common in rural areas of developing countries, these reserves will be held in the form of real goods such as food and supplies, gold, jewelry, or livestock. As responsive financial markets develop, liquidity reserves can increasingly be held in savings accounts and in unused credit potential. Both saving and borrowing help rural families synchronize their expenditures and receipts over time. Institutions that accept savings deposits and extend loans intermediate between savers and borrowers, making it possible for some to spend expected income before they receive it, and for others to hold funds safely and profitably for future use. Both savers and borrowers gain from intermediation when these institutions function properly.

Rural communities typically have a continuing demand for effective financial intermediation because of the heterogeneity of rural households. A high percentage of rural residents are engaged in farm or farm-related enterprises which produce large seasonal and year-to-year fluctuations in their cash incomes and the payments they must make. Since all rural families experience periodic deficits, they will hold reserve assets much of the time. Borrowing is not nearly so universal as saving: because of birthright, skill, luck, or a combination of circumstances, some farm families are capable of financing all liquidity deficits out of accumulated savings. Normally, most people borrow at some time during their lifetime, but it should not be assumed that all households need credit all of the time. In communities where financial savings facilities are conveniently available, often perhaps three-quarters of the families hold savings accounts at any one time, while only about one quarter have loans outstanding.

Forms of Saving and Borrowing

Saving is normally thought of as the acquisition of currency or liquid instruments such as bank deposits. Borrowing is often viewed as a formal contractual arrangement whereby the creditor advances funds in exchange for the borrower's promise to repay. These concepts of saving and borrowing are too narrow: saving occurs whenever part of one's current income or wealth is reserved for future consumption; borrowing occurs whenever current expenditures are paid for out of future income.

A comprehensive definition of accumulated savings would be the value of all assets held, including financial assets, inventories, livestock, equipment, and land, less any debts outstanding—in other words, the net worth. This balance-sheet definition still excludes some nonconventional forms of asset: labor or other services owed by a neighbor in return for favors provided, for example. In many societies, children assume an implicit, open-ended obligation to care for their elderly parents; this obligation is a form of asset for the parents. In both examples the assets may be regarded as the result of prior "saving," in that personal consumption was in some sense deferred. Though not normally included on a balance sheet, the neighbor's debt of labor and the children's pledge of old age security are examples of debt that often carry stronger repayment obligations than a bank loan.

The many forms of saved assets differ in the degree to which they can be mobilized for use in lending. Bank deposits and other liquid forms of savings can be readily mobilized in financial markets; the size, liquidity, risk, and location of savers' funds can be transformed by financial intermediaries to meet the opportunities facing diverse borrowers. In contrast, the hoarded cash, the neighbor's labor, or the children's obligations to parents cannot be mobilized for lending to other people. In some rare instances these kinds of transactions can be pledged to a third party, but in general they lack the marketability needed for effective mobilization.

Role of Liquidity Reserves for Rural Families

Rural households use their reserves of credit and savings in many ways: to adjust to seasonal patterns of income and expenditure, to adapt to technological change, to protect themselves from adversity, and to balance their income and expenditure over their life cycle.

As noted above, firms and households experience seasonal variations in receipts and expenditures. Farmers have high expenditures at the beginning of each growing season and high receipts after harvest. Those who sell farm inputs or who buy, market, or process farm produce also experience seasonal concentrations in receipts and expenditures. Credit and savings help these various groups adjust to their seasonal variations.

The adoption of new technology, increasingly a fact of life, is likely to shift or disrupt cash flow patterns. New seed varieties, fertilizers, and chemicals tend to be more expensive than the techniques they replace. Machines are relatively large investments which pay off over several years, whereas the hand labor and animal power they replace are more divisible, current expenses. Investments in irrigation and drainage generally should be accompanied by higher outlays by farmers for seed, fertilizer, and pesticides. Many forms of technology, such as tractors or combine harvesters, also involve some expansion of the farm operation to spread overhead costs and capture potential economies of scale.

Unanticipated medical bills or drops in income because of crop failure, depressed product prices, or lack of seasonal employment play havoc with cash flow patterns. These risks cannot easily be insured, and reserves of savings and credit are needed to finance consumption and business expenses during periods of adversity.

Reserves of credit and savings also enable households to balance expected earnings and expenditures over their life cycle. The financial dimensions of a family's life cycle can be described in four stages: establishment, growth, consolidation, and decline. During the first two phases, expenditures typically exceed current earnings: there may be large outlays for housing and getting established in a farm or nonfarm business; and outlays for food, clothing, and medical care are high during the years of bearing and rearing children. In the consolidation stage, expenditures typically stabilize or decline while earnings continue to increase. In decline, earnings decrease and reserves are used to meet current expenditures.

Financial intermediation can accommodate lifetime income and expenditure patterns. Young families typically rely on credit to finance deficits. As they mature their use of credit typically stabilizes or declines, and they accumulate savings to cover deficits during old age.

Sources of Liquidity

Expenditures differ in their size and frequency, and there are corresponding differences among the sources of funds used to make these expenditures. The sources and uses of funds may be matched in terms of their cost and flexibility. Cash offers great flexibility, since it is divisible and involves negligible transactions costs; however, the costs of holding cash include the danger of theft, forgone interest earnings, and, over longer periods, inflationary loss. Since these costs may sometimes be significant, many people hold only enough cash for such small daily expenditures as food, personal items, and bus fare.

The most flexible alternative form of liquidity is demand deposits against which checks may be written. In poorly developed rural financial markets, however, demand deposits are not readily available and the negotiability of checks is limited. The next best alternative often consists of savings deposits, and payments are made either in cash or by transfer instruments such as money orders. These instruments are used when cash payment is not convenient because the expenditure is too large or the buyer and seller are too far away from each other.

The use of cash, checks, and money orders takes on added dimensions when credit is also involved. One dimension is substitutability. Credit may be made available in various forms, ranging from cash obtainable on demand within the limits of a borrower's "open" account, or cash supplied in a single payment, to vouchers which the borrower exchanges with a dealer for a particular product such as fertilizer. Open-account credit extended by sellers to their customers, for example, can replace cash sales. Cash advances are often disbursed in the form of a check for the convenience of the borrower. When credit is tied to specific uses, substitution may occur if a borrower sells the required product (fertilizer, for example) and uses the money so obtained for more attractive purposes.

A major distinction is customarily made between formal and informal credit. Formal credit involves written contracts for loans from formal or chartered lending institutions such as banks or cooperatives. Informal credit, by contrast, includes loans from relatives and friends, and also from merchants, wealthy landowners, or full-time moneylenders offering small commercial transactions on open account without legally binding contracts. Most efforts to promote rural development through credit projects operate in the formal realm. An examination of the characteristics of formal credit may provide insights into its limitations as a development tool.

Formal credit is generally inflexible and costly. Although the interest rates on formal loans are typically low in comparison with those charged by informal commercial lenders, the costs to borrowers for paperwork, travel time, legal fees, commissions, or bribes are typically much higher. Added complexity means long delays between the application, approval, and disbursement of loan funds. The usefulness of formal credit for liquidity management may be further diminished when loans are extended in kind, because this restricts the borrower's choice of product, especially when rigid quotas are applied such as fixed quantities of fertilizer and seed per hectare of cropland. By contrast, informal loans are typically approved and disbursed promptly, and their specific use is freely determined by the borrower. Because it is more flexible and obtained more quickly, informal credit is valuable to many farmers for liquidity management. Formal credit is typically used for large nonrecurring expenses where other sources of liquidity are insufficient; major purchases such as land, breeding livestock, machinery, and equipment are often financed with formal credit.

Implications for Credit Policy

It is widely believed that the savings capacity of low-income rural people is quite low. In fact, however, their capacity to save appears quite high. They *must* save to accommodate seasonal variations in receipts and expenditures, to manage uninsurable risks, and to even out the cash flow over their life cycle.

The belief that they cannot and do not save may be based on the observation that small-farmer households frequently hold only small amounts of financial savings or none at all. Sometimes this is due to a lack of dependable or convenient deposit services in rural areas, where deposits or withdrawals are complicated by delays, paperwork, long distances, and poor communications. Another important reason for low financial savings rates is that many banks and other financial intermediaries pay low rates of interest on small deposits. Minimum size requirements for deposits and transactions, service charges on deposits, and the low, often negative real interest rates make other forms of savings more attractive. Inventories, jewelry, land, and other real assets are then preferred over saving deposits, and direct exchanges of labor and other services may substitute for monetary exchange. The family's security fund is a large number of children rather than a financial accumulation.

In most cases rural financial markets would perform better if small savers were paid positive real rates of interest. Savers could substitute their holdings of less productive real assets for deposits, and these could in turn be more effectively mobilized as a source of credit to others.

Characteristic of formal credit programs is a high incidence of default. Informal lenders tend to be flexible about repayment timing, while formal lenders have fixed due dates. Postponing a loan repayment is a liquidity management tool; and since formal credit is less valuable than some other liquidity reserves, the costs of losing its availability as a result of nonrepayment are relatively low. Current consumption, the repayment of informal loans, or the replenishing of liquid assets and inventories will often take precedence over repayment of formal loans. Relatively few penalties are severe enough to cause borrowers to reorder these priorities.

Another common failure of formal credit programs is that most loans go to a few, relatively wealthy borrowers. One reason is that low interest rates force lenders to ration limited funds, frequently on the basis of risk. The incentive to reduce risk, as well as transaction costs, favor users of large amounts of credit. Transaction costs per dollar borrowed are lower for lenders in the case of large loans, and wealthy borrowers are more likely than poor ones to be making large, "lumpy" investment expenditures. In addition, formal credit provides a comparatively low-cost liquidity management tool for wealthy borrowers.

Conclusions

The potential demand for effective financial intermediation in rural areas appears to be strong. A heterogeneous population, seasonal incomes and expenditures, technological change, and high risks suggest that even the poorest rural people would participate in effective credit and savings mobilization programs.

The behavior of most rural people suggests that they perceive the savings and credit services now offered as inadequate. Despite storage costs, spoilage, and theft, many households hold relatively large amounts of real goods and relatively small amounts of liquid financial savings. Savings in the form of real goods are often unproductive and cannot be mobilized to support loans to those desiring credit. Where formal credit programs have been introduced, most are characterized by low participation and high default rates; despite its significantly higher interest rates, informal credit is widely used. Typically, formal credit programs are simply too costly and too rigid to play a major role in liquidity management. Where a program has comparatively little value to its borrowers, many of them see little point in repaying loans.

Low participation in savings and credit services in rural areas is explained by four factors: (1) They are often inaccessible: depositors and borrowers may have to travel long distances to carry out routine transactions. (2) They are costly to use: excessive paperwork, delays, fees, and bribes are common. (3) They are too rigid: many savings and loan activities have minimum transaction requirements, and some credit is extended in kind rather than cash, in amounts based on quotas that bear little relationship to the borrower's liquidity situation. (4) Most savings and credit programs have low and often negative real rates of interest. Low interest rates force potential depositors to turn to less productive savings alternatives, and they induce lenders to ration limited funds to relatively few of the more wealthy borrowers.

11. *Financing Rural Nonfarm Enterprises in Low-income Countries*

Richard L. Meyer

[A neglected element in rural finance is the support of nonfarm activities. These have been generally short of capital, among other things. Credit institutions should develop more innovative approaches to adapt their services to small nonfarm enterprises.]

A number of low-income countries, especially in Asia, are placing increased emphasis on off-farm employment to alleviate rural poverty. Although rural incomes have improved in some countries, there is growing frustration with strategies that have had only limited impact on rural welfare. Capital-intensive industrialization has failed to generate significant increases in employment to absorb the available labor supply. Technology-oriented agricultural development strategies have eased food constraints, but the supposed trickle-down of benefits to small farmers and rural workers has been limited. Although some small-farmer programs appear promising, most have yet to demonstrate a significant effect on poverty. Policy makers are therefore turning to off-farm employment as an additional way to improve incomes of farm households.

As development strategy shifts in this direction, a logical question must be: how can the small-scale sector be assisted? In many countries, expansion of the small-scale sector depends on restructuring the rules of the financial game which favor large-scale firms. After such a restructuring, however, the question still arises as to what specific programs and policies will facilitate the creation and expansion of small-scale firms. The purpose of this chapter is to review the financing of rural nonfarm enterprises and analyze how rural financial markets can better serve these activities.

Extracted from *Problems and Issues of Agricultural Credit and Rural Finance* (Dhaka: Bangladesh Bank, Agricultural Credit Department, 1979), pp. 117–25; also published by *Development Digest* (July 1980), pp. 92–100.

Off-farm Work and Rural Nonfarm Enterprises

Before discussing finance, it is useful to summarize briefly some of the recent literature concerning the rural nonfarm sector. Two research themes are most relevant. The first concerns the nature and extent of off-farm work for rural households. At one time, this issue was largely ignored by agricultural economists; part-time farming was seen largely as a transitional phenomenon. Part-time farmers were viewed as a problem in efficient resource allocation, and policy was largely directed toward speeding their adjustment from part-time to full-time status.

More recently, however, the part-time farm household has begun to be viewed as a permanent fixture of the rural setting. In such widely divergent settings as the United States and Japan, rural residents typically earn incomes from both farm and off-farm sources. In the United States the proportion of farm household income derived from off-farm sources grew steadily from 43 to 59 percent between 1960 and 1976; in Japan this proportion grew from 48 to 62 percent from 1964 to 1975. Off-farm income is much more important for small farmers. Over 80 percent of the household income of U.S. farmers selling less than US$2,500 in gross sales came from off-farm sources in 1976, up from 60 percent in 1960. In Japan, farm families with less than 0.5 hectares in 1973 earned almost 90 percent of household income from nonagricultural sources, while that percentage was only 30 percent for those with more than 2.0 hectares. And the importance of off-farm work is not limited to high-income countries. Farm records, surveys, and village studies in such widely divergent areas as Thailand, Taiwan, Republic of Korea, Sierra Leone, Nigeria, and Egypt show that farm families receive income from a wide variety of off-farm or nonfarm activities. Problems of rural-urban income gap and rural income distribution would be much worse if low-income rural households did not engage in such off-farm activities.

The second theme found in the literature concerns the nature, extent, and potential of nonfarm enterprises in rural areas. In many areas 20 to 30 percent of the rural labor force is engaged primarily in nonfarm work. The share was reported as 51 percent in Taiwan in 1966, 40 percent in the Philippines in 1970, and 25 percent in Korea in 1970. One-half to two-thirds of all nonfarm employment opportunities in Asia were found in rural areas and towns. Similarly, small-scale firms, the majority of which are located in rural areas, represent a major share of total employment in a number of industries. For example, Harry T. Oshima ["Labor-Force 'Explosion' and the Labor Intensive Sector in Asian Growth," *Economic Development and Cultural Change*, vol. 19, no. 2, January, 1971, pp. 161–83] found for the Philippines in

1961 that firms engaging fewer than ten persons accounted for 93 percent of the employment in construction, 94 percent in commerce, 76 percent in manufacturing, 64 percent in transport and communications, and 95 percent in services. Several studies that have tried to assess the characteristics of different size firms suggest important advantages for small-scale enterprises. They are less capital-intensive, are more geographically dispersed, offer more opportunities for unskilled and family labor, have greater linkages with the agricultural sector, and have greater export potential than frequently assumed.

Assistance to Small-scale Enterprises

Most countries employ a variety of industrial promotion techniques, including customs exemptions, preferential foreign exchange rates, tax incentives, and concessionally priced credit. Unfortunately, these techniques are principally geared to large capital-intensive firms, and small firms frequently are not benefited. Some promotional efforts must be pinpointed more specifically to their problems. The specific needs and approach will vary from country to country, but various options have been suggested.

• Infrastructure. Social and economic infrastructure may have a substantial impact on the development of nonfarm activities. Rural areas typically lack communication, transportation, electricity, and other facilities.

• Trading services. Small firms frequently lack adequate input and product markets. Healthier cooperatives or trade associations can help obtain a steady supply of lower-cost inputs and stimulate production of goods of appropriate quality for domestic sales and exports.

• Research and technical assistance. Much of the research in many countries is conducted in urban-based institutes, with results that have limited relevance for small rural enterprises. Some of this research could be better located in rural areas, where it would be more directly accountable to the intended clientele. Nonfarm extension services could be developed, similar to existing farm extension programs, to encourage the spread of innovations.

• Vocational training. Most training in specific skills occurs in small-scale enterprises through apprenticeships and on-the-job training. This should be complemented by formal training that provides basic instruction in management, record keeping, and marketing.

• Industrial estates. Providing services over wide geographical areas can be prohibitively expensive. Several countries have tried to achieve economies of scale by creating industrial estates that provide infrastructure, facilities, and in some cases even the shells of buildings for firms. The Indian experience shows, however, that high-cost, poorly located estates will not be fully utilized.

• Financial services. Most studies identify credit and other financial services as a constraint and propose credit programs for nonfarm enterprises, frequently in conjunction with technical services.

Existing Financial Services

The literature clearly suggests that small-scale firms suffer from inadequate institutional financing. Three types of evidence are frequently given in support of this claim. First, small businessmen customarily identify finance as one of their key bottlenecks when asked about their business.

Second, small enterprises are frequently started and later expand largely with equity capital obtained from savings accumulated from other activities or from within the firm itself. For example, Carl Liedholm and Enyinna Chuta ["The Economics of Rural and Urban Small-scale Industries in Sierra Leone," African Rural Economy Paper no. 14, Department of Agricultural Economics, Michigan State University, 1976] report that approximately 60 percent of the funds used to establish small-scale industries in Sierra Leone came from personal savings from agricultural activities, trade, or business. The 1973 Accra manufacturing survey [cited in William F. Steel, *Small-scale Employment and Production in Developing Countries: Evidence from Ghana*, New York, Praeger, 1977] showed that over 90 percent of the firms were started with personal savings or loans from relatives. Banks, however, frequently play a more important role in the finance of larger firms in many countries. The limited use of credit by smaller firms can be seen as evidence of discriminatory credit rationing.

Third, when credit is used, it frequently is obtained from informal sources (other than friends and relatives) such as input suppliers, purchasers, and moneylenders. The interest rates charged are usually higher than those charged by formal credit sources. For example, David Kochov and others [*Financing the Development of Small-scale Industries*, World Bank Staff Working Paper no. 191, Washington, D.C., November, 1974] report that small industrial enterprises in Korea borrow at rates of 35 to 40 percent from informal sources, compared with 17.5 percent from official banks. It is concluded that small businesses are denied adequate formal credit and are forced into more costly, informal sources.

Supply constraints offer one plausible explanation for the limited use of formal credit. Two other explanations from the side of demand also may be important. First, complicated procedures inconvenient or uncongenial to borrowers are often introduced by lenders to assist in rationing scarce loan funds. Thus, total costs to the borrower of obtaining small bank loans include much more than just the interest on the loan. Second, there may be little demand for bank credit by small-scale firms because their economic environment is so uncertain that they have little incentive to grow and expand. Input supplies may be uncertain and of poor quality; product markets may be easily saturated with increased production. In such conditions, assumption of loan repayment obligations may appear unwise.

Determining which of these explanations is most appropriate is a complicated undertaking beyond the scope of this chapter. The answer will vary by country and by industry, and firms existing side by side in the same industry may have quite different credit demands. Several reasons on the supply side, however, may explain the limited amount of credit offered to small firms. Understanding these reasons and relaxing the supply constraints will help clarify the issues on the demand side.

Factors Affecting Credit Supply

Nonfarm enterprises in the rural areas may suffer from inadequate credit because of the heavy emphasis on farm credit in many countries. Through regulations, quotas, rediscount arrangements, special funds, and other means, many countries have tried to increase the flow of funds to farmers, and especially to small farmers. When these efforts are successful, lenders may spend so much effort and funds to meet the farm credit objectives that they have little time or funds left for rural nonfarm enterprises. Some of these specialized lending institutions are even legally prevented from making nonfarm loans. Furthermore, low, inflexible interest rates, set by custom or usury laws, keep profit margins low in small rural lending operations.

Farms are heterogeneous, but in specific agricultural regions most farms will likely use similar technologies and production practices. Thus, lenders can develop procedures and rules of thumb to guide farm credit operations that will be fairly valid within the immediate area. Within that same market area, however, nonfarm enterprises can be expected to vary widely—perhaps a blacksmith, bicycle repair shop, bakery, tailor shop, cement plant, and textile firm, and only one or a few of each. It is difficult for the lender, therefore, to acquire familiarity with each type of firm and understand its unique problems well enough to feel confident in granting credit and technical assistance.

Lenders generally perceive high risks in small-enterprise lending, just as they do with small-farmer credit. Small-scale businessmen almost by definition have limited reserves to withstand adversity. Although the small-scale sector may appear to have considerable resiliency as manifested by a large number of firms, the turnover of firms is often high and bankruptcies are common. These firms can provide only small amounts of collateral, and the value of such collateral may be low because of their limited markets. The success of small-scale nonfarm enterprises may be inextricably tied to the fortunes of farming: when harvests and prices are good, farmers have income with which to pay old bills and contract for new goods and services, but when yields or prices are poor, so is the market for nonfarm firms. Thus, loan repayment will likely follow a similar pattern for both farm and nonfarm firms, so that the rural lender will have limited opportunity to reduce substantially the risk of his total portfolio through nonfarm loans.

Finally, the administrative structure of some larger banks works against making many loans in rural areas. Banks often give little authority to branch staff to make decisions on loans. The branch staff see their function as largely to collect and channel deposits to urban areas, not aggressively to seek loan customers in rural areas.

Directions for Improvement

The limited amount of funds going to rural nonfarm firms, and the problems encountered by countries that have tried to increase formal credit supplies, suggest a need to rethink how financial services can be effectively provided in rural areas. Several issues need to be faced:

• The current emphasis on implementing credit projects rather than strengthening rural financial markets contributes to fragmenting rather than integrating financial services. A few borrowers are favored by a specific project, while many are neglected. Services to firms outside the project may even deteriorate as staff and agencies strive to service project beneficiaries. Rural financial markets must be opened up to a wider range of clients. Borrowing and savings services must be broadened, and appropriate incentives given to financial intermediaries.

• Discussion has focused on the type of institution that would effectively provide financial services to rural nonfarm enterprises, but this issue is probably not worth all the attention usually given to it. Studies of farm finance show a striking similarity in the performance of various types of institutions in different economic environments. The key appears to be the working objectives and interests of the institutions, not their particular form or ownership. For example, Costa Rica, Jamaica, India, and Bangladesh have nationalized commercial banks to alter their performance. Yet studies suggest that these nationalized banks continue to serve approximately the same clientele as they did before nationalization. The nationalized banks tend to share most of the same decision-making criteria used by private banks. Fortunately, many countries have a fairly well-developed set of intermediaries. The challenge is to develop appropriate incentives so that these intermediaries will service nonfarm firms, not to create new special-purpose institutions.

• More innovative thinking is required to reduce the cost and risks of lending to small farms and nonfarm firms. Lending procedures, like deposit operations, need to be streamlined. Risks may be reduced through guarantee funds and loan insurance. Group lending experiments may suggest ways to reduce costs and improve repayment performance. Loan repayments can be scheduled differently; for example, a bicycle shop may logically make daily or weekly loan payments which a farmer could not do because of distance and seasonality of income.

• Increased attention must be given to the terms and conditions of loans. Amortization schedules must be made more flexible. Incentives are required to encourage rapid payments, but simple provisions are also necessary for extending loans and scaling down payments when planned production and sales conditions are not met. Interest rates must be set to reflect the scarcity of capital in the society and offer an attractive return to the lender.

• Training and technical assistance are required for both the lender and borrower. Lenders need assistance in improving loan services to keep pace with the efficiencies obtained by some institutions in servicing deposits. Loan officials need information on the problems and the potential of various rural nonfarm enterprises. Lenders might also provide important noncredit services to borrowers. Most small businesses have little or no record keeping; lenders are logical sources of information on how to establish and maintain accounts, and how to use such information for decision making. Indeed, this information might be more useful for the long-term survival and expansion of the firms than the credit itself.

12. *Financing Small-farm Development in India*

Chester B. Baker and Vinay K. Bhargava

[Small-farm credit is promoted to replace the moneylender and to finance increased productivity through modernization. Expectations, however, often exceed performance. Indian research suggests the discrepancy may be traced to a failure to take liquidity management into consideration. Programs designed to account for household liquidity management can help modernize and improve the viability of small farms.]

The Role of Credit

Recent literature suggests that government credit programs have limited success in reaching small farmers. Cooperative credit societies have often failed to survive, and survivors have often failed to reach substantial numbers of small farmers. Nor is the record significantly better for commercial banks or specialized agencies. Some suggest that small farmers' response to economic opportunity is limited or even negative. There is evidence, however, that small farmers do in fact respond sensitively and positively to economic incentives.

In India a large majority of small farmers have not adopted high-yielding crop varieties because of lack of capital. Since credit is visualized as reducing this capital constraint, it is generally argued that more credit, reduced cost of loans, and more technical assistance would accelerate the economic growth of small farms. Credit programs in India have tried to do just that: provide loans at low interest, move toward a "credit package," and link loans to the provision of production inputs and repayment to output. Yet loan defaults increase at an alarming rate.

In common with most credit programs for small farmers, India's programs limit the use of loan proceeds to the purchase of improved inputs. But small farmers must finance both production and consumption activities. Operating at a near-subsistence level, they must also

Extracted from *Australian Journal of Agricultural Economics*, vol. 18, no. 2 (August 1974), pp. 101–18.

provide for adverse contingencies in their businesses or households, and they face the problem of managing seasonal cash deficits and surpluses.

In their production activities, small farmers can diversify and keep their resource organization flexible. In their marketing activities they may have options in forward commitments. But in both cases their alternatives are limited. Some crops must be produced to meet food consumption requirements; the farm is already diversified. Moreover, diversification and flexibility provide at best the means to counter uncertainty in production, not uncertainty that affects consumption. The best and perhaps only way to provide for adverse outcomes in consumption is in liquidity—the ability to generate cash on demand.

A Theory of Liquidity Management

It is useful to conceive of a farm as a business firm with a collection of assets. The aggregate value of these assets to the firm exceeds the sum that could be obtained if they were sold separately. In a rationally organized firm, an asset with an expected sale value greater than its contribution to firm value would be sold. In practice, virtually all assets will be found to have (separate) sale values that are less than the values they contribute to the firm. This analytically useful concept provides the logical basis for ascribing liquidity values, as well as production values, to assets.

Even cash in the balance sheet of the firm may contribute more to firm value than the actual sum of money. Cash in hand is accessible immediately and at zero transaction cost, which gives it a liquidity value. Firms borrow even while retaining cash balances. As assets such as crops and livestock mature, the expected value of the cash proceeds from their sale increases relative to their value in current (noncash) form. As the firm's cash supply increases, the liquidity value of further increments of cash diminishes.

In general, an asset in the balance sheet of a firm makes two contributions: it produces an expected stream of income and contributes to *credit*—that is, money the firm can borrow when it can show an asset-holding position. [*Note*: In this chapter, the world *credit* is italicized when it refers to borrowing capacity, as opposed to the usual meaning of money actually lent.] *Credit*, defined as borrowing capacity, can substitute for cash as a source of liquidity, even though *credit* does not appear in a conventional balance sheet for the firm. *Credit* can be used to produce loan proceeds without actually disposing of balance-sheet assets. Given an increase in reliable access to loans, the small farmer can be expected to commit more cash to production and to rely on unused credit as a contingency source of cash.

In developing countries, sources of liquidity for small farms are limited. Insurance, even against common hazards, is scarce. Assets—such as land or bullocks—are generally fixed and essential for the farm's operation. Since these assets are not very salable and are subject to high transaction costs, they have limited liquidity value. Conventionally defined, the liquid assets of a farm include cash, gold, and jewelry. Cash is a nearly perfect source of liquidity since it can be converted to use with zero transaction costs. Gold and jewels are subject to transaction costs that may be excessive. Hence *credit,* if reliable, versatile, and easily accessible, provides an unusually valuable source of liquidity. But small farmers typically are denied such *credit* except by moneylenders. Generally they are forced to restrict their cash purchases to preserve some liquidity.

Such behavior explains the high percentage of liquid assets in the financial organization of poor farmers. Moreover, it explains the widespread failure of government credit that is restricted in its use and is perceived as temporary and unreliable by the small farmer. So conceived, credit programs fail to replace informal lenders who are regarded as a source of liquidity reserve.

The behavioral assumptions in liquidity management can be represented as in figure 12-1. In each case, the value of liquidity, shown on the vertical axis, is related to the amount of cash (A) or *credit* (B) used (read left to right) or reserved (read right to left) as shown on the horizontal axis. The relation is shown as nonlinear to reflect the plausible assumption of diminishing returns as the percentage reserved increases. When the firm is drained of liquidity in either form, however, it is plausible to expect the liquidity value to reach extremely high levels. An interesting implication of figure 12-1 is that the rational firm may borrow in the presence of a positive cash balance (such a result could not be explained by conventional firm theory with a rate of interest greater than zero).

The heights and slopes of relations such as those of figure 12-1 reflect subjective responses of the decision maker to uncertainties in his economic environment. For the cautious, the relations will be higher and perhaps more steeply sloped than for the less cautious. For an aggregate of assets with a high liquidity content, the height of the relations in both A and B will be lessened, other things being equal. Moreover, the more secure, versatile, and cheaper the access to credit, the lower would be the function in A, relative to the function in B.

Modeling a Typical Small Farm

We have introduced this theory of liquidity into the model of a small farm typical of Badaun District, Uttar Pradesh, India. In table 12-1 we list the conventional constraints and requirements that condition alternatives open to the small farmer. Badaun District has two distinct

Figure 12–1. *Behavioral Assumptions in Liquidity Management*

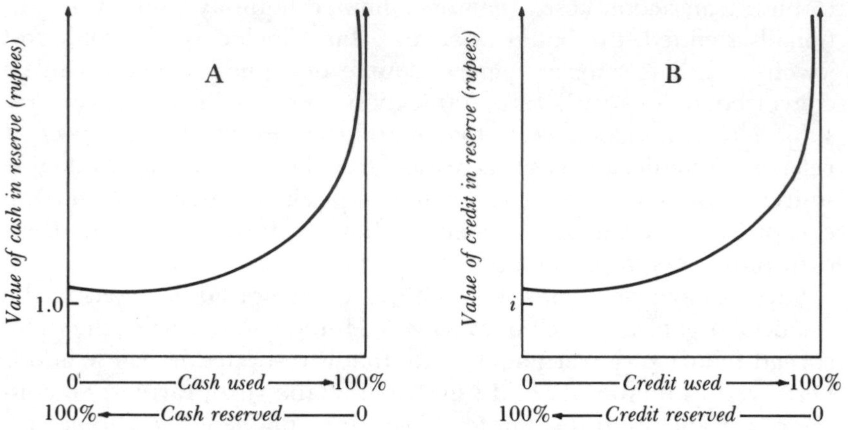

crop seasons: a wet season from June to November and a dry season from December to May. Hence the model year is specified from June 1 through May 31 and divided into two equal intervals. Land for crops is 1.7 hectares, of which 0.57 is committed to sugarcane contract, leaving 1.13 hectares to be allocated among the other crops listed under "Crop inventories."

Allocable labor resident on the farm amounts to 132 man-day equivalents in each season. The year is started with Rs1,000 in cash, plus the inventories in the "Quantity" column. In this semisubsistence unit, seasonal household requirements are given for maize, paddy, and wheat. In addition, cash is required as indicated. (It is an accounting convenience, as well as a precision measure, to identify the last day, May 31, separately from the rest of the dry season.)

The alternatives for the use of these resources and for meeting specified requirements are: paddy and maize are wet season crops; wheat, dry season; sugarcane uses land in both seasons. Alternatives in maize and wheat are differentiated between local and high-yielding variety (HYV) seeds, the HYV further differentiated by two levels of intensity in resource use. At level 1, HYV maize uses 155 days of labor and Rs161 per hectare to produce 10.61 quintals. Level 2 maize uses 229 days of labor and Rs275 per hectare to yield 15.87 quintals. Comparable requirements for level 1 HYV wheat are 135 days of labor and Rs389 per hectare; for level 2, 176 days and Rs593. At level 1, the HYV wheat yield is 29.306 quintals; at level 2, 40.727 quintals.

Table 12-1. *Constraints and Requirements for a Small Farm Typical of Badaun District, Uttar Pradesh*

Row description	*Season*	*Relation*[a]	*Quantity*	*Unit*[b]
Land	Wet	L	1.7	Hectares
	Dry	L	1.7	Hectares
Labor	Wet	L	132.0	Days
	Dry	L	132.0	Days
Crop inventories				
Local maize	Wet	E	1.0	Quintals
	Dry	E	1.0	Quintals
HYV maize	Dry	E	0.0	Quintals
Paddy	Wet	E	1.35	Quintals
	Dry	E	1.35	Quintals
Local wheat	Wet	E	10.0	Quintals
	Dry	E	0.0	Quintals
HYV wheat	Dry	E	0.0	Quintals
Sugarcane	Dry	E	0.0	Quintals
Household crop requirements				
Local maize	Wet	E	1.5	Quintals
	Dry	E	1.5	Quintals
Paddy	Wet	E	1.35	Quintals
	Dry	E	1.35	Quintals
Wheat	Wet	E	5.50	Quintals
	Dry	E	5.50	Quintals
HYV wheat inventory limit		E	5.0	Quintals
Sugarcane contract		E	0.57	Hectares
Household cash requirements	Wet	E	500.0	Rupees
	Dry	E	500.0	Rupees
Cash available	Wet	E	1,000.0	Rupees
	Dry	E	0.0	Rupees
	May 31	E	0.0	Rupees

a. L means equal to or less than; E, equal to.

b. A hectare equals 2.47 acres; a quintal equals about 220 pounds; and in 1974 a rupee equaled US$0.12.

Sales of maize provide cash in the dry season, as do sales of paddy. Wheat sales do not provide cash until the last day of the model year. The same is true for sugarcane. Hence, although wheat and sugarcane sales add to the farmer's eventual income, they do not add cash that can be used within the model year. The model provides for the purchase of maize in either season and for wheat in the dry season as an alternative means of meeting the consumption requirements specified in the model. The other crop consumption requirements can be met only by on-farm production. Labor can be hired in each season at Rs2.70 per day.

Table 12-2. *Summary of Selected Results in Solutions with Varied Specifications in Financial Environment of Small Farm in Uttar Pradesh, India*

Plan number	*Specifications on financial constraints of the small farmer*	HYV *wheat*		*Rupees borrowed*		*Cash reserved (rupees)*	*Net cash flow*
		Area (hectares)	*Sales (quintals)*	*Money-lender*	PSCP[a]		
No liquidity specifications							
1.	Moneylender only	0.82	17.55	674			1,252
2.	Moneylender and PSCP	0.82	17.55		656		1,391
Liquidity specifications							
3.	Moneylender only	0.39	4.14	541		317	578
4.	Moneylender and restricted PSCP[b]	0.43	4.81	341	189	317	640
5.	Moneylender and nonrestricted PSCP	0.77	11.01		680	209	1,010

Note: Beginning cash is Rs1,000 unless otherwise specified.

a. Public sector credit program.

b. Solutions from these specifications are in rough accord with averages from a survey of randomly sampled small farms in the district. Plan 4 provides for more HYV wheat than the actual average (0.43 versus 0.15) but the total in wheat is much the same (0.74 versus 0.72).

Model Solutions

In table 12-2 we summarize some of the results from solutions of the model under five basic plans. In Plans 1 and 3, credit from the public sector credit program (PSCP) is set at zero to represent the financial environment of the small farmer without such a program. In Plans 1 and 2, the liquidity reserve requirements are set at zero, and no values are given for liquidity reserves. Hence Plans 1 and 2 are consistent with results from "conventionally" specified linear programing models. In models that include liquidity management requirements and vectors, Plans 3, 4, and 5 and their variants, the objective function contains coefficients in activities that value liquidity sources in reserve—cash and *credit*. The farmer's net money income is termed "Net cash flow."

In Plan 1, without liquidity management vectors or requirements, the small farmer has access only to informal lenders, that is, moneylender credit. At the optimum, the small farmer produces the required minimum amount of sugarcane, reaps paddy and local maize sufficient for household requirements, and plants 0.82 hectares to HYV wheat. The wheat crop produces the household requirements and 17.55 quintals for sale. In this specification, the small farmer borrows Rs674 from the moneylender. Net cash flow amounts to Rs1,252.

Plan 2 retains the "naive" assumption of liquidity management—zero value for liquidity and no liquidity requirements. A PSCP is introduced into the financial environment of the small farmer (with properties similar to the actual program in the district). In the solution, the small farmer switches his borrowing to the PSCP and borrows Rs20 less than in Plan 1. Even so, he keeps 0.82 hectares in HYV wheat and his net cash flow increases by about Rs140. If the small farmer responds in this naive manner, we could predict a higher cash flow from introducing the PSCP but no change in the production organization of the small farm. We stress, however, that there is little reason to accept this version of small-farmer behavior. Indeed, it is precisely the falsity of this assumption that most likely accounts for the generally disappointing record of credit programs.

In remaining versions of the model, a total liquidity requirement is specified at a minimum of Rs1,000. The amount, which accords in general with observed values in liquid assets, is increased with the adoption of HYV to reflect the risks added by increased requirements for labor and for cash to buy fertilizer and seed. For example, the liquidity requirement for the dry season was increased by Rs293 per hectare of HYV wheat. HYV maize increased the liquidity requirement in the wet season by Rs263 per hectare. The liquidity requirements could be met with either cash or *credit* or by a combination of the two. In fact, both sources of liquidity are valued at "prices" that increase as the amount of liquidity diminishes.

In Plan 3 the small farmer is restricted to the moneylender as a source of loans. In the optimum plan, with the more realistic specification on liquidity management, HYV wheat is reduced to 0.39 hectares. Wheat sales are reduced to 4.14 quintals. The small farmer borrows Rs540 from the moneylender, reserving Rs1,959 and Rs317 of *credit* and cash, respectively. A cash flow of Rs578 is produced by the optimum organization, less than the cash with which he began the year. But to the cash flow must be added the Rs317 held in reserve.

In Plan 4, a PSCP is added to financing alternatives available to the small farmer, though with zero value for PSCP *credit* held in reserve. The solution is especially interesting in that it roughly accords with the sample average of surveyed small farmers in the district. HYV wheat is planted in 0.43 hectares, providing sales of 4.81 quintals. The small farmer borrows Rs341 and Rs189 from the moneylender and PSCP, respectively, reserving Rs317 in cash to contribute to his liquidity requirements. His net cash flow is Rs640, to which we add the Rs317 in cash reserve, to compare with the Rs1,000 with which he began the year.

In Plan 5, loans at the PSCP agency are made available without constraint as to use of loan proceeds. Hence the value of liquidity in the form of PSCP *credit* is increased. The new specification increases the area in HYV wheat to 0.77 hectares, which approaches the level reached with the "naive" specifications of the first two versions of the model. Sales amount to about 11 quintals. Borrowing is confined to the PSCP at about Rs680. Reserved cash declines to Rs209. An important objective of the PSCP is to induce a larger commitment of small-farmer resources to the farm. The model reveals the linkages required to produce this result: a more highly valued credit source that allows *credit* in reserve to substitute for cash in reserve. This is the only specification that produced a net cash flow as great as the beginning cash specification—even without adding the reserved cash.

Policy Implications

When liquidity requirements and values are ignored, as in Plans 1 and 2, the model solutions suggest that public sector credit programs are likely to have little effect on the introduction of HYV wheat. The results attainable with such programs may therefore be seriously understated. With the more reasonable behavioral assumptions of Plan 3, however, the area planted to HYV wheat is sharply reduced, as is the net cash flow. Indeed, the net cash flow plus cash reserve is less than the beginning cash supply in the results of Plan 3. In Plan 4, introducing a credit program with limitations on the uses of loans by farmers modestly increases the area planted to HYV wheat and nearly restores beginning cash (net cash flow, Rs640, plus cash reserve, Rs317). As noted, this result is of special interest because it roughly accords with small-farmer behavior observed in Badaun. Hence we can use it as a basis for comparing results from a "synthesized" improvement in credit programs.

Plan 5 presumes a program that leads the cultivator to value *credit* in reserve. This could be due to the greater reliability of the loan source, easier or cheaper access, fewer restrictions on the use of loan proceeds, and so on. The results are rather dramatic. Plan 5 nearly doubles the area planted to HYV wheat and generates a net cash flow that exceeds beginning cash and still provides a small cash reserve at the end of the year.

The model results do not in themselves produce foolproof prescriptions for improving government credit programs. They do, however, suggest payoffs attainable if these programs can be improved. It is apparent from elsewhere that fewer restrictions on access to loans and on the use of loan proceeds might well be improvements. Sanctions would be needed to hold down defaults, but defaults might be reduced if the program were more highly valued by the cultivator.

13. *Voluntary Rural Savings Capacities in Taiwan, 1960–70*

Marcia L. Ong, Dale W Adams,
and I. J. Singh

[Economic planners and policy makers often assume that small farmers in developing countries have very little capacity to save. This article supplies evidence that small farmers in Taiwan saved substantial amounts in the 1960s.]

A large amount of attention has been given to mobilizing capital in and from rural areas of low-income countries. In most cases involuntary techniques, such as taxes or price manipulation, have been used to do this. Rarely have policy makers considered voluntary techniques for stimulating rural savings. In part, this is due to the stereotype that depicts rural households as having low incomes and very high consumption propensities. The lack of adequate household data on income, consumption, and savings has discouraged research that might test these assumptions.

In the following, we provide information on rural household savings and some of its determinants in Taiwan during the 1960s. Taiwan was one of the few places that for several years systematically collected farm household data that were detailed enough to allow such analysis. In addition, the agricultural sector in Taiwan had experienced rapid economic and social development. Overall, agricultural output had increased at a rate in excess of 5 percent a year since the early 1950s, while the value of agricultural exports more than tripled. The benefits from this rapid growth were relatively equitably spread. Furthermore, Taiwan provided one of only a handful of examples of aggressive mobilization of voluntary savings in rural areas.

Data Used

The household data used in this study came from a farm record-keeping project. Households voluntarily recorded their economic ac-

Extracted from *American Journal of Agricultural Economics*, vol. 58, no. 3 (August 1976), pp. 578–81.

tivities daily, and supervisors carefully checked and aggregated this information on a regular basis. Consistency checks on the data showed it to be more complete and reliable than information collected by most cross-sectional household surveys. Household members usually have a difficult time recalling small, fragmented consumption decisions that cover extended periods of time, whereas these farmers recorded events each day. Most households underreport income in surveys.

As might be expected, households that voluntarily participate in record-keeping projects are not completely representative of the population. A comparison of the participating households with households in representative, island-wide rural sample surveys in 1962 and 1967 shows some important differences. For example, record-keeping households owned 20 to 30 percent more farm land than the average farm family. There was little difference in average family size between the two groups. In 1962 record-keeping households had average incomes and consumption expenditures that were 60 to 47 percent, respectively, above the average survey household. In 1967 incomes were 29 percent greater and consumption expenditures only 2 percent greater than survey household figures. Since, as was suggested earlier, survey households are likely to underreport their income, the real differences between the incomes of the two groups is probably less than these percentages indicate. Given the relatively homogeneous nature of farms in Taiwan, the record-keeping households come closer to representing the entire population than would many similar accounts elsewhere.

Methodology

Savings are defined as total net household income minus total household consumption. Consumption includes the value of all purchased goods for the household as well as products produced and consumed on the farm. This includes costs for household operations, education, and health, and purchases of consumer durables. To remove the effect of family size, income and consumption information was converted to per capita figures by dividing by the number of people in the household.

Propensities to Save

Yearly per capita income and consumption figures for the record-keeping households are shown in table 13-1. Average per capita income of the record-keeping households increased in real terms by almost 50 percent over the eleven-year period, a compounded rate of 4 percent a year. Household expenditures also increased substantially over the period, though at a slightly slower rate than did incomes. This resulted in a gradual increase in the average propensity to save (APS)

Table 13-1. *Household Income, Expenditure, and Average and Marginal Propensities to Save, Taiwan Farm Record-keeping Data, 1960–70*

		1970 New Taiwan dollars			Estimated coefficients[c]			
Year	Number of households	YBAR/N[a]	CBAR/N[a]	APS[b]	a_0	a_1	R^2	MPS[d]
1960	95	4,609	3,784	0.18	739.3	0.623 (13.9)[e]	0.68	0.38
1961	207	5,358	4,364	0.19	1,219.8	0.542 (21.0)	0.68	0.46
1962	233	5,731	4,504	0.21	1,355.7	0.488 (18.8)	0.62	0.51
1963	227	5,750	4,421	0.23	1,675.6	0.432 (16.2)	0.49	0.57
1964	535	5,691	4,346	0.24	1,364.7	0.496 (30.6)	0.64	0.50
1965	501	6,151	4,702	0.24	1,013.6	0.580 (29.3)	0.63	0.42

1966	430	6,711	4,840	0.28	2,426.0	0.315 (17.4)	0.42	0.69
1967	402	6,784	5,136	0.24	1,372.6	0.541 (22.0)	0.55	0.46
1968	416	7,122	5,140	0.28	1,850.9	0.457 (23.6)	0.57	0.54
1969	411	6,388	5,645	0.12	1,433.4	0.649 (20.9)	0.52	0.35
1970	404	6,778	5,409	0.20	1,813.0	0.531 (21.1)	0.53	0.47

a. *YBAR* equals average net farm family income; *CBAR* equals average household expenditures, and *N* equals number of individuals residing in the household during the year. Current New Taiwan dollar (NT$) figures were converted to 1970 prices using general index of prices received by farmers published by the Bureau of Accounting and Statistics, Provincial Government of Taiwan: 1960 = 81.0, 1965 = 89.2, and 1970 = 100.0.

b. APS is the average propensity to save calculated at mean farm family income and household expenditure levels for each year (1 − *CBAR*/*YBAR*).

c. These are estimates of the linear per capita consumption function $(C/N)i = a_0 + a_1 (Y/N)i$.

d. MPS is the marginal propensity to save calculated at the arithmetic mean income and expenditure levels for each year $(1 - a_1)$.

e. Figures in parentheses are *t*-values for the slope coefficients. All coefficients are significant at the 1 percent level.

Source: Marcia Min-Ron Lee Ong, "Changes in Farm Level Savings and Consumption in Taiwan, 1960–1970," Ph.D. dissertation, Ohio State University, 1972.

Table 13-2. *Average and Marginal Propensity to Save by Farm Size and Income Source for Record-keeping Households in Taiwan, 1960–70*

Group	*1960*	*1961*	*1962*	*1963*	*1964*	*1965*	*1966*	*1967*	*1968*	*1969*	*1970*
					Average propensity to save[a]						
Farm size (hectares)[b]											
0–1	0.15	0.14	0.16	0.21	0.17	0.18	0.19	0.19	0.23	0.07	0.13
1.01–2	0.16	0.21	0.22	0.21	0.25	0.26	0.28	0.25	0.27	0.10	0.23
2+	0.28	0.19	0.26	0.30	0.32	0.30	0.39	0.29	0.34	0.19	0.24
Ratio of farm income to total household income											
0–0.7	0.09	0.18	0.24	0.14	0.16	0.22	0.22	0.30	0.23	0.07	0.14
0.7+	0.19	0.19	0.21	0.25	0.26	0.24	0.30	0.26	0.29	0.15	0.24
					Marginal propensity to save[c]						
Farm size (hectares)											
0–1	0.60	0.42	0.49	0.68	0.40	0.46	0.50	0.46	0.44	0.48	0.34
1.01–2	0.26	0.45	0.54	0.49	0.43	0.40	0.68	0.45	0.48	0.40	0.56
2+	0.78	0.51	0.50	0.50	0.61	0.40	0.77	0.46	0.63	0.21	0.46
Ratio of farm income to total household income											
0–0.7	0.32	0.53	0.60	0.34	0.28	0.36	0.60	0.27	0.41	0.15	0.26
0.7+	0.39	0.45	0.49	0.59	0.56	0.45	0.70	0.56	0.58	0.52	0.56

a. Average propensity to save equals 1 − household expenditures/household income.

b. One hectare equals 2.47 acres.

c. Marginal propensity to save is calculated at the arithmetic mean income and expenditure levels for each year. As in table 13-1, results are from a linear function form.

Source: Ong, "Changes in Farm Level Savings and Consumption in Taiwan."

over the 1960–68 period. The very high APS of the record-keeping households during this period is impressive. In the early 1960s households were saving roughly one-fifth of their incomes; in the 1964–68 period rates of saving increased to roughly one-quarter of total income.

The sharp downturn of APS in 1969 was in part because adverse weather seriously affected agricultural production and incomes. Part of the decrease in APS in 1969 and 1970, however, may also have been because very attractive consumer goods began entering rural markets in the mid-1960s. In addition, the lower rates of return to on-farm investments in the late 1960s could have further discouraged household saving.

Estimates of the short-run marginal propensities to save (MPS) throughout the 1960s were fairly high (see table 13-1), ranging from one-third to two-thirds of additional annual income. There was substantial variability in MPS from year to year, but in general the marginal savings appear to have been quite high.

Other Determinants of Savings Capacities

Studies by Toshiyuki Mizoguchi ["Consumption Functions and Savings Functions for Japanese Farmers' Families in Post-War Japan," *Rural Economic Problems*, vol. 4, 1967, pp. 20–35], Tsutomu Noda ["Savings of Farm Households," in *Agriculture and Economic Growth: Japan's Experience*, Kazushi Ohkawa, Bruce F. Johnston, and Hiromitsu Kaneda, eds., Tokyo, University of Tokyo Press, 1970, pp. 352–73], and others have suggested that savings performance among households may vary considerably with farm size (often used as a proxy for income) and source of income. To test this, the Taiwan households were grouped into three categories: those with less than one hectare, one to two hectares, and more than two hectares. A second classification of the households was based on the ratio of income derived from on-farm agricultural activities to total household income. Average and marginal propensities to save among these different subgroups for 1960–70 are presented in table 13-2.

A review of the average propensities to save by farm size shows that the APS almost always increases with farm size. In part, this reflects the favorable impact on savings of higher incomes, which in turn are associated with farm size. The generally higher APS and MPS among the larger farms also suggest that households with more farm land may have had more profitable on-farm investment alternatives for their savings than did smaller landowners. Nevertheless, there are relatively high APS and MPS among households in the smallest farm-size group, and the marginal savings behavior of households with small farms was not vastly different from that of households with larger land areas.

Also shown in table 13-2 is a breakdown of APS and MPS by income-source ratios: households with the highest ratios received a larger part of their total income from on-farm agricultural activities than did households with low ratios. These APS and MPS fairly consistently showed better savings performance among high-ratio households. These results tend to confirm Noda's findings in Japan that households close to doing full-time farming tend to have larger savings propensities than do those with higher proportions of outside income.

Implications

As indicated before, the data used in this study tend to overstate average rural savings capacities in Taiwan: the households studied have higher than average incomes and are headed by progressive farmers. We feel that this upward bias is largely offset, however, by our exclusion from savings of all expenditures on education and consumer durables. During the 1960s the average record-keeping household used 10 to 15 percent of its total consumption in these activities. Half or more of the expenditures could have been defined as savings with strong justification. These data, plus other indicators, reinforce the conclusion that very large voluntary savings capacities emerged in rural Taiwan during the 1960s. The large increase in financial savings in all rural areas and the rapid increase in total on-farm assets are strong evidence of substantial savings capacities. The well-documented transfer of capital out of the agricultural sector, the sharp increases in rural human capitalization, and the widespread accumulation of consumer durables in rural areas lend further weight to the argument.

It might be argued that the large savings capacity found in Taiwan during the 1960s is a special case, that Taiwanese are somehow culturally endowed with large doses of frugality. We feel that this is not the major explanation of Taiwan's remarkable savings performance and that the increases in rural incomes during the 1960s are not unique to Taiwan. Individual farm households and major agricultural regions in other developing countries are also experiencing high rates of growth in incomes. We conclude that Taiwan's savings performance is due to appropriate policies rather than unique behavioral characteristics. Household savings were strongly stimulated by two sets of incentives. The first set included price policies, new technology, marketing facilities, land tenure adjustments, and public investment programs that gave strong incentives for on-farm investments. The second set of savings incentives flowed to farmers through financial markets. The physical presence of savings institutions in most rural areas (farmers' associations, postal savings, and commercial banks) gave rural people the opportunity to save and provided the convenience, stability, liquidity, and security necessary to attract savings. Furthermore, Taiwanese policy makers were aggressive in using attractive interest rates on deposits to induce savings.

The Taiwan experience during the 1960s seriously challenges the stereotype of low savings capacity that has been routinely applied to rural households. A more realistic notion of rural savings behavior should be adopted in the development profession and in economic planning.

14. *Agricultural Development without Credit*

C. J. Howse

[Credit for poor farmers is often not necessary and may do more harm than good. Even the poor have money which can be mobilized when they join savings clubs that encourage good resource management and good husbandry. Savings clubs can help poor farmers progress without institutional credit.]

I would like to suggest that the provision of agricultural credit to people with a low income and poor educational background is not generally warranted. It is today widely accepted that peasant farmers can become more productive only if given the opportunity to borrow someone else's money. In his 1973 address to the Board of Governors of the World Bank in Nairobi, Robert McNamara said:

> For the smallholder operating with virtually no capital, access to credit is crucial. No matter how knowledgeable or well motivated he may be, without such credit he cannot buy improved seeds, apply the necessary fertilizer and pesticides, rent equipment or develop his water sources. Small farmers generally spend less than 20% of what is required on such inputs because they simply do not have the resources.

While agreeing that credit is sometimes necessary at a later stage in the farmer's development, I cannot agree that peasant farmers must have access to credit before they can put one foot on the ladder to increased productivity and income. In my view credit is a privilege—not everyone's right—and that privilege must be earned. The greatest need today is for a system that teaches peasant farmers how to develop by using the resources they already have and that gives them confidence in their own ability to affect their status in society.

The provision of credit to the peasant agricultural sector, even as part of a fully integrated project, almost invariably runs into great difficulties. Credit card systems, single channel marketing, stop orders,

Extracted from *Agricultural Administration*, vol. 1 (1974), pp. 259–62.

and the like are designed to make sure that credit is in fact used for planned purposes and that repayments are collected. In almost every case, however, within a couple of years of the implementation of the system farmers are selling their produce "by moonlight" or under other members' names to escape the stop order system, and there are many, often very clever subterfuges to escape repayment. Those in charge then recruit more credit controllers, court cases are initiated, and assets are confiscated. Frustration rises, and eventually either the project is run along military lines or it dissolves into an administrative nightmare.

A second fallacy commonly believed is that the peasant farming community has no money. In reality there is money. For those who truly live the hand-to-mouth existence of a beggar the absence of money is a reality, but for the average person this is not the case. Peasants can and must be taught to save some of their income to meet anticipated future expenditure. Everyone, whether earning $60 a year or $60 a day, finds it difficult to save and has a thousand excuses to offer. But it is an inescapable fact that the necessity to save is greater for the poor than for the rich. If people do not save some money, no matter how little, they will always remain poor. The answer is not to give them credit year after year, as happens all too frequently in many agricultural projects, but to wean them off credit as soon as possible—if one is forced to give credit at all. We must at all costs not cause people to live in perpetual debt.

To persuade a poor person to save is a daunting task for the majority of people concerned with development. But savings clubs, acknowledging that the majority of the poor are illiterate and unsophisticated, yet not unintelligent, seem to succeed where all else has failed. Savings stamps of low denomination are purchased for cash at regular weekly meetings of the clubs and have a very strong visual appeal to the saver. The stamps are stuck onto a card which, when full, is exchanged for a savings certificate, which is stuck into the member's savings book. The secret of the savings clubs is, first, the simplicity of the system, which enables maximum membership participation and comprehension and reduces the possibility of fraud; second, the regularity of weekly savings days; and third, the policy of "saving for a purpose," which makes much more sense than "saving for saving's sake," which quickly loses its appeal. If the work of the extension services is combined with the savings clubs, the members can be shown the purpose of saving, and as long as the goals are financially within their reach and the message is the right one, people will catch on.

A package program that identifies the essential inputs necessary will ensure the success of a particular project and the cost of implementing it. In poor areas a package program might start off with the essential ingredients for growing a quarter of an acre of maize, an eighth of an acre of groundnuts, or an acre of cotton or for purchasing a pair of breeding rabbits or ten laying hens. Each time the cost involved must be within financial reach to encourage adoption. Part of the proceeds from that crop or enterprise must be saved so that the following year a larger area or a bigger enterprise can be undertaken. The participants will grow as fast as their motivation and ability will allow, and they are self-financing as long as the savings element is constantly pushed.

These savings clubs can become small nuclei for area development and a focal point for the extension service that otherwise is usually rather ineffective. Self-sufficiency is encouraged at all times, and the members of the savings club are strongly encouraged to obtain the supplies necessary for project implementation themselves. In this way club members growing crops, for instance, will purchase their supplies in bulk, simplifying the transport and possibly qualifying for discounts. The marketing of the resulting produce can also be done communally. All the supplies taken by members must be paid for by tearing the relevant number of certificates from a member's book and cashing them. There is no such thing as a bad debt and no worry about collection of credit. Change for certificates not fully spent can be given in the form of stamps. Eventually bulk suppliers of agricultural commodities could be encouraged to accept certificates rather than cash to simplify the process.

The security of the members' savings is most important. Although the system does eliminate almost any chance of fraud on savings days, the safekeeping of each day's savings until they can be deposited in a bank or other institution is very important. Where clubs operate in an organized project area, a mobile banking agency could probably be arranged one day a week; in nonproject areas trusted local missionaries often guard the savings. Government officials are very rarely involved in this aspect. Workers are needed to promote the formation of clubs, but here again the simplicity of the idea enables ordinary men and women to act in this capacity; local people who are paid relatively low wages can cover perhaps six clubs from a home base by using a bicycle. Continuous in-service training is necessary to give these fieldworkers full insight into the potential of the clubs.

Financial control of the clubs is the responsibility of a central organization which distributes the stamps and certificates. To ensure regular reporting, sufficient stamps for only four to six weeks' operation are issued at any one time, and replenishments are sent only on receipt of the completed financial forms. In this way many clubs can be controlled by a small central organization, and financial returns are guaranteed. Another advantage is that the stamp system can be used by any organization or group to encourage its members to save money.

Women's clubs, young farmers' clubs, church groups, fishermen's groups, and others can utilize the system and benefit enormously from the additional buying power it brings.

The system at present operates in Zimbabwe, Lesotho, Zambia, and Malawi, but is still very much in its infancy except in Zimbabwe, where there were over 300 clubs by 1974. The early reports on the 1973 season from these indicated that the demand created for agricultural inputs was so strong that it temporarily outstripped the available supplies of hybrid maize seed, groundnut seed, and fertilizer. While this is an undesirable occurrence, it shows what can happen when the peasant farmer is properly motivated. It has all been done in two and a half years, and the word "credit" is never heard!

15. *Women at the Cameroon Development Corporation: How Their Money Works*

Virginia DeLancey

[Women wage earners at a tea estate in Cameroon, along with a group of non-wage-earning women in the same area, were interviewed regarding their incomes, savings, and family assets. It is clear that savings can be significant among a relatively uneducated group of mainly manual workers in Africa. Such savings should be mobilized for development.]

This chapter describes some efforts to accumulate capital by women employed by the Cameroon Development Corporation in southwestern Cameroon. It does not attempt to provide a case study of outstanding women who are successful in accumulating capital; it examines all members of a group of women selected on the basis of their principal economic activity and location, whether or not their performance was exceptional. Data were analyzed to determine whether these wage-earning women must immediately consume their relatively stable earnings to maintain their family and household, or whether they are able to save for future consumption or investment. Do these earnings allow them to purchase durable goods, to invest in profitable business, or to educate their children?

Setting and Background

The Cameroon Development Corporation (CDC) is under the jurisdiction of the government of the United Republic of Cameroon. Its operations were formerly concentrated in the coastal area of the Southwest Province, with emphasis on cultivating oil palm, rubber, bananas, tea, and pepper. Of the 13,000 permanent employees, more than 1,000 are female, about half of whom work at the Tole Tea Estate on the slopes of Mount Cameroon. The majority labor in the fields, some

Extracted from *Rural Africana*, no. 2 (Fall 1978), pp. 9–33.

are headwomen in charge of a group of laborers, and a few work in the factory or in clerical jobs.

The data for this study were collected in 1975 and 1976. Interviews were requested with each married woman living with her husband and employed by the CDC at Tole Tea Estate, a total of 175 persons. Fifty-three non-wage-earning women were also interviewed, including women with income from trading or other self-employment and two with no income. The wage-employed women averaged 30–34 years of age, the non-wage-employed 25–29 years. The women in general are not highly educated. Eighty-six percent of the wage employees and 53 percent of the non-wage-employed had no education at all, and only 4 percent of the wage earners and 21 percent of the nonwage earners had completed primary school.

The 175 employed women earned an average of CFAF9,767 ($39) in wages or salaries per month (table 15-1). Most of these women received additional income, for example, from a family allowance from the Cameroon National Social Insurance Fund, earnings from petty trading or sale of excess "chop farm" produce, or in the form of the market value of food they grow and consume. Total incomes averaged CFAF17,354 ($69) per woman per month, more than twice the average of CFAF8,250 ($33) for the 51 out of 53 nonwage earners who received an income.

The Possibility of Saving

Studies of the African labor force in the past have emphasized problems such as the "target worker," who works long enough to obtain cash to buy a particular radio or pay taxes and then goes home. They have dwelt on the phenomenon of a backward-bending supply curve of labor; if it existed, it would allow some employers to attempt to justify low wages in the belief that a per unit wage increase would only cause the workers to work less because they would be able to earn the same amount as before with less effort. With this widespread concern that wage laborers might be less than diligent or stable in their work habits, one would not suspect that such persons would actually save any of their earnings.

Table 15-1 indicates that 98 percent of the wage earners interviewed were savers. Accumulated financial savings averaged CFAF48,042 ($192) per wage earner, or CFAF49,166 ($197) per person saving money. Table 15-1 also indicates that 81.1 percent of the non-wage-earning women were able to save. Their average was CFAF6,348 ($25) per nonwage earner, or CFAF7,824 ($31) for each of the nonwage earners who saved. If one compares averages of savings with incomes, one can see that the wage-employed women had savings equal to about 4.9 times their monthly wages, or 2.8 times their total monthly income.

Table 15-1. *Monthly Income and Financial Savings of Women at Tole Tea Estate*

	Wage earners		*Nonwage earners*	
Item	*Francs (CFAF)*	*U.S. dollars*	*Francs (CFAF)*	*U.S. dollars*
Total wages	1,709,266	6,837	—	—
Average wages	9,767	39	—	—
Total income	3,036,912	12,148	420,742	1,682
Average income	17,354	69	7,939	31
Total savings	8,407,315	33,629	336,440	1,346
Average savings	48,042	192	6,348	25
Average savings of those who save	49,166	197	7,824	31
Number in sample	175		53	
Number who save	171		43	
Percentage who save	97.71		81.13	

— Not applicable.

The nonwage earners, in contrast, had savings averaging from 0.8 of their monthly income to the equivalent of their monthly income.

To discover outlets for earnings other than consumption for subsistence or financial savings, the women were asked about durable goods—the assets within their homes—and a simple count was made. Of all household assets, three were most prevalent in both sample groups. More than two-thirds of wage-earning women and up to 90 percent of non-wage-earning women lived in homes having at least one watch. About two-thirds of the women in both groups lived in households having a radio. Third in frequency were sewing machines, some of which may be for personal use while others are investments for earning additional income. One-third of the wage-earning women and more than one-fourth of non-wage-earning women lived in homes having such machines. (Non-wage-earning women seem to live with more assets than their wage-earning sisters; a greater proportion of the husbands of non-wage-earning women are in higher employment categories than the husbands of the wage earners.)

Nearly three-fifths of wage-earning women and more than two-fifths of nonwage earners live in households that have invested in their own home. In addition, about one-fifth of both wage earners and nonwage earners live in households owning rental structures, and nearly two-fifths of both categories live in households that have purchased land on which there is a completed structure or on which they propose to build one. More than half the women live in households that have purchased farm land. The proportion of such investments is particularly significant because the Cameroon Development Corporation provides housing for its permanent employees, and corporation land is generally turned over to the employees for temporary use as "chop farms" for their own food supply.

Thus, a very large proportion of all of the women save at least some of their incomes; the wage earners manage to save a much larger amount per woman and a much greater proportion of their average income than do the nonwage earners. Many families of both groups are able to purchase durable assets, particularly watches, radios, and sewing machines, and many also invest in their own homes, rental buildings, land, and farms.

Reasons Given for Saving

In his 1953–55 study at Tole Tea Estate, W.A. Warmington ["Savings and Indebtedness among Cameroons Plantation Workers," *Africa*, vol. 28, October 1958, pp. 329–43] found that more than half the saving reported was actually short-term, the money soon being spent on clothes, entertainment of visiting relatives, purchase of household goods, or payment of rent, litigation expenses, or outstanding debts. Only a few of his sample used their savings as trading capital or for apprenticeship fees. Saving for educational purposes was not worthwhile at that time, because primary education was provided for all the children at the expense of the corporation.

When Mark W. DeLancey conducted research in the same location in 1969 and 1970 ["Voluntary Associations in a Rural Area: The Case of the Cameroons Development Corporation," paper presented at African Studies Association Annual Meeting, 1973; and "Institutions for the Accumulation and Redistribution of Savings among Migrants," *Journal of Developing Areas*, vol. 12, January 1978, pp. 209–24], he found 90 percent of the male employees saving, mainly to meet unexpected trouble (illness, funeral expenses, unemployment), for education, to marry, to buy things (such as clothes, motorcycles, radios, and bicycles), or to build a house. These reasons imply short-term as well as long-term saving. Education had become an important reason by that time; fees had been instituted in many primary schools, and opportunities for secondary education were more prevalent if money for tuition was available. DeLancey found that 33 percent of the purposes stated could be classified for development, 26 percent for welfare, and 41 percent for consumption.

The results of my research are shown in table 15-2. The women were asked to give two reasons why they would save if they were able to. Wage-earning women were most concerned with saving for educational purposes: 24 percent of all reasons given were for education,

Table 15-2. *Reasons for Saving by Women at Tole Tea Estate*

Reason	Wage earners			Nonwage earners		
	Number	Percentage of reasons[a] (N = 379)	Percentage of savers[b] (N = 171)	Number	Percentage of reasons[a] (N = 91)	Percentage of savers[b] (N = 43)
Social security or welfare						
General trouble	23	6.1	13.5	5	5.5	11.6
Sickness	65	17.2	38.0	25	27.5	58.1
Trouble and sickness	(88)	(23.2)	(51.5)	(30)	(33.0)	(69.8)
Transport home	6	1.6	3.5	1	1.1	2.3
Court cases	0	0	0	2	2.2	4.7
Funeral expenses	15	4.0	8.8	8	8.8	18.6
Unemployment, retirement, old age	30	7.9	17.5	5	5.5	11.6
Plan for life, help for future	6	1.6	3.5	1	1.1	2.3
Bequest to children	18	4.7	10.5	3	3.3	7.0
Help for family	7	1.8	4.1	0	0	0
Total	170	44.9		50	55.0	
Investment or development						
Education	89	23.5	52.0	16	17.6	37.2
Help for children to get employment	5	1.3	2.9	0	0	0
Help for children or brother to get ahead	2	0.5	1.2	1	1.1	2.3

Business	6	1.6	3.5	3	3.3	7.0
Farm	1	0.3	0.6	1	1.1	2.3
Corn mill	3	0.8	1.8	0	0	0
Engine saw	2	0.5	1.2	0	0	0
Rental structure	3	0.8	1.8	0	0	0
Own house	20	5.3	11.7	6	6.6	0
Taxi	7	1.8	4.1	0	0	0
Total	138	36.4		27	29.7	
Consumption						
Food and clothes	18	4.7	10.5	6	6.6	14.0
Maintenance of self and children	23	6.1	13.5	5	5.5	11.6
Durable assets[c]	10	2.6	5.8	1	1.1	2.3
Sewing machine[d]	7	1.8	4.1	0	0	0
Durables and sewing machine	(17)	(4.5)	(9.9)		1.1	2.3
Automobile	4	1.1	2.3	1	1.1	2.3
Bridewealth	4	1.1	2.3	0	0	0
Entertain visitors	0	0	0	1	1.1	2.3
Family enjoyment	4	1.1	2.3	0	0	0
Other	1	0.3	0.6	0	0	0
Total	71	18.8		14	15.4	
Grand total	379	100.0		91	100.0	

a. The number citing each reason as a percentage of the number of all reasons cited.
b. The percentage of savers giving each reason.
c. Bicycle, radio, pots and pans, iron bed.
d. Sewing machines may have been purchased either for personal use or for investment.

Table 15-3. *Usage of Savings Institutions*

	Wage earners			*Nonwage earners*		
	Persons using the institution (N = 175)		*Number of uses as percentage of total uses*	*Persons using the institution (N = 53)*		*Number of uses as percentage of total uses*
Institution	*Number*	*Percent*	*(N = 479)*	*Number*	*Percent*	*(N = 83)*
Njangi[a]	107	61.1	22.3	10	18.9	12.0
Meeting	140	80.0	29.2	30	56.6	36.1
Bank	21	12.0	4.4	0	0	0
At home	89	50.9	18.6	34	64.2	41.0
Credit union	105	60.0	21.9	4	7.5	4.8
Loans	5	2.9	1.0	3	5.7	3.6
Cooperative	0	0	0	1	1.9	1.2
Other, unknown	12	6.9	2.5	1	1.9	1.2

a. Rotating savings and credit association.

and 52 percent of the women responding mentioned education as one purpose. Second in importance was saving for sickness: 17 percent of the reasons given were for this, and 38 percent of the women respondents mentioned it. Other important reasons for saving among the wage-employed women were for subsistence in the event of being fired, for old age or retirement, or for undefined trouble. Non-wage-employed women placed sickness as the most important reason for saving and education second. Twenty-eight percent of the replies of these women and 58 percent of the women respondents mentioned sickness; 18 percent of the reasons and 37 percent of the women mentioned education as a purpose of saving. Third in importance was funeral expenses.

The reasons for saving in table 15-2 have been grouped into categories of social security or welfare, investment and development, and consumption. Forty-five percent of the reasons given by the wage-employed women and 55 percent of those of the non-wage-employed were for security and welfare purposes. This is interesting in view of social insurance benefits extended to employees in the past few years. Thirty-six percent of the reasons given by the wage-employed and 30 percent of those by the non-wage-employed were for reasons classified as investment and development. Within this category, schooling for children was by far the most important to these women. They were intent on seeing both male and female children continue in school as long as possible, and they often paid school fees or secondary school tuition when their husbands did not or could not. Investment, chiefly in housing, was of minor importance to the wage-employed women and was only slightly more important to the non-wage-employed. This may be partly a result of the security of wage employment for the families of both categories of these women. Consumption purposes had quite a low priority for wage earners and for the others.

Institutions for Saving

The magnitude of funds available for development projects may be estimated from an examination of the institutions in which savers have deposited their funds. Table 15-3 shows the number and percentage of women using each type of institution for saving. Most women used at least two or even more institutions; for that reason, table 15-3 also shows the usage of each institution as a percentage of total usage.

The institution most frequently used by wage-employed women and second most frequently used by non-wage-employed women was the "country" or "family" meeting. Eighty percent of wage-employed and 57 percent of non-wage-employed women saved in this way. The two most common types of meetings consist of a group of persons from the same ethnic group in the case of the country meeting, or from the same immediate or extended family or lineage in the case of the family meeting. The members meet once or twice a month, often the first Sunday after pay day, to discuss matters of importance to the ethnic homeland or sometimes to decide on the possibility of carrying out a community development project at home. An important part of the meeting is the deposit of money by members into the meeting bank, after which most of the sum is deposited into a savings account in a commercial bank. Most commonly it is "broken" once a year, the deposit removed from the savings account and the individual savings returned to the members. The total amount saved in this way (CFAF648,250 = $2,593 by wage earners, and CFAF95,300 = $381 by nonwage earners) is significant, although the average deposits are small. Some wealthy members, often the self-employed, will make large deposits.

The next most frequently used savings institution by both groups of women was the *njangi,* or rotating savings and credit association. Sixty-one percent of the wage-employed and 19 percent of non-wage-employed women saved in this way. [See the description of rotating saving and credit associations by Bouman, chapter 30 below.] Amounts saved by wage earners in njangis were generally larger than in meetings. The total amount of money generated by njangis (CFAF3,125,000 = $12,500 for wage-employed, and CFAF86,000 = $344 for non-wage-employed) was greater than that by bank accounts (CFAF967,000 = $3,868) among these women. Among the wage-employed, njangis generated the greatest total amount of money.

Preference for banks ranked fifth, although the total sum (CFAF967,000 = $3,868) accumulated by the 12 percent who saved in this institution was third in total monetary value. Non-wage-employed women did not use banks at all. Reasons for the infrequent use of banks are: a savings account cannot be opened with less than CFAF5,000 ($20); the nearest bank requires a long uphill walk or the cost of a taxi ride; and there is a CFAF100 ($.40) service fee for each deposit. Interest received is both low and taxable.

A new savings and credit institution has swept the area in recent years: credit unions now operate on many of the CDC estates, as well as in the towns. Although only 7.5 percent of the non-wage-employed women at Tole saved in the credit union, 60 percent of the wage-employed were members, nearly as many as belonged to njangis. The average amount saved was only CFAF5,800 ($23) for the non-wage-employed, but CFAF27,185 ($109) per wage-employed woman. The total amount saved was minor for the non-wage-employed women, but it reached CFAF2,854,415 ($11,418), nearly as much as from njangis, for the wage-employed. Most employed women members have a monthly amount automatically deducted from their wages and deposited.

The only other significant type of savings was cash kept in individuals' homes. Fifty-one percent of the wage earners and 64 percent of the non–wage earners claimed to save in the house, but the amounts were small.

Conclusions

Data have been presented to show that attempts to save by individuals may be much greater and more common than has been thought. This survey shows that nearly every wage-employed woman interviewed had savings of some amount. The majority of non-wage-employed women in the same location also saved, although in much smaller quantities, for different reasons, and in different institutions. Although roughly half the reasons given for saving were stated in terms of social security and welfare, most of the other reasons were defined as investment and development, chiefly the improvement of human capital.

It is impossible to continue to believe that Africa cannot generate capital internally because the people do not save. The above case study of women employed at just one of the many estates within the Cameroon Development Corporation demonstrates that these women, as well as resident non-wage-employed women, live in households that have been able to purchase an assortment of durable assets and make various types of investments. It also shows that women of both categories have been able to retain personal financial savings. The wage-earning women achieved far greater average savings and had at least a greater intention to save for investment and development purposes, particularly for the schooling of their children. When confidence builds in the government social insurance scheme, it is possible that additional amounts of savings may be released from welfare and social security purposes and transferred to investment and development purposes. Saving for old age and retirement might take the form of saving to purchase or develop a farm or food-processing operation or a business for post-CDC days. It is the wage-employed women who used savings institutions that have greater potential as intermediaries in the extension of credit to others for economic development.

Recommendations for Further Reading

Adams, Dale W, and G. I. Nehman. "Borrowing Costs and the Demand for Rural Credit." *Journal of Development Studies*, vol. 15, no. 2 (January 1979), pp. 165–76.

Barry, Peter J., John A. Hopkin, and C. B. Baker. *Financial Management in Agriculture*. 2d ed. Danville, Ill.: Interstate Printers and Publishers, 1979.

Johl, S. S., and T. R. Kapur. *Fundamentals of Farm Business Management*. Ludhiana, Punjab, India: Lyall Book Depot, 1973.

Lee, Warren, and others. *Agricultural Finance*. 7th ed. Ames: Iowa State University Press, 1980.

Long, Millard F. "Why Peasant Farmers Borrow." *American Journal of Agricultural Economics*, vol. 50, no. 4 (November 1968), pp. 991–1008.

Miller, Leonard F. *Agricultural Credit and Finance in Africa*. New York: Rockefeller Foundation, 1978.

Mizoguchi, Toshiyuki. *Personal Savings and Consumption in Postwar Japan*. Shinjuku, Tokyo: Kinokuniya Bookstore Co., 1970.

Roberts, R. A. J. "The Role of Money in the Development of Farming in the Mumbawa and Katete Areas of Zambia." *Small Farmer Credit in Africa: AID Spring Review of Small Farmer Credit*, vol. 6 (February 1973).

Shahjahan, Mirza. *Agricultural Finance in East Pakistan*. Dhaka, Bangladesh: Asiatic Press, 1968.

Issues for Discussion

1. Loan applicants A and B are identical. A receives a loan in cash, while B receives one in kind. What differences, if any, would you expect between the behavior of A and the behavior of B?
2. How can lenders constructively accommodate fungibility in their lending programs and relationships with borrowers?
3. How useful are farm plans, farm budgets, and supervised credit in ensuring efficient loan use? Are farm budgets more useful to the borrower or to the lender? What are the types and levels of the costs of supervised credit?
4. What is an unutilized credit reserve? Since it is unutilized, does it have any value? Do formal credit institutions typically provide rural borrowers with higher unutilized credit reserves than informal lenders? How does the availability of unutilized credit reserves affect the willingness of borrowers to maintain good credit ratings with lenders?
5. How do farmers use credit in their management of risk?
6. Do all farmers or managers of nonfarm rural firms want or use loans all the time? If not, why not? Under what conditions can farm households use loans in a socially desirable manner?
7. Do farmers typically use loans to finance most of their investments and operating expenses? If not, how do they finance these outflows?
8. What evidence is there to support the argument that there is more voluntary savings capacity in rural areas in low-income countries than most policy makers realize?
9. What policies commonly used in low-income countries tend to reduce voluntary rural savings? What policies tend to reduce the flow of savings into formal financial institutions?
10. Under ideal policy conditions, how important would deposit accounts and attractive deposit account facilities be for the rural poor in low-income countries?
11. The "household" and "farm" are abstractions used for analytical purposes. Does their use complicate or simplify the evaluation of credit impact?
12. Saving is defined as deferred consumption. Does rural saving tend to reflect the short-term or long-term deferral of consumption?
13. What financial services are most highly valued by nonfarm rural firms? Does the heterogeneity of these firms make it difficult for formal lenders to provide these services?

PART IV

URBAN FINANCIAL INSTITUTIONS IN RURAL MARKETS

Parts IV and V of this book deal with rural financial market institutions. This part takes up two types of banks that lend to farmers: the general-purpose commercial bank, and the special-purpose agricultural credit institution (almost invariably government-owned). Both are urban-based entities that extend into rural areas. Commercial banks are normally oriented to an urban clientele but may also have rural branches and customers. Special-purpose farm credit organizations are, of course, intended to operate in farming areas, but they are usually designed in urban terms and are not indigenous to the countryside. By comparison, the financial institutions discussed in Part V are either wholly indigenous (informal lenders and savings organizations) or more locally oriented and run (cooperatives).

Both the commercial banks and the specialized farm credit organizations encounter problems when they operate in rural areas. To some extent these difficulties may be traced to urban characteristics that inconvenience many rural clients and discourage potential clients. This is especially true of commercial bank procedures for loan approval that are geared not to rural people, but to the urban firms that represent the bulk of the bank's business. These procedures require borrowers to have bank accounts and certain kinds of collateral, and to use special application forms. As with loans, so with savings deposits; conventional commercial banks do not appear to be appropriate for serving large numbers of rural people. Banks have generally shown relatively little interest in soliciting small rural savings accounts. The high cost of processing these accounts is a factor, but often a disinterest, based on low expectations and cultural distance from rural mores, tends to inhibit urban-bred branch managers from seeking savings deposits or developing innovations that could attract more rural funds.

Although commercial banks do make agricultural loans, these loans are often to large landowners or plantation operators whose assets and other characteristics meet bank standards of creditworthiness. In some countries, commercial banks serve small farmers through cooperatives that deal with the banks. Banks are also effective lenders to marketing boards or agribusinesses purchasing from, or selling to, small farmers. Except for their relations with large-scale producers, the contribution commercial banks make to the developing rural economy is largely indirect, through services to others who link farmers and rural entrepreneurs with the rest of the economy.

Concern with accelerating agricultural development, increasing access to credit, and alleviating rural poverty has led governments to create specialized agricultural lending institutions. Many of these specialized banks do not, however, broadly improve farmers' access to credit, because they tend to serve a limited clientele of large borrowers. In addition, they frequently experience high defaults and incur costs that exceed revenues, so that they require large subsidies from the government to stay in operation and expand. They often invite political interference. This list of negative traits does not apply to all specialized farm credit organizations, but almost all of them show one or more of the weaknesses described, as suggested in the articles that follow.

The problems of these two types of institutions in rural financial markets may be summarized as: limited access to, and high cost of services to farmers and other rural people, absence of savings facilities, undermining of repayment habits, and a lack of cultural compatibility of banks and customers. Limited access is especially a problem in commercial banks. Two approaches other than selective credit controls are used to stimulate them to lend to more farmers. One is to encourage private banks to finance agriculture by offering them preferential discount (and guarantee) facilities for their agricultural loans, either from the central bank or through another special intermediary. This process has been extensively tried in Mexico, for example, with only modest results. The other widely used method is the development of guarantee funds (without preferential discounting), either by organizing group responsibility for repayment at the local level or by organizing a loan insurance structure from above. There has been insufficient experience in developing countries to judge the potential of this innovation to expand access to more rural producers.

The special-purpose lenders present a knottier set of problems. Unlike the commercial banks, whose activities are geared to successful survival in urban areas, single-purpose agricultural lenders are a government creation, operated by civil service employees or their equivalents who may not be concerned with institutional viability. This can be true even when a special-purpose subsidized farm credit operation is set up within an otherwise solvent and successful commercial bank. The lack of motivation can show up in various ways, notably in lax debt collection and indifference to the creditworthiness of borrowers. The government's attachment to other priorities, such as expanding total loans to farmers or lending to political clients, can take precedence over financial soundness.

Several approaches to the problems commonly experienced by urban institutions in rural financial markets are explored below (and in Part V as well). In Nicaragua a program to expand small-farmer access to credit to achieve economies of scale in administrative costs used computerized recordkeeping to monitor performance. This effort had a promising start, although other factors may prevent its full potential from being tested in Nicaragua.

A second idea for reforming agricultural lending is to combine the advantages of informal lending with those of government agricultural banks. Informal lenders are geographically and culturally close to their local rural clients. They should be better judges of the individual creditworthiness of neighborhood farmers than would a more distant bank loan officer. They should also be in a better position to collect loan repayments. It has been proposed that agricultural credit institutions rely on local village agents who would use bank-supplied resources to conduct a semiformalized loan operation. These agents would be given latitude in their selection of borrowers and in the details of their operation, but they would be subject to the control of bank branch managers who would enforce standards of honesty and adherence to bank policy directives. One such experience in Malaysia is described in this section. The idea has not often been tried, and results could vary widely.

Other aspects of the performance of formal institutions in RFMs are dealt with more fully later in the book. Most prominently, the prevalence of low interest rates that undermine the viability of lending institutions and the scarcity of financial savings facilities in rural areas are treated elsewhere. So, too, are potential economies in group lending and competition among different types of institution in the same RFM.

Commercial Banks

The three articles on commercial banking in rural areas begin with a description by Green (chapter 16) of what commercial banks have and have not done in financing agriculture in developing countries, and how their outlook may be shifting. He speaks from experience with the large London-based Barclay's group and its activities in Africa and the Caribbean. He explains why such a bank is active in certain areas and avoids others. His viewpoint reflects considerations of profit and loss that also apply to many smaller banks and to banks owned by nationals of developing countries.

Romero Chavez (chapter 17) gives an account of the elaborate institution building that has taken place in Mexico to expand financial support to agriculture. Repeated reorganizations attempted—never fully successfully—to increase the outreach of the banking system to the smaller, less commercially oriented farmers. An innovation of particular interest is the preferential rediscounting of agricultural loans by private banks in a two-tiered system: specialized intermediary bodies were organized by the government to deal with private lending institutions and the central bank and to promote activities by the farmer.

Another innovative feature described by von Stockhausen (chapter 18) is the use of special funds for at least partial guarantee of repayments to encourage banks to accept the unaccustomed risks of lending to small farmers or other small-scale entrepreneurs who would not qualify under the usual screening procedures. Here, too, a two-tiered system would be appropriate as the system expands. The author makes clear, however, that repayment insurance cannot work unless actual creditworthiness is built up. He discusses the problems of establishing group accountability on a local basis, and the considerations governments must take into account in supporting the system. Von Stockhausen concludes that subsidized restoration of defaulted sums must be avoided.

16. *The Role of Commercial Banking in Agriculture*

G. J. B. Green

[The role of commercial banks in financing agriculture has traditionally been limited by considerations of risk and operating expense. Banks prefer lending to larger enterprises, including cooperatives. The author's views are based on the experience of Barclays Bank DCO and Barclays Overseas Development Corporation Ltd., mainly in the Commonwealth countries of East and West Africa and the West Indies, through 1970.]

A commercial bank administers the day-to-day financial requirements of a country by lending to one person the money of another—with safety, skill, and speed, and at reasonable cost to its customers and profit to itself. In many of the overseas countries where Barclays Bank DCO operates there are, as yet, relatively few specialized financial institutions. The banks are thus extremely important in the monetary affairs of those countries. They offer a wide range of financial services and cooperate with the central banks in the execution of monetary policies.

The Bank's Funds and Lending Policy

The composition of the funds in Barclays Bank DCO is shown in table 16-1. Aside from share capital and reserves, almost all the funds (liabilities) are current deposits, term deposits, and savings accounts. Most of this money can be withdrawn on demand (though in any one period only a small and predictable proportion probably will be); thus, banks borrow short. Unless a bank wins and retains complete confidence, such deposits will not be made. The bank has to balance the liquidity of its assets (so that it can meet withdrawal demands) against the profitable use of deposited funds. Banks therefore tend also to lend short, keeping a certain proportion of their assets as cash and easily realizable assets; hence, most of the money lent is soon deposited again and is available for fresh advances. Loans are usually restricted to

Extracted from *Change in Agriculture*, edited by A. H. Bunting (London: Gerald Duckworth, 1970), pp. 515–24.

Table 16-1. *Composition of Funds of Barclays Bank DCO and Proportion of Funds Lent*
(millions of pounds)

Composition of funds	*1939*	*1952*	*1967*
Liabilities			
Current liabilities[a]	108	442	1,269
Loan capital	—	—	15
Share capital	5	9	24
Reserves	2	8	22
Total	115	459	1,330
Assets			
Current assets[b]	48	191	384
Advances	34	155	697
Investments	30	105	211
Trade investments and investment subsidiaries	—	2	15
Bank premises	3	6	23
Total	115	459	1,330
	1935–39		*1963–67*
Average percentage lent (whole bank)	33.60		52.50

a. Current deposit and other accounts, reserves for contingencies, and balance of profit and loss.

b. Cash, money at call, treasury bills, bills eligible for rediscount, and other trade bills.

sectors of the economy that are already flourishing. Banks must avoid unnecessary risks in lending to maintain trust and keep the cost of money to borrowers reasonably small; they protect themselves and their depositors by covering loans with tangible securities. For all these reasons banks are generally more ready to finance commerce and industry than agriculture.

Methods of Bank Financing for Agriculture

In the agricultural sector, British overseas banks formerly limited themselves largely to providing comparatively short-term, self-canceling seasonal loans. They did this by switching surplus funds from one country to another so that slack periods in one were offset by the demand peaks of another. But foreign exchange control regulations have made this practice increasingly difficult. Fortunately economic expansion, new investment opportunities, and growing deposits have enabled the banks to rely more on local sources. At the same time, the proportion of bank loans to agriculture has declined in relation to total advances.

In many developing countries, long-established firms or agents with sound security have been largely replaced in agricultural marketing by cooperatives and government marketing boards. Marketing boards, with their statutory monopoly, require large amounts of short-term money to buy crops at harvesttime. Working together, the banks can usually supply this from local resources along with drawings from London or from the country's central bank. Advances closely match the course of purchasing and delivery in the field. There are usually three main stages; each is covered by security, and repayments are continual as the produce changes hands. If sales are slow or increased stocks are held from one season to the next, this system can be considerably disrupted.

The commercial banks have generally encouraged agricultural marketing cooperatives and cooperative banks by lending them short-term crop finance, which they in turn lend to local cooperative societies. In this way much of the risk, administrative cost, and difficulty of handling many small payments is borne on the spot by a cooperative movement which is directly in touch with the farmers. The reserves and assets of some cooperatives are sufficient to provide normal commercial security. Some use a first and second payment system; others (where prices are fixed by law) borrow on the security of the crop itself, with irrevocable instructions so that all receipts are paid into the banks. For less well-established cooperatives a government or marketing board guarantee provides security.

Commercial crop buyers are usually either large companies or produce merchants and traders originally from overseas; they are usually well known to the banks and have good security. Large expatriate companies tend to buy export produce not controlled by boards; the others buy direct from farmers. In Nigeria, there are now indigenous produce buyers; since they have little security, their repayments are guaranteed by government boards.

Large plantation estates (often companies) and well-to-do farmers are the bank's main customers for seasonal short-term production credits or working capital. They are well organized financially and have land or other assets as security. The accounts are large and the seasonal turnover regular, so that the loans need little supervision and therefore cost less. Processors of agricultural products (which may be cooperatives) also have good security and management and therefore qualify for bank loans of working capital.

Small farmers have generally had little direct help from banks. They are often unable to pledge their land, because they do not own it. Their yields are small and uncertain, and their farms are numerous and scattered, which adds to the cost and difficulty of lending and collecting money. (Some progress has been made in Kenya, where many small farmers now have title and other sources of regular income.)

Banks have given production credits to small farmers through cooperatives (notably in Cyprus) or under government guarantee (as in Nigeria).

Changing Attitudes to Financing Agriculture

As part of the growing interest throughout the world in advancing agriculture in developing countries, Barclays set up an agricultural section consisting of a credit adviser and assistant in London with three field officers, one each in East Africa, West Africa, and the Caribbean. It has given particular attention to longer-term agricultural finance.

Commercial banks generally regard long-term lending as the business of specialized national or private institutions, aid agencies, land and development banks, finance corporations, and so on, financed by soft loans, nonrepayable loans at low interest, or government grants. Both borrowing and lending are long, since there is no need to hold cash for withdrawal on demand, and in national institutions security is generally less important.

In commercial financial corporations engaged in medium- and long-term finance, repayment, and consequently security, are essential. (An example of such a corporation is Barclays Overseas Development Corporation Ltd., a subsidiary of Barclays Bank established in 1946 to provide long-term development finance.) Their equity investments must show a profit, and long-term debenture loans must be repaid promptly. Hence the object of the loan must be proved sound and the management competent, and the borrower must put in a substantial contribution of his own. Such conditions are more commonly satisfied in commerce and industry than in farming, and consequently agricultural loans form a relatively small part of total loans (table 16-2). They tend to go mainly to large company estates or well-to-do farmers. Many good farmers are unable to make convincing financial projections, and banks tend to have less knowledge of technical agricultural matters than of industrial and commercial ones. The agricultural officers in our bank, who can bridge this gap, appear to have increased the bank's lendings to individual farmers.

Table 16-2. *Loans Made to Agriculture by Barclays Overseas Development Corporation Ltd., 1962–67*
(thousands of pounds)

Advances	*1962*	*1963*	*1964*	*1965*	*1966*	*1967*
Total	12,872	12,755	13,525	13,407	13,632	14,157
To agriculture	2,253	2,419	1,990	2,183	2,075	2,021
To agriculture as percentage of total	18	19	15	16	15	14

Commercial banks have always, in effect, provided medium-term finance for farmers in the form of overdrafts—renewed annually, but with a hard core persisting over some years. Where bank reserves and savings have increased and other lending outlets are limited, perhaps because of competition, these banks are now moving cautiously into the field of explicit medium-term loans (up to eight years or so), mainly to large commercial farmers. Security, participation of the borrower, good management, and the ability to repay remain essential criteria in judging borrowers. Under supervision by an agricultural officer, medium-size farmers should now also be able to borrow, but commercial banks cannot do much to help farmers in countries where social and economic institutions have not produced farming entrepreneurs with valuable land as security.

Institutional Substitutes for Private Enterprise

In some countries banks may be able to assist national agricultural development corporations or specific, specially supervised projects. Barclays agreed, for instance, to make a fairly substantial eight-year loan, in local currency, with a four-year grace period, to the Agricultural Development Corporation of Kenya for the production of improved in-calf dairy heifers for sale. In this way the bank can help meet local costs where external aid has provided the foreign exchange costs.

Banks may also be able to participate in World Bank agricultural development projects. In some projects in Latin America banks have lent money to farmers, partly or wholly at risk, but are able to offset the loans by drawings on a central state monetary authority, which in turn is funded by a World Bank loan. The interest on these drawings is arranged in such a way that the banks make more profit as their contribution increases, which encourages them to lend to agriculture rather than to other sectors. Good management is assured by the technical and supervisory staff of the project, and security may be based on tangible assets (in which case the bank may assume the whole risk) or on government guarantee or insurance schemes. Such loan schemes also tend to help mainly medium- to large-scale commercial enterprises.

Production Loans to Small Farmers

When a monopoly marketing board ensures repayment, banks are sometimes able to help small farmers by lending to selected cooperative unions, which in turn lend to their affiliates and members. The loans represent a percentage of the previous season's crop, and a matching percentage of the board's sales is paid to the bank. The cooperatives meet the administrative costs, and their members know that if the borrowers do not pay up, part of their own sales may be called on instead. This can be done only with well-run societies. It has the virtue of avoiding government guarantees, which lead both borrowers and lenders to care less about repayment.

Critique

It is said that banks do not lend enough to agriculture. It is often forgotten that although commercial banks are not usually able to provide funds for development purposes, they do in fact provide important amounts of short-term agricultural finance; seasonal advances for crop purchase and processing provide valuable aid to agricultural growth. In some countries as much as a quarter of the banks' total advances may be for such purposes. This total frequently equals the share of the government's budget which is devoted to agriculture. The international activities of banks help cover both the local and the foreign exchange components of the costs of export.

Direct loans to small farmers are risky and expensive and are often not repaid. Consequently they will probably remain strictly limited. Cooperatives and other institutions, however, can enlist the help of banks to finance production and purchase crops from small farmers. Bank advances consequently tend to go mainly to a small number of large-scale farmers, but the contribution of these farmers to total farm output is often considerable, as in Kenya, Zambia, and the West Indies.

As farmers become successful on a larger scale, longer-term bank loans will tend to replace the help of specialized agricultural credit agencies and so release funds for smaller-scale development. This tendency will be particularly notable where close technical supervision and control can increase management skills and government guarantees can supplement security; where refinancing systems, perhaps backed by international aid, can maintain the banks' supplies of money and make their operations more profitable; and where the bank has an agricultural staff. But banks are unlikely to devote much money to long-term loans because most of their funds come from current or short-term deposits, which must always be secure if the bank is to hold public confidence and maintain its role as a multiplier of credit. Most long-term lending, particularly for small farmers, will still have to be handled by specialized institutions.

How far a bank can help the agricultural sector depends largely on how far the economy as a whole is commercialized. In developing countries the industrial and commercial sectors usually have both good management and sound security, whereas a strictly commercial approach may be impossible in the traditional agricultural sector. Where farming has become commercialized, and where processing and export businesses have developed, the banks may be able to provide their normal types of support. Though the outlook of banks is developing, as the appointment of agricultural officers by Barclays shows, spectacular progress is not likely without the growth or strengthening of specialized credit management agencies, new refinancing arrangements, and closer supervision of credit.

17. *Centralized Rediscounting and Loan Guarantee Facilities in Mexico*

J. Jesus Romero Chavez

[The Mexican government has tried to solve the problem of financing agricultural production through institution building and credit policies. The emphasis has been on expanding credit for agriculture by means of rediscount and guarantee facilities, which have helped the large modern commercial sector but reached few of the small farmers who are in the majority. Developments through 1980, before nationalization of private commercial banks in 1982, are the focus here.]

Institution Building

Special institutions for agricultural credit in Mexico go back to 1926 when the government established the Banco Nacional de Credito Agricola (BANGRICOLA). This bank was intended to function similarly to the Raiffeisen system of cooperatives in Germany, with local regional banks and central rediscounting facilities. The reality, however, was completely different from the plan from the beginning. The central bank started lending directly to farmers, and the regional banks aborted into simple loan agencies. Most borrowers had political influence, which eventually resulted in many bad loans.

In the following decade, a growing number of *ejidatarios* (members of collective farms called *ejidos*) obtained land through the agrarian reform. They have a right to use but not to sell this land. Since they were not eligible for the usual bank loans, they pressed the government to provide access to credit. In 1935 the government formed a new bank for ejidos, the Banco Nacional de Credito Ejidal (BANJIDAL).

During World War II and the Korean War, world prices of agricultural products went up, and the potential for Mexican exports grew considerably. The government decided to promote agricultural exports and gave the Banco Nacional de Comercio Exterior (BANCOMEXT) more resources to finance the agricultural operations of commercial, export-oriented producers. At that time BANCOMEXT and the Bank of Mexico (the central bank) were the institutions that provided BANGRICOLA and BANJIDAL with lines of credit.

The FONDO and Its Counterparts

During the 1950s, the government concluded that these banks were not channeling enough credit to agriculture and that private banks were little interested in financing risky operations among smaller farmers. To feed a growing population, the government created a trust fund in the Bank of Mexico in 1955 to rediscount and guarantee agricultural loans by private banks: the Fondo de Garantia y Fomento para la Agricultura, Ganaderia y Avicultura (FONDO).

Under the rediscount mechanism, banks submit to FONDO summaries of their agricultural loans. Against these documents FONDO issues advances to the banks through their accounts with the central bank. Interest rates charged the banks on these advances are below the rates the banks charge farmers on the loans used to secure FONDO advances. The banks are obligated to repay FONDO advances on specified due dates, whether or not farmers repay the underlying loans. Private banks may offset part of the risk of loan default by obtaining guarantees from FEGA, another trust fund (see below). FEGA guarantees cover up to 80 percent of the value of loans to farmers.

After a slow start, FONDO became a very prestigious institution. In 1962–63 it was chosen to channel aid resources from the United States through the Alliance for Progress. Later, the World Bank and the Inter-American Development Bank selected it as a channel for their agricultural credit loans. FONDO, however, did not perform all operations for which it had been authorized. Legal problems made it impossible for it to guarantee private bank loans which could not be insured by the mutual and cooperative insurance companies. As a result, private banks lent only to farmers who had collateral.

In the 1960s, crop insurance programs were improved and expanded through two types of institutions: the so-called mutual societies, controlled by the Ministry of Agriculture, and the Consortium for Crop Insurance, controlled by the Ministry of Finance and operated through a trust fund in the central bank. In 1964 both systems were merged and a national insurance company, ANAGSA, was created. Insurance was made compulsory for short-term borrowers from government banks.

In 1964 the government again felt that official banks had deteriorated and that insufficient loans were flowing to the agricultural sector. It decided to create a new system and eliminate the BANGRICOLA and BANJIDAL through financial starvation. Banco Nacional Agropecuario (BANAGRO), an agricultural central bank, was established to finance the operations of selected branches, agencies, and regional banks of the BANGRICOLA and BANJIDAL systems. Subsequent political pressures stopped the financial starvation of the two old systems, however, and BANAGRO then formed its own operating network of seven regional banks. The 1970s started with three competing government agricultural credit systems differing in their lending terms and procedures. As a result of a major policy change, FONDO was authorized to operate through all three systems.

To expand Mexico's access to resources from international institutions for medium- and long-term agricultural lending, a new trust fund was established in 1965, the Fondo Especial de Financiamiento Agropecuario (FEFA). FEFA is operated by the same management as FONDO and rediscounts loans made by public and private banks. In 1973 still another trust fund, FEGA, was established, under the same conditions, to guarantee loans made to ejidatarios by commercial banks and to reimburse the banks for their costs of technical assistance to farmers. These three funds in the Bank of Mexico became the FIRA system.

In 1969–70 the government established in BANAGRO a new trust fund, the Fideicomiso para Credito en Areas de Riego (FICAR), to increase production in irrigated areas. In addition, the government created in BANAGRO a trust fund for rural infrastructure (FOIR), which finances a portion of such development costs as land clearing, tubewells, fencing, and pasture improvement.

Organization of BANRURAL

In 1975 the government decided that to improve the flow of funds to the agricultural sector it was necessary to reorganize the whole rural credit system. For that purpose it appointed a board of directors and a single management for BANAGRO, BANGRICOLA, and BANJIDAL. By a 1976 law, these three banks merged to create the Banco Nacional de Credito Rural (BANRURAL), a central agricultural bank with twelve regional branches. This law defined types of borrowers and organized the entire official agricultural financing system. This includes BANRURAL, FIRA, and all other trust and development funds; the Financiera Nacional de Industria Rural (yet to be organized); and the Financiera Nacional Azucarera (FINASA), which traces its roots to 1931 when a special sugar industry organization was established. The law also covers the operation of the private agricultural credit system consisting of commercial banks and other financial institutions.

Financing Agriculture in 1980

Agriculture accounts for about 10 percent of Mexico's gross domestic product, employs nearly 40 percent of the total labor force of 17 million, and provides more than 15 percent of the country's exports.

Production grew at about 6 percent a year from 1945 to 1955, 4.4 percent from 1955 to 1965, and at less than 2 percent from 1965 to 1975; in 1976 growth was negative. Population increase, however, has been around 3 percent a year. Declining growth in production and increasing domestic demand have caused food imports to rise and the agricultural trade balance to deteriorate. Mexico is determined to alleviate this problem and has made great efforts to increase the use of public funds for agricultural development and to stimulate private investment by making credit more widely available.

Government policies have focused on the allocation of public resources to irrigated areas, in which about 500,000 farmers live, and have left most of the more than 4 million farmers in the rain-fed areas with limited public resources. About half the rain-fed producers are subsistence farmers with fewer than 5 hectares. Irrigated agriculture has prospered and now produces about 48 percent of the country's output, while rain-fed agriculture has stagnated. This policy has polarized Mexican agriculture into commercial and traditional farmers. It is necessary to remodel the credit system and agricultural pricing policies to improve the productivity and income of traditional farmers; otherwise, the gap between the two types of agriculture will continue to grow.

As of 1980, the financial arrangements for agriculture consisted of: a government agricultural banking system formed by BANRURAL and its twelve regional banks, FIRA, several intermediate institutions specialized by commodity—sugar, coffee, and tobacco, for example—and some other state-owned organizations; a private banking system of commercial banks, financieras, and other institutions that rediscount with FIRA; and a noninstitutional network of suppliers, relatives, friends, and persons who lend money to farmers. According to the Bank of Mexico, the consolidated flow of resources through the banking system to the agricultural sector amounted to Mex $84,900 million in 1978 and Mex $112,000 million in 1979, of which commercial banks financed 22 percent in 1978 and 19 percent in 1979, while BANRURAL and FINASA's share was about 50 percent (see table 17-1).

BANRURAL's main operation is short-term lending to organized groups of low-income farmers, ejidos, and individual smallholders. As of 1980 its annual lending covers more than 3 million hectares and benefits about 1 million producers; only 15 percent of BANRURAL lending is long-term. FINASA's operation is limited to short- and medium-term loans for sugarcane producers and sugar mills; FINASA lends to 114,880 farmers, of which 82 percent are ejidatarios. Commercial banks, backed by FIRA, finance short- and long-term loans to larger farmers, agribusinesses, and some ejidatario groups—an esti-

Table 17-1. *Financing of Mexican Agriculture through the Banking System*
(thousand millions of Mexican pesos)

Year	Total banking system[a]	Private banks		FIRA		Government banks[b]	
		Amount	Percent	Amount	Percent	Amount	Percent
1965	10.4	2.7	25	0.5	5	7.2	70
1970	17.7	6.0	34	2.1	12	9.6	54
1975	38.2	10.7	28	6.6	17	20.9	55
1976	44.8	11.5	26	9.5	21	23.8	53
1977	63.7	19.5	22	14.4	23	34.8	55
1978	84.9	18.9	22	23.4	28	42.6	50
1979[c]	112.0	21.4	19	34.4	31	56.2	50
1980[d]	145.0	27.7	19	47.6	33	69.9	48

a. Outstanding balances on December 31 classified as agricultural loans.
b. BANRURAL and FINASA (FINASA's lending amounts to roughly 10 percent of the combined total of both institutions).
c. Estimated.
d. Projected.
Source: Bank of Mexico.

mated total of about 200,000 beneficiaries. Institutional credit reaches only 30 percent of the country's cultivated area (mostly in irrigated districts) and about 20 percent of all producers.

Financing Agriculture in the Future

The new emphasis on rain-fed areas and the government's strategy for food self-sufficiency create a new frame of reference for the agricultural credit system. To increase the flow of funds to agricultural production, it is necessary to solve problems of both supply and demand. Changing the pattern of credit demand and preparing all farmers to receive and use credit implies important structural changes. Pricing policies, infrastructure, and input delivery systems, as well as the development of local technologies, are just a few of the areas in which improvements are needed in the short run to increase demand for institutional credit in productive uses.

Increasing the credit supply requires changes in the delivery system. First, the number of loan offices should be more than doubled. Second, the legal framework, the system of farmer organizations, and lending procedures must all be adjusted. Third, resource mobilization must be improved by changing the institutional structure. Fourth, farmer education and credit procedures geared to risk must be developed with government support to meet the conditions in rain-fed areas.

It is clear that central rediscounting facilities such as FIRA and FICAR are efficient under certain circumstances. "Second floor" credit operations (lending to lenders) are always simpler to control. FIRA, for example, charges commercial banks' accounts with the Bank of Mexico at specified due dates for its rediscounts; there are no collection difficulties. But direct credit operations with farmers involve real risks, are politically critical, and very expensive. Alternatives to agricultural credit banks, such as loan associations, credit unions, or credit cooperatives should be explored.

Conclusion

The Mexican agricultural credit system has been very dynamic for more than fifty years. Since 1955 it has been characterized by central rediscounting with operating regional and commercial banks; rediscounting through the Bank of Mexico became a significant reality in the 1960s. It has grown considerably and is in good standing thanks to the protection the government grants to both the central institution and the commercial banks. One main disadvantage, however, comes from the political situation that surrounds the system and makes lenders quite selective. Farmers not considered commercial are avoided, and the system's coverage is thus restricted.

Central rediscounting through specialized agricultural banks has had its ups and downs. When BANGRICOLA was formed, the government planned to develop regional operating banks and a strong central agricultural bank. Because BANGRICOLA had to grant loans to politicians and operate with below-market interest rates, however, financial weaknesses arose from low repayment rates and negative interest spreads. As a result, BANGRICOLA had to knock on the government's door for funds and fell into a vicious cycle of dependency. The same holds for the other parts of the system. This could happen to BANRURAL too unless there is a change toward decentralized operations.

Along with the strengthening of regional banks and the financial position of the system as a whole, new types of intermediary organization need to be developed. The weakest link in the chain—the one between small borrowers and local credit institutions—must be strengthened. Previous attempts to establish a cooperative credit system have failed, but no other form of intermediary has evolved. The objective might be reached if the government decides to revive the old dream of having relatively autonomous credit unions or cooperatives that would multiply the local or regional banks' effort to reach large numbers of farmers, supported by centralized rediscounting.

18. *Guarantee Funds and the Provision of Capital in the Self-help Sphere*

Joachim von Stockhausen

[Loan repayment guarantees can encourage the issue of credit to small-scale enterprises in general and foster the formation of self-help organizations. Credit guarantees reduce the risk to lenders and increase their willingness to lend to marginal groups, such as small farmers. Two-tier guarantee systems, with collective guarantees by target group members and counter guarantees by a government agency, are more effective in promoting self-help activities than are direct guarantees by a public authority.]

Guarantee Funds for Indirect Financial Assistance

Credit institutions are limited by statutory and regulatory requirements. For example, long-term loans can often be granted only against first mortgages on real property. In many cases, industrial and agricultural land can be used as collateral for loans only under certain conditions that exclude tenant farmers and owners lacking registered titles. When strict requirements for collateral are maintained despite the inadequate availability of collateral among small- and medium-scale borrowers, there is an inherent conflict between the lenders' need for security and the government policy of supporting small borrowers who often cannot offer sufficient security. Unable to provide sufficient collateral, small borrowers receive little credit, and the absence of sufficient collateral is, in turn, a result of their inability to obtain credit to enable them to grow larger—a vicious cycle. Critics assert that it would be easy to solve this conflict by reducing security requirements and gearing lending policy less to collateral and more to development. But this solution is not compatible with the general social need for banks to safeguard their liquidity.

This is where external credit security comes into the picture. The object is to ensure an adequate supply of credit to small-scale borrowers at the necessary maturities by converting into "real security" the ability of small-scale borrowers to service their debt. Guarantees by a third party separate the repayment of a loan from the actual repayment capacity of the borrowers. Guarantees help direct credit to deserving borrowers by converting their ineligible collateral into eligible collateral, or by converting an awkward bank requirement into a more convenient form. Guarantees stand in place of the collateral the borrower has difficulty providing.

Guarantees represent only one instrument for external or collective provision of collateral. Overall, there are two categories of collective collateral: institutional lender-borrower security, and institutional lender security. The first reduces not only the risk to the lender but also to the borrower. It is intended to increase not only the availability of credit but also the likelihood of its being used by the borrower, since some of his risk is now covered. The most important forms of institutional lender-borrower security are government price and purchase guarantees, life insurance policies for borrowers, and crop and livestock insurance.

Institutional lender security seeks merely to reduce the risk to the lender and thus increase his willingness to extend credit. All types of credit guarantee fall into this category of collective credit security.

Between these two categories of collective credit security is the modified deficiency guarantee. Under a normal deficiency guarantee the guarantor is liable only if the borrower actually fails to meet a demand for loan repayment. A modified deficiency guarantee, however, deals with default that may occur if a borrower's obligation has not been met in the stipulated manner—for example, because of crop losses in bad weather. Such a guarantee agreement could also be viewed as a precursor of crop insurance.

Collective guarantees by credit guarantee associations are still at a very early stage in developing countries. The explanation lies mainly in the difficulty of creating suitable institutional structures rather than in a failure to understand their significance for credit policy. That collective guarantees have been duly recognized as an adjunct to lending is indicated by the growth of loans to informal groups in rural areas. Individual credits to a group of borrowers are consolidated, and the group assumes full liability for the loan. Most of the groups are nonjuridical precooperative organizations that implement the collective guarantee in two ways: (1) A group member in default is expelled from the group, and the group is not liable for the obligations of that member. This system presupposes strong cohesive social ties among the individual group members. (2) The group accepts unlimited liability for the loans provided. This system may be regarded as a transitional form between an individual guarantee and a collective guarantee. Both forms are found in developing countries, but the amount of experience gained with them is still too limited for a general evaluation. Traditional forms of cooperation have yet to be developed into organized credit guarantee associations.

Guarantees can be paid for in several ways. If the insurance principle is applied, the guarantor organization charges for the service. This fee can be passed on to the borrowers. The same principle would apply to reinsurance or counterguarantees. In these cases, disbursements to cover nonrepayment of loans or other contingencies would be made from a fund accumulated for the purpose. Governments may subsidize some of these costs or put an initial payment into a guarantee fund if they wish to support the purposes of a guarantee. If a group of borrowers assumes full liability for each member's repayment, any payments to make good a default would be made entirely from within the group.

Guarantees can make more credit available to target groups in the short term and can also improve the effectiveness of banking systems in the medium term. By transferring credit risks from the lender they help build up a flow of capital between the target groups and the banking system. The banking system can then intensify its services for the target group: collection of money, transmission and transformation of capital, and handling of payment transactions. Guarantees, however, represent only half of this mechanism. They need to be supplemented by measures to promote savings, such as higher interest rates or schemes to insure deposits. This two-pronged approach is needed because the effectiveness and deepening of financial flows are determined by the continuing ability of the target group not only to service its debt obligations but also to save. Such an approach favors the growth of banks engaged in both deposit and lending activities with the target group.

Single-tier versus Two-tier Systems

In the promotion of small-scale enterprises in agriculture or industry, I distinguish between direct and indirect measures. Direct measures include grants to strengthen the resources of target group enterprises and additional credit rediscounting facilities to improve the availability of financing. Measures that indirectly help finance small-scale enterprises include separate insurance and guarantee arrangements. With indirect measures, there is less risk that public authorities will exert excessive control over the activities of the target group than in the case of direct measures. Thus, guarantees promote self-help among marginal groups of entrepreneurs.

The degree to which guarantees stimulate self-help is determined essentially by the type of guarantor and guarantee. For example, a public fund providing deficiency guarantees directly will have a smaller effect than would a credit guarantee association run by the target group in combination with a counter- or supplemental guarantee provided by the state.

Credit guarantee associations are, at the outset at least, often unable to meet their obligations without support from the authorities. The principle should be established that state assistance will be gradually eliminated. A suitable course is to establish a two-tier guarantee system, under which the authorities assume a counterguarantee for credit guarantee associations. This system is significant for the following reasons:

- Credit guarantee associations foster the idea of self-help; they should be specifically encouraged by institutions that promote self-help organizations.
- Credit guarantee associations offer the assurance that guarantee applications will be examined by representatives of the same branch of industry as the applicant. These individuals have a better knowledge of the technical problems and of their follow entrepreneurs than have bankers or outside functionaries. They can better judge the usefulness of proposed investments and consequently provide a technical guarantee in a relatively uncomplicated manner.
- The assumption of counterguarantees by the authorities reduces the risk to the credit guarantee association and lessens the possibility that the self-help idea will be undermined by financial overextension.
- Counterguarantee funds enable the authorities to obtain a direct picture of target group activities. It is thus possible to have an objective dialogue among the authorities, the participating banks, and the target group.

Conditions for Success

Despite the advantages of guarantee funds, too much should not be expected of them. They alone cannot solve the problem of outside financing for small borrowers. Guarantee funds can perform a useful function and perhaps even be necessary for getting institutional loans to some target groups. Their developmental impact, however, comes only when they are used in combination with measures to promote savings and to increase the creditworthiness of the target group by building it into an attractive partner for the banks.

Guarantees must not be allowed to degenerate into a new channel for subsidies. Edward S. Shaw, a prominent advocate of a liberal capital market policy, endorses credit guarantees and insurance schemes as an appropriate regulatory mechanism, provided the beneficiaries are required to pay premiums high enough to cover the costs: "Needless to say, it should charge for its services a price generally adequate to cover its costs and losses. Free guarantees and free insurance on the capital markets are indirect subsidies that twist and distort the allocation of savings. Moreover, prices charged for them are incentives to capital market development" [*Financial Deepening in Economic Development*, New York, Oxford University Press, 1973, p. 128]. The demand that guarantee systems cover their costs implies allocation of credit on the basis of banking criteria and a strengthening of internal credit discipline by the target group. Bad credits and lax repayment practices can destroy guarantee systems.

In guarantee systems there is a risk that the credit application process will become overly bureaucratized. This risk may be minimized if guarantees are viewed primarily as an instrument to assist self-help among marginal groups. The best possible way to keep a guarantee system free of red tape is for the target group to participate actively in the guarantee process.

Specialized Farm Credit Institutions

The analysis of specialized farm credit institutions (SFCI) is undertaken in general terms by Von Pischke (chapter 19). He outlines the reasons SFCI are established and the assumptions behind the policy. He shows how the impact of one-sided intervention into rural financial markets can have a series of unfavorable consequences. Loans get poorly distributed, repayment discipline suffers, and political interference is introduced. Some possible future trends are noted.

The default problem is discussed more fully by Sanderatne (chapter 20). He categorizes the reasons for the high rates of delinquency in repayment found in many parts of the world. One of the few comprehensive surveys of defaulters, conducted in Sri Lanka in 1971, indicated that defaulters tended to have lower than average yields in the year they were interviewed, and about a third had suffered crop failure. In other cases nonrepayment resulted from the attitudes of debtors or the perceived indifference of creditors. Sanderatne offers suggestions for improving repayment.

The next three chapters present examples of different experiences with SFCI. Graham and Bourne (chapter 21) present what may be an extreme case of successive financial failures in Jamaica, associated with an upturn in agricultural output in an otherwise declining economy in the 1970s. High arrears in repayment for public (but not private) banks were a principal weakness. Wharton's account (chapter 22) of twenty years of experience with the ACAR program in Brazil paints a somewhat more positive picture. Here the emphasis was on extension and technical education in a backward province, implemented through supervised credit. Elaborate individual farm plans were used at first, but supervision became less detailed as the program grew. The program was heavily subsidized: interest rates were well below rates of inflation and somewhat below the costs of providing credit, but repayment rates were excellent. The impact on production appears clearly positive among farmers in backward areas, although less so among commercial farmers.

The INVIERNO/PROCAMPO project in Nicaragua, initial stages of which are described by Bathrick and Gomez Casco (chapter 23), represents an effort to apply modern management techniques to an integrated program for large numbers of relatively poor and backward farmers. Elaborate planning and preparation, integration of credit with technical and marketing services, and computerized record keeping and monitoring of activities were features of this project.

19. *The Pitfalls of Specialized Farm Credit Institutions in Low-income Countries*

J. D. Von Pischke

[Why are specialized farm credit institutions established in low-income countries, and why do they frequently founder? This phenomenon of development finance is explored by analyzing the performance problems of these institutions with the use of financial logic and elements of political economy.]

Specialized farm credit institutions (SFCI) primarily provide loans for agricultural production. They have names like Agricultural Finance Corporation, Rural Development Bank, and similar titles. In contrast to other financial institutions, their loan portfolios consist almost entirely of agricultural loans; SFCI do not on any significant scale accept savings deposits or provide money transfer services.

SFCI are established by governments in low-income countries to provide finance for expanding agricultural production. They may cater to specific groups of farmers defined by farm size or crops; they are sometimes linked with land reforms. Their services may be directed toward the beneficiaries of projects for agricultural settlement or comprehensive rural area development. SFCI are usually expected to provide an impetus to agricultural innovation and to promote certain social aspects of rural development policy. Development assistance from foreign donor agencies is often important in shaping these agencies; substantial sums have been directed into SFCI by the World Bank, U.S. Agency for International Development, and European donors.

Specialized farm credit institutions in low-income countries have a checkered financial record. Their efforts to achieve institutional and financial viability and to expand their clientele are complicated by the vagaries of agricultural production and prices, and some of their activities have more in common with social welfare than with commercial practice. These lenders often find it difficult to recover enough

Extracted from *Development Digest*, vol. 18, no. 3 (July 1980), pp. 79–91.

loans to break even financially. Losses appear to be larger than would be expected from normal credit institutions.

Why are SFCI Created?

The assumptions behind the creation of SFCI are that the agricultural sector is not well served, that most rural families (or a target group) do not have access to credit from existing, usually urban-based institutions. Policy makers believe that supplying credit for agriculture or for the target group in question would be advantageous. This belief is based on four related views of rural people, the state of agriculture, the requisites of rural development, and the role of government. The first and most basic is that "farmers are poor." The second holds that little agricultural innovation or progress can occur without credit, so that poor farmers need credit. The third is the axiom that government should promote rural development or the welfare of target groups. The fourth is that supply-leading finance can stimulate agricultural development and productivity. Supply-leading finance means providing funds in advance of a demand for them in an effort to stimulate borrowers to risk new and useful activities [see chapter 5]. In agriculture, when credit is tied to new practices, such as improved inputs or a new crop, it is assumed that financing will accelerate the adoption of an innovation by the target group of intended borrowers.

Interaction of Interest Rates and Access to Credit

The complex of beliefs held by policy makers favors cheap farm credit supplied by the public sector. Its proponents state that credit should be provided at a "reasonable" rate of interest for purposes considered socially and economically imperative, and for target groups viewed as poor and needing credit to progress. Interest rates charged by traders or other local moneylenders are high compared with those found in banks, and it is considered objectionable to charge a high rate to farmers, the most disadvantaged people in society. Low rates of interest are sometimes thought to compensate farmers for their losses of income from government price ceilings on food products (which help consumers). The usual result is agricultural interest rates below or roughly equal to the going rates on loans to other major sectors.

Low interest rates on loans to rural people end, paradoxically, by restricting their access to financial services. Most rural people are costly for a lender to serve. They tend to deal in small transactions, which are relatively expensive for a credit institution to process, and they are frequently scattered geographically in areas with poor communications. The small size of the market around a rural credit office makes it difficult for lenders to achieve economies of scale. Rural people may not be accustomed to modern commercial practices and often are not so concerned about loan due dates as other customers, characteristics which raise the lender's management costs. Deposit-taking institutions with a clientele of small depositors who conduct business in cash must keep on hand relatively large amounts of cash which earns no interest—an additional cost of serving these clients.

The rural economy and farm prices fluctuate widely. Some poor harvests and some failures in the marketing system's capacity to absorb produce are to be expected. The amount of cash generated by agricultural output will vary since the marketed portion is a residual left after the relatively constant subsistence requirements of farm families are satisfied. This variability in income tends to reduce lenders' evaluation of the debt payment capacity of rural target groups. The unpredictability of loan repayment collections increases lenders' liquidity requirements, which raises their costs and reduces the supply of funds they are willing to lend.

Uncertainty concerning a borrower's future cash flow and his ability to service debt is viewed by the lender as a credit risk. One determinant of willingness to bear this risk is the interest rate, which affects the lender's expected income. Loans involving substantial uncertainty tend to be avoided by lenders unless they can charge high interest rates. When interest rates (used here to denote all fees levied by lenders) are kept low, lenders are not encouraged to expand into activities which incur higher costs—including the costs of greater uncertainty. Low rates thus encourage lenders to ration credit stringently according to commercial criteria of creditworthiness, that is, to lend to fewer borrowers than would be willing to pay their rates, and to refuse those who are conventionally seen as higher risks.

Credit rationing by existing financial institutions severely restricts rural access to financial services. This is seen in the paucity of rural offices of banks; in demands for loan security beyond the capacity of most rural households; in minimum requirements for the size of transactions and of deposit account balances which are high relative to normal transactions and incomes in rural areas; and in other arrangements or requirements imposing significant transactions costs on those seeking financial services. Adherents of the complex of beliefs favoring cheap credit from the public sector see this as grounds for remedial government intervention by establishing a special-purpose farm credit institution. This lender is intended to overcome alleged weaknesses in market performance and is not designed to be dependent on market resources. It is funded through the national treasury—frequently with support from foreign aid agencies.

By definition, a specialized farm credit institution is highly restricted in the services it provides, operating on only one side of the rural financial market. Credit access is considered the primary problem, and so deposit-taking and money transfer services are typically not developed. Rural savings capacities and liquid resources are usually thought to be small. Institutions already in place (post office savings banks or commercial banks) may be thought to be providing adequate financial services outside the credit sphere.

Effects of One-sided Intervention in Rural Finance

Intervention solely on the lending side of the rural financial market has consequences which are frequently overlooked. It tends to fragment these markets further: credit channels do little to stimulate rural savings. Such intervention may encourage a popular belief that formal sector credit is essential to progress, a view which could prevail at the expense of traditions of self-help.

Most important, dependence on the national treasury and external donors limits SFCI access to market funds and to the local information it would have if it performed other roles. Lack of such access alienates the institution from the communities it serves. Unable to act as a *rural* institution, intermediating between rural savers and borrowers, it serves merely as a one-way link between the government and rural sectors. Rural people are not regarded by SFCI as a market to be developed, but are seen as poor, exploited, or economically incompetent people requiring assistance. Rural people, in turn, do not view SFCI as something of their own, but as a benevolent intrusion to be exploited. In these circumstances a specialized farm credit institution is not well positioned to learn about rural financial flows, behavior, and local priorities—knowledge available only to those who enjoy sufficient rural confidence. Lacking such information and insight, SFCI management can develop only limited decision-making expertise. SFCI are not in a position to be stimulated by either the discipline imposed or the opportunities offered by market participation.

Without detailed information about the mechanics of rural finances, and limited by budgetary and operating constraints imposed by government sponsors, SFCI generally are forced to allocate or ration credit according to criteria different from those applied by commercial banks. Political criteria of some sort, broadly defined, are inherent in government programs to promote the welfare of target groups selected by nonmarket criteria.

Credit rationing by SFCI takes two forms, intensive and extensive. Intensive credit rationing involves lending to a relatively small target group and providing its members amounts of credit which are large in relation to the existing scope of their operations. For example, a farmer with two local cows may be given a loan to buy several high-grade cows. Intensive credit rationing has features attractive to aid agencies. The usual objective of intensive credit rationing is to increase the production and incomes of borrowers through technological innovation. The loan is so large that borrowers could not repay it with their preloan cash flow, so repayment must come from loan-supported investment. Lenders tend to be quite selective in allocating credit and frequently use elaborate mechanisms based on farm budgets to determine which farmers will qualify. An assumption underlying intensive credit rationing is that lack of finance is the binding constraint on production and incomes. If so, this implies that all other elements essential to increasing production and incomes, including the ability to accommodate the uncertainties involved, are in place or can be provided and made operative by finance. Intensively rationed credit is supply-leading finance par excellence.

Extensive credit rationing is intended to provide credit access to large numbers of farmers in broad target groups as well as to increase production. For example, all members of a cooperative or all commercial growers of wheat may have access to seed and fertilizer loans. Within SFCI budget constraints, however, broad access implies relatively small loans to numerous borrowers. Loan limits under extensive rationing are frequently specified according to rules of thumb or standard amounts per hectare, instead of the more complicated farm budgets used for intensive credit rationing. Extensive rationing is most frequently found in credit for seasonal inputs; small amounts issued to each borrower satisfy the production bias of planners while inspiring a broad appeal which is politically desirable. Programs using extensive rationing are usually funded by governments without support from donors except in area development projects, in certain aid for cooperatives, and in farm credit systems funded through centralized rediscounting agencies.

Each variety of credit rationing under political criteria contains the seeds of its own financial destruction. These seeds take root to the extent that extremes in credit rationing overwhelm financial considerations. Programs with either highly intensive or highly extensive rationing self-destruct most rapidly, other things being equal.

Intensively rationed credit attempts to perform the function of ownership capital in absorbing the impact of uncertainty. Intensively rationed loans are large relative to the financial status of the borrower, impose relatively large burdens of fixed debt service, and change the on-farm factor mix significantly by the addition of higher technology. Such loans can push the borrower's finances beyond his managerial and risk-bearing capabilities, especially during the period of adaptation to credit-supported change. In periods of adversity, the new activity may not generate sufficient cash flow to repay the loan which permitted its adoption; delinquency in repayment easily results. Borrowers, however, may not regard SFCI loan contracts very seriously:

they may view the lender as an alien institution with access to the "free" resources of government.

Extensive credit rationing can also lead to problems. In promoting wide access to credit, lenders offer it to some borrowers who cannot use it wisely, who have little intention of repaying, or who are so exposed to uncertainty or so close to subsistence that even small repayment obligations assume major proportions. In these cases, defaults are probable. For others who borrowed with the expectation that their agricultural incomes would be increased, the small sums of extensively rationed credit may present limitations. If the loan is a small fraction of the financial requirements of an improved input package, adoption of the package may be incomplete; improved seeds without enough fertilizer, for example, may not perform much better than traditional varieties. Access to extensively rationed credit therefore may not stimulate new practices, and the loans may be too small to engender either innovation or repayment.

Rationing by political favoritism easily leads to poor loan discipline, which can include delinquency, deceit, and diversion. Political lending may put little pressure on the favored borrowers to repay; incentives to build a good credit rating are lacking. Some ways of circumventing loan limits under extensive rationing are to apply for credit for a larger area than will be cultivated or to borrow simultaneously under different names. The large size of intensively rationed loans may tempt borrowers to divert the funds to purposes not envisaged by the lender; they may sell loan-supported purchases or disbursements in kind for immediate cash, or submit fictitious invoices from accommodating suppliers.

Repercussions of Poor Loan Discipline for the SFCI

Poor loan discipline impairs SFCI development. Funds which would have become available for relending as outstanding loans mature are locked up as arrears. As arrears accumulate, SFCI funds fail to revolve. Potential borrowers may increasingly find their access to credit delayed, restricted, or denied because of the declining liquidity of the lender. When funds for lending decline, intensively rationed credit becomes available to fewer new borrowers. Lenders may increase the average loan size to lower administrative costs and thus cater to still fewer large, low-risk borrowers. In contrast, lenders of extensively rationed credit may reduce the average loan size to maintain broad access. Arrears may be increased as these loans become increasingly trivial, especially in real terms when inflation raises the costs of modern husbandry.

Arrears have an opportunity cost. Funds that are not repaid cannot be lent to others at interest. Day-to-day collection problems occupy lenders' scarce personnel, often at the expense of planning, staff training, the development of management information systems and more effective services for rural people. The accumulation of arrears and the associated poor financial performance demoralize staff members, making it even more unlikely that the institution will become financially efficient. In the rural communities affected, overcoming a tradition of poor loan discipline by government lenders is difficult and has its own cost. Private financial intermediaries may be deterred from serving the poor because of bad repayment habits. They may be increasingly reluctant to extend credit in experimental or innovative ways because of the heightened political sensitivity surrounding the enforcement of rural loan contracts.

Poor loan discipline creates distrust. Defaulters, originally considered as poor farmers deserving financial assistance, are placed in an adversary position against their financial partner in development; the flow of communication between farmers and rural development administrators, extension agents, and SFCI staff is constricted. Distrust inhibits development programs by making consensus and cooperative action more difficult or by requiring the exercise of force to implement programs involving rural participation.

Widespread default demonstrates to rural people that the government is not able or not willing to enforce contracts. But cases taken to court by SFCI may strain the ability of the courts to dispense justice, especially if defaulters are numerous. The legal force of other contracts may be compromised by loan defaults. The accumulation of arrears also make SFCI more vulnerable to political interference. Those who formed the institution to assist the rural poor and gain popularity are seldom enthusiastic about expropriating poor farmers' property or denying further credit to a blacklist of defaulters. Interference, if across the board, permits all defaulters to take a longer free ride; if selective, it favors certain groups or individuals. Default can be a source of conflict between those who strain themselves to repay and those who do not and fail to suffer for it. To the extent that the pattern of default mirrors the rural power structure, equity is violated by the manipulation of collection activities.

The Future of SFCI

The preceding description, although it accents the negative possibilities, nevertheless reflects the experiences of SFCI in many countries in one degree or another. In view of the problems which plague specialized farm credit institutions in low-income countries, what is their future? Agricultural and rural development programs will continue to receive large amounts of funds from their sponsor governments and foreign aid donors because of their economic and political appeal, and much of this will go into credit. Less certain is the survival of particular SFCI and the complex of beliefs favoring cheap credit from the public sector. Four major influences may work against this complex of beliefs. First, it will be rendered irrelevant in some countries, eclipsed by a strong centralized control of agricultural production and of rural people and the transformation of the formal financial sector into a set of accounts for the planning authority. Second, rural development breakthroughs not involving supply-leading finance are likely to divert attention from the credit complex.

Third, the intellectual position of the complex will be eroded in some degree by trends apparent in recent research on rural financial markets. Empirical data increasingly challenge the assumptions that rural people are unable to save, that rural liquidity is negligible, that the informal credit market is characterized by usurious rates of interest, and that SFCI and low interest rates serve the best interests of rural people. Fourth, the complex can be undermined by the practical success of farm credit suppliers which operate effectively in financial terms at odds with the complex. These could include aggressive efforts to mobilize target group deposits and to build viable financial institutions not dependent on subsidy.

20. *An Analytical Approach to Loan Defaults by Small Farmers*

Nimal Sanderatne

[Failure to repay loans has often plagued government farm credit programs. This paper discusses the nature and extent of default and develops a conceptual framework to analyze the problem. The reasons for default obtained in a survey in Sri Lanka are analyzed. Types of policies which might resolve the problem are suggested.]

The inability to recover a significant proportion of funds loaned to small farmers is widespread. In many countries where credit has been given without collateral, farmers have tended to repay a declining proportion of loans over time. This places a serious financial burden on credit-giving agencies and governments. Without a steady inflow of funds, the capacity of a credit agency to maintain or increase its lending to small farmers becomes restricted. High rates of default decrease both the number of creditworthy borrowers and the ability of a small-farmer credit program to continue as an aid to agriculture.

Nature and Incidence of Defaults

Default rates are measured in various ways, such as the collection ratio for an accounting period, the percentage of the portfolio in arrears at a given time, the proportion of borrowers who repay, and the repayment index. This chapter is concerned with factors responsible for defaults, defined as loans overdue for repayment. It is difficult to determine how many of the overdue loans will ultimately be recovered. Generally, the longer the arrears, the greater the likelihood that the loan will not be repaid. Recorded arrears and defaults may not always indicate the actual level of defaults, as some overdue loans may be concealed by refinancing or extending the period of repayment.

In most small-farmer credit programs sponsored by governments, the credit agency deviates from banks' traditional insistence on collateral. The agency in some cases evaluates the capacity of farmers to repay and restricts its loans to "viable" farmers who would have an

Extracted from *Savings and Development*, vol. 2, no. 4 (1978), pp. 290–304.

adequate surplus. Such programs have had a lower rate of default, but their coverage has been limited. For instance the Bangkok Bank, a private commercial bank in Thailand, has operated a credit program for small farmers since 1963. It evaluates each farmer's holding with respect to soil capability, cropping pattern, costs, yields, and family expenses, and assesses his creditworthiness. It has had a high rate of recovery, and several other commercial banks in Thailand have begun similar schemes.

High rates of default ranging from 50 percent to as much as 80 or 95 percent have been reported in small-farmer credit programs in African, Middle East, and Latin American countries. Most South and Southeast Asian countries have had similar experiences with low recovery rates, yet in East Asia strong village cooperatives have enabled Japan, the Republic of Korea, and Taiwan to resolve this problem.

The general experience with credit programs not requiring collateral is that the rate of recovery is initially good but later declines. This may be due to less discrimination in the selection of borrowers, to less supervision of lent funds, or to more political interference and corruption as a credit program progresses. For instance in Indonesia, when the improved BIMAS Program commenced in 1970–71, about 95 percent of the funds were recovered in the first three years, but the level of recovery declined until only 64 percent of the funds lent were recovered in 1975. Several studies have found no conclusive evidence that the repayment record of small farmers is worse than those with large holdings. The World Bank, for example, has cited Bangladesh, Bolivia, Colombia, Costa Rica, and Ethiopia as countries where large farmers have poorer repayment records. Since large farmers tend to get more and larger loans from the institutional sector, a low repayment record implies that the better-off farmers benefit most from default. The large farmers' greater control of village organizations may account for the ability to avoid repayment.

A Conceptual Framework for Analyzing Defaults

The numerous reasons often given for the nonrepayment of loans may confuse the issues. A conceptual framework for analyzing loan defaults can provide an understanding of the underlying reasons for default, which is a prerequisite for appropriate policies to solve the problem.

The World Bank has categorized the reasons for default into three: the failure of farmers to use borrowed funds for production, the failure of the investment, and the refusal to repay. Six categories are used here: defects in farm production; variability in incomes caused by fortuitous, seasonal, or unforeseen factors; defects and inadequacies in the organization disbursing credit; attitudinal conditions not conducive to repayment; misallocation of borrowed funds; and other miscellaneous reasons. These categories are often interrelated, and a borrower may not repay for more than one reason.

•Defects in farm production. Poor productive conditions of the farming enterprise often make it difficult to repay. This defect is also expressed in terms of "nonviable farm units," which often refers to the small size of farms. The implication is that farmers are unable but willing to repay.

A defective production situation is encountered when the amount due for repayment exceeds the farmer's cash savings, which is the excess of farm income over family subsistence needs. Inadequacies of land resources and other agricultural inputs and deficiencies in supportive services are basic reasons for an income too small to repay loans. Land tenure conditions, the productive potential of the land, the availability of inputs, satisfactory marketing channels, and remunerative prices are among the important factors bearing on farmers' earnings. The defects in agrarian production regarded as an obstacle to repayment include only those that cannot be overcome by the use of credit. Without productive investment, short-term credit leads only to greater indebtedness to the lending agency.

•Variability in incomes. The farmer may be unable to repay his loan in a particular season owing to crop failure or the destruction of a crop by theft, fire, or other hazard. His inability to repay may also be caused by a sudden fall in prices or the unmarketability of his produce. Farmers in this category are normally able and willing to repay, and the organizational structure is capable of collecting the dues. Defaults in this category are thus abnormal and presumably temporary.

•Defects in the credit organization. Unlike the other two categories, the farmer in this case is able to repay and willing to do so, but since the organization giving credit does not pressure him to repay, he does not. The farmer may believe that he will neither suffer penal interest rates nor endanger his subsequent borrowing by his default; loopholes which enable a defaulter to borrow subsequently and abandoning attempts to collect earlier defaults would support this belief. Sometimes the staff of the credit agency itself might even encourage borrowers not to repay.

•Attitudinal conditions. Farmers who do not want to repay loans despite their ability to repay fall into this category. They often consider government funds as grants rather than loans. This cause is generally closely linked with defects in the credit organization's policies, such as abandoning efforts to collect unpaid debts under earlier schemes and the lack or weakness of any sanctions on borrowers who do not return loans.

•Misallocation. The use of funds for purposes other than those for which the loan was intended can interfere with repayment. Some persons may have invested loan proceeds in other activities which have proved a failure; or even if successful, there may be a lack of liquid funds to repay on time. Other misallocations include the use of borrowed funds for ceremonial needs, a sudden illness or death, or repayment of loans from other sources.

Empirical Evidence on Reasons for Default

Since few empirical studies identify the causes of defaults, the proportion of defaults or defaulters in specific categories cannot be estimated. The relative importance of certain reasons for default can be gauged from the character of the program and agencies disbursing credit, from differences in default rates in regions, and the performance of credit schemes over time. For instance, if a credit agency had a rate of default very different from that of others in the area, the implication is that weaknesses in the agency's policies or its officials were the cause. If the data on loan defaults are available by size of farm, it is possible to see whether the agrarian structure had an important bearing on defaults. Variations in default rates between normal seasons and those with a high rate of crop failure would indicate defaults caused by fortuitous circumstances.

Where credit programs have had a high level of defaults, studies should be undertaken to elicit data on the reasons along the lines suggested in this conceptual framework. These studies should enable the formulation of policies to reduce the rate of defaults. There are, however, inherent problems in obtaining such data from surveys. When the information is collected from defaulters themselves, there is likely to be a bias toward reasons which absolve them from blame, such as crop failure or faults of the credit agency. When data are collected by the credit agency, much of the blame would be placed on the farmer rather than on deficiencies in the agency or its program.

One of the few comprehensive surveys of reasons for default is that conducted in Sri Lanka in 1971 by the Central Bank of Ceylon. This sample survey interviewed defaulters of agricultural loans taken from 1967 to 1970, when the rate of default was nearly 30 percent. The survey interviewed 841 defaulting members of cooperatives and collected data on family size, cost of production, living expenditure, area cultivated, and the reasons for default. Seventeen reasons for default were elicited from the defaulters themselves. These have been reclassified in table 20-1 into the six categories developed in the conceptual framework.

•Defects in farm production. The survey data disclosed a high correlation between low incomes and defaults. Defaulters had much lower average yields in irrigated rice fields (two-thirds of the national aver-

Table 20-1. *Categories of Default*
(percent)

Category of default	*Defaulters*	*Loans*
Defects in farm production	19	17
Variability in incomes	26	33
Defects in the credit organization	17	12
Attitudinal conditions	16	18
Misallocation	15	15
Miscellaneous	7	5
Total	100	100

Source: Central Bank of Ceylon, *Survey of Defaults in the Repayment of New Agricultural Loans* (Colombo, 1972), table 18, p. 28, reclassified.

age), and the reasons given for the lower yields included, among others, either a lack of adequate irrigation or waterlogging, inadequacy or unavailability of inputs on time, and poor extension services. With inadequate incomes borrowers may use loan funds for their subsistence, or where they have used it for cultivation purposes any increased income may still be used for subsistence needs rather than the repayment of loans.

•Variability in incomes. The survey disclosed that one-third of the defaulters had not repaid owing to crop failure. This is probably an overestimate. Only 10 percent of farmers had used the provision in the agricultural credit scheme allowing an extension of the loan repayment period on account of crop failure; and the general statistics on crops during these seasons indicate a lower rate of failure than that implied in the interview results. It is likely that the farmers' tendency not to accept responsibility for their delinquency is a major reason for attributing defaults to this reason.

•Defects in the credit organization. Deficiencies in the credit organization accounted for 17 percent of defaulting borrowers. It is significant that 9 percent of defaulters said they would have returned the loaned funds if cooperative officials had not been indifferent, taking no active steps to recover loans. A further 8 percent of defaulters said they did not return funds because they felt cooperative officials would not return the money to the bank. The survey report is replete with observations on the lack of interest, poor supervision, and unsatisfactory record keeping of cooperatives.

•Attitudinal conditions. Despite the tendency of defaulters to attribute their delinquency to circumstances beyond their control or to blame it on others, 18 percent of the loans were not repaid because 16 percent of the defaulters felt no obligation to repay. These defaulters stated they considered loans outright grants, expected the defaults to be written off, or simply had no intention of repaying.

• Misallocation. About 15 percent of the loans were not repaid because 15 percent of the defaulters had used the money for unauthorized expenditures such as unforeseen expenses connected with an illness or death, legal and ceremonial expenditure, settlement of debts from other sources, or for other activities which were either not profitable or illiquid.

• Miscellaneous. Other reasons not easily categorized accounted for about 7 percent of defaulters and 5 percent of defaults. These reasons included alleged malpractices of government officials and political interference.

Policies for Reducing Defaults

Since the causes for default are interrelated, as noted earlier, resolving the problem requires an integrated approach. For analytical clarity, however, the measures for resolving each of the reasons for default are discussed separately.

Defects in agrarian production must be remedied by measures which overcome the specific defects. Where the basic problem is the small size of holdings, land redistribution may be necessary. Where tenancy conditions impose high rentals, land reform may provide relief. Inadequate marketing facilities may be remedied by the provision of new channels, improvement of roads and transport, and sometimes government purchase of produce at minimum guaranteed prices. Agricultural credit is only one facet of agricultural development, and credit policies by themselves will be ineffective if structural problems are not resolved.

Defaults owing to the variability in incomes caused by seasonal or fortuitous circumstances are more specific. Where there has been a crop loss, a postponement or rescheduling of the loan payment is one means by which the farmer's inability to repay could be handled. Crop insurance could also be used to enable farmers to repay loans from indemnities obtained at times of crop failure. Where the fall in farm revenue has been due to a sudden fall in prices, price fluctuations could be cushioned by a minimum guaranteed price for agricultural produce.

Improvement in the efficiency of the credit-disbursing organization is fundamental to decreasing the incidence of defaults. Improvements generally needed include better management and better-paid officials, a system of credit supervision, farm management data on borrowers, and proper accounting.

A reluctance to repay loans from the government or cooperatives has often been created by governments themselves. Political considerations have impelled administrations to abandon efforts to collect unrepaid loans; where such a policy has been adopted, borrowers tend to expect similar amnesties in the future. Therefore one essential need is for a clear and unambiguous position of the government that loans will not be forgiven.

The independence of a credit program from the government may ensure a better attitude among farmers toward repayment. Some countries have therefore transferred credit programs to the regular banking system and provided guarantees on defaults to encourage commercial banks to enter the field of lending to small farmers without collateral. This is necessary, as most commercial banks need to develop supervisory systems for this type of lending. Yet the continuation of guarantees at high levels could cause a lax attitude toward the recovery of loans, and the banks might fail to develop a capacity to deal with small farmers. Therefore guarantees should be used only to initiate lending by these institutions, and it should be made clear that these guarantees will be gradually withdrawn.

The inability of credit organizations to compel borrowers to repay and their lack of effective sanctions are major factors creating a lax attitude among borrowers, but the insistence on collateral is an unsatisfactory solution. Group lending has sometimes been adopted to ensure a sense of responsibility for repayment. The basis of this approach is that in some cultures the borrower would be reluctant to let down his fellow farmers who are liable in case he defaults. Even where there is no such orientation, it is argued that the joint liability would ensure group pressure on the defaulting members. At worst, the members of the group suffer the loss rather than the lending agency.

Three strategies appear to be necessary to resolve the problem of high default rates. First, fundamental deficiencies in the agrarian structure should be remedied, and supporting services developed to make small farm units viable. Second, policies should be developed to cope with fortuitous and seasonal crop failures, either by adjustment of credit repayment conditions or by a program of crop insurance. Third, and most important, the credit-disbursing agency should be strengthened; it must develop the capability to ascertain the creditworthiness of borrowers and must have a system of surveillance of funds.

21. *Agricultural Credit and Rural Progress in Jamaica*

Douglas H. Graham and Compton Bourne

[Public sector agricultural credit institutions in Jamaica show the extremes of an output planner's approach to credit as contrasted to a banker's approach. Agricultural output grew in the 1970s in an otherwise depressed economy, but all the government credit programs were swamped by severe delinquency problems.]

The agricultural credit system in Jamaica has experienced substantial growth, institutional changes, and financial difficulties in the 1970s. This history takes on special poignancy in the light of the island's economic difficulties in the post-1974 recession and energy-deficit world and the hopes, inspired in the early 1970s, that a new democratic political order with a socialist program would guide Jamaica's future. A political mandate for increased public sector activity and redistributive policies coincided with a shift in world economic conditions that severely compromised the island's growth potential. This was the context within which changes in rural credit institutions and strategies occurred.

Economic Growth and Stagnation

During the late 1960s and early 1970s, the Jamaican economy registered respectable rates of growth (6 percent for real gross domestic product), although this was not true of the agricultural sector, which declined at an average annual rate of 4 percent. During the mid-1970s, however, there was a severe economic recession. The gross domestic product decreased between 1973 and 1978 by an average of 2.8 percent each year. While manufacturing, construction, and commerce declined at average annual rates of 7, 10, and 8 percent respectively, agriculture was the only productive sector to experience positive growth at 3 percent.

Revised and condensed version of "Agricultural Credit and Rural Progress in Jamaica: A Development Dilemma," in *Borrowers & Lenders*, edited by John Howell (London: Overseas Development Institute, 1980), pp. 59–80.

This dismal economic growth experience was associated with sharp contractions in domestic savings and investment. Domestic savings which averaged 17 percent of gross national product between 1965 and 1970, averaged only 10 percent between 1971 and 1975, becoming negative thereafter. Real net capital formation contracted almost continuously from J$250 million in 1970 to J$29 million in 1977. A growing deficit in the balance of payments had a seriously debilitating effect on the economy. Net foreign reserves fell from J$130 million in 1974 to *minus* J$196 million in 1977 to place Jamaica on the verge of international bankruptcy. Annual inflation rates (with the consumer price index as the measure) rose from 9 percent in 1972 to 48 percent in 1978. Interest rates, ranging from 2 to 12 percent on bank deposits and 7 to 12 percent on government securities during these years, did not keep pace with inflation; negative real rates of interest of 8 to 40 percent prevailed.

In summary, the Jamaican economy experienced a long economic decline after 1972, with the agricultural sector the principal area of positive growth. The extent to which the substantial credit flows described below contributed to Jamaican agricultural performance is a matter of some controversy. We argue that fundamental weaknesses in the design and operation of the public sector credit programs undermined the effectiveness as well as the viability of rural credit institutions in Jamaica.

The National Network of Agricultural Credit

The five major sources of formal agricultural credit in Jamaica in the 1970s were the commercial banks, the Agricultural Credit Board, the Jamaica Development Bank, the Self-Supporting Farmers Development Program (SSFDP), and the Crop Lien Program. Commercial banks are the largest single source; this credit is largely short-term and goes to medium-size and large farmers with good credit ratings and limited risks.

The remaining agricultural credit sources are public sector institutions or programs. The oldest of these is the Agricultural Credit Board created in 1960. This institution has two portfolios: one serves large farmers through direct loans; the other, for small farmers, is channeled through the national network of small People's Cooperative Banks. Loans in both cases are largely short-term and seasonal and, in the case of the People's Cooperative Banks, small in value.

The Jamaica Development Bank began making large, medium- to long-term development loans to medium-size and large farmers in 1969. The SSFDP was also established in 1969 to make medium- to long-term loans to small farmers; limitations on farm acreage, gross sales, and assets have created a clientele for the SSFDP that can best be characterized as medium-size. Finally, there is the Crop Lien Program created by the government in 1977 and administered by the Ministry of Agriculture through extension agents in conjunction with the People's Cooperative Banks which disburse these loans. Crop Lien loans are strictly small, short-term, seasonal, and limited to domestic foodstuff producers and small farmers with little or no previous loan experience.

The value of loans outstanding from these five major sources grew almost sevenfold in nominal terms in eight years from J$25 million in 1970 to J$168 million in 1975. But as a result of the inflation this increase was only a doubling in real terms. In 1978 there was practically no change in amount of credit in nominal terms, and a pronounced contraction in real terms.

Institutional Shifts

Table 21-1 indicates the changing roles of the several institutions and programs making up the agricultural credit supply network during the 1970s. The sources are classified by the farm size that most typically reflects the majority of their portfolio. From this profile it can be seen that large farmers benefited handsomely from the agricultural credit initiatives in Jamaica during the 1970s. Commercial banks and

Table 21-1. *Total Agricultural Loans Outstanding at End of Year by Farm Size and Source, Selected Years, Jamaica*
(percent)

Farm size and source	*1971*	*1974*	*1976*	*1977*	*1978*
Large farmers and cooperatives	45.8	60.8	77.4	72.0	68.2
Commercial banks	39.1	44.2	60.2	54.4	48.8
Agricultural Credit Board (direct loans)	4.7	4.2	3.0	2.9	3.4
Jamaica Development Bank	2.0	12.4	14.2	14.7	16.0
Medium-size farmers	13.2	16.2	11.5	12.7	14.9
Self-Supporting Farmers Development Program	13.2	16.2	11.5	12.7	14.9
Small farmers	40.9	22.9	11.0	15.2	16.9
Agricultural Credit Board (People's Cooperative)	40.9	22.9	11.0	9.5	9.9
Crop Lien Program	—	—	—	5.7	7.0
Total (percent)	100.0	100.0	100.0	100.0	100.0
Total (millions of Jamaican dollars)	30.5	60.1	136.7	165.8	167.8

— Not applicable.

the Jamaica Development Bank increased their relative portfolio substantially until 1977 while, at the other end of the spectrum, the small-farmer program of the Agricultural Credit Board and People's Cooperative Banks was losing ground. In 1977 and 1978, however, there was an improvement in the credit share of small farmers. Two factors accounted for the later shift: first, the Crop Lien Program was established, and the People's Cooperative credit expanded; second, commercial banks reduced their lending to agriculture. The Crop Lien Program was the largest source of credit increase that year, eclipsing the customarily dominant role of commercial banks within the total portfolio. No doubt the substantial erosion of the older small-farmer credit line through the Agricultural Credit Board had caused sufficient concern and grievances that a new initiative was felt necessary to redress this imbalance. Unfortunately this initiative led to substantial problems of default.

A large proportion of the loanable resources of the Jamaica Development Bank and the SSFDP come from foreign sources—the World Bank, the Caribbean Development Bank, and the Inter-American Development Bank. Domestic sources were geared almost exclusively to short-term seasonal loans—through commercial banks, the Agricultural Credit Board, and the Crop Lien Program—whereas foreign resources were earmarked for medium- to long-term developmental loans. As the most rapidly growing source of funding for agricultural credit between 1974 and 1978, international financing was crucial to the expansion of total credit supply during the 1970s and, more important, indispensable in lengthening the term structure. Growing problems of delinquency and declining foreign exchange earnings, however, raise serious questions as to whether Jamaica will be able to secure new international financing for these activities.

Performance

Table 21-2 shows how total credit has been rising as a percentage of gross domestic product (GDP) in the 1970s, reflecting the growing rate of inflationary financing through substantial increases in the money supply. Agricultural credit constituted roughly 8 percent of total credit. The ratio of agricultural credit to agricultural GDP increased from 32 percent in 1970 to 53 percent in 1978.

The ratio of agricultural credit to agricultural GDP has been rising in recent years because many of the loans outstanding are deadwood, that is, in permanent default. Much of the loan capital was probably diverted to nonagricultural uses because of the growing stagnation in the economy as a whole. Credit may have been leaking out of the economy as capital flight, as well as into real estate, land, and other inflation hedges.

Table 21-2. *Credit Ratios for the Jamaican Agricultural Credit System, 1970–78*

Year	*Total credit/ total GDP*	*Agricultural credit/ total credit*	*Agricultural credit/ agricultural GDP*
1970	27.2	7.8	32.3
1971	30.8	7.6	30.7
1972	31.5	6.4	33.0
1973	41.2	6.8	38.2
1974	41.2	6.5	36.9
1975	46.7	9.1	55.8
1976	55.3	8.9	60.1
1977	61.1	9.9	62.6
1978	62.1	7.8	53.2

Sources: Bank of Jamaica, *Statistical Digest*, various years; Government of Jamaica, Department of Statistics, *Income and Product*, various years.

The final issue warranting discussion in this section is the implicit subsidy built into the current credit programs (see table 21-3). The interest rate charged for agricultural credit ranged from a low of 3 to 7 percent in government programs to 13 to 14 percent in commercial banks, and the average of about 10 percent was clearly below the rate of inflation (column 1). The net result was negative real rates of interest (column 3). The real rate of interest times the ratio of agricultural credit to agricultural GDP gives an estimate of the implicit credit subsidy as a percentage of agricultural GDP. Column 5 shows that in 1978 this reached 9 percent, a high level by any standard. If the currently defaulted loans are never repaid, the subsidy will be several times larger.

Thus, credit appears to be increasingly used in inappropriate (that is, nonagricultural) or inefficient ways, while the beneficiaries (borrowers) are enjoying a sizable subsidy. The social costs of this credit strategy are substantial, especially when relatively large landowners form an important fraction of the beneficiaries.

Arrears and Institutional Viability

In evaluating the performance of the Jamaican rural financial market, an important question is whether its institutions are financially viable. Central to the issue of viability is the loan repayment experience of lenders. Table 21-4 summarizes the arrears record for all the Jamaican institutions and programs. Although the commercial banks have respectable recovery rates (low arrears), all the public sector programs record alarmingly high arrears rates. This raises a serious question as to whether any of the latter programs are financially viable. To place this issue in context, the large-farmer and small-farmer programs are discussed separately even though arrears are high in both cases.

Large-farmer Programs

The arrears experience of the Jamaica Development Bank (JDB) is the classic case of the large-farmer delinquency problem. The JDB was established in 1970 to service fairly large capital-intensive activities through investments in dairy or beef herds, dairy equipment, tractors, pumps, new pastures, fencing, wells, irrigation, new plantation crops, and so on. These investments were financed by large loans, which made up the greater part of annual net flows of agricultural credit. Any serious problem in delinquency in this program affects an important component of the total credit portfolio and, moreover, one that is allegedly on the cutting edge of the modernization drive in Jamaican agriculture.

The JDB did not keep its accounts in a way that revealed the arrears until recently, when pressed to do so by its international creditors. Insufficient attention was paid to designing appropriate arrears measures and setting up the machinery for effective and timely collections. There was also a deficiency in loan appraisals, despite the early emphasis on staffing this division at the expense of the collection division; arbitrary interference with established loan review procedures was common. In retrospect, the institution has paid dearly for this behavior with rising arrears rates and low staff morale. One can only conclude that the JDB obtained more loan funds from international agencies than it could manage. Newspaper disclosures about the bank's management must have helped increase farmers' resistance to repayment. The macroeconomic situation also contributed to arrears problems by depressing gross incomes and the debt repayment ability of farmers.

Small-farmer Programs

Table 21-4 shows that the arrears performance of the small-farmer credit programs, with one exception, is no better than that for the large-farmer JDB program. The old line program of the Agricultural Credit Board and the People's Cooperative Banks records arrears on about 40 percent of the loans outstanding. The accounts are not designed to generate an arrears measure on amounts due; no doubt the latter are considerably higher, since there are medium-term loans in the portfolio.

The relative importance of the Agricultural Credit Board (ACB) program has declined, and its reputation suffered as a result of its long-standing arrears problem. Accounting and managerial practices are deficient, and loan appraisal and collection procedures perfunctory. The Self-Supporting Farmers Development Program, originally

Table 21-3. *Estimates of Real Rate of Interest for Agricultural Credit and Implicit Credit Subsidy as Percentage of Agricultural GDP*

Year	*Rate of inflation* (1)	*Average nominal interest rate on agricultural loans* (2)	*Real rate of interest (2) − (1)* (3)	*Agricultural credit/agricultural GDP* (4)	*Credit subsidy as percentage of agricultural GDP*[a] (5)
1975	15.7	10.0	−5.7	55.8	3.2
1976	8.2	10.0	+1.8	60.1	0
1977	14.0	10.0	−4.0	62.6	2.5
1978	27.9	10.0	−17.9	53.2	9.5

a. Subsidy as a percentage of agricultural GDP is estimated by taking the proportion of total outstanding agricultural credit to total agricultural GDP (column 4) and multiplying it by the negative rate of interest (column 3).

Sources: Bank of Jamaica, *Statistical Digest*, various years; Government of Jamaica, Department of Statistics, *National Income and Product*, various years.

Table 21-4. *Arrears Percentages for Selected Agricultural Credit Institutions and Programs in Jamaica, Middle to Late 1970s*

Credit institution and program	*Arrears as percentage of amounts due*	*Arrears as percentage of total loans outstanding*
Commercial banks, 1978[a]	4.4	4.4
Public sector agricultural credit programs		
Jamaica Development Bank (commercial window)		
1974	n.a.	2.2
1976	81.2	8.2
1978	82.6	19.6
SSFDP, 1978	38.0	18.0
Agricultural Credit Board (People's Cooperative Banks), 1978	n.a.	39.0
Crop Lien Program (Ministry of Agriculture), 1978	94.6[b]	94.6[b]

n.a. Not available.

a. From the files of a commercial bank in Jamaica in 1978. Commercial banks classify a debt as in danger or arrears according to a variety of factors in the judgment of a loan officer. The loan does not have to be formally due to be so classified and, conversely, a loan may be overdue but not be in danger of nonpayment.

b. Amounts due and loans outstanding are the same on this seasonal loan program.

Source: Loan files of the institutions and programs.

established within the ACB in 1969, was transferred to the JDB in 1974. When the Crop Lien Program was established in 1977, it was located in the Ministry of Agriculture instead of the ACB. Government budgetary support to cover the ACB's overhead, deficits, and new loan capital has diminished in favor of newer public sector programs, and the institution is now engaged in a holding action on a diminishing resource base.

The Crop Lien Program is the most recent initiative to reach the small farmer. Launched in 1977 in an effort to stimulate local foodstuff production and save on foreign exchange for food imports, the program was widely publicized and apparently did reach a large number of farmers. Roughly J$9.5 million were disbursed in short-term loans to some 30,000 farmers. Reportedly, farmers with loans from a commercial bank, the Jamaica Development Bank, or the SSFDP were ineligible. Repayments were expected to be voluntary with little if any inducement needed; but, as is clear from table 21-4, the program was a complete financial failure with only a 6 percent recovery rate after a year and a half of operation. Clearly a "grants mentality" was operating with no serious sanctions for default, nor any serious consequences for the officials responsible.

The SSFDP had arrears rates of 38 percent for the amounts due and 18 percent for loans outstanding. This is respectable only by comparison with the JDB, ACB, or Crop Lien Program. Moreover, the lower arrears ratio comes with a price, namely, a high cost of supervision that is largely absent from the other programs. A highly decentralized system of field officers with separate staffs for loan appraisal, technical assistance, and loan collection ensures close monitoring of loans by personnel close to the farmer and local conditions. By contrast, the JDB conducts all these operations out of one central office.

Conclusions

Jamaica in the 1970s vacillated between a planners' and a bankers' perspective on agricultural credit strategies. The plan-oriented Ministry of Agriculture has always viewed credit in terms of its end use. After the targets for agricultural output have been established, all policy instruments are directed toward those production goals, and credit programs are launched to service the production programs. The most recent example is the Crop Lien Program. Nonrepayment of loans is considered of lesser importance than substantially increased output of domestic foodstuffs. There is an implicit assumption that the opportunity cost of public funds is low.

The bankers' perspective is less concerned with production per se and more concerned with institutional viability. Bankers focus on the proper evaluation and administration of loans and on charging a sufficient rate of interest to cover costs; they are determined to protect their cash flow through low arrears (with emphasis on collateral and foreclosure) and tend to be pessimistic about the possibilities of lending to small farmers. The JDB and SSFDP credit strategies reflect this thinking in some degree. In the JDB, however, poor performance has not only damaged the institution but also compromised its credit strategy.

Delivering public sector credit to small farmers has proven difficult in most countries, and Jamaica is no exception. Quick and widespread dissemination of loans invariably transforms credit programs into ad hoc income transfers. Although careful supervision of small-farmer loans may reduce arrears, the high costs of supervision limit the scope of the program. In the end, a supervised program may not be much more cost-effective than a low-cost, unsupervised program with high defaults. More helpful would be a package of agricultural policies that distributes inputs in kind at subsidized cost and promotes minimum price programs and marketing arrangements that reduce income variance. Policies promoting off-farm employment and income opportunities in rural areas could also improve the economic welfare of small-farm families. In addition, informal credit channels are very likely providing funds to more small farmers than are the inequitably administered credit programs with high default rates.

Economic stagnation has constrained the prospects for financial reform and recovery in Jamaica. Under more normal circumstances the growing distortions in the financial sector, which cause negative real rates of interest and inequitable credit subsidies, could be dealt with through interest rate reform. The declining rate of savings and implicit taxation of small savers for the benefit of larger borrowers could be corrected in the same way. The constraint on this otherwise sensible strategy is the weak demand for loans in a severe economic recession. High liquidity in the commercial banks suggests that banks were unable to find customers at significantly higher loan rates while overall inflation rates were high and economic recovery not yet under way. These conditions create poor prospects for rapidly eliminating the inequitable and inefficient credit subsidies through negative real rates of interest. Savings continue to be penalized, and various forms of nonprice rationing allocate public sector credit.

22. *The ACAR Program in Minas Gerais, Brazil*

Clifton R. Wharton, Jr.

[The first twenty years of a rural development program suggest that extension education is much easier to expand than supervised credit, in terms of both the number of people reached and the number of services offered. Credit to early adopters appears to yield excellent returns, but no firm conclusions are possible.]

In 1948 the American International Association for Economic and Social Development (AIA, a nonprofit corporation based in New York), at the invitation of the state government of Minas Gerais, Brazil, organized a rural development program called the Associacão de Credito e Assistencia Rural, usually called ACAR. It was organized as a nonprofit society to give assistance to the farm families of the state, mainly through supervised credit and extension education. Five years after its establishment, ACAR was recognized as a successful approach to rural development and began to be widely copied by other states in Brazil. In 1956 a national organization, ABCAR (Associacão Brasileira de Credito e Assistencia Rural), was set up by AIA and the Brazilian government to develop programs similar to ACAR in other states. The experience with ACAR in Minas Gerais offers a useful case study of methods and techniques of planned change for low-income farmers in traditional agriculture.

The Low-income Farmer of Minas Gerais

The conditions of life of the typical small farmer in Minas Gerais are like those of farmers in other developing areas. His family lives in a small, unsanitary, and uncomfortable house, usually far from a supply of water. Poor nutrition, hygiene, and water undermine health and in turn limit the capacity for work. Isolation and lack of communication restrict the family to the small local community, except for a few religious ceremonies. If any member of the family receives any educa-

Extracted from *Change in Agriculture*, edited by A. H. Bunting (London: Gerald Duckworth, 1970), pp. 525–32.

tion, it seldom goes beyond the third grade. All the farm labor is provided by the family, and farming methods are entirely traditional, handed down from father to son following an ancestral chain of custom. Any small surplus of farm produce over what the family itself needs goes to the local merchant in exchange for needed commodities. Hence the farmer knows little of commercial marketing. Usually the net income is so small that no basic improvements can be introduced in farm operations or in the home. (There are also large commercial farmers in the area, not to mention some very big cattle ranches; these were not the target of ACAR activities.)

The agricultural practices of small farmers in Minas Gerais are essentially primitive. Slash-and-burn agriculture is common. On a single farmstead, only a fraction of the total land will be cultivated in any year while the rest lies fallow before being burned over for use once again. Draft animals are still the main source of farm power; simple hand tools such as hoes and sickles predominate; fertilizer is rarely used, and then inadequately. On most farms all types of capital are in short supply, and what little credit is available generally goes to the large farms. The bulk of credit for the small farmers flows through private channels—merchants, warehousemen, and affluent neighbors. Credit is usually short term, not exceeding two years, and is used to finance farm work or consumption. Such credit is rarely available for long-term investment or improved farm inputs.

Improved technology and credit formed the basic, initial core of the ACAR program, though its activities quickly broadened into other areas.

The ACAR Program

ACAR's general objectives have remained virtually unchanged since its inception: "To intensify agricultural production and to improve the economic and social conditions of rural life. This objective will be accomplished through the continuation of its linked system of: (a) rural extension to take to rural families, through direct educational action, knowledge for the betterment of their agricultural and home economics practices, as well as to promote changes in their habits and attitudes as a means to attain better economic, social and cultural levels; (b) rural supervised credit aiming to habilitate technically, economically and socially, small and medium farm families and to better their living conditions through the use of credit based upon farm and home management plans and the techniques imparted during the subsequent supervision" (agreement of February 1960).

Field activities are carried out by state, regional, and local offices. Each of the fourteen regional offices in the state takes care of an average of eight local offices. There are 120 local offices working directly with farm families and communities, each staffed by an agricultural supervisor, a home supervisor, and a clerk. In 1964 ACAR had a staff of about 550 and reached more than 3 million people a year through various activities, having expanded from a modest beginning with three local offices in 1949.

Extension Education

ACAR's activities in extension education reached a substantial fraction of farm people. In 1964 more than 50,000 meetings and demonstrations were held, attended by some 750,000 persons. ACAR has employed most of the known extension methods for diffusing new farm and home practices—youth clubs, women's clubs, nutrition and health projects, community exhibits, meetings and demonstrations, county extension committees, leadership training projects, technical bulletins, and radio programs.

The relative importance of extension education in the ACAR program has grown through the years. Although extension was included from the very beginning, the supervised credit program was initially more important. Today, ACAR functions mainly as a broadly aimed state extension service. It undertakes a wide range of activities only in selected areas rather than throughout whole counties (*municipios*). Individual and group activities are concentrated among those farmers and in those areas that seem to have better prospects for rapid development and that may serve as points from which to spread new practices, ideas, and technologies to nonparticipating farmers.

With the establishment of rural extension committees in 1961, the general approaches of ACAR in different localities were coordinated toward predetermined objectives. Through the committees, local participants in various aspects of the ACAR program were able to offer suggestions about problems in their own community and helped form programs to resolve them. Together with leadership groups and adult groups, the committee did a great deal to involve rural people actively in the program and to increase their experience with local organization to deal with community problems.

Supervised Credit

The ACAR program of supervised credit has moved through three phases. In the earliest days, the program used traditional supervised approaches, with detailed planning for each farm. Selected farm families received short-term operational or production loans, together with individual planning and supervision of their farm operation during the year. As the number of farm families increased, a form of "oriented" credit was inaugurated which omitted such detailed planning and supervision. Later, the emphasis shifted to credit for farm families identified as early adopters. Credit for housing and for youth was also introduced in recent years.

ACAR does not make the supervised loans from its own funds but through the Caixa Economica do Estado de Minas Gerais, a state bank. ACAR does the planning and educational work, while the bank is responsible for the banking functions. ACAR recommends the loans to the bank for approval, and actual amounts in each case are decided on the basis of careful study by the technician and the farmer. The loans are for one to three years, depending on their purpose.

The funds available for the program have gradually increased over the years. In 1964 the Inter-American Development Bank lent the Caixa US$6.4 million to be used exclusively for the ACAR program. Until the 1963–64 crop year, when oriented credit and credit for housing were introduced, the number of loans ranged from 118 to 1,734 a year; they averaged about 1,300 from 1955–56 on. The loan repayment record of the borrower families has been extremely good. As of November 30, 1964, 99.95 percent of matured loans had been repaid.

Criticism of the Credit Program

Three criticisms of the ACAR credit program question the subsidized rates of interest, the cost of the program, and the actual impact of the program on farmer and state production and productivity.

Subsidized Interest Rates

Interest rates on ACAR loans range from 6 to 8 percent a year. Since inflation rates of more than 10 percent have been continuous in Brazil for many years, these interest rates constitute a significant subsidy. From 1939 to 1953 the general price index for Brazil increased at 12 percent a year. During the 1950s the rate of inflation fluctuated between 15 and 25 percent, but by 1964 it had reached a peak of 120 percent a year. At such rates of inflation, persons securing ACAR loans were in effect securing credit subsidies in real terms. Subsidy rates probably accounted for the continuously increasing demand for loans and the recurrent credit squeezes, which had to be applied because the rate of interest charged was below the equilibrium level. They undoubtedly had effects on the allocation of resources on the farms securing the loans.

Program Cost

A second major criticism of the ACAR credit program has been its high cost: the total cost of the program divided by the number of families receiving supervised credit; the total value of loans outstanding compared with the total cost of the ACAR program (credit plus extension); and the cost per family served under a supervised credit program compared with the cost per family served solely by an extension program. The first two criticisms are beside the point, since ACAR was never solely a credit program and its total costs included noncredit activities. If only the true costs of the credit programs are measured, then it might be valid to compare the return derived from such an expenditure on credit with the return from extension activities without credit.

A careful, detailed cost study was made of the ACAR program for 1953, which revealed that credit costs represented between 7 and 11 percent of the value of the average loan. If this cost is viewed as an investment in human capital and is compared with the value of the total change in annual output per farm not accounted for by changes in factor inputs, its investment yield is 650 percent:

Proportion of change in output	
Accounted for by change in input	44 percent
Not accounted for by change in input	56 percent
Value of total change in annual output per farm not accounted for by change in inputs	Cr$7,800
Average annual cost of assistance program per family	Cr$1,200
Return in increased output per Cr$1 of investment in new knowledge	Cr$6.5

We have no study on the return for a comparable expenditure for extension alone, as a basis for comparison. Even if there were such data they would probably refer to different groups, since the credit program and the extension program tend to serve different types of farm families.

Program Impact

The first study of ACAR was made by A.T. Mosher [*Case Study of the Agricultural Program of ACAR in Brazil*, Washington, D.C., National Planning Association, 1955], who employed measures of productivity such as net income and production per hectare, secured from the records of borrower families. Since most farmers had participated for only a few years, the results tended to be mixed. But the records of eighty-one borrowers who had received three or more loans showed a general upward trend in their net worth, especially among subsistence farmers.

A second more detailed study was made in 1958 of 126 selected borrower families in two areas from 1949 to 1954 [C. R. Wharton, Jr., "The Economic Impact of Technical Assistance: A Brazilian Case Study," *Journal of Farm Economics*, vol. 42, 1960, pp. 252–67]. Two measures were used to evaluate two effects of the program on the farmers: the change in their agricultural output through time, and the changes in their output-input ratios through time. Both measures were tested against similar ones for the state of Minas Gerais and for Brazil. The index of aggregate output for the ACAR borrowers on semisubsistence farms revealed a growth rate between 21 and 32 percent a year and a growth rate in productive efficiency between 7 and 16 percent a year. In commercial agriculture, however, the combined growth rate in aggregate output lay between 7 and 11 percent a year, while productive efficiency decreased at a rate between 3 and 7 percent a year. Output growth for the semisubsistence farms was significantly higher than for the state or for Brazilian agriculture as a whole. In the case of the efficiency measure of output-input ratios, the differences were more mixed. On the whole, increases for semisubsistence farms continued to be significantly above the state and national trends, though not as dramatically as in the case of output, while commercial farms showed little difference.

The study of ACAR by E. R. de A. Alves ["An Economic Evaluation of an Extension Program, Minas Gerais, Brazil," M.A. thesis, Purdue University, 1968] used a measure of economic efficiency with two elements, price and technical efficiency (the relative ability to select the most appropriate technology). These measures were determined from a sample of sixty farmers who worked with ACAR and another sixty farmers not assisted by ACAR. Alves found that technical efficiency was greater and price efficiency smaller among the non-ACAR farmers than among the ACAR farmers, a result exactly opposite to what one would expect. Alves advances possible reasons for the contrary result such as noncomparability, errors in memory and enumeration, and difficulties in measuring difference in managerial abilities. Of the possible explanations, the one with the greatest logical and intuitive appeal is the probable effect of the subsidy rates of interest on ACAR loans in the context of general inflation. At the time of the Alves study the rate of inflation was around 80 percent. Under these conditions farmers who borrow may be trying to build up assets rather than maximize income.

Despite the positive and negative findings of the various studies, any overall assessment of the ACAR program would conclude that it has been quite successful in a number of ways and in a number of areas. In addition to the tangible evidence of the successful effect of ACAR, the program has expanded rapidly within the state and served as a model for similar programs in other states of Brazil.

23. *Innovative Approaches to Agricultural Credit in the INVIERNO/PROCAMPO Project in Nicaragua*

David Bathrick and G. Gomez Casco

[In its first three years, INVIERNO issued 20,000 loans to 8,500 small farmers in an integrated rural development project and suffered a delinquency rate of 10 percent. Project designers sought to provide a comprehensive set of services to project participants, supported by a computerized information system with integrated management for all project components.]

The purpose of this chapter is to describe an integrated rural development project developed in Nicaragua, originally called INVIERNO, which obtained some favorable results with the use of innovative methods that could be of interest in other countries. Modern managerial techniques made it possible to extend credit to large numbers of poor farmers with an unusual degree of efficiency.

Background

From the mid-1930s until the late 1960s, Nicaraguan development policies emphasized growth through the promotion of diversified export crops. Large amounts of agricultural credit were provided to large- and medium-size producers. This commitment to growth objectives gave Nicaragua the highest agricultural growth rate between 1950 and 1964 of any Latin American country. But little attention was directed to small farmers, and commercial credit institutions did not lend much to the small producer. Certain policies promoted the purchase of labor-replacing farm equipment. Beginning in the mid-1960s, rural unemployment increased, and rural wages in real terms began

For a detailed review of this project, see David Bathrick, *Agricultural Credit for Small Farm Development: Policies and Practices* (Boulder, Colo.: Westview Press, 1980).

declining. Yields for maize and beans, the basic domestic crops, declined.

In 1972, responding to this growing dilemma, the government undertook a major rural assessment. This two-year study served as the basis for a major change in agricultural policy. An expansion of the small-farmer sector, the study argued, would generate higher real income, which in turn would provide the effective demand for the basic goods and services produced by other rural dwellers; and this objective was adopted.

Such a strategy required a reorientation of public agricultural service institutions from serving large commercial farmers to helping the rural poor. It was decided a new institution was required to provide integrated development services combining banking with other activities. In May 1975, INVIERNO—the Peasant Farmers Development Institute—was created. Chartered as a development bank, INVIERNO was allowed to attempt a major transformation of rural Nicaragua. The project was funded by a government commitment of $33 million over a five-year period, complemented by a $12 million loan from the U.S. Agency for International Development. Given the broad mandate of INVIERNO, it is of interest to observe the innovative activities developed to address the inherently conflicting objectives of equity and efficiency.

Innovative Operational Features

The initial field activity was setting up an agricultural credit program with supporting services for extension, the supply of inputs, and the marketing of output. To test various systems prior to the large-scale provision of services, INVIERNO focused on a few regions, and some of the more innovative operational features were developed in a pilot area.

Because of poor rural roads, limited transportation facilities, the absence of basic agricultural inputs in the market towns, and the low level of agricultural technologies used, basic services had to be brought to the communities. All credit transactions were to be provided by mobile banks, and the communities would receive extension assistance, input supplies, and marketing services.

The original region served by INVIERNO had the largest number of small producers and the lowest rural family incomes in the country. The program's basic service could not be provided to all small farmers in this region. The areas selected for project services were less than twenty-five kilometers from the zonal office and had a minimum population density, proximity to a serviceable road, and some agricultural potential.

To minimize the costs within the eligible communities, a promotion campaign was undertaken to attract as many local participants as possible. This made field visits less expensive per client served. Community leaders were selected and instructed about the INVIERNO program in order to promote interest and to coordinate the scheduling of services with participants' needs.

Central Management Services

To ensure better control of the field operations in isolated rural communities, a series of centrally monitored management services was developed. A brief description of each follows:

• Project planning. Clearly defined annual project objectives were prepared as a basis for periodic cross-checks. An input-output planning approach provided management with reference points, ensured that required resources were programmed, and served as a basis for preparing operational instruction manuals.

• Operational systems manuals. Supported by a large in-service training program, manuals covering all aspects of field activities were prepared. Such manuals helped ensure that newly hired field personnel would have reference materials from which uniform services could be provided.

• Internal auditing. Attention was directed to the auditing of zonal office operations. The auditors talked with program beneficiaries. During the first year of field operations, 13 percent of the agricultural credit loans received a detailed audit of client and INVIERNO records. Such rigorous independent attention served to uncover administrative problems and to clarify clients' impressions of INVIERNO field operations.

• Cost monitoring. A system was developed to monitor the high social overhead—the nonbanking side of the INVIERNO program costs. Costs that would have been incurred if INVIERNO had functioned only as a commercial bank were separated from the promotional and social development costs—which normally would be funded from government resources. A distribution reflecting the allocation of staff time to each category was prepared for a master reference chart.

• Computer applications. One of the most innovative elements in the execution, monitoring, and evaluation of the project was the extensive use of computers. Beyond the traditional computer applications for standard accounting purposes, a series of programs was developed to facilitate the rapid and efficient processing of a large number of individual credit applications and to provide management information concerning input requirements and loan repayments. Such a system provided rapid data analysis to assist project management to make periodic adjustments.

Development of Skills

The INVIERNO program combined agricultural and social skills through the creation of the "Agromoc," a graduate in vocational agriculture who was given training in group motivation and organization. INVIERNO developed a four-month program for vocational school graduates that emphasized group dynamics and consciousness raising. This training program was designed to help extensionists convince groups of farmers of the importance of introducing changes in their agricultural practices. The program reduced the number of field staff required, since only one or two professional "social promoters" were assigned to each zonal office to backstop the Agromocs' work.

Credit System

Traditional supervised credit was thought inappropriate, too elaborate, and cumbersome, since the INVIERNO priority was the rapid economic improvement of many small farmers. Special systems were created to reach large numbers of isolated farmers lacking collateral and needing only small amounts of capital. Some of the features are the following:

• Loan application. As a result of using mobile banks, loan applications could be made in the local community. The application was a simple two-page form, using numerical codes to facilitate electronic processing. Basic information on land tenure, age, and farm plan was recorded. The review process attempted to ascertain, among other things, the creditworthiness of applicants. The application process was usually completed in one day.

• Loan processing. The applications approved by a community board were passed along for computer processing. Rapid approval of a large number of applications was made possible by the use of uniform decision-making criteria at a lower cost than most manual systems. All applicants were reviewed against a standard scale that established point rankings for acceptance or rejection. No follow-up visit by either party was required. The entire transaction was done rapidly: in early 1978 more than 10,000 applications were processed during a one-week period.

• Line of credit. To reduce loan transaction costs for both client and lender and to give clients a greater sense of security and a commitment to farm development, a five-year line of credit was established with an approved borrower. During the original application process, the client was determined to be eligible for a total amount, which was computer-processed at the time the loan was approved. The approved clients received a computer-processed contract specifying the amount that could be borrowed. The clients meeting contract conditions could, in each planting season, draw down the amount set during the application phase. The system avoided the additional costs usually encountered in processing additional loan contracts for the same client. By maintaining one comprehensive account per client, INVIERNO reduced operational costs.

• Loan disbursement. Loan disbursements were made in the community, and required inputs could be purchased at that time. Money was authorized for multiple purposes including oxen rental, contract labor costs, and family maintenance. The individual farm plans described in the application form were cross-checked against the computerized farm plan criteria so that standardized "recommended" purchases and amounts could be established. These recommended levels were then negotiated by the Agromoc with the client.

• Loan repayment. Traditional commercial loan repayment arrangements seldom take into account the uncertainties of agriculture. Consequently, both institution and client are very often forced to change loan repayment plans. INVIERNO handled this problem by adjusting the repayment terms to the client's estimated capacity to pay, which was based on average yields and prices in each area minus allowances for family maintenance. In unfavorable periods a reduced payment would reflect those conditions; and during periods of higher yields, larger amounts would have to be repaid. Over time, the bad and good times would balance out.

Outcome

A good measure of program success is farmer response. As of June 1978, over 20,000 loans had been disbursed to 8,500 small farmers. The average farm unit was under two hectares and received on the average a loan equivalent to US$175. Few projects can claim such a widespread participation of small farmers. During this period, maize yields per hectare doubled in comparison with the yields of traditional methods, and the use of modern technology increased appreciably. Unlike many small-farmer credit programs, loan repayment was quite satisfactory. A 1977 evaluation of the project reported a delinquency rate of 10.4 percent.

Because of high start-up costs and the large portfolio of small loans, immediate self-sufficiency of this program could not be expected, even with good repayment and an 18 percent interest rate. However, the operational systems being developed to reduce costs, the gradual expansion of the project, and the increasing emphasis on new technology to diversify farm operation and thus increase average loan sizes were moving this program toward financial self-sufficiency.

Another measure of the worth of the INVIERNO program, which was started before the 1978–79 civil war, is the response of the revolutionary government. It would have been natural to dismantle this program of the former government after the revolution. Instead, the new government chose to expand INVIERNO's scope substantially. Although its name was changed to PROCAMPO, much of the system remained intact.

Conclusions

This brief account is not intended to present a model for application to similar environments. More space would be necessary to permit full development of the many aspects that might have application elsewhere. Three general points, however, could be of value to professionals developing credit facilities for the rural poor.

The INVIERNO experience supports the opinion that programs designed to accelerate the modernization of agriculture should deliver comprehensive services at the community level. The provision of local services to as many farmers as possible not only facilitates the diffusion of technology but also reduces operational costs.

The program provides one of the first case studies on innovative computer applications to facilitate rapid and efficient processing of credit applications, improve loan portfolio management, and reduce operational costs.

Appropriate management systems are necessary to ensure the efficient delivery of a variety of complex development services to isolated rural communities. Detailed attention to system design, review, staff training, evaluation, and modification ensured that integrated services were provided at the appropriate times.

Rural Agents for Urban Lenders

The proposal discussed in the two following chapters moves in the opposite direction from that in chapter 23, by Bathrick and Gomez Casco, to achieve similar objectives. Both seek to increase poor farmers' access to credit and simultaneously to decrease lenders' administrative costs. The INVIERNO/PROCAMPO project established a highly centralized, elaborately supervised system for this purpose, while Miracle (chapter 24) proposes a highly decentralized and informal approach. He suggests that formal credit institutions extend loans through individual loan agents, who reside in rural villages and operate in some ways like traditional moneylenders with minimal requirements for paperwork and approval procedures and no staff or formal office. A central problem is the motivation of the agents and the shaping of their relationship with the bank so that incentives, rather than direct supervision, can be relied on to achieve bank objectives, including repayment.

Wells (chapter 25) describes an extensive effort to apply one variant of this idea in a systematic way. A Malaysian government bank established to serve smallholders decided to channel some of its loans via small merchants (who had been lending money to farmers) as an alternative to lending through farmer associations, which are not well organized in some areas. Both types of intermediaries were subjected to more formal controls in loan approval and disbursement than Miracle suggests. The results of using the two intermediaries can be compared: both issued loans rapidly; the private merchants' loans showed a higher ratio of credit used to that approved, and a higher repayment rate, than the loans through farmer associations. This vindicated the controversial decision to rely on the private sector to lend public funds.

24. *Economic Incentives for Loan Agents*

Marvin P. Miracle

[Since credit institutions have difficulties dealing with small farmers in developing countries, it is proposed that loans be extended through local village agents closely acquainted with borrowers. Agents would be paid commissions based on their collection performance and on other functions determined by government policy.]

Many developing countries have attempted to establish institutions to provide small-farmer credit, and an amazing diversity of institutions has been tried. Most of these attempts, however, have had at best very limited success. Only a small percentage of small farmers are being reached by credit programs; administrative costs are high; and delinquency rates tend to be at least 20 percent of funds loaned. The great majority of these credit institutions have been supported or sponsored by governments, and failure to achieve financial viability (without subsidy) may be related to this fact.

For the most part, private banks have not been very active in agriculture except in the case of loans to large-scale farmers, especially those raising export crops. [See chapter 16 for a discussion of commercial bank lending to agriculture.] The best-documented efforts to make greater use of private rural banks in reaching small farmers with credit is in the Philippines and (briefly) in South Vietnam. Although differing in detail, the central features of both these programs are that the government provides financial incentives to private investors willing to create rural banks to serve small farmers. Through such incentives the government regulates these small local banks, including the percentage of their total loans that are made to small farmers and the interest rates charged. For example, the government of South Vietnam matched the amount of capital raised by the investors with interest-free capital and gave them a tax exemption for five years.

Lessons from the Informal Credit Market

The great majority of private lenders to agriculture are too small to create formal banking institutions, and may be called informal lenders.

Extracted from *AID Spring Review of Small Farmer Credit*, vol. 19 (1973), pp. 223–33.

The informal capital markets for small farmers in developing countries are made up of a noncommercial segment—loans from friends and relatives often made without interest—and the commercial segment in which loans are made through a variety of channels such as crop buyers, input dealers (suppliers of pesticides and fertilizers), landlords, and professional moneylenders. This informal capital market probably provides over 90 percent of total credit received by the small farmers of most developing countries—though this share is decreasing. This credit system seems to have much lower administrative costs and default rates than the formal banking system. At the same time, it provides services seen by farmers as superior to those available through most institutions in the formal capital market; this helps explain why small farmers are sometimes willing to pay interest rates three and four times as high as those charged in the formal capital market.

Administrative costs in the commercial segment of the informal capital market are low because it is an extremely decentralized system of dispensing credit. Lenders in this market have little if any overhead cost for real estate; they keep few written records; they charge no loan appraisal fee. Probably as important as their low costs is the nature of the service they provide. They can extend credit quickly—often within minutes after it is requested—and therefore provide it exactly when it is needed. They are equally flexible concerning repayment. Borrowers can repay in small amounts and at any time; but what may be more important is that the lender, because he knows his clients well, often learns of any significant sales of crops or livestock by his clients and can press for repayment before the client's income is used for other purposes.

Another extremely important aspect of the operation is the "nonformal" atmosphere of lending in this market. In sharp contrast to most government and private lenders in the formal market—who frequently go out of their way to exaggerate differences in status and seem to delight in making the borrower feel ill at ease—lenders in the commercial segment of the informal capital market work in an atmosphere in which the borrower is comfortable. This usually means a minimum of formal requirements or protocol, use of the borrower's language or dialect, and a rural style of dress. Moreover, the lender is usually available close to the borrower's home or the commercial centers he typically frequents, whereas formal credit institutions typically force many of their borrowers to journey a considerable distance and present themselves in unfamiliar surroundings.

Many features of the commercial segment of the informal capital market might be incorporated into institutions in a formal capital market. Proposals made by Daniel Goodman and Thomas Stickley in the *AID Spring Review of Small Farmer Credit* (1973) move in this direction. Goodman proposes that formal credit institutions develop incentive systems so that loan officers will be rewarded for good performance, such as achieving low default rates. The incentives he mentions include salary increments, promotions, and extra vacations.

Loan Agents and Incentives

Stickley's proposal deals with loan agents outside credit institutions and with only one incentive—a commission based on the rate of recovery on loans. Essentially he proposes a decentralized lending system in which the lending agency learns as much as possible from the commercial segment of the informal money market. He suggests that lending institutions trying to reach small farmers lend primarily through agents or loan officers who would live and operate in villages and have little or no overhead and no offices. Paperwork would be no more than keeping a record of amounts loaned to each client and the amounts recovered.

Under this proposal, the village-based loan agent would be given full authority to decide the creditworthiness of farmers applying for loans, and he could grant loans on the spot if he felt the borrower's reputation and prospects were satisfactory. Should the loan agent feel he needed to know more about a prospective borrower, it would be up to him to determine how much effort to spend in investigation of creditworthiness.

The loan agent would get a relatively small salary supplemented by a commission which, if he performs well, would be large compared with both his salary and any potential income from alternative occupations he might undertake. Performance would be judged largely by the percentage of loans recovered: the higher the percentage of recoveries, the higher would be his commission. The commission might also be varied according to the percentage of loans made to small farmers or to borrowers employing new technology, in cases where those are important objectives of government policy. If commissions are set high enough, agents who perform well would realize an income considerably larger than they could earn in alternative occupations. They would then have little incentive to use for themselves the bank funds at their disposal, as they would be tempted to do if their future earnings from commissions were not clearly greater than other possible returns from the bank capital they were handling.

Stickley does not attempt to provide details on what these salaries and commissions might be. I have worked out an example using Kenya data. A loan agent receives the salary of an agricultural assistant, plus commissions of 3 percent of the loans that were fully recovered; if he extended thirty loans of about $150 each in a year and recovered all of them, he would earn about three times his salary in commissions. This administrative cost to the lending institution should be covered by interest paid by the borrower; if it were not, it would represent a 3 percent loss of lender capital through commissions. The capital loss through default in many programs, however, appears to be much higher than 3 percent. If loan agents were not able to achieve a 100 percent recovery of funds extended—say, only 95 percent—the capital loss to the lender through commissions and default combined might be as much as 7 percent; but this is still less than many losses through default alone—not to mention the saving in administrative costs.

Incentives to Foster Productivity

One advantage of a decentralized system based on strong monetary rewards for low default rates is that loan agents would have an incentive to learn not only the borrowers' dialect or language but also as much detail as possible about their farm potentials and constraints. Such agents would then see the virtue of introducing farmers to profitable innovations as soon as they become available, and they would have strong incentives to discourage farmers from trying innovations ill-suited to their situation. Unlike present extension agents, the loan agents in this decentralized banking system would stand to be personally and financially penalized for introducing methods which in fact were unprofitable to farmers.

At present the representatives of credit and extension institutions do not have an incentive to seek out farmers who have the interest and capacity to adopt innovations or to discover which communities or farms have conditions that make the innovations unsuitable. In part because of this, a single new crop variety or a single fertilizer recommendation is often promoted over wide areas with great diversity of soils and rainfall conditions and indiscriminately presented to farmers who cannot use it profitably, as well as to those who can.

Some blame also lies at the door of the laboratory researcher who develops new crops or practices. Typically, researchers in developing countries have a paternalistic approach to the farmer, and especially to small farmers. They decide what the farmers' needs are, usually without consulting with farmers; as a result, technologies are developed under experimental conditions that have little in common with those actually found in rural areas. These "innovations" are then presented to the farmer; if he rejects them because they are not profitable with his constraints and resources, new efforts are launched to "educate" him. For example, if a farmer does not adopt a crop variety which stores poorly, requires more water than he has available, or matures when all his labor is required for other enterprises, his reluctance is often blamed on ignorance. This situation is unlikely to change without considerable governmental effort. The gulf between farmers and researchers in language and culture, and the reluctance of researchers to leave their comfortable research facilities for tiring trips to villages having few amenities, suggest that most researchers are not likely to seek out the small farmer. The small farmer is in no position to make his needs known to the researcher and therefore is badly in need of a representative who has a vested interest in his prosperity.

The loan agents in the decentralized credit system outlined above would have a monetary incentive to see that researchers find answers to the actual needs of the farmers they serve. With a commission at stake, the loan agent would have not only an incentive to keep researchers informed about innovations needed in his area, but also a vested interest in seeing that farmers were informed of the correct method of employing new techniques. He would have every incentive to inform farmers himself when he knew the answers to their problems, or to get them in touch with someone else if he did not.

25. *An Input Credit Program for Small Farmers in West Malaysia*

R. J. G. Wells

[In West Malaysia a government bank lends to farmers through intermediaries which can be either selected private traders or publicly sponsored producer associations. The private sector intermediaries have better repayment records, have higher rates of utilization of their loans, and reach more farmers than the producer organizations. Rice production has grown with the increase in credit, but the program has financial weaknesses.]

This chapter evaluates a crop-based production input credit scheme operated in selected rice-growing areas of West Malaysia by the Agricultural Bank of Malaysia (Bank Pertanian Malaysia). This is a state bank established in 1969 to provide short-, intermediate-, and long-term credit to the smallholder agricultural sector and to act as the nucleus of Malaysia's institutional agricultural system.

The rationale behind the formation of such specialized agencies is well known: with increased attention to rural development programs and especially to modernizing the small-farm sector, it was thought necessary to enlarge the supply of institutional agricultural finance. Increasing credit assumed a greater urgency following the advent of short-term, high-yielding rice varieties and an extensive investment in large-scale irrigation and drainage schemes in "rice bowl" areas of West Malaysia. These developments permitted double-cropping on a much larger scale, which offered the potential for a rapid increase in rice production. The newly formed Agricultural Bank had as its first priority a credit program for rice production inputs.

The creation of a new specialized institution clearly presupposed a significant void in the existing organized rural credit structure. Private banking institutions had displayed a reluctance to finance smallholder agricultural production. Many primary producers had, to be sure, received a relatively elastic supply of loanable funds from noninstitu-

Extracted from *Journal of Administration Overseas*, vol. 17, no. 1 (January 1978), pp. 4–16.

tional sources, but on disadvantageous terms; the lowest interest rates charged by private lenders were thought to vary between 30 and 40 percent a year. While smallholder credit cooperatives had operated in the rural credit market since the early 1920s, their record was not highly regarded by policy makers. This was made explicit by the creation in the 1960s of directly competitive multipurpose farmers' associations intended to usurp many of the cooperatives' roles. These farmers' associations were inexperienced as of 1969, however, and most of them were not considered a suitable mechanism for financing the Green Revolution in West Malaysia.

Program Objectives

Since February 1970, the bank has operated a production input credit scheme aimed at small rice farmers who meet the bank's basic criteria of creditworthiness. The coverage of the scheme is determined chiefly by the availability of adequate water supplies and infrastructure. Initially, geographical coverage was restricted to the Muda River irrigation project area in the states of Kedah and Perlis, but it has progressively included other double-cropped areas. The bank's view is that individual farmer-borrowers must have an adequate land base and be able to repay loans.

The basic goal of the program is to make production credit available to individual farmers so they can acquire the inputs necessary for increased productivity and increase their net incomes. A subgoal is to provide an economical credit system which will stimulate the flow of credit into the production of paddy (unmilled rice) by activating both public and private agencies to supply inputs along with credit.

Under the scheme, short-term production loans are offered for a growing season of about six and a half months for specified nursery and field fertilizers, insecticides, mechanized plowing services, and hired labor for transplanting and harvesting. Loans are disbursed in the form of printed coupons validated for the recommended quantities of inputs. Coupons are issued at the commencement of the season and are exchanged by farmers for inputs from official suppliers within a prescribed time; in the case of labor coupons, cash payments to the farmers are made by local credit centers. Loan repayments are deducted from the value of the rice sales.

Organizational Structure

The bulk of the funds in the credit program are extended by two-step lending through a network of intermediary institutions called "local credit centers," which act as the bank's agents; the remainder of the funds are issued direct from the branches of the bank. Farmers' organizations and private traders operating in the rice-growing areas are appointed, after screening, to organize local credit centers. An interesting feature of the scheme is that both public and private agencies are used as channels for credit. The public sector participants consist of producer organizations (rural cooperatives and farmers' associations), while the private sector channels are rice millers, licensed paddy buyers, merchants, and shopkeepers who possess facilities for paddy collection and marketing and have storage facilities for farm inputs. Local credit centers are responsible for the initial screening of loan applications and for disbursing the input credit and securing repayment.

This organizational structure permits the farmer some element of choice in the selection of his local credit center, which increases his accessibility. It also allows competition between the suppliers of credit and production inputs, which is one of the goals of the credit program. Furthermore, the use of traditional private financiers means that many of the decisions about the supply of credit and tied inputs are made by community organizations which are better able than national agencies to assess the managerial performance of individual farmers and their repayment capability. At the same time, the administrative burden on the bank is lightened.

Private agencies have represented a significant proportion of the local credit center network. The considerable reliance placed on the private trading sector, although politically controversial, illustrates a judicious pragmatism. Under pressure to make the input credit scheme operational in the first paddy season in 1970, the bank made full use of organizations which had successfully operated at the local level. Private retailers and paddy agents were financially strong and already had intimate knowledge of conditions in their areas, so they were in a good position to screen loan applications. Use of producer organizations, however, had to be restricted to those that had proved to be financially viable and operationally efficient. The network of farmers' associations had only recently come into existence, and the rural cooperatives were subjected to severe screening in view of their past performance. Licensed paddy dealers, along with producer organizations of both types with a proven marketing capability, became the agents for collecting repayment in kind in conjunction with the sale of the borrowers' crops.

Local credit centers are assigned a wide range of responsibilities in the operation of the program. They are responsible for screening and processing loan applications, for determining loan size and input requirements, for enforcing contracts, and for the disbursement, supervision, and collection of loans. In essence, both the coverage and the prospects for repayment are greatly influenced by the loan appraisal methods employed. There are significant differences in the appraisal procedures of the three types of local credit centers. Credit investigation by private agents is highly informal; most prospective borrowers are existing customers well known to the agent, who can make a quick assessment of the farmer's character and creditworthiness. The borrower is nevertheless required to complete a loan application form and give details of his present land base, previous production, loan repayment records, and farm and nonfarm income.

Farmers' associations have a much more formalized loan appraisal procedure. Initial interviews are held and the loan application form completed at the small agricultural unit (SAU, a subunit at the village level of an area farmers' association, which typically covers at least six SAUS). Loan applications and reports are subsequently forwarded to the area farmers' association office where they are scrutinized by the general manager before submission to the credit committee. This committee normally comprises the chairman of the board of directors, the general manager, the chief of the credit section, and a representative of the SAU. The SAU representative will indicate to the committee his views concerning the creditworthiness of the applicant, and recommendation or rejection of the loan application will be decided by the committee. Various forms of credit limit are imposed; credit for labor expenses is not given.

Rural cooperatives operate a less systematic and less uniform screening procedure than do the farmers' associations. Loan applications from members are scrutinized by a loan committee of a varying number of officers; explicit attention is paid to the loan repayment record of the applicant. In the case of members applying for a loan for the first time, the officials' knowledge of the member and judgment of his character form the basis for assessing his creditworthiness. Credit limits are imposed, although no uniform set of criteria is employed; cooperatives also vary in their attitudes toward granting credit coupons for labor expenses.

Interest Rates

From the inception of the scheme the agricultural bank had two basic lending rates; 12 percent per season (approximately six and a half months) for unsecured loans and 9 percent per season for secured loans were charged until August 1972, when the rates were reduced to 9 percent and 6 percent per season for unsecured and secured loans respectively. Out of this a service commission of 4 percent—3 percent after August 1972—was paid to the local credit center for the risk involved in loan collection and for administrative costs. Since August 1972 an additional penal charge of 1 percent per month has been instituted on overdue loans.

The high degree of tenancy in West Malaysian rice fields signifi-

Table 25-1. *Number of Farmers and Acreage Covered by the Agricultural Bank of Malaysia's Paddy Production Credit Scheme*

Season and year	*Number of farmers authorized*	*Land area (acres)*	*Average acreage per farmer*	*Total credit disbursed (thousands of Malaysian dollars)*	*Total credit per acre (Malaysian dollars)*
1st 1970	431	1,894	4.4	58	30.8
2nd 1970	2,293	10,249	4.5	271	26.4
1st 1971	4,461	21,221	4.8	830	39.1
2nd 1971	7,477	34,638	4.6	1,271	36.7
1st 1972	8,424	40,665	4.8	1,751	43.1
2nd 1972	10,722	50,484	4.8	2,212	43.8
1st 1973	10,732	55,940	4.7	2,679	47.8
2nd 1973	11,837	62,678	5.2	3,091	49.3
1st 1974	12,454	59,876	4.8	4,522	75.5
2nd 1974	16,885	88,462	5.2	4,534	51.2

Source: Data from the Agricultural Bank of Malaysia.

cantly limits the availability of collateral acceptable to the bank. The scheme was designed on the premise that land titles would be the main form of collateral. Even in the case of owner-occupiers, however, such collateral is rarely available; administrative and legal problems involved in land charging and stamp duties are so cumbersome and expensive that neither the farmers nor the local credit center are prepared to undertake the exercise. In consequence, nearly all loans were issued on an unsecured basis, initially at the higher interest rate. But because of the dearth of suitable security, the bank abolished the distinction for the purpose of interest rate computation in September 1973 and reduced rates to 8.5 percent a year, or 4.25 percent per crop season.

There is a strong case for the lending rates to provide a sufficient margin above deposit rates to cover program costs and build up reserves so that delinquent loans can be accommodated. The dramatic 1972–73 reduction in rates conflicted with this aim. It was not intended to provide an overt income subsidy to farmers, but the program is indirectly subsidized from the profits of other loan programs. Its operating costs have been estimated to exceed income by about 2 percent. The economic case for realistic pricing of production credit is even more powerful than arguments based on political self-interest: low nominal rates and what are usually negative real interest rates make it virtually impossible to show a profit or to cover program costs, and they cause allocative difficulties. Moreover, low loan rates imply a low interest rate on deposits and discourage rural savings.

Evaluation

The short-term lending operations of the bank in rice farming are shown in table 25-1. The scale of lending under the scheme rose perceptibly in both monetary and real terms in its first five years; the number of borrowers and the double-cropped paddy acreage covered have increased rapidly. The bank has also become the major supplier of institutional credit to rice farming and has aided the adoption of high-yielding seed varieties and complementary inputs by participating cultivators. In the five main areas of its operations the bank is beginning to make an impact on the credit market. Its credit activity is concentrated in areas where large-scale irrigation facilities have been provided and there is considerable potential for augmenting production. Credit is disbursed mainly to above-average farmers: the average size of rice farms covered by the scheme is 4.4 to 5.2 acres, more than the average of 3.1 acres in the country.

Several factors restrict the bank's coverage. The inability to recruit a sufficient number of acceptable local credit centers is one impediment; future expansion in coverage will almost certainly necessitate enlarging the branch network to increase direct lending. Unless more private traders can be brought in, this would seem to depend on the continued evolution of a viable network of producer organizations.

The private sector, however, has a higher rate of credit utilization as a proportion of credit sanctioned than either of the producer organizations, and its repayment record is generally superior to that of the producer organizations. Private local credit centers have also provided access to production credit for nonmembers of producer organizations—a substantial proportion of the nation's paddy farmers. All this tends to vindicate the bank's controversial decision to utilize the private trading network. Incorporation of traditional rural lenders into the credit scheme provides an economical way to stimulate the flow of credit for rice farming without using government resources.

Undoubtedly, the agricultural bank faces formidable handicaps in increasing the disbursement of funds. There is a need for stricter loan appraisal procedures to minimize loan delinquencies where traditional forms of security are generally not available. Another restraint on the utilization of bank credit arises from the low incomes of many rice farmers, who often borrow for consumption purposes. Borrowing for consumption also results from the "lumpiness" of their income receipts—only twice a year for the majority of rice planters who double-crop. Their ability to stagger the sale of their produce is impeded by their lack of on-farm storage capacity and the frequent need to sell their crop at harvesttime to repay debts.

The bank is also faced with the problem of a relatively high rate of defaults and late repayment of loans. For the first season of 1971, the ratio of recoveries at the due dates about one month after the harvest was 77.7 percent. For the same season in 1972, the ratio had increased slightly to 78.9 percent, and by the first season in 1974 the recovery rate improved further to 82 percent. A delinquency rate of nearly 20 percent in a supervised credit program can hardly be deemed satisfactory. Of course, delinquency rates of 20 to 30 percent are often found in small-farmer credit in other developing countries, and it would be argued that some delinquency in loan repayments is not incompatible with a successful loan program if socioeconomic benefits arise from the infusion of production credit among small farmers. Nonetheless, delinquency rates remain an important quantitative indicator of program problems and usually require reducing if a psychology of default is not to be engendered. The overdue rate facing the bank suggests that it could experience future difficulties in reconciling the goal of increased coverage with the need to make only economically sound loans.

Recommendations for Further Reading

Abdi, Ali Issa. *Commercial Banks and Economic Development: The Experience of Eastern Africa.* New York: Praeger, 1977.

Bathrick, David D. *Agricultural Credit for Small Farm Development: Policies and Practices.* Boulder, Colo.: Westview Press, 1981.

Bhatt, V. V. "Interest Rate, Transaction Costs and Financial Innovations." *Savings and Development,* vol. 3, no. 2 (1979), pp. 95–126.

Datey, C. D. *The Financial Cost of Agricultural Credit: A Case Study of Indian Experience.* World Bank Staff Working Paper no. 296. Washington, D.C., 1978.

Sayad, Joao. "Controle de Juros e Saldos Medios." *Revista Brasiliera de Economia,* vol. 31, no. 1 (1977), pp. 229–48.

Shetty, S. L. "Performance of Commercial Banks since Nationalization of Major Banks: Promise and Reality." *Economic and Political Weekly,* vol. 13 (1978), pp. 1407–51.

Vogel, Robert C. "Rural Financial Market Performance: Implications of Low Delinquency Rates." *American Journal of Agricultural Economics,* vol. 63 (1981), pp. 58–65.

von Stockhausen, Joachim. *Credit Guarantees as an Instrument for Self-help in Developing Countries.* Bonn: Friedrich-Ebert-Stiftung, 1979.

Wai, U Tun. *Financial Intermediation and National Savings in Developing Countries.* New York: Praeger, 1972.

World Bank. "Agricultural Credit." Sector Policy Paper. Washington, D.C., 1975.

Issues for Discussion

1. Do all innovations in rural financial markets reduce the social costs of providing financial services?
2. Are commercial banks suitable vehicles for small-scale credit? Should commercial banks be forced to undertake business that is not appropriate to their cost structures? What steps may be taken to encourage commercial banks to expand their rural business on a voluntary basis?
3. What are the advantages and disadvantages of (a) specialized farm credit institutions, and (b) group credit, compared with other financial intermediaries?
4. What shortcomings on the part of lenders contribute to poor loan collection performance? How can a lending institution gain and maintain the respect of its clients, so that they will not want to default?
5. What scope is there for using local traders or informal financial intermediaries as the agents of formal institutions, with responsibilities for making small-scale loans and collecting repayments and small-scale deposits?
6. What types of problems are likely to develop from politically motivated supply-leading finance?
7. What are the causes of the reorganization of government-owned rural credit institutions and of changes in the institutions used by governments to provide rural financial services?
8. What are the limitations of loan guarantee programs as a means of inducing commercial banks to lend more to agriculture?
9. Under what circumstances do cheap central bank rediscount facilities for agricultural loans discourage formal lenders from mobilizing savings in rural areas?
10. What are the arguments for and against requiring banks to pay for the technical assistance to farmers under supervised credit programs?
11. What is the relationship between the quality of a lender's service to its customers and its loan collection performance?
12. Will governments or donor agencies provide subsidies indefinitely to agricultural banks to cover the costs of lending which are not met by interest income? In what circumstances would these sources of subsidy be most likely to increase or to decrease their contributions?

PART V

LOCAL RURAL FINANCIAL INSTITUTIONS

Having looked at urban-based commercial banks and specialized farm credit organizations, we now turn to more locally based methods of providing financial services. These fall in two categories: informal lending and saving methods, and cooperatives or other local groups involved in finance. To what extent do these mechanisms overcome the weaknesses in rural financial markets (RFMS) that the more formal organizations display? These weaknesses include limited access to rural customers, high cost of services, absence of savings facilities, financial nonviability, lack of active competition, and inability to expand services to respond to and create opportunities.

Informal Finance

The extent and importance of informal lending and saving are suggested by sample surveys. They indicate that the volume of informal finance is greater than the formal financial flows in rural areas of many developing countries. Informal lending appears to have advantages over institutional lending, especially among low-income groups and in the more remote and small-scale local RFMS.

Informal loans are supplied to farmers by relatives and friends at little or no interest, and on commercial terms by traders, large landowners, and others who may be full-time moneylenders. Informal finance also includes various traditional, noninstitutional ways of accumulating savings and extending credit, examples of which are given below.

The activities of informal commercial lenders (whom we will call moneylenders, though most have additional occupations) have a number of favorable features. Moneylending is never subsidized by governments, yet moneylenders' demonstrated ability to survive almost everywhere implies financial viability and an ability to adapt to rural conditions. Moneylenders supply services desired by their clients without the costly apparatus of buildings, papers, and staff, and they do this at low cost to borrowers because of proximity, their quick response to requests, and the flexibility they permit in repayment. There is no doubt about the broad access of low-income rural people to such credit, nor do cultural gaps separate lenders from clients. Informal lenders are often better judges of creditworthiness among their neighbors, and better at collecting debts from them, than are institutional lenders—certainly better than many government-owned banks. Whether they are active competitors with one another or tend toward collusion is conjectural and varies by location. But on the whole there are few barriers to entry to moneylending for those having sufficient funds, and moneylenders seem more prepared to act competitively than are the specialized farm credit institutions.

With so much to be said for them, why are they held in low esteem by many civil servants and policy makers? The most commonly given reason is that they charge high interest rates that are felt by many to be exorbitant and exploitive. In addition, some religions oppose charging interest. Another reason is that moneylenders frequently lend for consumption rather than production—that is, they are indifferent to what borrowers do with their loan receipts. This is disparaged by critics, both because it can put poor borrowers in debt without adding to their ability to repay, and because it does not boost agricultural output or serve "national development"—that is, serve the goals specified by planners—as governmental credit programs are supposed to do. A third reason, less often heard but pertinent to RFM analysis, is that rural moneylenders are associated with rural backwardness and are often considered unable to improve their services in support of a growing, modernizing agricultural sector.

In regard to moneylender interest rates, survey data suggest that median rates might be in the vicinity of 40 to 50 percent on an annual basis, which is higher than institutional rates; but, as will be argued at length later, the latter are generally much too low at present, especially with substantial inflation. Little research has been done on moneylender costs, however, which could distinguish causes for high interest rates. Singh (chapter 28) presents such data for seven north Indian village moneylenders; the average annual rate of interest they charged was 142 percent, and their average cost of lending was 134 percent. This supports claims that high rates are explainable and justifiable. About a quarter of this cost was for the risk of default, computed from past experience; over half the cost was a calculated return of 77 percent from alternative uses of the same money in local agriculture, which served as an opportunity cost to the lenders. It is apparent that this is a poor community in which investible funds are scarce relative to potential uses. It must also be in a quite small and isolated RFM; many investors elsewhere in India would be delighted to get 77 percent on their money if they could.

Singh's example is too limited to support firm generalizations, and it may represent a somewhat extreme case, but the direction of the evidence it presents does illustrate the nature of the problem. Moneylenders have a competitive advantage in many RFMs: they can provide financial services that clients want in areas where formal lenders cannot. Their relatively high rates of interest (on rather small loans) must cover the costs they incur.

If such RFMs had better communications and facilities, capital should flow more readily toward investments with prospects for high returns. This process should in time reduce marginal rates of return, and increased competition among lenders would reduce interest rates. But if the government's approach to this situation is that moneylenders are "evil" and should be eliminated or subjected to an interest rate ceiling, then capital will only get more scarce—or the ceiling will be ignored. Numerous chapters in this book show that formal institutions do not reach out effectively into rural areas. These considerations, taken together, should generate a greater respect for the services that informal lenders can provide.

There are, however, limitations to the potential for informal finance in rural areas—even if the prejudice against moneylenders should cease, and if governments could support their role through more constructive policies. Their very adaptability to RFM conditions, and the personalized element in their relations with clients, may make it difficult for them to fit into programs of modernization, growth, and competition. They could be out of place in a program that featured tied or conditional loans directing credit toward specified agricultural inputs. Efforts to control loan uses are often ineffectual, but governments may not wish to be seen encouraging consumption by directing resources through a group noted for giving consumption loans.

Nevertheless, the informal lender has a place in the spectrum of RFM activities. Informal lenders will continue to provide services that a great many people want and will pay for. Informal commercial lenders are a useful and legitimate part of RFMs, and their elimination should not be a government objective. Rather, the quality and prices of their services should be improved through increased competition.

Cooperatives and Group Lending

The organization of borrower groups has involved conventional and unconventional approaches. A number of governments have founded and supported cooperatives to pursue rural development objectives. Many of these cooperatives include credit as one of their functions, while credit unions are cooperatives that specialize in mobilizing savings and lending to members. In addition, banks may lend to temporary or semipermanent borrower groups whose only function is to assume joint responsibility for repayment.

Some of these organizations have succeeded. They have contributed to the most successful experiences in rural finance in developing countries. In the Republic of Korea and in Taiwan, cooperative organizations are found in virtually every rural community; they offer not only credit but savings facilities, as well as widely used technical and marketing services. They have been able to grow, adapt to and participate in the modernization of agriculture, and mobilize savings of rural nonfarmers in addition to those of farmers.

Elsewhere, cooperatives or farmers' organizations with other titles have had a very mixed record as RFM performers. A few of these experiences are presented in three chapters below that give some idea of the diversity of performance; two later chapters in Part VI also bring out pertinent aspects of cooperatives. In addition, two chapters below deal with groups of farmers which are formed for joint borrowing but cannot be called full cooperatives. (They are sometimes called "precooperatives," a term which presumes that more elaborate cooperative functions will come later.)

Cooperatives have the potential for reducing lender and borrower costs by serving as intermediaries for individual farmers, and for reducing defaults through joint responsibility for repayment and peer pressure against delinquents. They can also serve as middlemen in cultural mediation (explaining bankers to farmers, and vice versa), improve debt collection when this is tied to cooperative marketing, offer savings facilities for members, and serve as a conduit for technical advice, input supplies, and product marketing. These potentials have been realized only to a limited degree. Generally the organization of groups of borrowers does reduce lenders' administrative costs, but repayment rates on loans from cooperatives around the developing world have been very erratic. Unfortunately, few cooperatives have accumulated member savings on a significant scale. Integration of credit with other services has proved difficult to manage. While some groups have performed well, others have not. Certainly the potential for developing cooperative savings facilities could be far more energetically pursued.

Institutional Diversity

It does not appear that any single institutional form provides a panacea for all countries in attaining superior RFM performance. But the positive value of institutional diversity within RFMs is a much neglected subject. Too many development planners have approached rural problems or financial problems with the assumption that there ought to be one best institutional form. When it appears that no one form is all-encompassing or foolproof, despite successes in one or more areas, one might be led to feel that there is no "solution." But if it is assumed instead that RFMs bring together a variety of people with different requirements for financial services, it becomes easier to see how the coexistence of different kinds of financial institutions and informal lenders can give rural participants a wider choice. A diversified RFM can respond to many more opportunities than a single type of institution could.

Almost all the research and writing in this field has concentrated on one institution at a time, whether in case studies or in generalized discussion. The articles collected for this book reflect that tendency, for it has been almost impossible to find studies of the interactions of different kinds of institutions within the same RFM. One such study by Harriss covers the very active competition among RFM participants in southern India and is presented below.

The RFM studied by Harriss encompasses small traders in farm inputs or products, government-sponsored cooperatives, state commercial banks, pawnbrokers, and farmers of various kinds. She found active competition among lenders. Generally, unregulated interest rates were moderate—one attempt at monopoly pricing failed. She also reports widespread access to credit, as well as to farm inputs. These conditions, the author finds, allow for many small traders and sustain many small farmers who would otherwise be driven off the land.

In contrast to the virtues of uncoordinated diversity, it may be argued that the most desirable RFMs are those in the Republic of Korea and Taiwan, where careful planning and execution have enabled one dominant, officially supported institutional complex to serve a wide range of rural activity in a well-integrated manner. It does not follow, however, that the same pattern should or could be reproduced elsewhere with the same results. Informal finance (especially the rotating savings and credit groups described by Bouman in chapter 30) is active in both Korea and Taiwan, coexisting with official programs that fulfill many but not all opportunities for rural financial service.

As Argyle suggests (chapter 39), the search for the perfect institution should be deemphasized in favor of improving the overall adequacy of RFMs. Where inadequacies are found, they can be corrected in a variety of ways, by relying on nongovernmental and informal as well as official initiatives, and by encouraging rather than trying to restrain competition among different types of RFM participants.

Institutional Diversity and Interaction

The following chapter by Harriss, based on field interviews and observations in a district of southern India, presents a comprehensive view of the interactions among diverse lenders and institutions active in an RFM. The market includes many small rice farmers and a smaller number of larger ones seeking credit. It also consists of informal lenders—fertilizer and rice merchants, pawnbrokers, and large-scale full-time moneylenders—among whom competition is active. Interest rates are moderate, and differences among them are explained; some trends through time are noted. Among formal lenders, the nationalized commercial banks play an important role by lending to fertilizer dealers who then relend to farmer-buyers and expand the use of nutrients in agriculture. Loans from cooperatives, offered at lower interest rates than private loans, go disproportionately to big farmers and tend to be found more in areas where private credit is scarce.

One important result of these activities is to increase the availability of fertilizer to small farmers and thus to raise their productivity and solvency. Although this result corresponds to official objectives of the main public credit institutions, the banks and cooperatives, it could probably not have been effectively achieved by them without the coexistence of private lenders and the high level of competitiveness among them. Harriss provides an excellent illustration of the value of looking at financial markets as a whole rather than at single institutions.

26. *Money and Commodities: Their Interaction in a Rural Indian Setting*

Barbara Harriss

[This chapter examines a rural area in southern India where the money market consists of pawnbrokers, state cooperatives offering subsidized credit, and private traders who compete actively for farmers' purchases or sales by offering them loans on favorable terms. State banks actively lend to the traders so that they may relend to farmers; this results partly from government's effort to increase the use of fertilizers. One consequence of active competition among lenders is to keep many small farmers in operation who might not survive without credit.]

This analysis addresses itself to the complex nature of a rural money market in south India. Data are drawn from field research in 1973–74 on a random sample of 200 traders in agricultural commodities (rice), agricultural inputs (fertilizer and pesticides), and agricultural investment goods (pumps and irrigation accessories), and from random surveys of twenty village cooperatives and of 200 producers of paddy (unmilled rice) in twelve villages of North Arcot District of Tamil Nadu State. I examine the private rural money market, the money markets organized indirectly and directly by the state, the linkages between private and public finance, and those between the money market generally and the market for agricultural commodities.

The Private Rural Money Market

The unorganized money market is highly complex. There may be as many as 180,000 farmers in the rice-producing eastern region of North Arcot who market paddy to some 2,300 traders. Traders said they lend, in cash or kind, to about half their customers. High and

Extracted from a paper presented to the Workshop on Rural Financial Markets and Institutions, Wye College, Wye, England, June 1979; also published in *Development Digest* (January 1982), pp. 16–23.

increasing demand for production and consumption credit enables traders to discriminate among clients. Private sector money is not necessarily a substitute for cooperative loans; it may be a complement to them: "If a man can't get a government loan, he's likely not to be able to repay my loan."

Agricultural Traders

A farmer's eligibility for short-term loans is determined by traders' own criteria similar to those used by state-run cooperatives. Traders assess landholding, crop size, capital assets, and past repayment performance. The private money market is more physically accessible than is that of the state. A trader's shop is open from 6:00 A.M. to 10:00 P.M., loans are obtainable with no paperwork, and the request is usually speedily handled. No security has to be given, and borrowers can use the money for any purpose, agricultural or social.

Agricultural loans obtained on the private money market are rarely small. In the paddy and rice trade and in fertilizer dealing the lower limits average Rs200. The largest loans to individuals are between Rs2,000 and 3,000, about equal to the maximum permitted by the cooperatives. Traders may occasionally lend up to Rs10,000, but cultivators seeking large sums are usually advised by traders to apply to nationalized banks or "private parties"—the highly elusive, large-scale, full-time moneylenders in the back streets of many market towns. Loan ceilings also vary with the size of the trader's business, smaller traders tending to lend to smaller farmers.

The average annual interest rate for loans is remarkably consistent at 13 to 14 percent, slightly above the current legal ceiling of 12 percent. The ways in which interest is paid, just as with the principal itself, are quite varied. Normal repayment is in kind after harvest, although loans for pumpsets are allowed a longer repayment period. In some collecting centers, no interest is charged to those who supply the trader with more paddy than the repayment of their debt necessitates. In the town of Arcot an interest rate of 12 percent a year is universal. In Arni and Tiruvannamalai wholesalers subtract as interest between Rs0.5 and Rs2.0 per 75 kilogram bag of paddy from the market price, which amounts to a rate of 4 to 10 percent a year.

Interest rates climb if a farmer repays more than a month after harvest. It seems that about one-fifth of all loans take longer than agreed to repay. Slow payers are not necessarily the smallest farmers, sometimes being large farmers who have reloaned borrowed money. In cases of late repayment, interest rates vary from 12 to 25 percent. The markets where funds are least available have the highest rates of overdue payments. Great social pressure, moral—and occasional physical—intimidation is exerted on slow payers, and traders exchange information on "bad risks." According to traders, an average of 5 percent of borrowers default completely. Every trader allots time and resources to attempt to retrieve his money, weighing the costs of potential litigation against the size of the sum to be lost.

Interest rates higher than the legal ceiling are often attributed to a combination of inelastic and rising demand, the costs of borrowing, and the costs and risks of credit administration. It has also been contended that high interest rates have a component of monopoly profit. This is obviously not the case in North Arcot, where competition among the lenders is active.

A few traders attract small savings deposits. The trader uses this money in trade; he will reciprocate the farmer's good faith by giving him small quantities of money (Rs3 to Rs5 for a meal, medicine, or a bus fare) in lieu of interest payment.

Credit and moneylending do not appear to be the basis of an exploitive relationship between trader and farmer in North Arcot, partly because both cultivators and traders belong to the same two castes. There are strong ties of kinship as well as money between town and country.

Pawnbrokers contribute to the private rural money market in competition with the nationalized banks, which also lend on pledged jewels. Compared with the banks, pawnbrokers offer greater ease of access, speedier service, easier valuation procedures, and larger loans in proportion to the value of the jewel. They also charge higher interest rates, allow thumb impressions, lend on jewels as well as on gold, and lend to any owners of jewelry without restricting loans to those with bank accounts as the banks do. Pawnbrokers are becoming an important source of cash for agricultural production, and the years since 1968 have seen a massive increase in their number throughout North Arcot. Interest is higher than that charged by banks and traders, varying from 18 to 25 percent inversely with the size of the loan.

This recent increase in pawning comes largely from poorer farmers seeking loans of Rs50 to Rs100 to pay agricultural labor, hire bullocks, buy fertilizer, or repair pumpsets, and to a lesser extent from larger loans for well-deepening and for purposes such as weddings and gambling. Traders will not lend these sums. Demand is highly seasonal (January to May) so that money may be idle at other times, which is partially reflected in the interest rate. Although pawnbrokers are held in low regard by other lenders, they are a more accepted part of rural society than is the formal lending institution.

The evidence indicates a relatively competitive money market. On one occasion, because of high default rates and because of fears of state takeover of the grain trade, the Arni Paddy and Rice Dealers Association of the largest traders decided to act collusively and reduce moneylending to farmers. It was the only association in the district to take such action, and by no means all traders complied. Flows of money from the local marketplace declined during 1973–74. Some traders, anticipating drought, used their spare funds to stock paddy to the legal limit and above. At the same time, credit from fertilizer dealers also dropped in volume, first because fertilizer had entered a phase of short supply and promotional credit was unnecessary, and second because overdraft facilities for traders did not increase when the price of fertilizer they sold more than doubled.

There was a marked result on the money market. Whereas in 1965 there were 10 pawnbrokers, in 1973 there were 72, and by 1974 there were 88. Within the pawnbroking trade, demand for money for agricultural purposes trebled in 1972–74. As a result, not only did new pawnbrokers enter the market, but also minor government officials, teachers, and clerks became moneylenders charging 18 to 25 percent. Although the interest rates charged were illegally high, they were rarely equal to the net rate of return on capital from agricultural commerce, which averaged an estimated 24 percent. The money market is thus structurally flexible. Private intermediaries—traders, pawnbrokers, and jewelers—compete for the business of different types of cultivators, while traders' money substitutes for state loans for smaller farmers.

Agricultural Producers

A survey of 200 paddy producers analyzed by B. N. Chinnappa ["Adoption of the New Agricultural Technology in North Arcot Division," in *Green Revolution? Technology and Change in Rice Growing Areas of South Asia*, B. H. Farmer, ed., London, Macmillan, 1977] and anthropological research by John Harriss ["Capitalism and Peasant Agriculture: Agrarian Structure and Change in Northern Tamil Nadu," Ph.D. dissertation, University of East Anglia, 1977] lend support to the description above. Chinnappa's data on borrowing and farm size show that the proportion of farmers borrowing for cultivation expenses was very low among the bottom 14 percent cultivating less than one acre (0.4 hectare), while about half the members of all other farm-size groups borrow. In the group taking loans, borrowed money contributed just under half of cultivation costs. Private credit sources—including village moneylenders and pawnbrokers who charge interest, chit funds with disguised interest charges, and friends and relatives who may or may not charge interest—grew less important than banks with increasing farm size.

As already noted, traders do not lend amounts below about Rs100, and pawnbroking is becoming important at the poor end of the spectrum. Since the average loan is about Rs180 per acre, it is possible that small farmers are borrowing from traders rather than village moneylenders. Consumption loans may be obtained from traders, and to judge from the increase in the number of both agricultural traders and pawnbrokers, it is possible that moneylending is being increasingly concentrated in the towns. Certainly the moneylender is not so prominent in the villages, nor are interest rates so high, as in conventional characterizations of other areas of India.

Demand for money in agricultural production has greatly increased for two reasons connected with two rather different forms of production. First, among larger farmers, money is simultaneously lent and borrowed, with interest rates and relative risks juggled in an effort to make a profit. This is known as "rolling," and the English word is used. Second, among small farmers, the demand for cash has increased. This reflects the need for modern farm inputs including irrigation water, increased insecurity, contingencies such as crop failure or the need to replace a team of draft animals or a pumpset coil, and desire for consumption goods.

State Financial Institutions

The involvement of national banks in rural money markets began in North Arcot in 1967. It coincided with the ending of a cooperative monopoly in fertilizer marketing and with a point when fertilizer production exceeded demand and marketing agencies instituted vigorous competitive tactics.

Indirect Participation

The financing of agricultural production by the state began in the form of credit sales at no interest to private fertilizer dealers or agents, who repeated the procedure with interest to farmers. A state-owned distribution company was the first to experiment with this, soon followed by the private companies. At the height of this credit boom, a trader's security bore no relation to the loans which were extended, and by 1971 the distribution companies themselves had large debts. Repayment was slow, and many traders went out of business.

By 1973, however, credit competition had stabilized somewhat, largely because of the skillful intervention of the state through the big commercial banks which had been nationalized in 1969. An example of the terms of their involvement is that dealers in agro inputs could obtain credit for up to 80 percent of the value of goods bought for resale, up to a specified absolute ceiling. A dealer was also eligible for an equal quantity of 180-day crop production credit, both for his own crops and for those of farmers, with repayment after harvest. Dealers were required to deposit 20 percent of their sanctioned limit with the banks. They also had to offer their title deeds, hypothecated stocks, or promissory notes, and to pay interest at 10.5 percent. Dealers were strictly supervised, having to supply a monthly stock statement and submit to periodic inspection of accounts by bank agents and of stocks of fertilizer by representatives of the distribution companies. Dealers no longer had any privacy in their financial transactions with companies and banks.

In this situation of glut and severe competition, the balance of power shifted to the nationalized banks. The private distribution companies competed with each other (and with the cooperatives as well) for sales, while the banks operated virtually identical schemes through every company. Interest rates charged to farmers were unsubsidized and higher than for cooperative credit. This form of finance has been standard practice since 1972 in North Arcot, where private traders sell half the fertilizer used. All licensed dealers are compulsorily involved, and up to 80 percent of the value of trade can be financed in this way.

The Direct Role of Nationalized Banks

Private moneylending faces formidable competition from the state. The purely private moneylending activities of input dealers are swamped by credit extended by the nationalized banks through them. The banks also offer 180-day production credit directly to farmers with over two acres, at the rate of Rs250 per acre up to a ceiling of Rs1,000 to Rs2,500, depending on the bank. These standard loan limits are lower and the interest rates are higher than those of the Panchayat Union and cooperatives which also lend to farmers. The farmer has to prove ownership and show all production receipts. A bank manager explained that it was of course very large farmers who know about this source of finance and used it, often for relending. They were often tardy in repayment, since these delays were not penalized by a rise in interest, and default was a major problem.

Cooperative Credit

The major competitor with private trade remains the cooperative credit system financed by the Cooperative Bank, which is subsidized. As Chinnappa shows, the 47 percent of the 200 sampled cultivators in North Arcot who took loans got, on average, 32 percent of their production credit from cooperatives. Cooperative credit is disproportionately concentrated among large farmers. In the sample the share of cooperative loans in all production credit rose with farm size from 10 to 62 percent. A case study of one agricultural cooperative showed that, in the area covered, loans per person per season averaged Rs800 for cultivators with less than three acres, while for those possessing more than three acres they averaged Rs2,300—above the official ceiling. Interest rates vary between 8.7 and 9.7 percent a year on postharvest payments, rising to 12.6 percent (the legal ceiling) for overdue payments.

Statistics on cooperative loans for all village societies were obtained from the Central Cooperative Bank in Vellore. To a remarkable degree, cooperative credit operates where private credit is least abundant. In the district as a whole, cooperative credit amounts to just under half the quantity supplied by private trade, excluding pawnbroker loans for production. In spite of the public sector's advantages in low interest rates, other costs to borrowers reduce its competitiveness: These costs include inefficient administration, lengthy application procedures, untimely arrival of credit, inflexibility of repayment procedures, and necessity for proof of collateral, as well as the cost of bribes. All this effectively raises the cost of loans to about the level of those from private traders. Also, the ceiling of Rs2,000 on cooperative production loans forces the relatively few cultivators with landholdings in excess of ten acres to seek extra funds elsewhere if needed. The outright default rate on the production loans of twenty cooperative societies surveyed in the study area was 26 percent, rendering the defaulters ineligible for further production loans. Many of them were large farmers. During the election campaign of 1972 farmers were "promised" that a vote cast in the right direction would write off a loan. [See chapter 42 for a description of the historical interaction of politics and cooperatives in the region in which North Arcot is located.]

State Lending to Commodity Traders

The state encourages the nationalized banks to lend to fertilizer dealers but discourages loans to paddy and rice traders. This cannot be enforced, however, and the financing of intraseason paddy and rice stocks is a secure and profitable form of investment for a bank. Wholesalers and millers may therefore obtain bank loans if they wish. One much publicized case concerned a bank which lent large sums to pawnbrokers and to professional moneylenders in one of the towns in the district. Once this was discovered it was quashed, but there is no doubt that similar activities continue.

The result of such intersectoral linkages and competition is that the existence of cheap state credit increases the availability of money for agricultural production and exerts a restraining influence on private sector interest rates. This social benefit cannot be quantified but ought to be borne in mind when assessing the social effects of the cooperative subsidy that benefits mainly large farmers.

Results and Contradictions

This complex money market and the limited expansion of agricultural production that it supports have enabled many small traders to maintain themselves in business and to compete with each other and the big traders. One result of this competition is that money is loaned to farmers at rather low interest rates. Thus the small trader allows the small farmer to reproduce himself and survive. Why are there so many small traders?

Agricultural commerce is relatively crowded for at least six reasons: (1) Commerce remains more profitable on the average than any other sector of this region's economy and continues to attract entrants. New entrants to trade come increasingly from the wage labor force of the commercial sector itself, as well as from producers of the commodities sold. (2) Commerce may also be crowded because of demographic expansion. Traders' families are slightly larger than those of the average peasant producer, and family members need employment. Joint family businesses become managerially unwieldy and often split to provide each son with control over resources and funds for consumption and reinvestment. (3) Family businesses also split because tax legislation discriminates against multiple enterprises and joint family combines. There are powerful fiscal incentives for simple single-owner businesses, and many traders acknowledge having split their firms for that reason. (4) The personal knowledge of clients necessary in moneylending may limit the number of clients any mercantile firm can scrutinize and maintain. (5) The state encourages easy entry into commerce in other ways. In North Arcot the dominant form of intervention encourages competition through market regulation, reducing distributors' margins at minimum cost to public funds by maximizing the number in trade. (6) The central government's goal of expanding the fertilizer industry to increase food production has led to a spawning of small input dealers with only limited scope for concentrating their capital. The international companies distributing fertilizer and pesticides compete through several separate networks of private dealers, through the cooperatives, and even through the state's Department of Agriculture.

The expansion of commerce in inputs itself increases the marketed surplus, which feeds back into commerce again. Competition among traders for farm commodities also results in moneylending at relatively low interest rates; in this market the effect on interest rates of subsidized cooperative credit from state-supported institutions has not been negligible. All this helps small and marginal farms to remain in operation and to expand production within limited spheres. At the same time, investment in trade is relatively attractive because of commodity price levels and the opportunity to profit from market imperfections, which are often the perverse result of state intervention. The structure that has evolved—small farmers, a large number of traders, relatively cheap loans from competition in trade credit, and state intervention—reinforces itself and arguably constrains agricultural production over the long run. The tight link between the money market and the imperfectly functioning commodity market allows a high return from joint operations in both markets, as trader and lender.

Informal Financial Intermediation

The first three of the five chapters in this section deal with informal commercial lenders, or moneylenders. Bottomley (chapter 27) analyzes in some detail the lending costs of informal and formal lenders, illustrating the relationships among them by use of hypothetical numbers. He finds that informal lenders have a cost advantage over formal institutions for small volumes of lending; but if volume increases, formal institutions are better able to realize economies of scale.

Next, Singh (chapter 28) presents actual data on costs and interest charges for seven village moneylenders in northwestern India. The high interest rates they charge are largely explained by their costs, including a relatively high risk of incomplete or delayed repayment, as experienced in the past, and a high rate of return on funds used on their farms (all seven were farm operators). In chapter 29, Wilmington describes the conditions in rural Sudan as seen by moneylenders. He emphasizes the hazard of borrowers' evading repayment and the importance of patron-client relationships that involve more than simple economic transactions between lenders and borrowers. Although Wilmington does not quantify lending costs, his article supports the case made by Singh that the moneylenders' seemingly high interest charges can be understood if costs are viewed from the lenders' standpoint, and that informal lenders are very often unjustly maligned.

Chapters 30 and 31 describe customary ways in which financial transactions other than simple moneylending are carried out. Bouman discusses the rotating savings and credit organizations that appear in many parts of the world: the Far East, South Asia, Africa, the Caribbean. All who participate in such an organization contribute a small sum of money on successive occasions, and each of them takes a turn receiving the group total. This semirecreational activity can generate significant savings and sometimes lead to investments. Adegboye discusses a particular kind of loan security found in parts of West Africa: the borrower grants the lender the produce of a cocoa, oil-palm, or rubber tree until the loan is repaid. Although this system permits farmers with little cash income to pay such expenses as children's schooling or taxes, the terms of the loan agreement often prove unsatisfactory to one party or the other. The system could be improved, but it fills a need and will probably continue even as more highly organized alternatives evolve.

27. *Interest Rate Determination in Underdeveloped Rural Areas*

Anthony Bottomley

[The high cost of administering small loans and persistent repayment problems lead to high interest rates in informal rural money markets in the developing world. Village moneylenders or traders may be able to operate more efficiently than public credit agencies, especially in low-volume markets; but at some point the latter can benefit from economies of scale enough to compete at lower cost.]

There has been relatively little analysis of interest rates in the predominantly rural, informal money markets of the developing world. A framework for such analysis requires an examination of the four components of rural interest rates: the opportunity cost of the money involved, the premium for administering the loan, the premium for risk, and monopoly profit. These elements will be discussed in the text and illustrated in table 27-1, which presents hypothetical cost structures for a rural informal moneylender and an urban bank.

The Opportunity Cost of Money

What the opportunity cost of money will actually be is hard to determine. It may be the value to a rural saver of parting with liquidity, or of forgoing the opportunity to invest in his own farm, or of fulfilling his social obligation to provide a lavish wedding for his daughter—that is, the supply price of money in the community. Alternatively, it may be the sum of what it costs a rural lender to get outside money to lend to a farmer—a national supply price. For example, it could begin with the charges a bank levies on an urban wholesaler who, in turn, relends with further levies on the transaction to the village shopkeeper who buys his goods. If the shopkeeper is unable to synchronize his lending to farmers with his borrowing from a wholesaler, the interest he charges will have to compensate for the periods in which such money lies idle in the village shop. If, for example, a moneylender can lend for only six

Extracted from the *American Journal of Agricultural Economics*, vol. 57, no. 2 (May 1975), pp. 279–91.

Table 27-1. *Hypothetical Lending Cost Structure on Loans to a Representative Borrower with Constant Net Returns to Scale*
(all costs are stated as percentages of amounts loaned)

		Moneylender's cost					Urban bank's cost				
Loan size (dollars) (1)	*Borrower net income (dollars) (2)*	*Basic rate (3)*	*Average adminis-trative cost (4)*	*Default (5)*	*Overall risk premium (6)*	*Average lending cost (3+4+6) (7)*	*Pure rate (8)*	*Average adminis-trative cost (9)*	*Default (10)*	*Average risk premium (11)*	*Average lending cost (8+9+11) (12)*
100	200	15	20.00	10.00	15.00	50	5	40.00	27.50	55.00	100
200	400	15	10.00	9.42	13.00	38	5	20.00	26.47	45.00	70
300	600	15	6.67	7.83	10.33	32	5	13.33	21.11	31.67	50
400	800	15	3.00	6.25	8.00	28	5	10.00	14.81	20.00	35
500	1,000	15	4.00	4.80	6.00	25	5	8.00	9.60	12.00	25
600	1,200	15	3.33	4.65	5.77	24	5	6.67	6.94	8.33	20
700	1,400	15	2.85	4.19	5.15	23	5	5.71	4.56	5.29	16
800	1,600	15	2.50	3.69	4.50	22	5	5.00	2.65	3.00	13
900	1,800	15	2.22	3.12	3.78	21	5	4.44	1.50	1.66	11
1,000	2,000	15	2.00	2.50	3.00	20	5	4.00	0.91	1.00	10

months (from sowing to harvest) and his money lies idle in consequence for the rest of the year, he must charge twice the alternative annual rate (on, say, government bonds) for the duration of the loan in order to cover the opportunity cost of his money. By the time the village shopkeeper comes to relend to peasant customers, the cost may have risen from a hypothetical "pure rate" of 5 percent, which is assumed in column 8 of the table, to a "basic rate" of 15 percent, which is assumed in column 3. Unlike the other components of the rate of interest, these two elements are unlikely to vary as loan size in column 1 increases.

All this does not imply that rural lending is entirely in the hands of merchants and shopkeepers. Larger landowners play a substantial role, as do relatives and friends. Landowners have a cost for their money which corresponds to opportunities forgone in alternative investments, and they will charge accordingly. Relatives and friends who lend money also sacrifice these opportunities, but interest is rarely levied on such transactions.

The Administration Premium

It is reasonable to suppose that the village shopkeeper or landowner who lends to the small farmer places an opportunity cost on his time, even if he does no more than sacrifice leisure, and sees a cost in any unavoidable souring of relationships which may occur between lender and borrower. These are valued at $20 on a $100 loan in the first row of column 4 in the table. This so-called administrative premium of $20 a year per loan to a representative borrower is assumed to be a constant amount, regardless of the size of loan. The processing of a loan of $500, and the pursuing of the borrower at repayment time, need not be much more time-consuming or arduous than when $100 changes hands. Thus, it is assumed in both columns 4 and 9 that when the size of a loan is doubled, the premium for administration is halved as a percentage of the loan amount, and so on through the range of loan size recorded in the first column.

There is a major difference between a village shopkeeper or petty lender and an urban bank. The bank's apparatus for lending—buildings, paid clerks, and so on—means that the administrative premium on each unit loaned is higher in the formal than in the informal money market, as indeed it must be when banks safeguard other people's money. In the table, the cost of lending for urban banks in column 9 is assumed to be consistently twice that of, say, the village shopkeeper in column 4. The latter can attribute some of the cost of his shop and his time to loans and some to his normal trade.

The Premium for Risk

Risk premiums are hard to estimate. Although it is assumed that default is outright for the sake of simplicity, most cases are less clear-cut. Payments are delayed, partial payments are received, renegotiation is requested, and so on. The percentage charge on each unit loaned arises from, but is not the same as, the percentage of default. This is illustrated by the differences between columns 5 and 6 in row 1 of the table.

If $100 is loaned and a net 10 percent of borrowers in this class are in default (that is, current defaulters minus past defaulters who now repay), then the 90 percent who do repay on time will need to pay a risk premium of $15 per $100 borrowed, not the 10 percent shown in column 5. This is because the lender parts with a principal of $100, of which only $90 ($100 – [$100 × 10%]) is repaid on average, and incurs basic rate opportunity costs plus adminstrative costs (in columns 3 and 4) of $35. Of this $35, only $31.50 is recovered ($35 – [$35 × 10% default]). Thus, for every $100 which he lends, $13.50 ($10 + $3.50) is lost to the village moneylender through default on the principal plus the opportunity and administrative costs incurred but not covered by earnings during the period involved. As a proportion of the amount actually repaid, the opportunity cost arising from a 10 percent default is $13.50/$90 or 15 percent, which appears in column 6. The appropriate formula is then:

$$\text{Risk premium} = \frac{\text{assumed default rate} \times (\text{principal} + \text{lending costs})}{\text{principal actually repaid}}.$$

The total assumed cost to a moneylender of supplying $100 worth of credit is $15 basic, plus $20 administrative premium, plus $15 risk—see columns 3, 4, and 6 of the table. Hence, this moneylender cannot cover his costs unless he charges an annual interest rate of $50 on a $100 loan (column 7), or 50 percent, to individual borrowers of the type depicted here.

This, however, is by no means the end of the inquiry into the intricacies of the premium for risk. The discussion so far has done no more than establish the mechanical relationship between default and risk. But what causes default? That is the real question, and may be answered by a discussion of nine distinct considerations.

Causes of Default

• Loan size. Other things being equal, the more a man borrows, the larger will be the probability of his being unable to repay.

• Borrower net income. There appears to be a systematic tendency for larger farmers with greater assets and higher incomes to borrow more than smaller, poorer farmers throughout the developing world. If their net incomes resulting from borrowing (see column 2 of the table) increase more rapidly than the cost of borrowing, their ability to repay will automatically increase. Therefore, there will often be a positive relationship between increases in borrower net income and levels of repayment, although this correlation is not always as great as one might expect. Nevertheless, rates of default (in columns 5 and 10) are assumed to decline as the volume of borrowing and associated net income grows (in columns 1 and 2). Declining default rates in the table are predicated on an increasing ability to repay, with unwillingness to repay remaining a major separate issue. It should be noted that although there are some data on delinquency and income levels in institutional lending, there are none for the informal lender.

• Debt-equity ratio. The ratio of debt to equity will probably be lower for high-income farmers than for low-income farmers who have little owned property, even though the better-off farmers generally borrow more. The lower the ratio of borrower's debt to equity, the lower the risk to the lender and therefore the lower the interest rate which the borrower will probably have to pay.

• Value of the collateral. The collateral offered will normally be of greater value in the case of the higher-income, higher-asset farmer. This will bear on default risk in much the same way as the debt-equity ratio. As borrower income rises, the normal expectation would be for the debt-equity ratio to fall and the value of any collateral offered against a loan to rise. These three considerations, acting together, lie behind the assumption of an inverse relationship between borrower income in column 2 of the table and default rates in columns 5 and 10.

In general, the provision of security will not be an important feature of lending in the informal money market. In India and Nigeria, for example, an estimated four-fifths of debt owed to professional and agriculturalist moneylenders was unsecured. In Ecuador, 85 percent of individual moneylenders surveyed in 1966 required only a personal signature. Borrowers in poor countries often have no security to offer against a loan, and in many cases foreclosure would be socially, politically, or legally difficult to enforce on defaulting farmers.

• Defaulters brought to court. The percentage of defaulters brought successfully to court will, of course, have considerable bearing on the willful type of default. Strict repayment discipline must be established early in any rural credit program if default is to be kept within manageable limits and if borrowers are to graduate to the low-cost, urban commercial money market. The problem is that govenments often have neither the resources nor the political will to enforce repayment. In Thailand, for example, the government's agricultural bank had more than 14,000 borrowers in default, but only 64 of these had been brought to court. Under this kind of discipline, default rose more than thirtyfold between 1968 and 1971. There is widespread evidence of increasing delinquency on loans as borrowers come to realize that a particular government credit agency need not be repaid. Government credit is particularly prone to high rates of default in the absence of determined efforts to bring delinquents to book.

• Income variance. Variations in borrower incomes may be a major cause of inability to repay. Two kinds of variance affect credit risk: differences in income among farmers in a given area in any given year, and variations from one year to another because of weather or natural disasters, plant disease, price declines, or whatever.

• Administrative costs of collection. The cost of administering collection efforts may have some bearing on the rate of default. Time spent on pursuing defaulters costs money, and some lenders consider it more worthwhile than others. It is sometimes argued that steps to ensure that borrowers use their loans for productive purposes will reduce the risk of inability to repay. This is open to debate, and certainly it involves higher costs of administration. Some believe that if a farmer sees the point of adding fertilizer, he will use whatever credit he can to this end, whether supervised or not. There is some evidence of better repayment rates in government programs that stress supervision and improved inputs.

• Real rate of interest. The money rate minus the rate of inflation gives the real rate of interest on a loan. Nothing will reduce default more than a low money rate of interest coupled with a high rate of price increase; if the government lends at 10 percent during a period when the cost of living rises by 60 percent, then it is paying the borrower 50 percent to take its credit. Providing the borrower repays, he can expect such gifts to continue. To default and cut off this source of credit would be to kill the goose that lays the golden egg.

• Type of lender. The premium for risk will alter according to who makes the loan. Whether the lender is a village moneylender, an urban commercial bank, a cooperative, or governmental credit agency will affect delinquency. There is probably a tendency for default to increase from the first to the last on this list. The village moneylender is likely to have the lowest default rate on small loans. He knows the character and repayment capabilities of his clients at firsthand and he can fix would-be defaulters with a beady stare every day of their lives or even arrange for them to be beaten up. This is why it is assumed in column 10 of the table that the default rate for an urban bank will be initially a good deal higher for the smaller loans than that of the moneylender in column 5, although local moneylenders do sometimes lose quite heavily.

It is sometimes argued that extending official credit to cooperatives will reduce default on official credit since they duplicate many of the advantages of the local moneylender. The whole membership of the cooperative can be made responsible for an individual's default, and social coercion to repay can be strong. But if the government remains unwilling to treat the entire membership strictly, the group as a whole may encourage even worse overall repayment.

Monopoly Profit

Monopoly is traditionally believed to be the major cause of high informal interest rates, and no doubt it often occurs. Theoretically, a monopolist will lend up to that volume at which his marginal lending costs equal the value of the borrower's marginal product on the loan, and he will levy a rate of interest equal to this value of the marginal product. But investigators should not be misled by interest rates which do not appear to reflect the value of marginal products. The true rate is often incorporated in the prices at which the village trader sells his goods to the farmer, or at which he buys his borrower's output in cases where such transactions are associated with a loan. Loans are characteristically used to facilitate trade; it should not be assumed that they are necessarily usurious as a result. In general, it seems likely that a borrower will welcome credit and that a lender will be happy to extend it in order to ensure that farmers will sell their crops through him.

At small loan sizes and associated low income levels, the village moneylender probably has a competitive advantage over lenders from outside the village. But from the discussion of the probable relation between increases in loan size and higher net borrower income, with the associated reduction in the borrower's debt-equity ratio and increases in the value of collateral he can offer, it does seem that private urban banks could break any moneylender monopoly in the higher income ranges. This point is illustrated hypothetically in the table at a level for individual loans of $500 and an interest rate of 25 percent. Here the urban bank's 10 percent advantage in opportunity costs (columns 3 and 8) just compensates for its 10 percent disadvantage in administrative and risk premiums compared with the village moneylender (columns 9 and 11). The urban bank can thus tolerate a default rate (in column 10) at 9.6 percent of a $500 principal, which is twice that of the village moneylender in column 5. For larger loans the bank's advantage becomes more marked.

The declining average lending cost in column 12 illustrates the bank's potential for entering the rural money market in competition with the village moneylender when more than $500 is loaned per borrower. This does not mean that such a potential will always be realized, but if the hypothesis is accepted, the bank will enter into competition with the village moneylender at a loan volume of $500 and an interest rate of 25 percent. Any monopoly profit which may have accrued to the latter will then disappear—although this will not ensure against the possibility of monopolistic practices on the part of the urban banks.

Conclusions

In general, administrative costs per unit loaned should decline as loan size increases and loan term lengthens. Yet the premium for risk is also very important in the total cost of lending. If borrowers are able to repay, that is half the battle; but they may well remain unwilling to repay unless they are forced to do so, which adds to administrative cost. Governments should be prepared to support their credit agents in foreclosure. Failing that, they should ensure that a lending agency also controls the marketing of the crops on which loans are made so that repayments may be recovered from the sales.

Yet even where these things are done, the administrative expense of lending small amounts to farmers who resist repayment will still be high, particularly where trained staff are in short supply. If the village moneylender-trader can undercut this, taking into account any lower prices he may pay for a borrower's crop, let him continue to provide the necessary finance. There is no apparent reason a government should transfer income to farmers in the random manner which widespread default allows, or by charging low rates of interest which fail to cover costs. If farmers see that credit has productive uses, they will usually want to borrow. They will be able to repay principal plus costs and should be made to do so.

28. *Structure of Interest Rates on Consumption Loans in an Indian Village*

Karam Singh

[Empirical analysis of cost components for farmer-moneylenders in an Indian village shows that what seem to be very high interest rates are largely explained by high opportunity costs and risks. Monopoly profits are quite minor.]

It is often claimed that the level of interest rates in underdeveloped rural areas is mostly due to the monopoly profits of lenders. This becomes especially difficult to judge for consumption loans because their unproductive nature means the lender has a higher risk. Since capital is the scarcest factor in underdeveloped rural areas, there are many alternatives for one's money. Interest rates in underdeveloped areas are, therefore, determined by the opportunity cost of the loaned money, the risk cost, and other administrative costs that the moneylender has to incur. This leads to a consideration of the moneylender's costs and revenues: any interest rate which more than covers these three costs will contain an element of monopoly profit.

In India approximately half of total rural borrowing is reported to be for family expenditures. The present study attempts to distinguish the various cost components of interest rates for consumption loans in the village of Bahoru, Amritsar District, Punjab. Some better-off people give rice or maize to farm workers in January and February; they recover it in the form of wheat in June and July after the wheat harvest, in amounts equal in value to one and a half times the quantity of the maize or superior rice (Basmati) or one and a quarter times the quantity of the inferior rice that had been advanced to the farm workers. Some discrimination in the interest rates charged to different borrowers is exercised, which depends in most cases on the working relations of the borrower with the lender and the farmer's past loan repayment behavior.

Extracted from *Asian Economic Review*, vol. 10, no. 4 (August 1968), pp. 471–75.

Method of Study

All seven lenders of the village who extended this type of loan during January and February 1967 were interviewed. To calculate the opportunity cost of the money supplied in loans, the major business of each lender was analyzed; all the lenders were farmers. The net returns from farming with existing capital were deducted from the net returns possible using that capital plus the loaned money, estimated by linear programing, to give an opportunity cost. Only major activities during the *rabi* season, the period for which loans remained out, were considered.

The study recorded the quantities of money loaned and recovered from 1963–64 through 1966–67. The total quantity not recovered during this period was taken as the basis for a percentage risk. The costs of distribution included the labor cost of the lender for loaning and collecting, the cost of maintaining records (if any), and so on. The opportunity cost, the distribution cost, and the risk cost were deducted from the total interest, and the balance was considered the monopoly profit.

Results

Only a small quantity of grain per borrowing family, varying from 20 to 80 kilograms, was given on loan. The principal of the lender, expressed in terms of the total value loaned by him, varied from Rs96 to Rs281 with an average of Rs169. The total amounts recovered by each lender ranged from Rs176 to Rs491 (average Rs299) and the amount of interest from Rs80 to Rs210 with an average of Rs130. The average interest rate was 143 percent a year, ranging from 134 to 159 percent (table 28-1).

The 143 percent interest rate seems to be very high, but whether this high rate is justified requires examination of its cost structure. The amount that could be attributed to each component of the interest recovered by each lender is shown in table 28-2, expressed in annual percentage rates based on the principal loaned out for the season.

The farmer-lenders give loans at a time when their own farms are starved of capital, and since the marginal value productivity of capital on these Indian farms is relatively high, any increase in capital would increase the farm income substantially. In the present study, the farmer-lenders could increase their farm incomes by amounts that would have been on the average 54 percent of the interest they received on the consumption loans they extended. In terms of annual rates of return, a 77 percent rate could be attributed to the opportunity cost of lending money. Thus, the opportunity cost of giving the loan

Table 28-1. *Principal, Time, and Rate of Interest of Different Lenders*

Lender	*Principal (rupees)*	*Amount recovered (rupees)*	*Interest (rupees)*	*Average time loan remained outstanding (days)*	*Annual rate of interest (percent)*
1.	281	491	210	190	143
2.	96	176	80	192	159
3.	139	251	112	200	146
4.	125	213	89	193	134
5.	147	262	115	200	143
6.	163	289	126	197	143
7.	231	412	181	207	138
Total	1,183	2,096	913	1,379	—
Average	169	299	130	197	143

Note: Column totals and averages may be affected by rounding.

represented a very important cost and consideration, assuming that the lenders behaved rationally.

The cost of distributing the loaned money included items such as the cost to the lender for his time solely associated with the lending business and the cost of maintaining accounts, if any. This cost consumed Rs12 to Rs30, or an average of 21 percent of the loaned principal. This amounted to 15 percent of the interest received.

As with all businesses, a certain amount of risk has to be undertaken. In some instances, it is not possible for a lender to recover all or a part of his principal. He must therefore recover it from the interest re-

Table 28-2. *Components of Interest Rate Charged by Different Lenders Expressed as Annual Percentage Rates on Amounts Loaned*

Lender	*Interest rate*	*Opportunity cost*	*Cost of distribution*	*Risk cost*	*Monopoly profit*
1.	143	95	14	43	−8
2.	159	100	24	25	9
3.	146	87	31	23	6
4.	134	54	22	35	24
5.	143	62	23	40	18
6.	143	72	20	36	15
7.	138	65	23	39	11
Average	143	77	21	36	9

Note: Column averages may be affected by rounding.

ceived from other borrowers, which will of course increase the interest rate he must charge. In one case reported, none of the principal could be recovered; and in 29 other cases out of the 45 a part of the interest was not paid. The risk cost to individual lenders in the study varied from Rs12 to Rs62. This came to an average of 25 percent of the interest received and would correspond to an annual charge of 36 percent on capital loaned (see table 28-2).

After meeting the opportunity cost, the distribution cost, and the risk cost out of the interest, only nominal sums remained that could be termed monopoly profits. In one of the seven cases, these costs were even higher than the interest received by the lender, thereby putting him at a loss of Rs11 (− 8 percent on an annual basis as shown in table 28-2). In two other cases these profits were only Rs4, or 9 percent and 6 percent of the amounts loaned. In the remaining four cases, the monopoly profits were from 11 to 24 percent. The average monopoly profit accounted for no more than 9 percent of the amounts loaned.

To sum up: in terms of components of the interest charged, opportunity cost accounted for more than 50 percent, risk cost some 25 percent, and distribution cost about 15 percent of the interest charged by the village moneylenders on their consumption loans. Monopoly profits accounted for only 6 percent of the interest.

Since the size of the sample is small, no generalized inferences should be made. However, because the loans carry high risk for the lender and the opportunity cost of capital in Indian farming is also high in some areas, high interest rates on the kind of loans in rural areas that were investigated by the study are quite predictable. Monopoly profits do not explain the high rates and may account for only a negligible proportion of the interest.

29. *Aspects of Moneylending in Northern Sudan*

Martin W. Wilmington

[Village merchants, landowners, and persons with no other occupation commonly lend money to small farmers in the developing world. Their interest rates tend to be very high, and they are often denounced by intellectuals and city dwellers. But their costs and risks are also high, and their services are adapted to their clients. This chapter gives the moneylender's side of the picture.]

Samuel Johnson once described the popular concept of the creditor as a man of evil appearance and intent, always eager to squeeze the last ounce of life out of the jovial, good-natured, charitable, and innocent borrower. Though much is heard about the alleged profits and characteristics of the moneylender, little is known about his problems or the nature of his role in society. Yet without an attempt to appreciate more fully his side of the story, it will be difficult to approach realistically the need for credit reform. It is frequently overlooked, for example, that many personal loans in Asia or Africa are made not for productive purposes but for lavish wedding feasts and dowries, on which no formal credit institution would extend credit to low-income borrowers but which nevertheless answer an urgent psychological need. No thought is given to the lack of debtor ethics which makes collection a strenuous and costly affair. Nothing is said about "bad debts" and the annual losses they cause the moneylender in countries where most borrowers are only inches removed from destitution; high residential mobility—particularly between city and country—which produces a high incidence of debt evasion; and low life expectancy coupled with the general absence of insurance that make every medium- and long-term debt a special hazard. No consideration is given to where the moneylenders themselves obtain funds for business; they, in turn, may have borrowed at exorbitant rates from a tight capital market or abstracted funds from profitable pursuits in other lines.

Extracted from *Middle East Journal*, vol. 9 (1955), pp. 139–46 (the Middle East Institute, Washington, D.C.); also published by *Development Digest* (July 1980), pp. 71–78.

Many people believe that moneylenders get enormously wealthy from profits extracted from the poor. Yet the apparent wealth of such lenders may come from occupations other than lending, which is often a subsidiary business for a merchant or landowner. Moreover, a great many moneylenders, despite the exorbitant rates of interest reported, do not seem to lead the prosperous life one might expect. Finally, an explanation must be given for a widespread phenomenon: Why do private moneylenders frequently enjoy the continued patronage of poor rural and city workmen, even after socially oriented credit facilities managed by cooperatives or the state have been made available to them?

Seeking a more balanced study of the economics of the moneylending profession, I made a preliminary investigation of the problem during a stay in northern Sudan, populated by Arabic-speaking groups of predominantly Islamic faith; it may have some validity for the Middle East as a whole. To get the moneylender's side of the story is no easy matter. Most of the time he keeps no detailed records and has only the vaguest notion of the relationship between revenue, cost, and yield. His own calculations are based on hunches and rules of thumb rather than conversion tables. If he does have the facts and know-how to answer a Western-style questionnaire, he is too suspicious and secretive to expose himself. My principal source of guidance, therefore, was government officials familiar with rural problems of the country. One of them had been reared in the house of a moneylender and had observed the family business at close range.

Pattern of Borrowing

Rural credit in northern Sudan is by and large in the hands of merchants and, to a smaller extent, landowners. In contrast to India and Pakistan, few people in Sudan make moneylending to cultivators their exclusive or principal business. Major banks such as Barclays or the Ottoman Bank steer clear of the small farmer.

Generally, the merchant-lender extends credit as an advance in money or kind against the next crop, an ancient system called *shayl.* Several types of shayl are practiced. The oldest form is an advance of grain or seed valued at a price substantially above the estimated price at the next harvest. The borrower must settle the loan by returning at harvesttime enough grain to make up the money equivalent of the loan. If a good crop follows a bad crop, with a resulting drop in market prices, the lender may get back as much as five to six times the volume of goods he loaned out. Another type of arrangement under shayl is more in the nature of a middleman's service. Cultivators may find it difficult to market their crops for lack of funds to purchase sacks and meet transportation costs. The merchant will agree to take over the crop at the market price less an amount approximating the rate of short-term advances on crops.

Still another form of shayl involves the advance of money against future crops. At the beginning of the season the cultivator will solicit a sum of money (or sometimes consumer goods) to be repaid in a specified quantity of produce, say an ardeb (5.6 bushels or 196 liters) of beans. The lender will set the amount to be loaned against the future delivery substantially below the last harvest price or the anticipated value at the forthcoming harvest, whichever is lower. Thus, when the borrower delivers the pledged quantity of beans, the higher valuation of the market should, if the lender's hunch was correct, give him a considerable profit from the operation, namely the difference between the harvest value of the commodity pledged and the shayl value set by him.

What rate of interest does the lender expect? The amount varies, of course, from year to year depending on price fluctuations. Probably the best indication of lender expectations comes from data collected when grain prices were relatively stable, thanks to government controls, so that the lender could foresee with greater assurance what the next harvest price would be. A typical transaction was as follows:

	Egyptian piasters
Value of ardeb of beans, end of season	360
Shayl value of beans, start of season	200
Gross profit of lender	160

In other words, at the start of the crop year the borrower received 200 piasters on loan. About ten months later, at harvesttime, he was required either to deliver an ardeb of newly harvested beans or pay their current market price. Owing to government controls, the lender probably knew that the harvest price would be 360 piasters; the borrower therefore was expected to pay 160 piasters for a ten-month loan of 200 piasters. This would mean an annual rate of interest of approximately 100 percent.

The Moneylender's Problems

What arguments could the moneylender present if called upon to justify this high rate of interest? The case cited above involved a village merchant engaged in moneylending as a subsidiary business. In such instances the return derived from the use of capital for loans to cultivators—rather than for retail trade—must be in some relation to the yield of capital investment in retail trade. In wholesale and retail trade in the Sudan the markups may be as much as 50 percent or more, and the turnover of capital in trading is rapid; a merchant may roll over his capital as many as five times during one year. If he immobilizes a certain amount of his capital, say 100 piasters, by lending it out to a cultivator for a year, he may forgo the opportunity to earn a substantial return on several times the amount of the loan, say 500 piasters. The rate of interest on the loan, therefore, will reflect the alternative profit in trading thus sacrificed. This will be true even though he may be lending out idle capital, for the year-long immobilization of idle funds may deprive the lender of trading opportunities that turn up in two or three months. Social pressures described below, however, and the desire to maintain a large market for his trading business will induce him to use some of his capital for loans to his cultivator-customers despite the attraction of other trading ventures.

In addition, protection must be provided against a miscalculation of market conditions at the next harvest. If, because of a bumper crop, the price of beans should drop below the shayl price, the quantity delivered by the borrower in repayment of his debt will be worth less than the amount of the loan. The discount must therefore be adequate to cover the wide price range within which agricultural commodities tend to fluctuate and provide a cushion against losses from unforeseen price declines. A crop failure, although it drives up commodity prices, may also be detrimental to the moneylender, for the cultivator may not reap enough to spare an ardeb of produce for loan repayment. He needs, after all, a minimum of grain for food and sowing; and the lender would incur communal ostracism if he tried to press his claim at the price of starvation or dispossession of his client. If there is a succession of bad crops, the lender's claim may remain uncollected for several years.

Often the condition of the cultivator after a bad harvest may be such that he has to borrow still more to feed family and flock and continue cultivation. The lender then will have to increase his investment in an already delinquent client if he wants to salvage his stake at all. To offset the loss, the shayl fee is compounded upon renewal or increase of the outstanding loans to double and triple the original rate. A vicious circle soon lifts the debt to astronomical levels. The borrower now may find himself enmeshed in a lifelong pattern of annual produce deliveries to the lender, only to be terminated by his death or unusual market conditions. This lifelong servitude of the rural debtor demonstrates two facts: the collection of debts in full after the lapse of contractual terms is no easy matter, and the high contractual rates of interest decried in many studies of moneylending are often not collected in full.

The Sudanese cultivator, for his part, often does not enter into debt with the notion that it is distasteful and a moral obligation to be discharged as soon as possible. He does not necessarily save or plan a more modest wedding or dowry because of a debt load. On the contrary, he may exert much resourcefulness in avoiding payment and withholding or concealing his crop from the grasp of the lender—like his counterpart in other parts of the world. Moreover, many cultivators manage to avoid repayment by joining the thousands of their countrymen who have found employment in Egypt. Once away, the debtor can seldom be traced; he will soon be swallowed in the vast crowds of Cairo, where he starts a new existence with a new occupation and a new wife. Debt evasion, therefore, is a risk of special magnitude to be calculated in setting the shayl rate.

Much has been said about the ineffectiveness of laws to protect the debtor. There are, of course, courts in Sudan to enforce laws against usury, but the debtor knows that once he appeals to them he may never get a loan again in his community. The lenders are a tightly knit guild; they not only abstain from competing against each other by offering lower interest rates, but also promptly join in the boycott of any cultivator who seeks his day in court. The lender is reluctant to go to court, although the law affords him certain rights, lest he awaken the borrowers to the existence of legal recourse. He knows that he can recover in court only a small part of the claim he considers justified, since the law limits the rate of interest. As in other parts of the Middle East, land and property titles are often too confused to offer a reasonable prospect of success to foreclosure proceedings. Moreover, the lender may face a communal boycott of his other business if he persists in foreclosure of a poor cultivator's land.

Services Offered by the Moneylender

Not all the interest collected by the creditor is profit and risk insurance. Certain expenses and outlays have to be recovered, certain services rendered to the borrower must be compensated. Often the lender pays out of his own pocket the local taxes due on the crop delivered by the borrower. Often he must supply sacks and transportation to effect the removal of shayl produce from the borrower's field. He must store the delivered produce until it is sold and pay the cost of transportation to the market; storage expenses and losses loom large among the many hazards of the region. A staff must be maintained to do all this work and roam the countryside on collection and check-up duty.

Frequently, the creditor uses the services of a guarantor, who cosigns a loan granted to a borrower weak in resources and credit standing. The guarantor is usually a man of better financial position than the borrower and linked to the lender by an informal arrangement to perform this chore whenever needed. He is not, however, really expected to be responsible for the loan in case of default. He is used first of all to witness the transaction itself if the borrower cannot sign his name, and second to impress the borrower with the seriousness of his obligation. If default does occur, the guarantor will be sent to exert additional pressure on the delinquent or ascertain the validity of his excuses. If the borrower's plea is accepted, the guarantor will merely be required to cosign a loan renewal without any firming in his commitment. For all this he is paid a commission by the lender—another expense to be covered by the interest collected.

Some of the services which the creditor supplies are technical; for instance, he will often supervise and advise the cultivator so that the farm work is done with care and efficiency to protect the lender's stake. (Supervision at harvesttime is also intended to make sure that none of the debtors conceal or steal the mortgaged crop.) Other services extend beyond the immediate commercial relationship between lender and borrower. By communal tradition the borrower is not merely a client but in many ways a social responsibility of the lender. The latter may be expected to lend extra money for medical emergencies, weddings, and birth ceremonies regardless of the status of outstanding loans. It has been mentioned that the lender must, because of social pressure, make further loans to a delinquent cultivator—even though he might be ready to write off the debt—if the cultivator's livelihood depends on it. Some lenders are known to have continued making interest-free loans to old customers long after they have retired from business, knowing that the cultivator had come to depend on this money and would perish without it.

Another aspect of the lender-borrower relationship in Sudan and other parts of the Middle East is that, in accordance with traditional practices fostered by the Islamic prohibition of interest, the lender considers himself not a banker but a partner of the borrower. One may argue that the Sudanese lender labels himself a partner only to circumvent the laws of state and religion; yet the many social and communal obligations which surround him make him more than a "lender" in the Western sense.

Conclusions

Such, then, would be the arguments of a Sudanese moneylender in justification of his business practices. No actual business accounts were accessible for study to show the range of profits and losses in moneylending; but in view of the many intangibles in the transaction between lender and borrower, it is doubtful that figures could tell the whole story. Government officials want to provide rural communities with inexpensive, socially oriented credit facilities. But they know it is difficult to replace the intimate knowledge, the social niche, and the supervisory work in lending and recovering loans which the village merchant can give. They know that city banks would laugh off most of the loan applications the rural moneylender accepts every day as a matter of course, and that state or cooperative credit agencies find it difficult to replace some of his social services. Government programs cannot easily cope with the rural borrower's ingrained distrust and dislike of institutions and red tape as the moneylender has done for centuries with his personal and informal touch. Attempts to provide rural credit facilities devoid of the well-advertised excesses of private moneylending have very often been disappointing. Some will ascribe this to ignorance and fear. But quite a few observers suspect that the reason may be the farmers' appreciation of a relationship whose full extent no accounting by double entry can show.

30. *Indigenous Savings and Credit Societies in the Developing World*

F. J. A. Bouman

[Organizations of farmers or townspeople who periodically contribute money in small sums and receive one large amount at one time in rotation constitute an informal mechanism that mobilizes savings and in some cases supports productive investments. The range and flexibility of these organizations are described, and their potential as a form of financial intermediation is discussed.]

A rotating savings and credit association is a group of participants who make regular contributions to a fund which is given, in whole or in part, to each member in turn. When there are ten participants, each contributing $10 monthly, each one in turn will receive $100 at every monthly meeting—the individuals chosen in turn by some method such as drawing lots. After ten months everyone will have received $100 and the cycle is closed. This is the simplest form, where no deductions are made to compensate the organizer for his responsibilities, no competitive bidding for the fund takes place, and no other agreement interferes with the fund's distribution or volume.

The first collector receives an interest-free loan from all the others. The last in line is saving money as he extends credit to his fellow members. The others alternate between debtor and creditor positions. The term rotating credit association has been used for these organizations; but it is not only the credit that rotates, the savings positions rotate too. Therefore, I prefer the term "rotating savings and credit association"—ROSCA, for short.

Ingredients of ROSCA Success

ROSCAS are a worldwide phenomenon, appearing in many parts of Africa, East and South Asia, both Americas, the Caribbean area, the Middle East, and even in early Europe. What accounts for their popularity among cultures as diverse as Ethiopia and Indonesia, Benin and

Extracted from *Savings and Development,* vol. 1, no. 4 (1977), pp. 181–214; also published in *Development Digest,* vol. 16, no. 3 (July 1978), pp. 36–47.

India? Common ingredients of ROSCA success include its accessibility, simple procedures, flexibility, and adaptability to many purposes. Any village, hamlet, or even family compound can form its own association. This easy access contrasts with formal finance institutions, to which large segments of the rural population have no access at all, while many others find access difficult. The geographical isolation of rural inhabitants, the psychological barrier arising from the impersonal approach, institutionalized suspicion, and the red tape of formal lending agencies scare away many prospective clients. In addition, commercial banks often demand minimum deposits and minimum loan sizes to stave off unprofitable transactions. In sum, the administrative machinery of the formal banking system in the developing world usually is not attuned to the poor, while ROSCAS are open to even the poorest.

ROSCA procedures, simple, flexible, and rather informal, contain effective mechanisms which regulate membership eligibility, credit rating, and repayment. The smallness of the group—commonly between ten and thirty participants in rural areas—ensures members' knowledge of each other's characters. Coupled with social control, this is an important barrier against fraud and defaulting. Almost all observers agree that obligations are taken very seriously.

Most African groups, for example, collect contributions in public at meetings of the full membership; failure to contribute is immediately noticed and met with expressions of collective disapproval. This contrasts with default on institutional loans.

The foremost appeal of a ROSCA is probably the contractual savings element. Through the regularity of small deposits, which otherwise might be spent on trivialities, one is able to accumulate more sizable sums for a worthwhile cause. The fact that loan repayments are also in installments appeals to participants. This contrasts favorably with short-term institutional loans that usually have to be repaid in one lump sum at maturity, which may inconvenience borrowers.

Flexibility is the hallmark of ROSCAS, and there are innumerable variations to the basic pattern outlined above. Participants may range from a handful to a few hundred; they can have one or more shares in one association, or two members may agree to share a turn. In large Asian cities, some people participate in up to five clubs at the same time. The order of rotation may be decided by lot, consensus, seniority, auction, negotiation, even by bribery, or by decision of the ROSCA president (this mostly in Africa). Different criteria are also used for membership eligibility, credit rating, payment obligations, and sanctions. Contributions may be in kind, but are generally in cash, ranging from a few pennies to more than US$100 equivalent per meeting.

Payments may be daily, as with shoeshine boys in Addis Ababa or the market traders and street vendors in India, or they may be weekly, monthly, or any other agreed period. The lifetime of a ROSCA and, concomitantly, the duration of a loan or savings period depend on the number of players and the length of intervals, and some can be very long lasting. The longer the duration, the greater the risk of default and of inflationary effects. The types most frequently encountered run from one to two years.

ROSCAS must often accommodate to a changing environment. Before the introduction of Western currency and monetization of the economy, the *djanggi* in Cameroon operated on brass bracelets, livestock, food, and other commodities, but then shifted to money. Liberian ROSCAS substituted money for rice in the 1920s after the Firestone plantation started paying employees in cash. These societies flourish not only in a traditional rural setting but also in towns and cities of all sizes, often as a focal point for ethnic enclaves, new occupational groups, or recent settlers and migrants; they form a link between the rural and urban worlds. While ROSCAS originally were instrumental in collecting dowries and meeting traditional expenses for religious ceremonies or funerals and weddings, members now use them to save for education fees, brick and zinc-roofed houses, sophisticated furniture, and yearly taxes.

Savings and Investment

Contractual saving appears the prime mover of these societies, but the credit element seems to become more important with the promise of economic opportunities. In such conditions the lottery selection system has been replaced by a system of competitive bidding for the fund in some cities. In parts of India the traditional *chitty* has blossomed into a modern banking enterprise based on written rules and a constitution, records and accounts, title deeds and promissory notes; a similar line of evolution can be seen in East Asia.

In Africa, developments have been less spectacular. The *djanggi* meetings at Babanki, Cameroon, for example, still follow traditional patterns, mixing business with pleasure. Being president of a society is still a matter of trust and prestige rather than of business acumen and economic gain. In nearby Nkongsamba, however, *tontines* have already introduced the auction system, and a fertilizer fund has been introduced.

ROSCAS are better able to perform these economic functions because they are also social institutions. Meetings of ROSCAS are both festive and business occasions and foster community solidarity and group interaction. These associations keep alive traditions and yet accommodate change, placating both the more conservative older and the impatient younger generations. Because they assist group cohesion, they have a potential mechanism to maneuver a community through a period of socioeconomic transition. This is particularly important for migratory groups of urban workers. Kinship networks find expression in these societies and cover both the urban enclave and rural area of origin. Meetings are used to exchange news from the countryside, to assist newcomers in finding employment and lodgings, to celebrate members' successes, and to solve quarrels among the group or disputes between a member and outsiders. The societies are also a vehicle to social status and prestige, while the allocation of turns in chairmanship and committees can foster education in money handling and business acumen.

Examples of Investment from ROSCA Proceeds

ROSCAS have provided entrepreneurs with capital to start a business, replace trading stock and machinery, buy or repair a fishing boat and equipment, or open a restaurant or retail shop. It is quite common for women in Cameroon to pool their savings for the purchase of a cornmill to relieve themselves of the tedious task of grinding maize; the time gained is often devoted to agriculture or petty trade. Investment in the education of one's children via participation in a ROSCA may be seen as part of its development function. [See chapter 15.]

Mutual aid societies and ROSCAS may also transfer capital from cities to villages. Members of urban societies privately invest in the purchase of rural land and housing; ethnic groups also collectively put money into self-help schemes and development projects in their native hinterland.

Effects of ROSCAs on Saving and Investment Behavior

Most development economists no longer uphold the once popular stereotype that peasants in developing countries cannot and do not save. The role that indigenous savings and credit associations play in stimulating savings is hard to assess with present knowledge. But by and large, available evidence suggests that they do play a significant role in generating rural and urban savings in many areas. Ethiopia's 1968–73 development plan estimated the annual savings volume in *ekubs* between E$200 million and E$250 million (equivalent to US$90 million to US$115 million), representing 8 to 10 percent of gross domestic product. This is a formidable performance for indigenous ROSCAS in a low-income economy commonly recognized as stagnant. In Kerala State of India, chit funds form 20 percent of all bank deposits. Extraordinarily large amounts of cash are involved in typical merchants' ROSCAS in both urban and rural environments.

The uses to which ROSCA funds are put—investment, consumption, or hoards—have been still less studied than the amounts saved. K. Harteveld ["Saving and Credit in the Grassfields," unpublished manuscript, Wageningen University, Netherlands, 1972], analyzing sixty-nine *djanggi* in Cameroon, summarizes the uses to which funds are put:

	Percentage of total
Family consumption	28
Education fees	17
Tax	14
Medical care	8
Dowries, obligation to in-laws	8
Trade and investment	7
Zinc roof	4
Debts (djanggi, 7 percent; others, 6 percent)	13

From his 1976 survey of two villages in Benin, R. Verhagen [personal communication] deduces that people attach high value to expenditures that enhance status and prestige. He lists the uses of tontine proceeds, in order of priority, as the purchase of a house, a wife, a bicycle, a watch or radio, and a zinc roof. After ROSCA members meet their primary objectives, their preferences grow in diversity: some are eager to obtain modern conveniences, others invest in apprentice contracts or go into business and trade. Time preferences for production and consumption vary with age; Verhagen's conclusion is that status is preferred early in life, productive investment later.

D. Levin [*Susu and Investment in Trinidad*, Research Paper no. 8, Trinidad, Central Statistical Office, 1975] investigated the uses of *susu* funds in Trinidad in 1975. He concludes that, as the fund gets larger, the greater is the tendency of members to invest the proceeds. The size of a fund increases with the number of participants; prospective investors who cannot afford large contributions will therefore join a susu with many participants. Levin further notes that blue-collar workers and self-employed artisans invest more often than white-collar workers. There is a marked difference among various age groups: no susu participant below the age of thirty encountered by Levin, whether blue- or white-collar worker, invests. This resembles Verhagen's findings in Benin.

Traditional and Modern Institutions—a Case for a Merger?

Governments, bankers, and students of development have reservations about traditional savings and credit systems, in spite of evidence demonstrating the ingenuity and improvisation with which villagers and urban migrants successfully manage to organize savings and credit facilities. Lack of knowledge about indigenous savings and mutual aid societies can lead to misapprehensions. According to S. Ardener ["The Comparative Study of Rotating Credit Associations," *Journal of the Royal Anthropological Institute*, vol. 94, no. 2, 1964], government circles in Ghana regard the ROSCA as a social evil, dangerous, and primitive, and the same has been noted in Nigeria and Cameroon. Rumor has it that ROSCA meetings are occasions for drunkenness and display of conspicuous consumption, that fraud and embezzlement are the rule, and that default becomes widespread once migration becomes easier. This negative outlook is supposedly fed from several sources: belief in the propriety of modern institutions; preoccupation with nation building, which discredits local associations as tribal; and opportunism among those who stand to gain most from modern financial intermediation.

Apparently, most development theorists remain skeptical about the potential contribution of traditional institutions to development, partly because much information about ROSCAs is sketchy and inaccurate, with little detailed analysis. Some of the arguments raised against ROSCAs are: (1) Traditional institutions are apt to maintain the old power structure. But do modern institutions do anything different? (2) Improved communications and increased migration will weaken internal social control and encourage defaulting. But empirical evidence from the most critical urban environments does not support the assertion. (3) The individual participant has no influence over the size of his fund. This usually is true, but there are choices: one can take more than one share, participate in several groups at once, or try to organize a new ROSCA closer to one's taste. (4) In the lottery and some other schemes the individual cannot decide the exact time he will receive his money. But this is why competitive bidding has been introduced in some areas. (5) Savers do not receive interest on their deposits. In some cases, however, they do; and the first drawers, of course, can always use their funds in the local capital market. (6) Contractual savings may embarrass a participant who suddenly finds himself without income. But this problem is present in any kind of contractual obligation.

What are the prospects for indigenous savings and credit associations and for their integration with the modern financial sector? Institutional organization of ROSCAs has advantages for both parties. For a bank, a ROSCA could mobilize savings and attract a new type of clientele, normally too shy to cross its threshold. Commissions and fees from running a chitty can be quite handsome. For participants, affiliation with a bank would bring the benefits of organizational expertise, efficiency, and financial reserves. Experience in India shows that the rate of failure caused by a lack of reserves to cover defaults is lower for chit funds organized by banks than for those established by individual ROSCA promoters, and that banks charge lower commissions than individual organizers.

A massive influx of outside resources into a rural area has potentially dangerous repercussions on the social framework if not carefully related to the absorptive capacity of the community. The more one moves away from what is traditionally acceptable, the greater the chance of disrupting the fabric of affinity and of social control in face-to-face relations. Liberal financial assistance to development can easily provoke fraud, jealousy, corruption, and evasion of obligations and thus destroy the potential for the development of a new "commercial ethic." To a certain extent this has already been the fate of some state-sponsored agricultural credit programs. Provision of credit has to be kept within the context of the socioeconomic environment of the borrower, and here there is much to learn from traditional credit suppliers.

If the channeling of public funds via traditional circuits requires handling with great care, what about the reverse—the channeling of rural savings mobilized by traditional institutions into the formal capital market? Typically, the formal capital market has largely chosen to ignore the existence of traditional savings and credit associations. As catalysts of rural savings, these associations could link the informal and formal money markets. But is such a link desirable? It would not necessarily increase the amount of savings; it could merely transfer resources from the informal to the formal capital market. This, in itself, is no guarantee of optimum use of resources. ROSCAS are the poor man's bank, where money is not idle for long but changes hands rapidly, satisfying both consumption and production needs. Where banks, cooperatives, or credit unions have tried to serve people at this level, low repayment rates and substantial losses have often resulted. But under the triple shelter of local knowledge, collective support, and social control, traditional institutions usually avoid such disasters.

Rural people commonly preserve liquid assets as insurance against future calamity, and if they think they will need "instant" capital they may keep these assets out of traditional channels of savings and credit. Here the institutional market could provide a safe place to deposit money where it earns interest. Banks in India and the Republic of Korea demonstrate that it is possible to attract savings accumulated via the ROSCA.

The formal and informal capital markets in developing countries are serving the interests of different types of clientele. Integration of the two under present circumstances might not benefit the weaker section of the economy, a section for which the formal market has not shown much concern in the past. The survival of the ROSCA over the years, and its persistence even in sophisticated city economies, suggests that there still is a need and a place for this institution alongside the more modern financial intermediaries. There is a vital lesson here for the advocates of building stronger institutions on traditional forms of savings and credit. If the case is sometimes made for modernizing traditional institutions, surely an even stronger plea can be made for traditionalizing modern institutions.

31. *Procuring Loans by Pledging Cocoa Trees*

R. O. Adegboye

[The use of cocoa trees as loan security and a source of income to lenders is widespread in western Nigeria. The terms and conditions of these loans have changed greatly over time. Borrowers pledging cocoa trees reported at the time this study was undertaken that school fees constituted the most important reason for borrowing. Although these loans involve written agreements between borrowers and lenders, performance by both appears to vary greatly, and certain reforms could improve the quality of these informal market transactions.]

Financial difficulties sometimes lead people to borrow money. And since the borrower's interest in borrowing is no less than the lender's interest in the repayment of the money borrowed, the method of carrying out the lending-borrowing transaction must be acceptable to both parties. One such method over the years in western Nigeria has been the pledging of land or of trees on the land. The use rights to a borrower's trees are enjoyed by the person who lends the money until his money is returned.

In the past a loan repayment involved, among other things, an "installmental work rate" assessed by the lender to be equivalent to interest rate until the principal was paid. The borrower, alone or with his entire family—that is, the husband, wife or wives, and children—would live at the lender's village to work on the lender's farm from sunrise to about 4:00 P.M. The borrower was generally given a plot to farm for himself if he did not already have plots in the area. The proceeds from any crops raised on the borrower's plots were generally applied to the liquidation of the loan. The lender would refuse repayment if it were made too soon, that is, if the lender had not realized sufficient interest on the loan. The loan might be written off, however,

Extracted from a reprint in October 1972 by the Agricultural Development Council (New York) from the *Journal of the Geographical Association of Nigeria*, vol. 12, nos. 1 and 2 (December 1969).

when the lender felt that the borrower either had worked sufficiently or would never be able to pay the debt.

From the above the *Iwofa* system evolved, whereby the borrower needed only to pledge his son or nephew to the lender until the money was paid back. When there was no son or nephew who could perform such obligations, the borrower himself had to report to the lender periodically for farm assignments generally lasting no less than five days at a stretch and usually no more than three times a year. The help from such a borrower was generally obtained during the peak seasons of clearing, planting, and harvesting. Even if loans were given without the usual pledge, the borrower occasionally felt obliged to help the lender in his farm work as a customary gesture of appreciation.

Trees such as cocoa, oil-palm, and rubber have gradually become important items in pledging. They have in recent years taken the place of a borrower's pledging himself or a close relation. There is virtually no village within the Western State of Nigeria where people do not practice the art of pledging cocoa trees. It is not necessary for the pledgee to come from the same village or even the same state as the pledgor. In fact, studies have found that better business relations occur when the only contact between the pledgee and the pledgor is brought about by pledging.

The purpose of this study is to observe the reasons for pledging tree crops, particularly cocoa trees in Nigeria; to describe the process by which the creditor-debtor relationship is established; to evaluate the use of pledging as a loan-procuring mechanism with respect to redemption problems; to explore some alternative loan-procuring opportunities; and to suggest ways by which the pledging system can be improved. Seventy villages were randomly selected from six principal cocoa-growing areas in the Western State. No less than five and no more than ten people were interviewed in each village. The respondents were those who had taken or were taking cocoa trees as collateral for a loan. These lenders will be referred to as pledgees, while their corresponding debtors are called pledgors. In all, 600 pledgees were interviewed.

The pledgee typical of this study does not generally fit the description of a professional moneylender. Invariably he is an artisan interested in cocoa trees for supplementary income. He may be a teacher, carpenter, tailor, palm-wine tapper, photographer, council clerk, or a produce buyer. He is not a rich man but is not poor by the village standard. He is in many cases a stranger to the pledgor.

Reasons for Pledging Cocoa Trees

Pledgees were asked to rank from the most important to the least important the principal reasons their debtors have for pledging. Many reasons are known not only to the pledgees but also to the whole neighborhood; funerals, marriages, litigation, and prolonged illness are customarily accepted as the main causes of borrowing. Their order of importance as ranked by pledgees was as follows.

1. Children's education. It was expected that marriages or funerals would be the most important reason for pledging cocoa trees. The biggest surprise in this study is the number one rank given to children's education. Out of a total of seventy villages in the study, at least one respondent in each of sixty-eight villages named children's education as the most important reason for pledging. In twenty-four villages the entire 192 respondents ranked children's education highest.

The reason behind this newly found support for children's education is that education is now looked upon as an investment, and children benefiting from the loan raised through pledging would most likely help in redemption of the pledge.

2. Marriage and funeral ceremonies. Iwo, Ife, and Ijesha divisions attach great importance to the celebrations that customarily accompany marriage and death. It is, however, a happy note that children's education is given a higher rating.

3. Litigation. Boundary disputes and sometimes chieftaincy contests often lead to prolonged court cases, which in turn force owners to pledge when they cannot sell their property. Since both sides of a court case cannot win, there is bound to be a financial loss on at least one side. It sometimes happens that the declared winner may not be the happier for it if he has to count the costs and returns in economic terms. Instances of prolonged litigation were cited as an important reason for pledging in most of the villages studied.

4. Old age and sickness. Even though it cannot be localized, old age and sickness are mentioned as a reason for pledging less frequently among literate and probably retired pledgors than among others. In the Egba-Egbado division most pledgors earn some form of pension and therefore do not count old age and sickness as strong enough reasons to pledge their cocoa trees.

5. Tax payment. The Flat Rate in western Nigeria is £3 5*s*. (values are for the late 1960s). To this is added the other rates and levies for self-help and community amenities, which would on the average add another £2 to it, thereby making the income tax something like £5 5*s*. This tax would look small to the average wage earner in western Nigeria but not to the many farmers who realize less than £50 cash income a year from all their farm activities. Furthermore, some of the farmers concerned had to pay an additional tax assessment which is seldom if ever based on the true value of assets.

6. Moving out of agriculture. Very few people ever move out of agriculture in the Western State, partly because employment opportu-

nities outside agriculture are very limited. Agriculture is insurance. To move out of agriculture is therefore not a popular reason for pledging cocoa trees. The most that owner-artisans would do is to rent out the cocoa trees if they found it difficult to operate the plots with hired labor.

7. Agricultural improvement. There are instances from the study where a farmer would pledge part of his cocoa trees for money to buy equipment and improvements, such as a spraying machine and spray, to increase the yield on the remaining trees. However, there was no instance of a farmer's pledging cocoa trees to buy fertilizer for yam or maize production. Most land for food crops had been put into cocoa in most of the cocoa-growing areas.

The Process of Pledging

If a farmer wishes to establish a pledgor-pledgee relationship, the first problem is to locate a pledgee. In some areas reputable money-lenders are interested in cocoa trees as collateral; they may be organized into cooperatives or may operate as individuals. Those in this study were usually strangers in the town or village concerned. Occasionally it is the fairly rich people of the town who loan money to the less fortunate ones in exchange for use rights over cocoa trees. In general it is not difficult for farmers who need money to locate pledgees, whether through the help of someone else or from the would-be pledgor's past experience.

Before signing the agreement, certain information is sought both by the pledgor and the pledgee. The pledgor is interested in the pledgee's past record of leniency with his debtors, that is, whether he would seek foreclosure or would help the debtor achieve his goal of redeeming the cocoa trees. The pledgee would seek information about whether the trees were communally or individually owned, whether the trees had been pledged out or sold to someone else, the age and health of the trees, the number of trees or the size of plot concerned, the specific reason for the pledging, their location and distance from the village or town, and the repayment ability of the pledgor. Neighbors give answers on creditworthiness, leniency, state of ownership, and the specific reason for pledging where necessary. In addition, the pledgee and the pledgor arrange an inspection visit to the plot to be pledged.

There may be differences in the provisions made in agreements from village to village. The following provisions are common:

- The pledge price per cocoa tree is 1 *s*. Circumstances such as old age, poor health of trees, and urgency in borrowing can make pledgees pay less.
- Net proceeds during the pledge period are treated as interest payment on the pledgee's loan.

- A minimum period of one year is expected to enable the pledgee to realize some interest.
- Only cocoa trees may be harvested by the pledgee; other permanent trees such as kola nut and palm trees that grow on the same land as the pledged cocoa trees would remain the property of the pledgor.
- The right of entry and exit is accorded the pledgor.
- Repledging the already pledged trees can be done only with the consent of the pledgee.
- Redemption of the pledge is always possible.

There was provision for foreclosure in some of the agreement papers, but according to informants the foreclosure clause is rarely enforced. In some places pledgees take a cash payment of interest in addition to harvesting the cocoa trees of their debtors; examples of this were found in Iwo and Ife divisions. In Ilesha division a pledge is treated as a lease by which the pledgee can harvest the trees for a certain number of years depending on the amount of money involved relative to the size of plot. This type of arrangement is common among old pledgors who may be unable on their own to redeem the pledge. The cocoa trees in this case are self-redeeming.

All 600 respondents in this study possess some form of signed document. These agreements vary in their legal validity. Three main types were noticed during the course of study: The first involves a letter writer who writes the agreement, makes two or more copies, reads it to the contracting parties, and makes them sign by affixing their thumb prints, generally on a postage stamp fixed to the agreement, which is regarded as evidence of government authority. The second type requires each of the contracting parties to have a witness, and the document is signed in a lawyer's office with the lawyer acting as letter writer and witness. A total of five people are required to complete the signing. In the third type a surveyor is employed to sketch a map of the plot in question and witness the agreement in addition to all those procedures mentioned for the second type.

Redemption Problems and Prospects

Redemption of the pledged cocoa trees is hindered by several factors. If other disasters follow closely that which caused the original pledging, the pledgor may seek additional money from the pledgee to turn the transaction into an outright sale. If all the pledgor's cocoa trees, or all his best trees, have been pledged out, he may be unable to raise enough of another crop to pay the loan. Cocoa is in many areas the chief income-earning crop.

The pledgor may die, leaving children and relatives who are unable or unwilling to redeem the pledge. Those who could take on the right of redemption may not know of the pledge. In Ijesha division most pledges are kept secret because a pledgor is regarded as a disgrace to the entire family. Upon learning that a relative has pledged his cocoa trees, a family member may become angry and fight to effect a quick redemption of such a pledge. Sometimes trees are repossessed without repayment of the loan.

Hazards of Pledging

Often when creditors are not interested in agriculture, or cocoa trees in particular, the potential output of cocoa is not realized since cultivation, spraying, and harvesting are not given adequate attention. Pledgors who were once the owner-operators of cocoa tree plots become less and less eager to redeem their plots when they have deteriorated. Although the right of redemption passes to the heirs of the pledgors and the right of use and retention could pass to the children of the pledgees, both rights decrease in value if damages suffered by the cocoa trees through neglect appear to be greater than the potential earning capacity of the plots. And if the agreed period of redemption is short, the pledgee would not like to make any permanent improvement unless guaranteed an adequate compensation—a proposition beyond the means of the poor pledgor.

The creditor also suffers some hazards. Sometimes the profit derived from operating the cocoa plots may be less than the rate of return elsewhere, but his capital is tied up indefinitely until the loan is repaid. He does not enjoy much good will from the debtor, who may occasionally steal from his old plot. At other times, a creditor may become the pledgee of a plot with dubious ownership and thereby forfeit both the principal and expected interest.

Alternatives to Pledging

Other ways of raising loans need to be explored, since pledging cocoa trees does not seem to be the best answer, particularly in view of redemption problems. There is no doubt that the value of cocoa is attractive to the lenders, and that the pledge of cocoa crops helps the business of produce buyers. Litigation could be avoided if both the creditor and the debtor would face the repayment problems with honesty—that is, if the creditor would treat the pledge as a lease and consider his net gains on the harvest each year as part of the repayment. It may be argued, however, that this would remove the inducement to lend money, since a normal lease would not give the creditor any interest payment. Pledging seems to be the only method acceptable to the lender because trees serve as collateral. Wealthier neighbors and relations would probably make loans to their poorer friends without any collateral were it not for the difficulty of repayment. Thrift societies could reduce the need for pledging if members do not often pull out of the society shortly after it is their turn to collect the savings [see chapter 30 on the nature of these societies]. Produce buyers, like other petty traders, would advance money to their customers in expectation of buying the customers' products, but frequent defaults and desertions render this method less appealing. Agricultural cooperatives could probably come the closest to minimizing, if not removing, the hazards of pledging. Efficient cooperatives financed by monthly contributions from members (as in Ondo) could turn farmers away from exploitive moneylenders and help restore pledged cocoa trees to their original owners. Some borrowers would like to keep their borrowing secret, however, and would rather pay a higher rate of interest to a private lender than face the publicity of a cooperative loan.

A certain amount of pledging will continue, and improvements in the system should be considered. The government should regulate the relationships between the pledgor and the pledgee. All pledging could and should be made public, so that taxes could be assessed on the true income of both the pledgor and the pledgee. The government could empower the local councils to supervise pledging where necessary. It should print standardized forms (to save the cost of the letter writer), employ the services of the Court Registry before the Commissioner for Oaths, and even provide lawyers at low cost.

The government could legislate that instead of yielding use and control of the pledged property to the pledgee, the pledgor could continue as owner-operator and pay the lender an interest rate equivalent to the local bank's rate until the principal is repaid. The land would then be in the care of someone who has a life interest in it and who can make improvements as need arises. Another approach would be to avoid foreclosure by fixing a time—say, five years—when the cocoa trees become automatically redeemed; that is, the government would deem the pledgee to have realized enough profit through good management to cover his principal and interest within the fixed period.

Financial Intermediation by Cooperatives and Borrower Groups

Of the five chapters in this section, the first two deal mainly with small groups of borrowers formed primarily to manage a loan jointly, while the last three concern cooperative organizations with a wider range of activities and a more stable membership. [Additional analyses of cooperatives are found in chapters 41 and 42.]

Schaefer-Kehnert (chapter 32) gives an account of the highly successful experience with group lending in Malawi, following failure to establish a more ambitious type of cooperative. Repayment performance has been excellent, and the government plans to use this approach throughout the country. Desai (chapter 33) surveys experiments with group lending in ten countries, some of which have borrower groups with more elaborate functions than those covered by Schaefer-Kehnert. He finds a variety of experiences and somewhat inconclusive results. Generally the grouping of borrowers does reduce costs for lenders and borrowers, but its effect on repayment rates is mixed, and some other anticipated benefits have usually not appeared.

Lee, Kim, and Adams (chapter 34) describe the activities of well-established cooperatives that include 80 percent of farm households in the Republic of Korea as members. Savings and credit facilities, along with technical services, farm inputs, crop marketing, and mutual insurance are provided through this officially sponsored cooperative federation. By 1970, savings deposits equaled half the funds loaned by cooperatives, and the proportion grew further. High real interest rates on deposits in most years were a major reason for saving, but convenience of facilities and official promotion helped the cooperatives mobilize these savings. Savings deposits were important in making possible the level of other services received by members.

Illy (chapter 35) describes the very unsuccessful performance of officially promoted credit cooperatives in Cameroon. After a few carefully supervised loans for farm inputs, which were largely repaid, the credit program moved into a period of very rapid expansion; supervision of loan use became less intense and was finally undermined by allowing "social credit"; defaults mounted uncontrollably. The author finds reasons for failure in administrative methods, in the incentives for extension workers to promote the formation of cooperatives and to inflate loan amounts, and in the misconception of planners as to the reactions of farmers—who unexpectedly came to regard the loans as gifts.

In chapter 36 Von Pischke outlines the success of coffee growers' cooperatives in Kenya in introducing a method whereby members could accumulate savings in accounts with the cooperative. Payments for coffee delivered were deposited directly in these savings accounts. Deposit balances grew rapidly, which the author believes indicates that the facility satisfied an important need. The cooperatives offered greater convenience and better terms than had been previously available. Elements of successful rural savings schemes are noted.

32. *Success with Group Lending in Malawi*

Walter Schaefer-Kehnert

[The Lilongwe Land Development Program initiated a method of lending to small groups of farmers that has been highly successful, especially in loan repayment. Farmers' clubs formed to assist extension work have also dealt successfully with small-farmer group credit.]

The high cost of lending to individual small farmers is a major concern in rural development programs. In Japan and parts of western Europe before industrialization, when their agrarian structures were characterized by small farms, this problem was solved by the formation of cooperatives. In addition to credit, these organizations supplied farm inputs and produce marketing services at lower costs than those charged by private trade. Efforts to introduce such multipurpose cooperatives in developing economies have often failed (with outstanding exceptions in the Republic of Korea and Taiwan), and attempts are being made to find simpler and more manageable "precooperative" structures that provide at least part of the services of the classical farmers' cooperative. One type of precooperative organization is that for group credit, which has been introduced in a number of countries in recent years but with limited benefits. The case of Malawi provides one of the few successful examples.

Shortly after independence Malawi failed in an attempt to promote rural cooperatives. Because of this experience, integrated rural development projects made no use of farmers' cooperatives in their early operations, and not until 1973 was group credit introduced in the pioneer Lilongwe Land Development Program (LLDP) to reduce the costs of lending.

Farmers' cooperatives typically have several hundred members, whose dues can pay for a full-time secretary. Credit groups in Malawi, however, have only ten to thirty members each and rely on unpaid

Extracted from *Zeitschrift für Ausländishe Landwirtschaft* [Quarterly Journal of International Agriculture, Berlin], vol. 19, no. 4 (October-December 1980), pp. 331–37; also published in *Development Digest* (January 1982), pp. 10–15.

management, which keeps lending costs low. The administrative staff usually consists of a chairman who provides the leadership, a treasurer who ensures trustworthiness, and a secretary who maintains the records of the group. There are more than enough volunteers to fill these positions, because the farmers are not fully employed on their small holdings, and the posts provide social prestige.

In group lending operations the security for credit repayment is usually provided by the joint liability of group members. If a default occurs on obligations to the lender, credit to the whole group is stopped until the default is corrected (and legal action against an individual member may also be taken). This may cause the entire group to be deprived of farm inputs such as improved seeds and fertilizers for the next growing season, which would result in a drop in production. To avoid such losses the Malawi group credit scheme introduced a security fund.

Borrowing farmers pay 10 percent of the loan amount as a deposit into a common fund that is kept in trust by the credit institution for the group. If there is a default, the shortfall is made up by drawing on the security fund. Farmers are then free to apply for new credit as soon as the fund is replenished. The group can also evict the defaulting members. Originally 20 percent of a group's credit was to be deposited into a security fund, but Malawi experience indicated that a 10 percent deposit was sufficient to cover the risk.

A gradual accumulation of deposits over a period of years was originally planned, so that an insurance fund against crop failure could be initiated. The LLDP administration did not pursue this idea, however, because most farmers preferred to disband their groups after each season and establish new ones before the next season, so that the membership could be kept flexible. The flexibility was advantageous because as the number of credit groups quickly expanded, the membership of individual groups became increasingly concentrated in smaller locations. Village groups and eventually extended families chose to form credit groups. This structure guarantees a higher degree of loyalty from the members because it avoids the anonymity from which cooperative societies with a wider membership usually suffer.

Prior to the formation of the credit groups, another precooperative structure had been promoted by Malawi's marketing agency, ADMARC. This organization encouraged the formation of input supply groups through which farmers could order their fertilizer by the truckload. Members of these groups received a discount on the price of fertilizer and could have it delivered to the location of their choice. This scheme had been highly successful and encouraged LLDP to embark on the group credit scheme.

In areas outside the main projects, the government extension service initiated a drive to form farmers' "clubs" for the purpose of group extension. These clubs established demonstration plots, and club members helped each other introduce modern technologies. In some cases members also undertook communal projects, such as village firewood plantations. Gradually the services of these clubs expanded to include group input supplies and group credit, so that now they are almost equivalent to multipurpose cooperatives. In 1980 there were approximately 200 farmers' clubs, each with a membership of close to 100. Although the membership per club is larger than that of a credit group, only twenty or so members of a farmers' club actually take out loans in a season.

Group Credit Development and Performance

Group credit was first tried in the Lilongwe project and then spread into farmers' clubs outside the project areas. Other integrated rural development projects in Malawi have also experimented with group credit, but statistics on these operations are not available.

Table 32-1 shows the number of individual and group borrowers in the LLDP area from 1972–73 through 1978–79. Also shown are the number of credit groups and the average number of borrowers per group over this period. (The LLDP administration expected the number of credit groups to reach 2,000 in 1978–79, but the number actually fell short of the 1977–78 figure because the fertilizer being financed did not arrive on time in sufficient quantities.) There are now more group borrowers than individual borrowers, and it is expected that group borrowing will continue to increase rapidly. The government is even considering allowing only group credit in new development areas.

Table 32-2 shows the loan amounts borrowed under the LLDP by individuals and farmer groups, the average loan per borrower, and

Table 32-1. *LLDP Individual and Group Borrowers*

Year	*Borrowers (thousands)*			*Number of groups*	*Borrowers per group*
	Total	*Individual*	*Group*		
1972–73	21.1	21.1	—	—	—
1973–74	25.7	23.9	1.8	94	19
1974–75	25.1	20.5	4.6	242	19
1975–76	32.2	24.6	7.6	410	19
1976–77	36.8	23.5	13.3	670	20
1977–78	42.5	14.6	27.9	1,267	22
1978–79	51.5	23.1	28.4	1,217	23

— Not applicable.

Table 32-2. *LLDP Individual and Group Loans*

	Amount of loans (thousands of Malawi kwacha)			*Loan per borrower (Malawi kwacha)*		*Repayment (percent)*	
Year	*Total*	*Individual*	*Group*	*Individual*	*Group*	*Individual*	*Group*
1972–73	382	382	—	18	—	97	—
1973–74	481	460	21	19	12	98	100
1974–75	737	601	136	29	30	98	100
1975–76	859	624	235	25	31	96	99
1976–77	1,012	627	385	27	29	100	100
1977–78	1,292	453	839	31	30	100	100
1978–79	1,461	656	805	28	28	n.a.	n.a.

— Not applicable.
n.a. Not available.

repayment records. The total amount loaned almost quadrupled over six years, and group credit climbed from zero to more than 50 percent of the loan portfolio. The average amount borrowed per farmer is around MK30 (Malawi kwacha 30 = US$40) and does not vary significantly between individual and group farmers.

The repayment record for group credit—100 percent repayment in four out of five years—is most impressive. Repayment by individual creditors used to be at 96 to 98 percent, but this figure also rose to 100 percent in 1977–78 and 1978–79.

Outstanding Issues

The LLDP administration differentiated between individual and group credit by charging individuals 15 percent and groups 10 percent interest. There is no information available on what the actual cost difference is in administering the two types of credit. The project administration gives credit groups specialized training in self-accounting, so that eventually considerable costs are saved. If farmers have a free choice either to take individual credit or to join a credit group, the difference in lending costs should be reflected in the credit terms—assuming that there is no special reason to subsidize one form over the other. Therefore, plans are underway to investigate the cost difference between individual and group credit.

There appears to be no significant difference between the repayment records of individuals and of credit groups (table 32-2). Indications are, however, that much greater effort is needed to collect payments from individual farmers than from credit groups. This factor should be included in the cost comparison.

The security fund mechanism used in the Lilongwe group credit scheme is not utilized by the farmers' clubs because they have funds from members' dues and communal operations. These funds, however, are rather small and unlikely to give the same protection as the 10 percent security fund. To simplify credit administration, it would be desirable to apply the same credit mechanism in both the farmers' clubs and the credit groups.

There is no doubt that the farmers' clubs, with their greater continuity and the combination of group extension with group credit, are a higher form of precooperative organization. A distinguishing feature of farmers' clubs, for example, is that members not taking up credit still continue to participate in group extension. But farmers' clubs are more difficult to organize than the single-purpose credit groups. Therefore, it might be practical to introduce a kind of graduation process by which credit groups might be promoted to farmers' clubs and eventually to regular cooperatives.

In meetings held with several hundred members of credit groups and farmers' clubs, almost all expressed the desire to broaden the range of items that would be eligible for credit financing. Demand was strongest for cash to pay casual labor during the growing season. Most farmers' clubs also wanted to receive medium-term credit for farming implements and in particular for bullocks and dairy cows. These items are at present financed only with individual credit and on a very limited scale because most farmers cannot offer acceptable collateral. The clubs feel prepared to guarantee the repayment of these loans.

One of the clubs has started making loans from its own funds on a limited scale. When asked whether the club would consider accepting savings deposits to build up its funds and provide an additional service, the club members appeared receptive to the idea but were reluctant to make a firm commitment. They apparently were aware of the additional responsibilities that would be involved and were not sure of the legal implications. Members showed a definite interest, however, in making savings deposits. This idea appeared especially attractive in view of the interest rates possible if interest on deposits were determined by the lending rate minus the very low administrative costs of the clubs. This indicated that farmers' clubs are prepared to develop into real savings and loan associations.

Conclusions

This experience with group lending in Malawi has proven that precooperative institutions can be developed successfully in poor peasant societies, even in environments where efforts to develop conventional cooperatives have failed. Group lending in Malawi can be distinguished from conventional lending by the following factors:

- The credit groups offer clearly defined economic incentives such as lower interest rates, price discounts on inputs, and relief from individual loan processing.
- The formation of groups is left to the initiative of the farmers; government assists but does not interfere.
- Formation and disbanding of groups is simple and non-bureaucratic.
- Membership in the groups is kept small.
- Management is provided by elected group members who perform their duties without pay, principally for social prestige.
- Operation is limited and simple.
- Members are fully liable for an individual default.
- Group security against default is provided by an advance deposit which is refunded with interest at full repayment of the loan.

These features coincide with the principles of Raiffeisen, who founded the German cooperative movement more than a hundred years ago. When organizing the first primary societies among peasant farmers his principles were to have a limited and simple sphere of operation, unlimited liability of members, and management by unpaid volunteers. Using these principles, the Raiffeisen societies established a reputation of creditworthiness that enabled them to borrow from commercial lenders; only later did they broaden their sphere of operation to include input and output marketing, processing, and other services. Today they handle more than 60 percent of all agricultural trade in the Federal Republic of Germany.

Thus, the group credit scheme in Malawi started with a concept that has a history of success. In line with historical experience, this precooperative concept should not be considered an end in itself, but rather the preliminary stage of an institutional development that can expand and broaden into a genuine cooperative movement. Malawi's experience with a previous cooperative movement that failed—apparently while trying to accomplish too much in too short a time with too much political interference—should guide further development so that the same mistakes are not made again. It may be wise to use a graduated process, the final stage of which could result either in a savings and loan association or a multipurpose service cooperative.

33. *Group Lending in Rural Areas*

B. M. Desai

[Experience in ten developing countries indicates that group lending programs permit a moderate reduction in lenders' administrative costs, yield little if any improvement in repayment rates, but result in rather widespread reductions in borrowers' costs.]

In this chapter I analyze experiences with group lending in the Dominican Republic, Ghana, Malawi, Bolivia, Philippines, Thailand, India, Nepal, Sri Lanka, and Bangladesh. I first present a framework to evaluate group lending as an innovation in rural financial markets by considering its intended functions. I then discuss the conditions under which this innovation actually brings down the costs of lenders or borrowers or improves the quality of service.

Intended Functions of Group Lending

Three potential advantages of group lending are that it can reduce the credit transaction costs of both lenders and borrowers; offer scale economies in the provision of related technical assistance and other services which promote the productive use of additional liquidity resulting from a credit transaction; and reduce the risk of loan default by means of peer pressure and joint responsibility among group members.

These functions can help overcome two fundamental barriers to financial intermediation between lenders and the rural poor: high administrative costs and the high risks associated with rural banking. Lenders recognize these barriers easily. For the borrowers, higher costs of negotiating a loan and a lower probability of getting it reduce the demand for credit. Since group lending attempts to reduce both the lenders' and borrowers' costs, it has a potential to lower these barriers.

These three intended functions of group lending can affect credit supply and demand. Scale economies in the provision of both the financial and nonfinancial services could increase the supply of credit,

Extracted from a paper presented at the Second International Conference on Rural Finance Research Issues, Calgary, Canada, September 1979.

and the possible lower default risk associated with group lending has the same effect. The potentially lower transaction costs to group borrowers would influence demand. By transacting individual loans through a group, borrowers would save time, transportation costs, and the expense of obtaining documents and certificates and registering collateral. Another demand-influencing advantage could arise if groups were to get access not only to loans but also to such other services as savings deposit facilities, technical assistance, or the advantageous purchase of inputs and sale of produce. Developing such additional "organizational good" for group members would increase the value of group membership.

If these potential advantages are realized, a larger volume of credit would be sought and supplied. To the extent that this occurs, group lending is an innovation with positive value. However, this reform like any other can fail to live up to expectations. On the supply side, for example, group members may jointly agree not to repay loans, which would increase rather than decrease the default risk. The chances of such collusion might be higher when groups are formed only to get access to formal credit with no other organizational good. Other supply disadvantages might be higher costs from forming groups and a possibly lower repayment rate in the absence of lenders' selection and direct supervision of borrowers. On the demand side, potential disadvantages for the individual might arise from the loss of choice as a member of a group or from the cost of maintaining group membership.

Group Lending Experiences in Ten Low-Income Countries

The following discussion considers whether the intended functions of group lending have been realized in ten low-income countries and what may explain the results. The studies considered do not cover the same issues or examine similar groups of borrowers. In some of the countries group loans were provided to those who did not previously have access to formal credit, which prevents a comparison of results with and without group lending. Some studies did not examine nongroup individual borrowers as a control to compare with the group sample. Others selected such a sample but did not test the differences between the two samples for characteristics other than their borrowing status. Despite these differences, the results of group lending experiments are remarkably uniform among the ten countries studied.

Lenders' Costs

All the country studies except those on Ghana and the Philippines report partial or inconclusive results for the effect of group lending on lenders' costs; the Ghana study reveals lower costs for group loans, while the Philippines study indicates higher costs. Lenders in the Dominican Republic, Nepal, Bolivia, India, and the Philippines have enjoyed scale economies in the administrative costs of making group loans. They did not all experience superior repayment of these loans, however. Half the countries studied provide evidence of lender cost reduction, but for all but one this is a partial result.

The lenders' costs would have been higher for group loans in most countries if the costs of forming borrowing groups such as cooperatives and providing other services to them had been added to the conventional transaction costs. These other costs were borne by agencies other than the lending institutions: in the Dominican Republic they were borne by the refinancing agency, the Dominican Development Foundation; in Bolivia, Ghana, Malawi, Thailand, Bangladesh, Nepal, and Sri Lanka technical services were provided by the government. Sometimes, however, these overhead costs were borne by the borrowers themselves, as in the case in Ghana, the Dominican Republic, Thailand, and India where responsibility for forming groups rests with the borrowers. Lenders themselves might undertake the formation of borrowing organizations, using existing village organizations or traditional informal groups, and these might be more creditworthy; such an effort is not found in the countries studied except perhaps in Nepal.

Scale Economies in Other Services

Group loans in these countries have not usually resulted in auxiliary organization for noncredit services. Indeed, groups have been formed mainly to give access to credit alone. Exceptions were in Nepal and Malawi, where lenders required a deposit of 5 to 10 percent of the total value of the group loan before a loan is made. These deposits may earn interest for the group; they were also used to cover shortfalls in the repayment of the group loan. The organizational good derived from the savings function by group members in Malawi and Nepal seems to have resulted in better loan repayment and apparently in solidarity and stability. These studies do not, however, provide data on the costs of administering these deposits. Other services may not have been developed in most countries because of a lack of incentives to the lenders.

Default Risks

There is little evidence that group lending improved repayment, and the record in these countries is mixed. A low delinquency rate was experienced in the initial years in the Dominican Republic, but it was not sustained. In Nepal and Malawi, repayment was good; low delinquencies were partly a result of the deposit requirements.

In group lending the nondelinquent members are required, in effect, to repay loans of the delinquent members. In practice, however, most lenders find it difficult to enforce this requirement. This may be in part because of a lack of legal sanction behind the joint liability principle. More important, it could reflect a lack of any organizational good beyond borrowing for the group members. In the absence of such auxiliary benefits from group membership the lenders cannot exercise any leverage to promote peer pressure as a substitute for conventional collateral. Delinquencies in Bolivia, the Philippines, and the Dominican Republic reportedly increased because lenders' services were inferior and delayed. Without appropriate incentives, lenders will not take on a multifunctional role or offer better quality and more timely services to the group.

Borrowers' Costs

The country studies all report these costs to be lower for group loans except in India and the Philippines. Group borrowers in India had higher costs than a control group mainly because of differences in the distance from lenders and in technology factors rather than differences in the borrowing status of the two samples. In the Philippines group costs were higher because loan procedures were not simplified; delays in receiving loans necessitated temporary borrowings from moneylenders at very high interest rates. And while group borrowers in the Dominican Republic did benefit from lower transaction costs, their gains would have been considerably more had they received the formal loans in time to avoid temporary borrowing from moneylenders.

Group borrowers enjoy the cost advantages of savings on fees for registering collateral, on the formal and informal expenses of obtaining the certificates needed with the loan application, and on the time and transportation costs of visiting lenders. In the Dominican Republic and Bolivia, members of groups informally collect money to cover the expenses of leaders who negotiate the loan. In other cases these costs are shared by rotating the leadership.

Despite the cost advantages to the borrowers, country studies also report some disenchantment with group lending. This is found when members are forced to bear someone else's debt, when they are refused loans because of the delinquency of other members, or when they are forced to attend group meetings. Borrowers' gains from group loans can be perceived differently by different members. To a relatively well-off farmer a group loan may be a reward for patronage, while to a poor farmer it could represent a key to independence. When groups consisting of both kinds of farmers are formed, they may not succeed.

Even a comparatively homogeneous group is unlikely to persist if its maximum size is not limited, and if its members do not receive rewards (besides loans) to compensate for their collective repayment responsibility. Providing such rewards to group members may not be possible without undertaking a multifunctional role that includes collecting savings deposits.

34. *Savings Deposits and Agricultural Cooperatives in Korea*

Tae Young Lee, Dong Hi Kim,
and Dale W Adams

[Rural cooperatives in the Republic of Korea have a major role in mobilizing voluntary financial deposits. They have been assisted by the government's interest rate policy, the savings promotion activities of cooperative officials, and membership confidence. The provision of good financial services to members has brought increased business to cooperatives, and voluntary savings deposits have provided Korean cooperatives with substantial resources for their nonfinancial activities.]

The present cooperative system in Korea has three levels of organization: primary cooperatives at the township level, county cooperatives, and the National Agricultural Cooperative Federation (NACF) at the national level. In 1975 there were more than 2 million member farmers in over 1,500 primary multipurpose cooperatives and 141 special-purpose cooperatives. More than 80 percent of the farm households were members of primary cooperatives. The average primary cooperative had about 1,200 members; special cooperatives were about half that large.

This cooperative system conducts a wide range of activities to improve the social and economic well-being of farmers. These activities include supplying farm inputs, marketing farm products, and providing credit and savings deposit services, mutual insurance, technical assistance, and some education. These programs are closely tied to government agricultural development policies. The provision of financial services through the cooperative system has been one way in which the government implements its rural development strategy.

 extracted from "Savings Deposits and Credit Activities in South Korean Agricultural Cooperatives, 1961–75," *Asian Survey*, vol. 17, no. 12 (December 1977), pp. 1182–94; also published in *Development Digest* (April 1979), pp. 43–51.

Table 34-1. *Total Amount and Sources of Loanable Funds in Agricultural Cooperatives in Korea, 1961–75*

		Percentage of total by source					
Year	*Total loanable funds (millions of current won)*	*Government funds*	*Bank of Korea*	*Agricultural credit debentures*	*Deposits received*	*Foreign loans*	*Cooperatives' own funds*
1961	16,911	57	18	2	20	—	3
1962	22,499	63	2	12	19	—	4
1963	27,727	55	12	8	20	—	5
1964	30,968	51	17	6	21	—	5
1965	44,200	33	37	2	24	—	4
1966	61,427	29	33	1	34	—	3
1967	73,391	26	33	0	38	—	3
1968	103,087	23	30	0	45	—	2
1969	158,221	26	21	0	48	4	1
1970	192,183	25	17	0	50	4	4
1971	212,636	24	19	0	51	2	4
1972	252,340	24	17	1	53	2	3
1973	312,889	21	19	1	54	1	4
1974	419,809	19	24	1	51	2	3
1975	484,600	n.a.	n.a.	n.a.	n.a.	n.a.	n.a.

— Not applicable.
n.a. Not available.
Source: Unpublished reports by the National Agricultural Cooperative Federation (NACF).

Agricultural Credit Services

Over the past few years NACF and its county-level cooperatives have been allowed to conduct all types of banking business. This includes receiving deposits from and making loans to farmers as well as non-farm individuals. Government loans directed to farmers are made only through the cooperative system. As noted in table 34-1, in the early 1960s government funds and money borrowed from the Bank of Korea made up a large part of the loanable funds handled by the cooperatives. By the early 1970s, however, deposits in the cooperatives made up a majority of the loanable funds.

The table also shows that the total volume of loanable funds in the agricultural cooperative system increased from about W17,000 million (current won) in 1961 to about W485,000 million in 1975. In real terms, this was more than a fourfold increase. (The wholesale price index for all commodities in Korea, with 1970 = 100, went up from 35.1 in 1961 to 238.0 in 1975.) Expanded private savings deposits in the cooperatives provided a large part of these additional loanable funds. The funds were used mainly for loans to members of the cooperatives or for business operations of the agricultural cooperative system. Thus, most of the loans made by the cooperative system were for agricultural purposes; in 1962, 92 percent of the value of outstanding balances was in agricultural loans. By 1975 this was lowered to 75 percent, a reflection of the continued growth of nonagricultural economic opportunities in rural areas.

Interest Rates

Some of the most interesting features of recent development policy in Korea are the changes in nominal interest rates in formal financial markets. Before 1965, nominal interest rates were quite low. Formal agricultural loans, for example, carried interest rates of approximately 8 to 15 percent a year; rates on financial savings deposits ranged from 9 to 15 percent. In September 1965 many of the interest rates on formal loans and deposits were almost doubled (table 34-2). Time deposits of more than two years carried interest rates of 30 percent, for example. Since 1965 interest rate policies, especially on deposits, have been more flexible, with rates moving up and down depending on inflationary pressures. As can be seen in table 34-2, these changes in nominal interest rates have resulted in positive real rates of interest in most years after 1964—over 10 percent during 1966–71 on long-term deposits.

The interest rate reforms in the mid-1960s increased the average rate of interest charged on agricultural loans. In 1964 none of the agricultural loans made by the cooperatives carried interest rates of

Table 34-2. *Interest Rates and Financial Deposits in Korea, 1963–74*

				Financial deposits (thousand million of 1970 won)[c]		*Savings deposits*[b] *(thousand million of 1970 won)*[c]	
Year	*Contractual interest rates on long-term deposits*[a] *(percent)*	*Changes in wholesale price index (percent)*	*Real rates of interest on long-term savings deposits (percent)*	*Total*	*Percentage in agricultural cooperatives*	*Total*	*Percentage in agricultural cooperatives*
1963	15.0	20.6	−5.6	84.2	14	27.7	5
1964	15.0	34.6	−19.6	69.2	15	23.3	5
1965	18.0	10.1	7.9	114.4	14	44.6	9
1966	26.8	8.7	18.1	162.1	17	93.9	16
1967	26.8	6.4	20.4	259.3	14	162.3	12
1968	26.1	8.1	18.0	434.8	13	297.9	10
1969	23.8	6.8	17.0	676.0	12	492.9	9
1970	22.8	9.2	13.6	789.7	12	576.3	10
1971	22.1	8.6	13.5	900.2	11	652.6	9
1972	15.4	14.0	1.4	1,069.4	10	736.3	8
1973	12.6	6.9	5.7	1,324.5	10	917.0	8
1974	15.0	42.1	−27.1	1,119.8	10	770.8	8

a. These rates are for twelve-month deposits. When interest rates were changed during the year, a simple weighted average of months covered by the interest rate was used in the calculations.

b. Excludes checking deposits, other demand deposits, and short-term passbook deposits.

c. The price index used to convert to 1970 prices was the wholesale price index for the Republic of Korea. The exchange rate of won for dollars in 1970 was 316.

Source: Bureau of Statistics, Economic Planning Board, *Korean Statistical Yearbook*, vol. 16 (1969) and vol. 22 (1975).

more than 25 percent a year. In 1966 about 9 percent of the value of cooperative loans carried rates of 25 percent or more, and by 1968 almost 30 percent of the value of loans carried these higher interest rates. After 1968, however, interest rates were steadily lowered until 1973 when inflation induced policy makers to raise interest rates again.

Savings Deposits

Unlike many developing countries, rather heavy emphasis has been placed on mobilizing rural financial savings in Korea, and significant amounts of national savings have been deposited in agricultural cooperatives. As noted in table 34-2, after the interest rate reform in late 1965, financial deposits in agricultural cooperatives increased from 14 to 17 percent of total financial deposits in the country. The proportion of total savings deposits in the country held by agricultural cooperatives also jumped from 9 percent in 1965 to 16 percent in 1966. Because of the very rapid growth in nonagricultural economic activities thereafter, the percentage of total financial deposits in the country held in agricultural cooperatives declined from 1966 to 1974.

In part, the increases in real amounts of financial savings deposits in agricultural cooperatives in this period were due to ambitious efforts by the government. Three financial institutions in rural areas—agricultural cooperatives, the fisheries cooperatives, and the post office—are heavily involved in mobilizing savings. A nationwide campaign to promote rural savings has been carried out almost every year during the harvest season from September to December.

In most cooperatives around the world, involuntary share purchases by cooperative members provide a large part of the organization's operating funds. Share money plus foreign or governmental assistance usually provide the bulk of loanable funds handled by the cooperatives. In Korea, however, share purchases are small in comparison with private voluntary deposits; from 1963 to 1975 they were only one-tenth to one-fifth the value of voluntary deposits. This is about the same pattern found among the highly successful farmers' associations in Taiwan and Japan; financial deposits, not involuntary share purchases, were the cornerstones of these institutions.

Cooperative Members' Attitudes toward Savings

To explore the attitudes of members toward savings deposits, interviews were carried out with a random sample of 120 individuals, 40 members in each of three rural primary cooperatives. The interviews showed that almost all the members (92 percent) had deposit accounts in either the cooperative or a post office or both. Over one-third of those interviewed indicated they had opened a savings account at the urging of cooperative officials. In two of the cooperatives, officials were reported to have been instrumental in attracting at least half of the savings accounts opened.

During the interviews the cooperative members were asked to identify the source of money used to make their most significant recent deposits. Not surprisingly, over half of them said crop or livestock receipts. About 20 percent reported nonfarm or wage income as the source for the deposit. Another 13 percent reported frugal living as the source, and the remainder reported using money from several other sources. The interviewed members indicated that about half the deposits were intended for farm or household operations. The other half of the deposits, however, appear to be closely tied to specified saving-investment decisions: about one-third of the deposits were for educational purposes, another 16 percent for land purchases, while about 3 percent were directed to some other type of investment. Deposit behavior seems to be strongly influenced by the rate of return depositors expect from financial savings or by the source from which financial savings are accumulated.

In 1969 interviewed members held more than three-quarters of their financial deposits in post offices. By 1975, however, these same members held over 95 percent of their financial deposits in the primary cooperatives! It appears that the cooperative members now view the cooperative as a safe and convenient place to hold their financial assets, and that Korean farmers are doing an increasingly larger share of their economic transactions with the cooperatives.

Conclusions

Several interesting lessons can be drawn from the experience with mobilizing rural savings in Korea. The first is that well-organized cooperatives can play a major role in mobilizing voluntary financial savings in rural areas. U Tun Wai [*Financial Intermediaries and National Savings in Developing Countries*, New York, Praeger, 1972, pp. 85–98] has argued that three key elements are necessary before savings can be mobilized: people must have sufficient resources or income to *be able* to save; they must have secure and dependable *opportunities* to save; and they must have an *incentive* to save—the expectation that their savings will result in substantial future satisfaction. Agricultural cooperatives appear to have been particularly effective in providing secure and dependable opportunities for rural households to add voluntary financial savings to their assets.

The second major lesson is that government policies—especially those affecting interest rates but also savings promotion—can strongly affect the ability of financial institutions such as cooperatives to mobilize savings. These same policies can also strongly affect the incentives which rural households have to hold financial assets and to save in general (rather than consume). Most rural cooperatives in low-income countries mobilize very little voluntary or involuntary savings. Aside from a small number of cases, most cooperatives offer very low, or negative, real rates of interest on financial deposits, and many cooperatives act as retail outlets for credit without providing any deposit services for members.

A third lesson is that low-income rural people may have much larger potential savings capacities than previously estimated. Kong Nam Hyun found that rural households included in the annual Korean farm household economy survey saved surprisingly large parts of their income ["Aspects of Rural Household Saving Behavior in Korea, 1962–1974," M.S. thesis, Ohio State University, 1977; and K. N. Hyun, D. W Adams, and L. J. Hushak, "Rural Household Savings Behavior in South Korea, 1962–76," *American Journal of Agricultural Economics*, vol. 61, no. 3, August 1979, pp. 448–54]. In 1963 all households in the survey saved an average of 12 percent of their household income; by 1974 this had increased to 33 percent. Even households with the smallest farms and households with the lowest incomes were saving significant amounts in certain years. This substantial savings capacity resulted both from interest rate policies and because cooperatives and post offices were able to provide rural households with secure, convenient, and inexpensive ways to save financially. Rural savers did not have to walk long distances or pay for transportation to make a deposit since facilities were located in the depositors' neighborhoods.

A fourth lesson to be learned from Korea, Taiwan, and Japan is the importance of the right kind of credit-savings activities in building viable, small-farmer service organizations such as cooperatives. In all too many cases these organizations are called on to provide services in areas where they cannot initially compete efficiently. Informal marketing systems or other government-sponsored services may sometimes be more efficient than cooperatives in providing production inputs, education and extension, and marketing services. Furthermore, since many cooperatives are forced to offer credit at low interest rates, they tend to concentrate loans in the hands of the influential to minimize lending costs; many members or potential members are thus denied credit and find it is not worth their while to join in cooperative activities. In Korea, Taiwan, and Japan, however, the excellent financial services appear to have offered strong incentives to rural people to join and participate in cooperatives. Because of the savings mobilized and the realistic interest rate policies in force, most members of the cooperatives have had access to credit. With realistic national policies, it appears that cooperatives can efficiently provide these financial services. And these services not only strengthen the economic base of the cooperative, but also give members a strong reason for participating in other cooperative activities.

35. *How to Build in the Germs of Failure: Credit Cooperatives in French Cameroon*

Hans F. Illy

[The failure of a credit project in Cameroon was predictable, both from the particular policies adopted and from the cultural differences between the lending institution and its borrowers.]

A widespread belief has been that the small farmer needs credit to increase production and to raise his standard of living. Starting from this assumption, there was no reason to investigate existing mechanisms for capital formation through saving, either individually or collectively, or the uses of this capital. Colonial administrations quickly became aware that Africans could more easily be induced to cultivate export crops such as coffee and cocoa if there was some material incentive other than the price, especially in the launching period. Unfortunately, this attitude has created expectations of easy credit in French-speaking Africa, where no project can be started without having secured a substantial amount of credit. To ask if there is a real need for credit, and for a feasibility study, largely passes for heresy. The natural link between savings and credit becomes distorted if credit is so easily available that the beneficiaries can interpret it as gifts, the economic use of which is not self-evident. This logically serves to postpone indefinitely any large-scale capital formation in Africa, as illustrated by the case study that follows.

Credit programs were started in French Cameroon in 1931, but they benefited only the white planters and some richer Africans because small planters could not present a real estate title, the only possible guarantee for a loan. This European structure could not fit into a system of communal property, where individual families have only a hereditary right to use the land. But another administrative institution was at the service of the peasant, the so-called Société Indigène de

Extracted from *Rural Africana*, no. 2 (Fall 1978), pp. 57–67.

Prévoyance (SIP), financed by a compulsory contribution levied with the head tax. There is no doubt that the SIP did much to improve the material infrastructure (especially roads and wells) in agricultural production and provided seeds, fertilizers, and so forth to the producer. But instead of having to pay part of the expense, farmers received these benefits at practically no cost; at least, this was the final outcome when the outstanding debts had to be written off. Though the intentions of the colonial power were often quite different, a shrewd farmer was in a position to carve out for himself important advantages without paying much for them. This must have had repercussions on his attitude toward any subsequent credit system alleged to be suited to his needs and capacities.

Characteristics of the New Credit

In the mid-1950s a new system, the Coopérative de Crédit Mutuel (CCM), was developed by the Caisse Centrale de Coopération Economique (CCCE) in Paris. The CCCE was the official government organ to channel funds to French territories overseas. It introduced the CCM into Africa, with Cameroon as the pilot project.

The key problem was to find a sufficiently solid guarantee for the credits granted. This was determined to be the unqualified joint liability of the CCM members, a system blindly adopted from the first Raiffeisen cooperatives in nineteenth-century Germany [see chapter 32 for a brief sketch of Raiffeisen principles]. The local CCCE office chose Bafou, a Bamiléké village, in which to launch the first CCM. This was a homogeneous group of thirty-eight Arabica coffee growers, all desiring to expand their production. Later, a minimum of seven and a maximum of thirty members was specified to ensure a viable entity. If a member wanted a loan, he presented a detailed application to the CCM's board of directors. The general assembly then checked the economic justification of the loan purpose stated on the application (Bamiléké are especially meticulous in this respect) and finally approved it jointly before presenting it to the bank.

A CCM was constituted with capital stock (in Bafou, each member paid CFAF20,000), which was deposited in the bank, and it could obtain a total amount of credit up to ten times this capital. All this activity was carried out by the local agents of the bank; it was only after 1958 that some link was established with the agricultural services, which already had a dense network of extension workers in close contact with the farmers. All seemed to start on a sound and stable basis of mutual trust to the benefit of the farmer. After a period of experimentation, operating principles emerged which could be applied to a broader clientele. In 1955–56 seven more CCMs were created, three for the first time in the cocoa-growing region (Nyong and Sanaga). But then the quantitative expansion became spectacular, utterly uncontrollable, continuing through 1961–62 (see table 35-1).

Of the total of 2,364 CCMs in 1962 with nearly 30,000 members, about 2,000 could be found in the central region and only 70 in the west (Bamiléké). Whereas in the initial period only a small number of economically trustworthy farmers could obtain credit, CCM members applied intense pressure to extend the system, so that practically all cocoa farmers in the south became eligible for it if they fulfilled minimum requirements. It appeared desirable to reach the small farmer—and the average amount loaned decreased from CFAF250,000 to about CFAF10,000. But this raises the question of whether individual cases could still be considered thoroughly to ensure creditworthiness and administrative efficiency. One of the promoters proudly announced a "cooperative density of 30 percent" (three out of ten cocoa farmers are members of a CCM) in the Nyong and Sanaga region, but without investigating what this meant for the long-range stability of the program.

Technical Deficiencies

There was no joint action by the country's administrative services. The entire responsibility lay in the hands of the Banque Camerounaise de Développement (BCD), a government bank having no experience with small farmers. The solution was to use the services of the agricultural extension network. This was a bad solution because extension

Table 35-1. *The Development of Coopératives de Crédit Mutuel (CCMs)*

Business year	*Number of CCMs*	*Number of loans*	*Total amount of loans (thousands of francs)*	*Average amount of loans (thousands of francs*
1954–55	1	29	7,125	246
1955–56	8	144	36,630	254
1956–57	70	1,910	97,728	51
1957–58	543	11,681	178,829	15
1958–59	1,632	16,498	241,110	15
1959–60	2,001	11,504	109,880	10
1960–61	2,235	6,472	148,893	23
1961–62	2,364	12,535	128,406	10
Total		60,773	948,601	

Sources: Ekhehart Gabelmann, *Die Genossenschaften in Kamerun* (Marburg/Lahn: Eukerdruck, 1971), p. 156; and Jacques Marsan, "Le Crédit mutualiste dans l'agriculture africaine et malgache," *Notes et études documentaires*, no. 3073 (1964), p. 14.

workers had no experience in handling money and advising on credit management.

Extension workers were offered a premium of CFAF2,000 for every CCM constituted. One can vividly imagine how these extension workers passed from one village to another asking people to sign an application sheet. More than one chief gave several names offhand and signed for these individuals immediately; evidently he, and he alone, wanted to enjoy the whole sum of credit. The most harmful invention was to link this premium to the loan sum CCMs applied for, because extension workers availed themselves of this opportunity by inflating the demands from individual members. These measures alone would have sufficed to undermine the system. It was too late when BCD recognized that something had to be done to halt this avalanche. Thirty special credit advisers were trained to improve operations in the field, but they could not save the boat from sinking. The costs of this attempt were considered too high, and half the advisers were sacked within a year.

One might think that the field services of the cooperative department (Direction de la Coopération et de la Mutualité) should have had some say in the establishment of CCMs. But jealousy and ill-will were so paramount within the administrative setup that Coop/Mut was literally restricted to the registration of new CCMs. Coop/Mut's experience might not have saved the credit program from failure, but the department's frustration probably made CCM rehabilitation less effective. In such an atmosphere there was no room for adequate training of potential and active CCM members, nor was time allowed for creating a cooperative spirit. Instead, a race was on for money from BCD vaults.

What was this money used for? The initial care given to checking the incomes of the first CCM members and the intense advice they received on production methods could not be devoted to all the members of more than 2,000 CCMs. The link between credit and productive capacity was largely broken. But the decisive blow to the program came when the bank yielded to pressures to distribute loans for the construction of houses. This type of "social credit" was unproductive and not matched by higher income of the beneficiary from the marketing of cash crops. On the contrary, the use of insecticides dropped by 50 percent in the same period and all production loans fell sharply. Better housing has been a basic aspiration of people in southern Cameroon and is highly rated as an element of prestige, but it is in a completely different category from agricultural credit. The unproductive type of credit displaced and came to predominate over the productive loans that could help secure repayment of the debt.

The tragedy was inevitable: in 1958 there were only 1.2 percent outstanding debts in arrears; in 1960 this figure moved to 8.3 percent; in 1962 it was already 32.5 percent. In 1965 the BCD stopped the whole operation because of the impossibility of convincing people to comply with their commitments. On June 30, 1968, the total in arrears amounted to CFAF235,212,000 (nearly US$1,000,000). This debt is, formally speaking, still pending.

The Social Determinants of Failure

Some of the reasons for this striking breakdown of an agricultural credit program have already been noted: lack of coordination between administrative services, the rapid creation of too many CCMS, the dysfunctional premium system, the shift to housing credits. These characteristics alone provide sufficient evidence of the technical incompetence of the promoters of the program, both French and Cameroonian. Irrespective of the cultural milieu of the program, these deficiencies necessarily led to fiasco. But this case study allows us to go further in understanding the social limitations of such an experiment.

The CCCE experts in Paris harbored some naive and idyllic perceptions about the environment in which they were called to work. Jacques Marsan ["Le Crédit mutualiste dans l'agriculture africaine et malgache," *Notes et études documentaires*, no. 3073, 1964, pp. 3, 6] writes, "Africa maintains a collective mentality and the cult of solidarity—the cooperative remains within this context. Grafted onto the traditional groups, the old families, it preserves them, even consolidates them by giving them a kind of modern significance." This harmonious picture makes us believe that the CCMS are the ideal "modernized" version of the so-called traditional solidarity, a prolongation of existing values molded into a new organization. If this is correct, why such a tremendous failure of the credit program? It seems that things are not as easy as suggested by Marsan.

Cooperation implies some sacrifice of the managerial sovereignty of individual farm households, the sacrifice being justified as promoting their general well-being. In the case of a CCM, however, the reward was enormous compared with the sacrifice. Even in the most individualistic society a modestly rational individual could have participated in such a collective enterprise. In this context, it is rather superfluous to look for some "traditional solidarity"; there is not the slightest need for it, because the individual advantages are so attractive. Reactions to the nonrepayment of a loan by an individual member were, indeed, rather complex. When only some members of the CCM had obtained credits, there was immense pressure to come up to the expectations of the bank because the majority of the members were still waiting to collect the same benefits. But when most of the members had profited, this pressure was no longer felt. There emerged instead a kind of solidarity in the refusal to repay. Why should I pay off my debt if I could be liable to pay for a co-member too? It became utterly impossible to enforce the "unlimited joint liability," considered the foundation of the whole CCM system.

Another important factor was the nature of the link between CCM members on the one hand and the state (before 1960, the colonial power) on the other. The whole program was executed in a strictly authoritarian manner. The rules were fixed beforehand; once a CCM was constituted, all the accounting and administration of individual loans was managed by the bank and its branches. There was nothing left to be discussed by the CCM organs, especially the board of directors. It is not astonishing that a cooperative spirit could not be instilled, because no participation in the decision-making process was allowed. In essence, the CCM system had deteriorated into a machine for the more or less automatic channeling of money to farmers, considered vital to the colonial and postcolonial emphasis on export agriculture. The loan was tacitly considered a gift from the state; and since a national solidarity had not yet been shaped, farmers could not reasonably be expected to feel allegiance toward this entity. The CCM experience unfortunately coincided with a period of political upheaval, of rebellion and its repression, actively aided by French military intervention.

The people of Cameroon felt quite strongly that the CCM program was coming from outside. Instead of refusing it (their colonial experience gave sufficient evidence that *l'administration* was always stronger), they quickly realized its positive aspects. The European promoters started from the false premise that this inclination was based on some traditional solidarity and lulled themselves into the belief that nothing could go wrong. Funneling more money to Africa and committing a good many technical errors, they did indeed provoke the breakdown of the system. But they did not feel responsible because they saw themselves as well-meaning development experts doing their best for poor Africans. Disappointed, they went back to Europe blaming Africa for its ingratitude and perfidiousness. Sometimes it may be better to refrain from "helping"; the outcome of inconsiderate action could be disastrous.

36. *A Penny Saved: Kenya's Cooperative Savings Scheme*

J. D. Von Pischke

[In 1970 a savings program was established for cooperative unions in Kenya. Its basic element was that payments to growers for coffee deliveries were credited to their accounts with their cooperatives, rather than paid in cash. The scheme grew beyond planners' expectations, demonstrating a previously unfilled savings need among smallholders. The progress of the scheme through 1974 is discussed.]

Kenya's Cooperative Savings Scheme was started in 1970. Depositors are primarily small coffee farmers. Cooperatives enjoy a virtual monopoly on smallholder coffee production, which constitutes approximately half of Kenya's crop. Primary societies own and operate coffee-pulping facilities. District-level cooperative unions sell the crop to the apex Kenya Planters Coffee Union, which stores, mills, and grades. Export auctions are conducted by the Coffee Marketing Board. The Department of Cooperative Development in the Ministry of Cooperatives and Social Services closely supervises many aspects of cooperation, including budgets, staffing, training, and auditing. Signatures of department staff are required on all checks written by local societies.

Structure and Administration

The Cooperative Savings Scheme (CSS) was conceived as an adjunct of the Cooperative Production Credit Scheme (CPCS), which provides short- and some medium-term credit to cooperators. CSS supplements CPCS as a source of funds for lending, and complements it by offering savings facilities to cooperators. Societies participating satisfactorily in CPCS are eligible to join CSS when they have trained staff, standardized their accounts, established adequate security arrangements, and passed enabling resolutions by a majority vote of the membership.

Adapted from a paper presented to the Second International Seminar on Change in Agriculture, Reading, England, September 1974.

Requirements of this sort help ensure an accounting capability to handle savings deposits.

CSS operates through the individual accounts maintained for paying members for their crop deliveries and for recovering loans made to them by their societies. The addition of savings operations to an existing accounting system permits economies not available to a commercial bank, for example, which would have to open a new account for each new depositor. Members of non-CSS societies receive their payments in cash; in CSS societies payouts are credited to members' accounts, and each member may within certain limitations make withdrawals as desired. The basic requirement is a KSh50 minimum balance, built up by retentions of KSh10 from the first five payouts following the introduction of CSS (one Kenya shilling = US$0.14). During the week following a payout a member may withdraw the amount of the payout plus KSh200. At other times the withdrawal limit is KSh200 per day, subject to a KSh2,000 monthly maximum which can be waived if liquidity permits and by prior arrangement.

Members may make deposits and authorize inward transfers under standing instructions. In the Machakos Union in 1973, for example, outside deposits (those not originating from payments for coffee by the cooperative) ranged from 2 percent to over 90 percent of monthly deposit transactions in shillings. Interest at 4 percent a year, computed monthly on the lowest balance rounded downward to an even KSh20 unit, is credited to accounts annually. A service fee of KSh1 per payout is charged, and in some unions KSh1 is charged for the issue of a passbook.

Savings services are handled by the banking sections of the cooperative unions. Attempts to decentralize accounting to the local societies were abandoned because of cost, considerations of control, and in some areas members' fears that the confidentiality of their accounts would not be respected. Depositors may generally transact business on their accounts six days a week at the banking section office, usually located in the district headquarters town, operated by the union to which their local society belongs. Unions also provide banking services at local society offices or other rural places on scheduled days or to coincide with coffee payouts, which are made approximately five times a year.

Operating Results

In 1972 CSS entered the implementation phase. By the end of 1973 it included seven unions and over 110,000 accounts belonging to members of affiliated primary societies. Total balances exceeded KSh36 million, an average of over KSh325 per farmer account (see table 36-1). Spot checks conducted by department staff suggest that over

Table 36-1. *Cooperative Savings Scheme Balances and Participation, 1970–73*
(total savings balance in thousands of Kenya shillings; average balance in shillings)

Partici-pating union	*Progress indicator*	*November 30, 1970*	*December 31*		
			1971	*1972*	*1973*
Kiambu	Total savings balance	1,053	2,308	4,514	9,080
	Number of accounts	7,000	n.a.	17,106	17,200
	Average balance	150	n.a.	264	528
Embu	Total savings balance	—	—	589	1,460
	Number of accounts	—	—	14,471	14,500
	Average balance	—	—	41	101
Machakos	Total savings balance	—	—	2,084	4,500
	Number of accounts	—	—	14,000	14,800
	Average balance	—	—	149	304
Murang'a[a]	Total savings balance	—	—	3,946	13,400
	Number of accounts	—	—	20,387	33,000
	Average balance	—	—	194	406
Kirinyaga	Total savings balance	—	—	1,180	5,000
	Number of accounts	—	—	17,088	17,000
	Average balance	—	—	69	294
Masaba[b]	Total savings balance	—	—	—	80
	Number of accounts	—	—	—	2,600
	Average balance	—	—	—	31
Meru South	Total savings balance	—	—	—	3,370
	Number of accounts	—	—	—	13,400
	Average balance	—	—	—	251
Total CSS	Total savings balance	1,053	2,308	12,314	36,890
	Number of accounts	7,000	n.a.	83,052	112,500
	Average balance	150	n.a.	148	328

— Not applicable.

n.a. Not available.

a. The Murang'a Union absorbed a credit and savings society which began operations in 1967.

b. The Masaba Union consists of pyrethrum marketing societies, whereas the others are primarily oriented toward coffee.

Source: Department of Cooperative Development, Government of Kenya.

half the accounts contain approximately the minimum balance, indicating that some farmers save enthusiastically while others do no more than what is required. This behavior does not appear to move any local societies to withdraw from CSS and revert to cash payouts.

Criticisms of CSS Performance

CSS may be criticized on three counts. The first might be that it was too successful. Balances accumulated rapidly and in 1972 surpassed the amount of CPCS loans outstanding—an event which had been

Table 36-2. *A Comparison of CSS Balances and CPCS Loans Outstanding, 1970–73*
(thousands of Kenya shillings)

Unions	*Members' accounts*	*November 30, 1970*	*December 31* 1971	1972	1973
Kiambu	Total savings balance	1,053	2,308	4,514	9,080
	CPCS loans outstanding	2,167	5,081	1,790	3,630
	Net savings	(1,114)	(2,774)	2,724	5,450
Embu	Total savings balance	—	—	589	1,458
	CPCS loans outstanding	—	—	701	688
	Net savings	—	—	(112)	769
Machakos	Total savings balance	—	—	2,084	4,500
	CPCS loans outstanding	—	—	561	1,000
	Net savings	—	—	1,523	3,500
Murang'a	Total savings balance	—	—	3,946	13,400
	CPCS loans outstanding	—	—	1,916	4,400
	Net savings	—	—	2,030	9,000
Kirinyaga	Total savings balance	—	—	1,180	5,000
	CPCS loans outstanding	—	—	796	1,400
	Net savings	—	—	384	3,600
Other CSS unions	Total savings balance	—	—	—	3,450
	CPCS loans outstanding	—	—	—	1,050
	Net savings	—	—	—	2,400
Total CSS unions	Total savings balance	1,053	2,308	12,314	36,890
	CPCS loans outstanding	2,167	5,081	5,765	12,170
	Net savings	(1,114)	(2,774)	6,549	24,720
Non-CSS unions	CPCS loans outstanding	—	3,456	2,299	2,540
Total	CSS balances less CPCS loans	(1,114)	(6,230)	4,250	22,180

— Not applicable.
Note: Parentheses indicate negative savings.
Source: Department of Cooperative Development, Government of Kenya.

projected for the millennium but which occurred quickly in all CSS districts (table 36-2). Planners evidently failed to understand that most peasants in the cash economy can save, while few are "creditworthy." All members of participating societies have CSS accounts, but the proportion having CPCS loans rarely exceeds 50 percent.

Profitable and appropriate employment for the CSS balances not needed for funding CPCS loans and for liquidity is difficult. Suitable investments allow only a small spread above the 4 percent paid to the depositor. The temptation to obtain higher returns from speculative and illiquid investments has arisen. The accumulation of funds has also subtly weakened hierarchical control, which is based to some extent on the expectation that each level, from cooperator through union, would be financially dependent on the next level up and ultimately on the cooperative bank. Indeed, not all "surplus" CSS balances are on deposit at the cooperative bank—most unions keep a portion of these funds, in excess of operating requirements, at commercial banks.

The second criticism concerns union control and accounting performance, which is grossly inferior to banking standards. CSS balances are to be used only for banking purposes, but in a few cases have been used for union working capital. Reconciliations are frequently not current, and audits are as much as three years in arrears. Consequently management information is imprecise, funds are not efficiently managed, interest income is forgone, and it is difficult to compute CSS operating income and expenditure. Accounting laxity endangers depositors' funds—a danger easily underestimated. The state of accounting information makes it impossible to judge CSS performance on a comprehensive and consistent basis.

The third criticism is that depositors' balances have not been insured against insolvency of the union banking section. Efforts to establish a deposit insurance fund remained in the discussion stage for several years. Banking history is of course replete with cases of insolvency. This business risk, compounded by problems of accounting performance, suggests that CSS enjoys no immunity from the possibility of a crisis, although none has yet developed.

Interpretation of Operating Results

Whether the accumulation of CSS balances represents net additional savings is unknown. To the extent that these balances are offset by depositors' depleting commercial bank and post office savings bank accounts, they would constitute a transfer of resources to the cooperative sector; this may increase their impact on rural development. To the extent that they are substitutes for cash hoards, they constitute an activation of dormant financial resources and an increase in the potential contribution to national development.

What accounts for the growth of CSS? Its expansion beyond the KSh50 average minimum balance per account into the realm of completely voluntary savings behavior suggests that it fills real needs. CSS appears to have decreased the costs of liquidity among its clientele. It offers an apparently safer alternative to cash hoards. The minimum balance required is well below that of most banks, and the rate of interest has been 1 percent above that offered by banks and the post office. The CSS-CPCS link is also a positive factor: the minimum CPCS loan is KSh100; the post office savings bank makes no loans, and commercial banks rarely lend less than KSh1,000, which is beyond the creditworthiness of many smallholders. Cooperative banking has apparently developed a market for financial services among previously unserved "barefoot" savers. The automatic crediting of crop proceeds to CSS accounts is probably the most important contribution to its growth, and it has reportedly dampened the orgiastic consumption cycle connected with cash payouts.

Saving is conventionally defined as "deferred consumption." Even if the lag between receipt and disbursement is only a week, there is an opportunity to put these balances to work. In the Machakos Union in 1973 the average month-end level of balances equaled 1.64 times the average monthly amount of deposits made, representing a forty-nine-day lag. Saving is too often thought of only in terms of long-range behavior allegedly beyond the capacity of peasant cultivators. CSS demonstrates that smallholders can and do save and that their savings can strengthen rural institutions. That the growth of CSS was highly dramatic during a favorable period for Kenya's coffee producers does not detract from the accomplishment. Indeed, that may be the whole point: if farmers do not save a portion of any real increase in their incomes, a valuable opportunity is lost.

Elements of a Successful Rural Savings Scheme

What lessons can be drawn from CSS experience? It appears that rural savings schemes have the greatest chance of success when:

- They are linked with growing cash income flows (for example, through marketing channels for a cash crop), a link ensuring a stream of deposits as well as only an incremental clerical burden, since sellers' accounts are already maintained.
- They are linked with credit, which provides an incentive for participants and an avenue for the local employment of funds.
- They deal in quantities appropriate for smallholder agriculture with respect to such requirements as minimum balance and loan size.
- They offer new opportunities to savers and do not merely duplicate services offered by other financial institutions.
- They are operated by organizations capable of planning, promotion, implementation, and control.
- They enjoy depositors' confidence. Institutions operating only at the village level may not inspire confidence. Confidence is demonstrated by the majority vote of the membership required for a society's entry into CSS. Majority rule also ensures that at least half of a society's members participate on a *voluntary* basis. Forced savings programs deprive farmers of part of the fun of rural development.

Recommendations for Further Reading

Begashaw, Girma. "The Economic Role of Traditional Savings and Credit Institutions in Ethiopia." *Savings and Development*, vol. 2, no. 4 (1978), pp. 249–64.

Bouman, F. J. A. "The ROSCA: Financial Technology of an Informal Savings and Credit Institution in Developing Economies." *Savings and Development*, vol. 3, no. 4 (1979), pp. 253–76.

Bottomley, Anthony. "Interest Rate Determination in Underdeveloped Rural Areas." *American Journal of Agricultural Economics*, vol. 57, no. 2 (May 1975), pp. 279–91.

Due, Jean M. *Costs, Returns and Repayment Experience of Ujamaa Villages in Tanzania, 1973–1976*. Washington, D.C.: University Press of America, 1980.

Firth, Raymond, and B. S. Yamey. *Capital, Saving and Credit in Peasant Societies*. London: Allen and Unwin, 1964.

Ghatak, Subrata. *Rural Money Markets in India*. New Delhi: Macmillan Co., 1976.

Kato, Yuzuru. "Sources of Loanable Funds of Agricultural Credit Institutions in Asia: Japan's Experience." *Developing Economies*, vol. 10, no. 2 (June 1972), pp. 126–40.

Minkes, A. L. "The Decline of Pawnbroking." *Economica*, NS, vol. 20 (1953), pp. 10–23.

Miracle, Marvin P., Diane S. Miracle, and Laurie Cohen. "Informal Savings Mobilization in Africa." *Economic Development and Cultural Change*, vol. 28, no. 4 (1978), pp. 701–24.

Nayar, C. P. S. *Chit Finance*. Bombay: Vora & Co., 1973.

Raiffeisen, F. W. *The Credit Unions*. 8th ed., 1966, trans. by K. Engelmann. Neuwied on the Rhine, Germany: Raiffeisen Printing and Publishing Co., 1970.

Technical Board for Agricultural Credit. *A Study of the Informal Rural Financial Markets in Three Selected Provinces of the Philippines*. Manila: Presidential Committee on Agricultural Credit, 1981.

Issues for Discussion

1. Under what conditions is a cooperative likely to be successful in mobilizing member deposits and issuing credit on terms that permit the cooperative to be self-sustaining?
2. What economies and improvements in loan quality are possible in group lending?
3. Are rural cash flows relevant to project design? What types of information useful for credit project design could be obtained by examining the flow of money into, within, and out of a specific rural area?
4. Are the interest rates quoted on moneylenders' loans identical to returns on moneylenders' loan assets? What allowance must be made for the moneylender's cost and losses from bad debts?
5. Both formal lending institutions and informal moneylending have several possible uses for their funds, one of which is lending to rural clients. Rates of return on the other alternatives may be quite high. What level of interest on loans to farmers is required to make rural lending worth their while?
6. What are the relative advantages of ROSCAS, from the point of view of participants, compared with formal intermediaries such as commercial banks?
7. Why do politicians and government officials often believe that moneylenders do not perform a legitimate economic function?
8. Certain lending institutions with rural retail operations have difficulty remaining solvent, while moneylenders have remained viable providing credit in the same kind of environment. What lessons can the moneylenders offer these lending institutions?
9. What evidence is there to suggest that liquidity in rural areas is generally higher than might be expected?
10. What measures may be taken by governments and external assistance agencies to lower informal interest rates in rural areas?
11. Why is the role of women often very important in informal financial arrangements and relatively minor in formal finance?

PART VI

GOVERNMENT POLICIES TOWARD RURAL FINANCE

Financial transactions invite political intrusions and government regulation and supervision. Politics almost always plays a large role in credit allocation, financial market development, and savings mobilization. There are several reasons for this. One is that interest rates, along with foreign exchange rates, are the most important prices in many countries. Through their control of interest rates and portfolio regulations, governments influence general price levels, credit supply, and the total volume of activity in an economy. The political system may also attempt to use selective credit controls to reward certain groups for their political support. Political control also occurs because credit involves moral issues. The charging of interest, for example, has long been a thorny religious and philosophical problem in many cultures. Regulation of financial markets may also reflect a government's vested interest, as a major borrower, in ensuring relatively cheap funds.

Regulation occurs increasingly as finance becomes complex. Financial development requires public confidence in the financial system. When gold and silver coins were used in commerce, the problems of confidence could be met by examining and testing the weight and purity of coins offered in payment. A higher order of confidence is required for the acceptance of paper money and checks. Governments play a key role in providing the climate in which paper instruments can circulate and maintain their value.

The activities in rural financial markets that are outside formal financial institutions are largely beyond the direct control of governments. Some governments try to overcome this limitation by attempting to reduce, control, or eliminate informal lending. There is little evidence that these attempts are very successful or desirable. In any case, the types of lenders and activities in informal markets that governments often try to eliminate tend to decline in relative importance or to move into the formal sector as development progresses. Governments have been much more successful in regulating formal rural financial markets through lending quotas and interest rate restrictions. In part this is because many of the modern institutions in these markets are government-owned and depend very heavily on funds provided by government or external assistance agencies.

Regulation is evidence of the intimate relationship between financial markets and political systems. A little-discussed feature of financial markets is that they are an attractive channel for distributing political patronage. It is very obvious when land reform, for example, is used to reward one group in the society and to penalize another. It is much, much easier and less visible for political leaders quietly to reward their allies by arranging special credit programs. The group benefited may realize a subsidy if concessionary interest rates are applied to the loan, as often occurs in formal agricultural credit. Loans can end up as income transfers if real rates of interest are negative, and especially if the political system tolerates loan defaults. A big advantage to the politician of rewarding groups through financial markets is that those who are disadvantaged by these actions are diffused and usually unaware or unperturbed that they are being harmed by special credit programs. At the same time, benefits are highly concentrated and visible to recipients.

Manipulation or direct control of interest rates is a major feature of traditional intervention in rural financial markets. Changes in interest rate policies are the cornerstone of new thinking about rural financial markets. This new thinking also stresses the distinction between nominal and real rates of interest. The nominal interest rate is that specified in loan contracts, and the real rate is the nominal rate of interest adjusted for changes in the purchasing power of money. Although traditional thinking about rural financial markets largely ignores changes in the price level, the new thinking argues that the real rates of interest are primary determinants of savers' behavior and strongly influence the performance of financial markets and the behavior of large borrowers.

In many low-income countries real rates of interest on formal agricultural credit were negative during much of the 1970s. In some countries, such as Brazil, real rates of interest have been negative on rural loans and deposits for much longer periods. Critics stress that low real rates of interest produce undesirable results. They cause financial intermediaries to concentrate cheap credit in the hands of relatively few borrowers. They also make it very difficult for the financial system to mobilize voluntary savings. This in turn creates dependence on the government or outside donors and renders financial institutions very vulnerable to political pressures. By discouraging deposit mobilization and by making agricultural loans unattractive to commercial lenders, low real rates of interest push the formal financial system serving agriculture toward being a one-way channel for cheap credit from the central bank to the ultimate borrowers.

New thinking about rural financial markets also stresses the importance of voluntary savings mobilization. Economists of all political views agree that savings must be mobilized if development is to be rapid. A majority of policy makers, however, have employed involuntary techniques such as taxation, inflation, price ceilings, and distorted exchange rates. Only a handful of countries have relied on financial markets, which are more voluntary in nature, to stimulate and mobilize savings.

A few of the reasons for not using financial markets to stimulate savings are readily apparent. For example, in some regions few formal financial institutions exist in rural areas. In addition, many formal institutions providing credit in rural areas do not accept deposits. Concessionary interest rates applied to most formal agricultural loans make it impossible for institutions accepting deposits to offer strong incentives to savers, and concessionary rediscount facilities at central banks often diminish lenders' incentives to mobilize savings.

Why have policy makers often chosen to impose, or not to correct, methods that impede the ability of organized financial markets to attract savings? Part of the explanation may be found in the way governments, reinforced by donor agencies, go about forcing the pace of rural development. They often direct large amounts of funds for the development of the agricultural sector into credit programs. These programs preempt more balanced uses of financial markets that include savings mobilization. It is also apparent that many economists and policy makers strongly believe that rural people, and especially the rural poor, cannot or will not voluntarily save significant amounts. These attitudes are residuals of misconceptions about the rationality of rural people that fascinated the development profession during the 1950s and 1960s.

Economic training in Western countries has often reinforced these attitudes. Neoclassical economics focuses on consumption rather than saving, and stresses investment to maintain or increase employment rather than investment to increase the capital base. Neoclassical economics uses interest rates to stimulate additional investment so that underutilized capital can be more fully employed. Little attention is given to how these interest rate policies and the overall use of financial markets to stimulate consumption affect household decisions to save, the vitality of financial markets, and capital formation.

These attitudes lead to self-fulfilling prophesies; rural people are thought to have negligible voluntary savings capacity, and then little or no opportunity or incentive to save is provided in rural areas. Furthermore, involuntary methods of mobilizing savings, such as low product prices offered by parastatal commodity boards, often reduce rural incomes. With reduced incomes, weak incentives, and little opportunity to save, little rural saving has been directed toward formal financial markets.

Financial savings have attractive features for the rural economy. Many rural households, for example, find it difficult to manage their liquidity because of price changes, disease, and weather risks associated with farming. Crop production also is characterized by surges in liquidity following harvests and illiquidity before harvests. Small incomes limit the range of assets many rural households can acquire and hold, especially assets that are relatively large and lumpy. This does not mean that their desire and need to save are not great; the poorer the family is, the more desperately it needs the protection against emergencies provided by liquid assets and by unutilized credit reserves with extended family members, informal lenders, or patrons.

Financial markets are especially useful for the poor because these markets can provide low-risk savings instruments that are highly divisible and liquid. The only asset that is more divisible and more liquid is cash. Too much money on hand, however, has drawbacks: it can be borrowed by relatives, readily consumed, lost, or stolen; it does not yield interest and probably deteriorates in value with inflation. Financial markets have the potential to address these problems of the rural poor by offering attractive savings instruments that provide an alternative way of managing liquidity and risk.

Little is known about voluntary savings capacities: it is difficult to measure potential when most of that potential is not exercised. Few incentives, a lack of formal financial institutions, and low incomes keep voluntary savings from emerging in financial form. There are, however, two ways to obtain insights into how much voluntary savings capacity could exist in rural areas. The first is to experiment with conditions favorable for saving. The second is to examine savings performance of rural households in the few areas where conditions stimulate voluntary saving and where modern financial institutions have attracted substantial amounts of rural savings. Japan, Taiwan, and the Republic of Korea appear to top this list, but evidence from Kenya [as presented in chapter 36] and Peru suggests a considerable potential under rural conditions quite different from those found in East Asia.

Policies

The close relationship between politics and credit has often been ignored in the design and evaluation of rural credit projects. It has also been widely assumed that credit controls can be highly effective in achieving publicly stated goals. The chapters in this section illustrate some of the ways governments try to regulate financial markets, how financial intermediaries respond to these regulations, and the part the external donor agencies play in this process.

Kane (chapter 37) analyzes how political and economic power mix in financial markets. He identifies the reasons for regulation of financial activities and points out that government controls on credit allocation are a result of dynamic forces in a society. Innovative financial intermediaries and borrowers, however, are often able to evade much of the original intent of regulations that are not in their best interests. These reactions cause unintended results. They also increase the cost of financial intermediation; time spent trying to locate and exploit loopholes in regulations is not available for devising innovations that would make financial intermediation more efficient.

Johnson (chapter 38) outlines the main policy options that governments use in their attempts to manipulate banks. He goes on to argue that credit controls are not an effective way of achieving many goals. Although easy to apply, many of the controls do not work because of widespread evasion.

Development assistance agencies have been prominent in agricultural credit. Argyle (chapter 39) describes how donors typically provide this assistance. He stresses that there is no single institutional form that works best in providing financial services in rural areas. He argues that government policies and the overall economic environment are the main determinants of credit project performance.

37. *Good Intentions and Unintended Evil*

Edward J. Kane

[When political power is introduced into economic affairs, it prompts a series of adjustments in markets to rechannel regulatory restraints. Those who are regulated attempt to circumvent the regulations by exploiting loopholes and disobeying the law. Avoidance and evasion absorb resources and raise the cost of performing the regulated activities. The conflict is seldom resolved without a wasteful cycle of further controls and market reactions.]

Relying on Adam Smith's concept of the "invisible hand," every economist can explain how markets react to individual economic power. Markets shape and reshape themselves to neutralize self-interested economic power by coaxing it into channels that serve the public good. But economists have devoted less attention to analyzing how markets systematically counteract the political power of coalitions of individuals. Regulatory restraints imposed by the "visible hand" of political power shape markets just as surely as economic power does, but in ways designed to create or perpetuate economic power.

Introducing political power into economic affairs initiates a dialectical process of adjustments and counteradjustments. In what resembles reflex action, markets rechannel regulatory power as regulatees short-circuit regulators' intentions both by finding and exploiting loopholes and by the simpler expedient of disobeying the law. Avoidance and evasion absorb resources (especially lawyers and administrators) from other uses and raise the costs of performing the previously unregulated activities. All this frustrates the coalition sponsoring the regulation and puts pressure on bureaucrats and legislators to seek new administrative remedies. The dialectical conflict can resolve itself in numerous ways, but seldom before the nation has experienced a wasteful cycle of political and economic reactions. Typically, bureaucratic

Adapted from *Journal of Money, Credit, and Banking*, vol. 9, no. 1 (February 1977), pp. 55–69, by permission.

controls and market adaptations chase each other round and round, generating additional problems, confrontations, and costs for society at large.

The Demand for Regulation

Underlying this dialectical concept is the idea that political power finds economic expression in demands for public goods, for direct or indirect government subsidization of certain activities, or for government regulation of the market behavior of categories of people whose actions are believed to reduce the welfare of others. Of course, specific political demands typically cut across these categories. The principal reason for suggesting a three-way taxonomy is to provide a fuller perspective on the third class of demand—that for government regulation of someone else. The very existence of this demand creates a "political market" for regulation and establishes incentives for politicians and bureaucrats to supply regulatory services.

The demand for credit allocation is a demand by, or on behalf of, frustrated borrowers for government intervention in their favor. It is a demand to change the rules of the economic game to assist so-called losers in credit markets—those who seek housing loans, small businesses, and nonwealthy households. (Of course, many kinds of regulation are also sought by economic "winners.") Whether and how the rules are ultimately changed is determined in the political arena, with economic analysts playing only a small advisory role on both sides. The economists' role is essentially to assist participants to sort out and articulate how their sectoral self-interest would be affected under alternative institutional arrangements. Professional sorting out is required because credit allocation works far less predictably than proponents presume, and its long-run effects are quite different from its short-run effects. The popular conception of how government economic programs work is marred by a naive tendency to project the effects of government actions wholly in line with the *intentions* of their sponsors. Voters (and legislators) are prone to wishful thinking about what governmental good intentions can accomplish in the market economy. Conversely, they are prone to blame difficulties in making controls effective on the bad intentions of identifiable groups or on the incompetence of some bureaucratic system.

Faced with rationing or price controls (which in the United States include city rent controls, the wage-price controls of 1971–73, the prohibition of alcoholic beverages in 1919, and the ceiling on savings deposit interest rates in the 1960s), affected parties can be expected to protect their economic interests—to probe opportunities to get around the controls or to turn them to their net advantage. This effect is all too often assisted by poorly designed administrative incentives that lead bureaucrats to act directly against a program's avowed purposes. Citizens' and bureaucrats' efforts to minimize the burden placed on them by government regulations generate unintended effects. Unlike a control's intended effects, its unintended effects usually are not desired by the coalition sponsoring the regulation, and they tend to become more and more important the longer a given control remains in force.

In debating the economics of any proposed new system of rationing or price control, proponents stress the intended short-run benefits while opponents stress the unintended long-run costs. Given the gaps in their respective outlooks, each side finds its case so strong that it comes to doubt the intellectual honesty or basic competence of its rivals.

Just What Is Credit Allocation?

The precise techniques of credit allocation are manifold, including any kind of subtle or unsubtle penalty or inducement to reduce or enhance a particular group's access to funds. The most straightforward programs employ explicit tax or subsidy inducements to change borrower or lender incentives. Allocational programs that rely on moral pressure or behavioral restraint show a penchant for going astray. Except for their costs of administration, restraint programs (so-called selective credit controls) generate no explicit cost or subsidy entries in the government budget. The costs associated with these programs are implicit rather than budgetary. They fall on the public at large and take the form of inefficient uses of productive resources, for example, additional activities required to comply with, enforce, or circumvent the restraints. The principal social costs—and even the benefits—of these programs are far from obvious and do not register as budgetary outlays or receipts. Selective credit controls and tax inducements represent a seductively simple way to promote any economic goal. A policy maker has only to promote the flow of credit to those who purchase or produce the "right" goods and services and retard the granting of credit to those who deal in the "wrong" ones. But the unintended effects of such policies must never be forgotten.

Forms of Selective Credit Allocation

Selective credit programs are designed primarily to redistribute economic opportunities, although some arrangements stress other kinds of benefits. Many of these programs are designed to offset the unintended distributional effects of aggregate stabilization policies. Explicitly targeted programs include loans to small businesses, rural businesses, farmers, exporters, disaster victims, and businesses owned by specific ethnic groups; loans or guarantees to large companies in financial trouble; and a wide variety of measures aimed at increasing credit for housing. Programs in the United States that offer large benefits to a lucky few have been marked by frequent scandals—allegations of corruption, payoffs to inspectors and influence peddlers, and fraud. Usually programs whose benefits are spread widely operate more serenely. These include government insurance for bank deposits and mortgages, differential interest ceilings and reserve requirements on various types of financial-intermediary deposits, and regulations governing the eligibility of collateral. But if one looks closely, serious unintended effects exist in these programs, too.

One frequent form of allocational technique is known as "moral suasion." It consists of intermittent communications from government officials urging financial institutions to regulate themselves in specified ways that favor or disfavor particular classes of borrowers during some crisis. These efforts seldom spell out what penalties, if any, will be imposed on recalcitrant institutions or what benefits cooperative firms may expect to reap. Approaches run the gamut from explicit suasion (formal letters signed by central bank officials and direct but undocumentable informal contacts, including telephone calls) to reputed suasion (rumors circulated by and for the benefit of troubled borrowers and lenders). Whether true or false, rumors sometimes have the impact of the real thing. Efforts at self-suasion from within financial circles can also develop, either as a grudging response to a manifest political threat or as an enlightened reevaluation of the ethical considerations at issue. These efforts may focus on effective remedies or promote placebos—that is, medication that looks real but has no effective ingredients. Even placebos can disarm adversaries and take politicians off the hook.

If everyone is using these financial controls, they must be good for something. But for what? For helping the economy or for helping politicians get themselves in power? The probability of obtaining or remaining in office is enhanced by pressing for actions that the voters or important people perceive as improving the performance of the economy. Even if a policy is not beneficial in fact, or is beneficial only in the very short run, supporting it can improve the odds of winning office so long as the bad effects do not become clear until later.

Economic controls are conceived, sustained, and occasionally abandoned in the political arena. In the economic arena, ways are devised to make them less effective. Good economic laws should survive the collision, and market adaptation helps to force the eventual reversal of bad laws. Though time-consuming and economically wasteful, this dialectic of bad economic laws is straightforward: controls are a payoff for successful political activity. Individuals who are dissatisfied with the outcome of some market process unite to press for governmental intervention. When these individuals assemble enough political influence, relief is granted in the form of rearrangements in the structure of taxes and subsidies or in the form of governmental controls on the price or quantity of the goods or service traded. As long as supporters of such measures remain united and politically powerful, the balance of true social benefits and costs remains secondary to the intended benefits. For a long while, unintended distortions caused by controls can be portrayed as consequences of educational or administrative difficulties, summarized in the phrase "imperfect enforcement." After a while, however, unintended effects tend increasingly to reduce the intended benefits and to expand a program's social costs. This process simultaneously undermines the sponsoring coalition and strengthens a growing countermovement. For controls to be jettisoned, the countermovement must beat what is left of the sponsors at their own game.

The Gap between Intended and Unintended Effects

Economic controls are designed to coerce citizens and firms to act against their perceived self-interest, supposedly for the common good. Enforcing such behavior is difficult and not always worth the trouble. As with legal prohibitions against alcohol or sex, the penalties cannot work without community consensus. The longer controls remain in force, the more time there is for interested parties to undermine that consensus through educational and political activity. The more controversial the problem that controls are intended to solve, the more unstable the operative consensus is likely to be and the more energy is likely to be directed to undermining it.

On the economic front, strong biting controls build up sizable rewards for those bold enough to defy them or clever enough to devise ways around them. The longer controls remain in effect, the more time evaders and avoiders (black and gray marketeers) have to search for loopholes, to perfect their enterprises, and to inform the public about the alternatives their operations create. Unless reinforced by strong community disapprobation, enforcement efforts tend to lag seriously behind those of the regulatees both in time and in quality. Without broad community support, regulating the flow of forbidden goods and services becomes like trying to make a school of hungry fish swim away from food falling through the water.

Once installed, however, systems of economic controls are seldom abandoned quickly or gracefully. A set of controls typically feeds on its initial failures. The less effective a set of controls appears in its first few months, the tougher and more widespread its penalties and reporting requirements tend to become. In large part, this follows from officials' penchant for viewing the success of such programs as a test of both their sincerity and their authority. Adaptive market responses that minimize the personal cost of controls to individual transactors are seen as disturbing evidence of growing disrespect for the government and its laws. During a control's "honeymoon period," administrators' most pressing pursuit is to reorganize bureaucratic operations to root out and punish such behavior. Customarily a network of controls continues to expand unless and until the budgetary cost, social inconvenience, economic waste, and distributional inequity associated with the system become painfully obvious even to the ordinary citizen. This necessitates a political reassessment. If the controls have outlived their political usefulness, only self-interested parties and ideological diehards will support their continuance. But as long as the hard-core adherents are well enough placed, the controls will survive in some form or other.

Do Credit Controls Work Even in the Short Run?

Whether controls work even in the short run depends primarily on adjustment costs: the cost to players of having the rules of the game change frequently. The links between specific debt flows and sectoral expenditure patterns is by no means hard and fast. There are many ways to finance any given expenditure. Lenders and borrowers have shown a great ability to relabel their debt contracts quickly or to substitute other, less efficient, unregulated (even specially devised) forms of credit for the regulated ones.

Even as a short-run expedient, the case for rationing credit is weak. First, the major impetus for government credit rationing often comes from complaints about problems that are not soluble by such devices and could be better dealt with in other ways. Trying to direct the flow of real resources with restrictions on particular classes of credit is something like trying to push heavy stones around with a thin, flexible stick; such tools work against the user's intentions as much as for them. But even controls that work as well as possible still impose costs as well as benefits. Against the intended improvements on targeted dimensions of economic performance, one must weigh the inescapable adjustment costs and unintended inequities and inefficiencies introduced by forcing credit flows out of their customary channels.

Rational policy makers need to balance net favorable effects on one or more dimensions against unfavorable effects that develop elsewhere in the economy before initiating control measures. Moreover, because controls lose their effectiveness over time, policy makers need to monitor such tradeoffs continually. They must regularly assess and tabulate the net effects of any ongoing credit allocation policy and kill any program whose continuing benefits do not promise to exceed its continuing costs.

Conclusions

A supplementary "political" market for regulation services opens up as soon as economic forces finish their work. Transactions in this political market disturb the general economic equilibrium and push the market forces into action again. In the political market, contracting and recontracting absorb real resources and occupy real time. This requires analysts to focus explicitly on the transitional costs of moving from one equilibrium to another.

The analysis developed here indicates that a decision to establish government credit allocation would kick off a long cycle of market and political interaction. Credit rationing promises to make financial markets work less efficiently, to redistribute wealth in ways that could easily run counter to intentions, and to politicize further any intersectoral economic conflicts. It could seriously increase political and economic alienation among the less powerful members of society.

38. *Credit Controls as Instruments of Development Policy in the Light of Economic Theory*

Omotunde E. G. Johnson

[Governments impose credit controls on commercial banks to force them to lend for socially desirable purposes. Johnson argues that credit controls are inefficient because of the costs they impose on lenders, borrowers, and society. Taxes and subsidies could be designed that would be more efficient than credit controls: greater specialization in lending might also achieve some objectives of credit controls at less cost to society. Since this article was written, many countries have adopted credit controls requiring commercial banks to lend more to agriculture.]

In their quest for rapid progress, developing countries have diverted resources to areas that are considered more productive in some social sense. Commercial banks can influence the pace and pattern of development by the *efficiency* with which they mobilize and allocate savings, and by the *direction* of their allocation of these savings. Central bankers and others have noted that commercial banks have allocated a disproportionate share of their funds to certain activities; in particular, the banks have concentrated heavily on short-term, self-liquidating loans to finance foreign and domestic commerce. Medium- and long-term loans, especially for industry and agriculture, have largely been neglected. Moreover, the facilities of these banks tend to be available mainly to established concerns in the urban areas. According to this view, the imbalance in the allocation of commercial bank funds has produced, and threatens to perpetuate, an imbalance in the pattern of development. To stem the flow of bank funds into low-priority areas and divert them to high-priority areas, credit control policies have been urged.

Adapted from the *Journal of Money, Credit, and Banking*, vol. 6, no. 1 (February 1974), pp. 85–99, by permission.

In this chapter, I examine credit controls as attempts to equate private and social profitability and as tax-cum-subsidy schemes. I conclude that there is no logical basis for them. Instead, other kinds of policies could be introduced that would not only achieve the desired goals of credit controls, but also do so more effectively and efficiently. I do not criticize credit controls as short-term policies in times of inflation or other emergency conditions (such as wars or drought), nor do I focus on particular techniques of credit control. Instead, I address the basic rationale of credit controls as instruments of development policy.

The Nature of Credit Control

Credit controls in developing countries have tended to be of three broad categories. First, there are the *portfolio-ceiling* devices, which generally set a ceiling on loans for specified purposes or to specified sectors. The ceilings may be set as percentages of loans extended to different sectors or as maximum amounts of loans allocable to specified sectors. Another type of portfolio-ceiling device is an incremental ceiling that specifies the maximum increase allowed for loans for various purposes.

Second, there are policies tied to the *discount mechanism*. The central bank may offer preferential rates in rediscounting paper originating in high-priority sectors to provide an added incentive for the commercial banks to increase lending to these favored activities. Or the central bank may engage in discretionary changes in the list of eligible types of paper to take account of alterations in the intensity with which it wants to push credit into different areas from time to time.

The third set of credit controls are tied to *reserve requirements*. These most often link differential reserve requirements to the composition of commercial bank portfolios. Banks whose portfolios conform to the requirements of certain minimum percentages of loans to the high-priority areas are allowed to maintain lower cash or liquidity ratios than the normal ratio. Alternatively, very high reserve ratios are imposed, and banks are then given the option of keeping these reserves idle or investing them in certain specified assets. The prescribed percentages or the associated liquidity ratios, or both, may be changed as the central bank's emphasis shifts from one high priority area to another.

Credit Control and the Equation of Private and Social Benefits

The implicit theoretical basis for credit controls has been that the private profitability (to the commercial banks) and the social profitability (to the nation) differ with respect to loans granted to the different sectors. In order not to confuse issues, it will be assumed here that this thesis is correct. Thus, the case most favorable to credit controls will be considered. The question then becomes why the private profitability of loans to particular high-priority areas should differ from the true social profitability. One can conceive of at least three reasons this could be so.

First, the "true" creditworthiness of the particular users of funds in the high-priority sectors may be underestimated by commercial banks. This implies that it would be profitable for the commercial banks, using their own discount rates, to spend some resources in estimating the "true" creditworthiness and to extend more loans and advances than they now do to these high-priority areas on the basis of the newly acquired information. It can then be argued that banks do not attempt to increase their knowledge about creditworthiness in these areas because of inertia and conservatism. But suppose it can be shown that the rate of return on commercial banks' information-augmenting activities in these areas is very low compared with other normal uses of their resources. It may still be possible to show that commercial banks do not in fact have a comparative advantage in assessing the creditworthiness of certain institutions and individuals, and that these institutions and individuals are among the high-priority areas. Therefore, even though some of their funds would be more profitable if invested in these areas, commercial banks are inhibited by ignorance of this fact and by the relatively high cost of finding out the truth.

A second reason for a divergence between private and social profitability of extending loans to high-priority areas is the possibility of disparity between the commercial banks' desired rate of return on loans and the correct marginal social rate of time preference. Commercial banks, in short, might have too high a desired rate of return relative to the marginal social rate of time preference. Given such a divergence, one can argue that if all loans are discounted by the marginal social rate of time preference, some of the high-priority sectors will be found to warrant far more loans than they at present receive from the banks. This argument, however, can be dismissed as irrelevant. The high rate of discount used by the commercial banks, relative to the true marginal social rate of time preference, can be made a case for more loans in general, but not necessarily a case for altering the shares of loans going to different sectors. Even if banks did grant more loans on the basis of the correct marginal social rate of time preference, there is no reason to expect they would not simply grant more loans to the same areas as in the past.

Still another reason can be listed to explain a possible divergence between social and private profitability of extending a greater fraction of bank loans to the high-priority areas. The long-range and wider impact of the development of these sectors on the economy as a whole may not be sufficiently incorporated into the private calculations of the banks, since neither the banks nor the particular firms and individuals of the high-priority sectors are able to capture the positive externalities of the latter's activities at sufficiently low cost.

Credit controls are seen as desirable in developing countries to direct the nation's resources into the most socially profitable uses. Fundamentally, the case boils down to this: First, commercial banks (or financial institutions in general) either underestimate the creditworthiness and overestimate the risk, administration, and collection costs associated with extending loans to certain sectors, or they have costs of assessing creditworthiness and risk and of administering and collecting loans in these sectors higher than the true social cost. Second, commercial banks do not take into consideration the external benefits which expansion of the high-priority sectors will yield for the rest of the economy.

The Distribution Effects of Credit Controls

By reallocating credit to alter the market-determined allocation of real resources, credit controls become implicit tax-cum-subsidy schemes. There are two methods by which they achieve this. One works through inflation, and the other alters the profits of banks and their traditional clients to make the high-priority sectors more attractive.

Consider the case of inflation. Policies tied to the discount mechanism, such as differential discount rates, work through inflation. Preferential central bank discount rates for paper originating from the high-priority areas, or preferential treatment for such paper in rediscounting, enable private financial institutions to give added credit to the high-priority areas without serious threat to the credit available for their traditional clients. The policy induces banks to increase their demand for paper issued by the high-priority sectors at any given interest rate, as well as to give such instruments more favorable treatment in any credit rationing. The result is increased purchases of these instruments by commercial banks. They will be expected to rediscount, at the central bank, the instruments they would not normally purchase without the preferential treatment. The funds are then again available for their traditional clients. Thus, commercial banks become simply media through which the central bank purchases paper originating from the high-priority areas. The net effect is expansion of the money supply.

The increased money supply allows the preferred sectors to bid away resources from other firms. The consequence is rising prices. The differential discount rates thus engender inflation, which is the mechanism by which the other sectors of the economy are taxed to subsidize the preferred sectors. The incidence of the inflation tax will depend on the distribution of financial claims, the structure of contractual relations, and bargaining strength; the secondary distributive effects of the inflation may not be desirable in the eyes of the authorities.

When credit-control policies do not tax and subsidize through inflation, they do so by implicitly taxing the banks and their traditional clients to subsidize the high-priority sectors. This is especially associated with portfolio-ceiling devices and reserve requirements. The aim of these policies is to augment the ratio of loans going to high-priority areas to the total earning assets of banks. Assume banks were in equilibrium before the credit controls. Such high-priority loans would then be less attractive to banks than other earning assets, because they are either less liquid or less profitable. Forcing banks to increase their ratio of high-priority loans to total earning assets would reduce the liquidity and profitability of their earning assets. The reduced liquidity would cause banks to alter the composition of their non-high-priority earning assets so as to increase liquidity, which would often mean substitution of government securities and large business loans for consumer debt and small-business loans. The ultimate result would depend on how greatly the high-priority loans differ from others. But two things are clear: First, profit considerations could lead banks to alter their portfolios of non-high-priority loans to favor the big, well-established firms at the expense of small firms, consumer credit, and low-yielding government securities. This readjustment of banks' portfolios may not be socially beneficial. Second, as long as the high-priority loans are not as liquid as the earning assets they replace, the banks will not be willing to substitute among their earning assets enough to neutralize the adverse effects on their profitability. This reduced profitability of their earning assets is the implicit tax on banks.

Since the implicit tax on banks restricts their ability to compete for loanable funds in the open market, loanable funds from ultimate suppliers are diverted toward the open market and away from banks. This is a further tax on the banks. The reduction in bank funds going to the banks' traditional clients causes these clients to turn to other sources of funds—open-market domestic, foreign, or internal. If they turn to open-market sources, the traditional clients bid up the prices of these funds in the attempt to attract them away from others. A rise in interest rates ensues. The effect is an implicit tax on the banks' traditional clients and a redistribution of wealth—away from net borrowers toward net lenders.

Thus, the policy of compelling banks to increase the proportion of high-priority loans in their portfolio leads to a twofold redistribution of wealth. First, the policy redistributes wealth away from banks and their traditional clients toward the high-priority borrowers. This is accomplished by forcing banks to lend to the high-priority areas, so that their wealth is reduced; by forcing the banks' traditional clients to turn to higher-cost sources of funds; and by enabling the high-priority sectors to borrow from banks at lower cost than under competitive conditions. Second, the policy redistributes wealth away from net borrowers to net lenders of open-market funds.

The Welfare Costs of Credit Controls

The more efficient financial institutions are in mobilizing savings and allocating them to competing investors, the more one will find increased interest payments to savers, lower interest rates to investors, and reduced transaction costs in getting funds from surplus to deficit units. Thus, savings and investment, as well as the social rate of return on society's investment resources, are augmented.

The implicit tax imposed on financial institutions by credit controls lowers the rate of return on the intermediary function and reduces the supply of financial instruments. The result is a lower rate of interest on savings, higher interest costs of investment, and greater transactions costs to society for transmitting funds from surplus to deficit units. Lower savings and investments, more direct financing, and lower returns on investment are the ultimate consequences.

The Alternatives

There are two kinds of externalities connected with the demand of high-priority sectors for bank credit. In the first case, the effective demand of these sectors for resources including bank credit is low because, in their productive activity, they are "unable" to capture profitably the full value created by their activities, and the noninternalized portion of this value is significant enough to warrant much more use of the society's resources in these activities. In the second case, banks underestimate the true effective demand of these sectors for bank credit because banks are "poor" in estimating this effective demand.

Once the issue is put in this form, it is clear that credit controls are not the answer. Rather, an explicit tax-cum-subsidy is appropriate in the first case. Required in the second case is the creation of financial institutions with greater capabilities than banks for assessing the creditworthiness of these sectors and for administering and servicing loans to them.

Consider the first case. It is the whole society that captures the positive externality flowing from the activities of the high-priority areas. For optimal internalization of these externalities, it seems desirable that the whole society should pay for these external benefits. This calls for an explicit tax imposed on the rest of the community, with the proceeds used to give an explicit output subsidy to the high-priority sectors in accordance with the estimated external benefits conferred.

In the second case, what is wanted are institutions with a large comparative advantage in assessing creditworthiness and in administering and servicing loans to the sectors considered high-priority, so as to reduce the cost of acquiring a given amount of information and of effecting a given amount of servicing. Working through such institutions could also ensure that the "right" amount of resources goes into assessing creditworthiness and administering and servicing loans. These new institutions could borrow funds from the commercial banks at market rates of interest and lend these funds out to the high-priority sectors, or they could be given substantial initial working capital from state funds and then be left to work on their own. In this second case, there is no need for subsidization of the high-priority sectors since the activities of the new financial institutions are socially and privately profitable. In both alternatives, the central bank is not at all involved. All the welfare costs and other disadvantages of credit controls discussed above are avoided.

39. *Development Assistance, National Policies, and Lender Type and Performance*

D. Brian Argyle

[Donor agencies greatly increased their attention to agriculture during the 1970s, and one expression of this is rural credit projects. These projects have financed farm-level investments that have generally been remunerative. Financial intermediaries of various types, each having its own strengths and weaknesses, have disbursed project funds. The success of credit projects depends not so much on the type of farm lender, however, as on the government policies and political factors that determine interest rates, the incentives for good loan discipline, and the intensity of loan collection activities. Several problems are typically associated with farm credit projects and institutions, and innovations in design could increase project impact and institutional effectiveness.]

Donor agencies increased their commitment of aid funds to developing countries at a rapid rate during the 1970s. As their aid increased, so did their interest in agriculture; donor agencies increasingly focused more direct assistance on agriculture as opposed to indirect help such as building roads or railways to serve rural areas. The extent of this shift is illustrated in the lending of the World Bank Group. Between 1970 and 1980, total Bank commitments for projects rose about four and a half times from $17,000 million to $80,000 million, while that for agriculture rose tenfold from $2,000 million to $20,000 million. In recent years, about one-third of Bank Group lending has been directly for agriculture, while substantial funds for infrastructure and industry have also been provided for the production of services and goods used mainly by agriculture.

Financial Institutions On-lending Donor Funds

To assist farmers, donor agencies have provided a range of inputs and services. The provision of investments and inputs may require a credit channel of some sort and a means of determining the inputs most appropriate for individual farmers. The types of credit programs and the institutional means used have varied according to the country and its financial environment, the institutions available, and the target group of farmers. The main channels have been commercial banks, specialized development banks, cooperatives, and project units.

In most developing countries, commercial banks were the earliest source of formal credit. Although their main interest has usually not been the financing of farmers, many commercial banks have had a long association with financing large farmers as well as various agricultural supply and marketing agents. In some countries the commercial banks have supplied credit to a much wider range of farmers, sometimes because governments have required that a specific percentage of bank portfolios be in agricultural loans. The advantages of commercial banks are that many of them have a network of branches and a reasonably competent financial staff who generally know their potential clients. Banks normally can provide short-term as well as medium-term credit and receive farmers' deposits, thus supplying an ample range of services. However, because commercial banks are interested in profits and in reducing risks, they generally favor lending to large farmers. In addition, they do not often have specialists such as agriculturalists to judge the merits of farm loan requests.

Donor agencies have frequently used commercial banks as a channel, often several banks in a single program. The donor usually lends to a central bank, which in turn lends to commercial banks. In many cases, the central bank supplies more than a simple discounting service. In Mexico, for example, a central bank agency, FIRA, provides discount facilities to commercial banks and to a government development bank for medium- and long-term agricultural loans. It also offers substantial technical assistance from a large staff of specialists in approving farmer loans and training bank staff. Through guarantees and attractive discount rates, it encourages loans to small farmers. FIRA has an important role in planning and preparing national credit programs. [See chapter 17 for a description of FIRA.]

In India a central bank offshoot, the National Bank for Agriculture and Rural Development (NABARD), discounts loans for commercial and cooperative banks. NABARD supports the operations of a large number of financial entities and coordinates overall credit strategy and requests for assistance. Other countries including Costa Rica, the Dominican Republic, Honduras, the Philippines, Ireland, Spain, and Portugal have utilized central bank rediscounting of assets either from commercial banks or from both commercial and state-owned development banks.

Development banks have been the channel for donor-assisted projects in some countries. These are usually specialized agricultural banks dealing with individual farmers. Sometimes, however, they act as apex institutions for cooperatives or other credit agencies. Most of these banks have been established in the past twenty years, but some have long histories, such as the Agricultural Bank of Turkey which is 110 years old. An interesting and well-developed institution is the National Agricultural Credit Bank (CNCA) of Morocco, which has a system of regional banks lending to medium-size and large farmers along with a large number of local banks lending to small farmers. The CNCA system reaches a significant percentage of all sizes of farmers.

Cooperatives are an important source of farm credit, particularly for small farmers. Although the cooperative movement is often linked to the national agricultural development bank or central bank, it sometimes has its own apex bank with associated local, state, and regional cooperative banks. Building efficient cooperatives capable of handling credit has proved difficult in many countries, despite the potential advantages of such a system. Utilization of cooperative marketing systems for credit recovery has sometimes proved effective.

In countries where the agricultural banking system is practically nonexistent or completely inadequate for achieving the objectives of development projects, a special project unit may be created to provide credit services. Sometimes these units are connected with a bank, but in other cases the credit component is kept completely outside the banking system. The use of a project credit unit is frequently linked to an intensive extension effort to improve farmers' practices through supervised credit. World Bank–assisted projects in Africa have used this approach. It frequently has a high operating cost but can achieve good loan recovery rates.

Informal credit has not played a significant role in donor-supported projects. Cooperation between informal lenders and formal projects has been hindered by suspicion. It seems quite certain, however, that informal sources of credit are affected by the inflow of donor agencies' resources. Informal lenders charge higher interest rates than do formal credit agencies, but they provide prompt, efficient service that most farmers continue to use.

The type of government, the local culture, and the general financial and economic environment determine which sort of institution is likely to be most effective. In many countries, there is little real choice of credit system for a project: an existing institution dominates the sector or subsector and thereby precludes the possibility of establishing alternative institutions except at great cost.

Environmental Determinants of Institutional Performance

A number of widespread problems can be as important to the performance of a credit project as are the institutional strengths and weaknesses. While agricultural output is inherently variable because of the weather, this is not the main cause for slow payment, arrears, and nonpayment of farm debts. Of significance is that when arrears are high, they are usually high for both large and small farmers, for rich and poor. In many cases farmers could afford to repay but do not do so; the credit is available at low cost, and farmers know (or think) that government and the credit institution are not prepared for political reasons to pursue defaulters. Politicians often argue for a lenient attitude on arrears, either because of political pressures or because they believe farmers deserve special consideration—particularly if they face low government-controlled produce prices or other constraints. Many countries, however, are able to control arrears. In India, for example, some institutions have few arrears as a result of firm institutional and government actions, while others are in a completely opposite condition.

In recent years the problems of low interest rates have escalated. As inflation has increased in most countries, governments have not been prepared to increase interest rates in line with inflation rates. This has had an extremely negative impact on the real values of lending institutions' assets and portfolios. Governments have endeavored to increase the funding of their credit institutions, but the additional resources are often not sufficient to maintain the real level of lending, and deterioration or stagnation follows. It is difficult to convince many governments (and even some people in the development field) that subsidized credit leads to far more problems than it solves.

Donor agencies have encouraged governments to lend to smaller farmers for reasons of equity and because frequently there is greater scope for increased production per unit of land on small farms than on large farms. Many governments provide credit to small farmers at a lower interest rate than to other agricultural subsectors or to the general community. Such policies put the credit institution in a difficult position, because it does not have an effective means of reaching small farmers cheaply and must either restrict such lending or lose money. Some World Bank–assisted projects require that a certain percentage of credit funds be allocated to the poorer sections of the farming community. Unless such conditions are coupled with a requirement that the institution's overall portfolio will move toward smaller farmers, these requirements may not be very significant because of the ability of an institution to transfer its own funds from category to category.

In some countries, governments have relied on cooperatives or borrowing groups to reach small farmers. This has been fairly effective in Turkey, where the Agricultural Bank of Turkey is able to lend to village cooperatives and groups based on very long- and well-established cultural practices. It has also been effective in some states in India and in several other countries. However, cooperatives frequently have been very inefficient and unsuccessful in reaching small farmers or collecting loan repayments.

In considering the effectiveness of various types of credit institutions, donor agency staff have often been concerned by the lack of accounting data and slowness of receipt of audited financial statements. This problem implies that managements of some credit institutions do not have the necessary data to make sound decisions. Substantial efforts have gone into improving accounting systems. There has been some success, but also disappointment. Many managers are not yet convinced that good information is the basis of good management.

Conclusions and Prospects

A review of farm credit projects reveals at least five effects: (1) In most cases, farmers receive significant financial benefit from investments for which donor funds are provided. Although some of these investments would have occurred without the donor-supported project, the alternative investments or the value of emergency reserves cannot usually be measured. (2) To the extent that agricultural interest rates are significantly below other rates in the financial sector, the possibility of diverting funds away from agricultural uses appears to increase. (3) The role of governments and politicians is vital in maintaining good credit discipline. If they falter, credit discipline easily deteriorates. (4) A significant number of project entities, particularly development banks, lose money on their projects. (5) In many cases, interest rates are negative, and institutions are struggling to maintain the real value of their assets. This puts considerable strain on these institutions, as their need to borrow increases.

In looking at future lending for credit purposes, donor agencies and institutions in developing countries continue to face significant problems:

• How to reach small farmers more effectively? Although the obvious answer appears to be some form of cooperative or borrower group, this approach requires much development in most countries as well as sound credit policies by government. In some countries, an increase in small farmers' interest rates plus other incentives may be sufficient to encourage credit institutions to lend more enthusiastically to small farmers. Use of the informal sector may have prospects but needs more study and trial.

• How to maintain the viability of the institutions and their lending in real terms without making them continually dependent on government handouts? This usually means raising interest rates and using more efficient methods.

• How to move away from a narrow approach of lending for specific purposes toward a broader approach of sectoral lending? This depends in most cases on credit institutions' developing sounder overall policies and improving and using more effectively their accounting systems. The use of donor funds to finance certain investments can provide a useful impetus in initial projects, but continuous reliance on such funds indicates either a lack of progress in building a sound institution or a difference in objectives between the institution and the donor agency—a likely cause for problems.

• How to mobilize the considerable sums of money available in rural communities? First, there is a need to provide services for accepting savings deposits; second, for many institutions an increase in their lending rates is essential if they are to provide services and pay attractive interest rates on deposits.

Patronage

Rural financial markets are often used to allocate rewards, favors, and other political benefits. The command over resources provided by credit, plus defaults and negative real rates of interest, provides the basis for patronage. The rewards are often not highly visible to society at large, while the social costs of the patronage are diffused and usually not clearly apparent, at least until the political power which provided the patronage is spent and the rules change. Ladman and Tinnermeier (chapter 40) show how politics and formal intermediaries in rural financial markets interacted recently in Bolivia. They reinforce many of the points made by Kane, Johnson, and Argyle in the preceding section and illustrate the forms that political intrusions take. They also suggest that funds from development assistance agencies may help sustain the political use of financial markets.

Youngjohns (chapter 41) and Robert (chapter 42) expand on this theme by discussing political considerations that have permeated cooperative credit. Although cooperatives are often promoted as grass-roots organizations that enable the rural poor to gain economic and political leverage, Youngjohns notes that the bottom-up organization of cooperatives that would permit this seldom occurs in low-income countries. Instead, a top-down organization typically emerges when cooperatives are organized and directed largely by forces outside the local area, usually national governments. Outside influence has often destroyed the commercial viability and financial integrity of cooperatives by forcing them to undertake activities on terms and conditions that do not generate revenues sufficient to cover costs. To survive, cooperatives in these situations rely on subsidies, which leave them open to political interference. Instead of being independent and self-sustaining, they frequently fall into patronal relationships with government agencies.

Robert points out that credit cooperatives used to channel cheap loans to their members are vulnerable to internal takeovers by local elites. Gains from access to cheap credit, especially if significant rates of default are tolerated, are quickly recognized by local elites, which colonize these organizations. His review of the cooperative credit system in a major region of India from 1900 through the 1930s shows how such a system can be captured and used for political purposes. How would these cooperatives have operated if savings mobilization, rather than disbursement of cheap credit, had been their main objective?

40. *The Political Economy of Agricultural Credit: The Case of Bolivia*

Jerry R. Ladman and Ronald L. Tinnermeier

[Although agricultural credit programs have economic objectives, they are often very appealing to governments for political reasons. An example of credit as a political instrument in Bolivia is described. It is pointed out that when resources are allocated to satisfy political objectives, less than optimal results for long-term development can be expected.]

The political economy of agricultural credit is important for five reasons: First, governments typically control the supply of formal agricultural credit, and they can strongly influence its distribution and allocation. Second, a concessionary interest rate, which is almost ubiquitous in the official agricultural credit programs of developing countries, provides an attractive income transfer to borrowers. Third, when governments tolerate long-term delinquency, as is not uncommon in developing countries, the nonrepaying borrower also receives an income transfer. Fourth, when inflation is present, concessionary and delinquency income transfers are magnified. Fifth, the advantages of obtaining these transfers are sufficiently attractive that they can be used by governments to gain the favor of borrowers and, conversely, cause borrowers to influence government.

Credit programs are particularly alluring for political purposes. They are easy to establish and administer; they have very legitimate economic objectives; and because money is fungible and because of the hidden transfers, the true uses of such funds are difficult to identify. Thus, credit lends itself to being used for political purposes under the guise of economic development.

The extent to which credit allocation decisions are influenced by political factors, or vice versa, is difficult to ascertain. The Bolivian case

Adapted from *American Journal of Agricultural Economics*, vol. 63, no. 1 (February 1981), pp. 66–72; also published in *Development Digest* (January 1982), pp. 24–32.

is particularly useful to study. This country is an archetype of underdevelopment and, as one of the world's poorest nations, has received large infusions of foreign assistance. Moreover, the country is small enough so the flows in financial markets are more easily identified than in larger and more complex countries.

The Political Elements in Farm Credit

Commercial financial institutions in developing countries have shunned lending to agriculture because of the high costs and risks embodied in these loans. Thus, pressures arose to provide alternative sources of financing. The passivity of the agricultural sector suggested a supply-leading financial approach, and government agricultural banks were commonly established. Yet when it became obvious that government institutions could not adequately finance agriculture, means were sought to force the private sector to lend to agriculture. Central bank rediscount mechanisms, loan guarantees, and loan portfolio requirements were common policies. Almost without exception all these agricultural credit programs incorporated a feature transferred from the U.S. Farmers Home Administration credit model: the low and concessionary interest rate. Foreign support for these programs is evident both in the advice and in the capital supplied in volume by donor agencies. Little attention has been directed, however, to the tremendous political leverage that the concessionary transfer offers.

A Framework

Figure 40-1 presents a country-wide demand curve DD' for credit from agricultural lenders to be used for agricultural purposes when interest rates are equalized throughout the economy. If the prevailing real interest rate is r, farmers would want to utilize OC_1 credit. Suppose, however, that the government subsidized agriculture by means of a concessionary interest rate, r_1, for agricultural loans but left interest rates for nonagricultural loans at the previous levels. Two effects would occur. First, borrowers would increase the quantity of funds demanded for agricultural purposes from C_1 to C_2 and, if nonprice rationing were not employed, would simultaneously receive a subsidy or income transfer (the concessionary transfer) of r_1rab.

Second, since money is fungible, credit can be ostensibly borrowed for agricultural purposes but be diverted to nonagricultural activities such as consumption or investment. This gives rise to agricultural illusion—that is, some loans appear to go to agriculture but in fact are used elsewhere. With the relatively lower interest rates for agricultural loans, it would be expected that borrowers would behave in this manner—especially those with multiple occupations and knowledge of

Figure 40–1. *Demand for Credit from Agricultural Lenders*

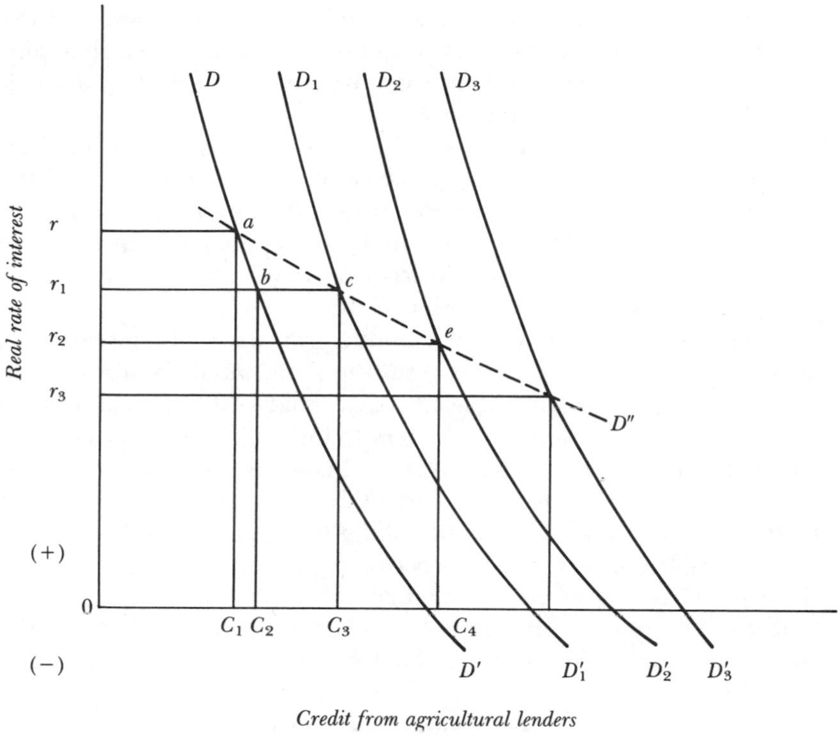

their investment opportunities—and the demand for credit from agricultural lenders would shift right to D_1D_1'. Borrowers would want to use C_2C_3 quantity of credit to practice agricultural illusion, and the concessionary transfer now becomes r_1rac.

If further concessions were granted (r_2, r_3, and so on), there would be yet further demand shifts to the right (D_2D_2', D_3D_3', and so on). The horizontal distance between any D_iD_i' and DD' at any r_i would represent the amount of credit demand from agricultural illusion arising from the concessionary rate. Therefore, the locus of all equilibrium points for all r_i and D_iD_i' traces the illusion demand curve for agricultural credit when concessionary interest rates are employed in that sector. It clearly demonstrates how agricultural illusion increases the concessionary transfer.

Delinquency provides another possibility for an income transfer. A delinquency transfer may be temporary when farmers do not repay their loans on time or permanent when they never repay. In the case of the temporary transfer the farmer gains from improved income or reduced costs resulting from control over cash flow. The permanent transfer is equivalent to the real value of the loan principal plus the real value of interest charges less any real amounts repaid on the loan principal and as interest. In terms of figure 40-1, the amount of the permanent delinquency transfer would be the $0C_3$ loan principal plus $0r_1cC_3$ interest, assuming a concessionary interest rate of r_1, agricultural illusion, and no repayment.

With inflation, the real rate of interest may be quite low or even negative. The effect is to enlarge the concessionary transfer and the temporary delinquency transfer (because of the lower real value of the loan when repaid). When inflation is anticipated by farmers the amount borrowed will increase in accordance with the demand schedule and will further enlarge both transfers.

Clearly the concessionary and delinquency transfers themselves and the additions to these transfers resulting from inflation are coveted. Therefore, a government with control over agricultural credit institutions can use these potential transfers to induce certain types of economic activity or to reward certain behavior among borrowers. Moreover, borrowers, in their competition for access to and a share of the transfer, will undoubtedly be willing to bargain with the government. Thus, there is an interplay between government and farmers in which political factors may take on considerable importance.

Heavy delinquency and default rates may be symptomatic of the degree to which political factors have entered into a loan program; when the government does not take legal measures to bring pressure on borrowers to repay, this indicates an unwillingness to bear either the economic or political costs of such action. The mere existence of these concessionary transfers and the possibility of an easy default transfer create a potential for corruption. Government officials could easily appropriate part of the transfer for themselves by directly or indirectly lending to themselves or by receiving kickbacks from borrowers.

Concessionary interest rates lead to suboptimal social allocation of credit, of real resources, and of the production of goods. Experience demonstrates that nonprice rationing schemes to offset suboptimal social allocation are difficult to enforce and are even more unworkable when political factors intervene. If inflation is present, the additional inflationary transfer enhances the attractiveness of using credit for political objectives and exacerbates the resource allocation consequences.

The concessionary and the delinquency transfers will affect income distribution. Those with access to them will gain at the expense of others. Inflationary conditions will increase the benefits of those who receive these transfers. Concessionary interest rates lead to lower interest revenues for the lending institution if the demand for credit is inelastic or the supply of loanable funds is restricted over the relevant range of the demand schedule. This, in combination with the well-recognized high costs of administering agricultural credit programs, will seriously jeopardize a credit institution's financial viability. Further, political lending will lead to erosion of loan funds because of the extensive delinquency inherent in such loans. The result is that to maintain or increase its loanable funds, the institution must be subsidized by government or obtain foreign loans or assistance.

Foreign Donors

Foreign economic assistance programs have contributed to the use of credit as a political instrument in two ways. First, they have provided considerable economic assistance for agricultural credit programs. Second, they have supported the policy of concessionary interest rates with the direct effect of creating concessionary transfers. As a consequence, they have been an indirect contributor to the use of credit for political purposes, which has led to other transfers. This is particularly true in the case of loans for general agricultural sector development, where credit typically flows to the larger and more sophisticated farmers and agricultural illusion takes on large dimensions. Even where foreign aid funds are earmarked for small farmers, however, the additional funds increase the size of the lender's portfolio and might permit some substitution, releasing other funds for other, often political, purposes.

Economic Solution and Political Cost

The obvious economic solution to all these distortions is to raise interest rates and decrease default. Why, then, have policies of higher rates not been put into effect? Furthermore, why do many lenders not use their legal power to limit default? The suggested answer is that the political cost is too great: governments would lose a means of bargaining for political support; farmers would stand to lose their transfers; and where corruption occurs, officials would lose these sources of income.

The Case of Bolivia

The framework is applied to Bolivia during the government of General Hugo Banzer, 1971–78, when the regional distribution of agricultural credit was highly skewed to the tropical lowlands in the department of Santa Cruz. Between 1973 and 1978, 68 percent of commercial bank loans went to that department. Between 1971 and 1978, 64 percent of the volume but only 23 percent of the number of Bolivian Agricultural Bank (BAB) loans went to Santa Cruz. In contrast, according to the 1976 General Population Census, only 12.6 percent of the rural population lived in that department. Further, for 1964–71, only 43 percent of BAB credit from regular credit lines went to Santa Cruz.

Several interdependent factors explain the highly disproportionate share of agricultural credit going to Santa Cruz in the Banzer period. First, the petroleum and agricultural boom in the region was viewed as the leading edge of the Bolivian economy. Rapid gains in food import substitutes and agricultural exports were expected from the commercial farms, whereas these possibilities were not foreseen for the small-scale traditional farming areas in the highlands. Second, geopolitics was another factor. With the new petroleum development, Bolivia viewed the growth of Santa Cruz as a buffer to further encroachment by Brazil, which had previously taken considerable territory in the rubber boom of 1899.

Whereas both factors were important in explaining the disproportionate credit flows, we suggest that domestic political events were also important in the credit allocation. President Banzer had risen to power in a military coup with the support of a coalition of interests of which a very important element was farmers in Santa Cruz. Hence Banzer was obliged to these persons not only for his sudden rise to power but also for their continued political support.

Institutional and Policy Structure

During 1971–78, 59 percent of bank credit in Bolivia came from BAB. In addition, the government-owned State Bank, a commercial bank, loaned approximately another 20 percent. The system was very amenable to government control. Credit was the chief policy instrument to "lead" agricultural production by means of special credit programs established by the government and donors of foreign aid. Key features of credit policy were concessionary interest rates and central bank rediscounts to the banking system from special credit lines for agriculture.

Foreign assistance provided a steady inflow of funds which freed government funds for lending to some major enterprises such as cotton (little foreign assistance was used for this crop), as well as for liquidity which the financial institutions needed in view of soaring, heavy delinquency. From 1967 to 1978, $146 million (all figures are in current U.S. dollars) in foreign assistance was committed for agricultural credit. A conservative estimate is that at least 45 percent of bank credit (BAB and commercial banks) came from this source.

From 1971 to 1978 BAB loaned $80.9 million in Santa Cruz in 3,348 loans. Of this amount $45.9 million went to cotton in a total of 726 loans. A much smaller amount, $4.1 million, was directed to 118 farmers for soybeans. The average size loan for cotton and soybeans was $63,169 and $34,525 respectively, much larger than the $5,287 national average. Credit for the two crops, which represented 41 percent of the national BAB loan portfolio, went to only a few farmers (6 percent of BAB loans). These loans were made primarily to the larger farmers of Santa Cruz, many of whom belonged to that region's elite or to powerful regional interest groups such as ADEPA (the cotton growers' association).

Income Transfers

The recipients of BAB cotton and soybean loans received total income transfers of at least $44.5 million over the period, an amount only slightly less than the $49.9 million of principal originally loaned. The average transfers for cotton and soybean loans were $55 thousand and $39 thousand respectively.

Almost $6.2 million of these transfers resulted from interest rate concessions of 12 to 15 percent for BAB clients relative to the rates charged by commercial banks for commercial loans. Since the commercial rates are maximum rates established by the Central Bank, they are likely to be less than the true opportunity cost of credit. To the extent this holds true, the concessionary transfer is understated.

The effect of inflation is to reduce the real interest rate and therefore to provide an additional transfer to the borrower. With the exception of 1973 and 1974, inflation in Bolivia was mild, yet the income transfer associated with inflation was very substantial, estimated at $8.2 million.

From 1971 to 1978, BAB delinquency worsened. At the end of 1971, 15 percent of the loan portfolio was overdue; at the end of 1978 it was 43 percent overdue after reaching a high of 47 percent in 1977. Had many loans not been refinanced or extended the figures would have been much higher. The delinquency is concentrated in Santa Cruz; in 1978, 68.8 percent of the total BAB delinquency was in that department. Both cotton and soybeans contributed to the high proportion of the volume of delinquency.

By the end of 1978, the delinquency transfer associated with cotton and soybeans was $30.1 million. Before June 1977, the government would not permit BAB to pressure farmers for repayment; the government issued Supreme Decrees to buy some private banks' delinquent portfolios and transfer them to BAB so that these lenders would not pressure farmers. In June 1977, Banzer issued a Supreme Decree which extended all BAB and State Bank cotton and soybean loans for periods of eight to twelve years. If the loans are paid back as scheduled, the borrowers will pay back virtually nothing in terms of real value because of the depreciating effects of inflation—the equivalent of a permanent income transfer.

The large BAB income transfers for borrowers for the two crops in Santa Cruz cannot be attributed entirely to political factors. Poor client selection, bad weather, insects, and marketing difficulties are other reasons. But political intervention in marketing also led to sizable transfers. For example, in 1973 BAB and commercial banks financed large quantities of cotton, and ADEPA made forward contracts to sell cotton on the world market. When the world price exceeded the forward price, ADEPA refused to sell. The government supported the refusal, and Banzer established a minimum price by Supreme Decree. World buyers refused to pay this minimum, which was higher than the contracted price, and much cotton remained unsold while delinquency soared.

The case of BAB is suggestive of what also happened in the State Bank. Unfortunately, the data available do not permit a breakdown of transfers for credit from that institution. They are, however, sizable. This institution also began to lend heavily for cotton and soybeans in Santa Cruz after 1972. By 1977 they had discontinued lending to agriculture because of heavy delinquency. In 1978 they had $22.4 million in 232 past due loans, most of which were for cotton and soybeans. Clearly, income transfers associated with these loans were also substantial.

Consequences

The use of credit as a political instrument to benefit the Santa Cruz commercial farming elite undoubtedly contributed to political stability during the Banzer reign. However, the elite's access to credit and the associated income transfers gave them a larger share of national income. Their ability to practice agricultural illusion through investment in real estate, commerce, and conspicuous consumption further enhanced their income and worsened regional and personal income distribution. For example, the highland peasants gained little, and if it had not been for foreign aid for small-farmer credit, which began in 1975, this large mass of farmers would probably not have received much credit. It is very plausible that such inequities were important factors in the defeat of the government's candidate in the 1978 elections.

The long-run viability of financial institutions was seriously harmed. After 1976 the State Bank withdrew from agricultural lending because of the high costs associated with its heavy delinquency. In March 1979 BAB had to be rescued from bankruptcy by a $41.5 million government bond issue that permitted BAB to meet its financial obligations.

Implications

What lessons does the Bolivian experience provide for the design or redesign of credit programs in developing countries? Ways to reduce political elements in agricultural credit would be to lower inflation, eliminate the concessionary interest rate policy, and decrease default. The elimination of government agricultural credit institutions would be a stronger move, but that would be going too far, given the historical evidence of commercial banks' reluctance to make agricultural loans, especially to small farmers. The elimination of concessionary interest rates would put the cost of agricultural credit on a par with the opportunity cost of money in other uses, so that attractiveness of farm credit as a patronage measure would be diminished. Moreover, raising the price of credit would divert its flow to more productive uses and might stimulate increased savings.

There would, however, be considerable difficulty in raising interest rates. Borrowers are accustomed to receiving the concessionary transfer and would resist losing this benefit. The large farmer would get less cheap money for other uses; the small farmer would lose the preferential treatment he believes is owed him; from both farmer classes the government would expect resistance. Furthermore, it is doubtful that the government would be inclined to raise the rate, because that would seriously reduce its options in using agricultural credit as political patronage.

The Bolivian case is not unique. It is likely that political forces figure strongly in credit allocation decisions in most nations. Although patronage in distribution may contribute to short-run political stability, it is subject to abuse and has undesirable consequences for resource allocation, income distribution, and the viability of financial institutions. The degree to which credit can be used as a political instrument would be substantially reduced if concessionary interest rates were eliminated, a tougher stance on default were taken, and inflation reduced.

41. *Cooperatives and Credit: A Reexamination*

B. J. Youngjohns

[Cooperatives in the developing world have been instruments of government policy rather than business-minded organizations servicing their members. A common type of cooperative is the single-purpose farm credit society, which is often a losing business proposition. Credit unions and multipurpose cooperatives have done much better.]

Within the developing world, the modern cooperative movement originated in India around the turn of the century. Although other types of cooperative were considered, a conscious decision by the British authorities gave priority to agricultural cooperative credit societies loosely based on the Raiffeisen model in Germany. The Rochdale system of consumer cooperatives, which had been quite successful in Britain since 1844, was specifically rejected as more suitable for urban than rural conditions and as too sophisticated for India at that stage. The Cooperative Credit Societies Act of 1904 provided only for cooperative credit societies. The Cooperative Societies Act of 1912 permitted the registration of other types of cooperative and became a model for cooperative legislation throughout the (then) British dependencies and in many other countries as well. It set the pattern of a cooperative movement under the supervision of a government department, headed by a Registrar of Cooperative Societies, and set the tradition of viewing cooperatives not so much as worthwhile in themselves or to their members but as instruments for public policy. This "instrumental" approach to cooperatives has persisted and has spread throughout the world, having been taken up by postindependence national planning and development offices and by the bilateral and international aid agencies.

Adapted from *Borrowers & Lenders*, edited by John Howell (London: Overseas Development Institute, 1980), pp. 179–98; also published in *Development Digest* (January 1982), pp. 3–9. The author, now deceased, wrote this paper while serving as the cooperatives adviser in the Overseas Development Administration. Its contents, however, do not necessarily reflect in any way the official views of this Administration.

The central contention here is that, no matter how worthy a government's intentions, the instrumental approach to cooperatives is mistaken and is the root cause of failure and disappointment. It misconstrues the fundamental principles on which a cooperative is based. The allegation sometimes heard that the colonial authorities uncritically tried to transplant an organizational form from industrial Britain to rural India and Africa misses the point altogether. This is precisely what they did *not* do—if they had done so, the result might well have been better. To develop this argument, it is necessary to look again at some of the basic defining principles.

Cooperatives as Business

A cooperative is a voluntary, democratically controlled association of people with the purpose of conducting some kind of business. Voluntary associations are established for all kinds of social, political, cultural, recreational, or defensive purposes; a cooperative differs from others in being an association especially set up to go into business. Once established and registered, the cooperative becomes a body corporate with perpetual succession, and it belongs to the class of business firms.

The distinguishing feature of a cooperative business is that it is owned by its members who are either its customers, its suppliers, or, in the case of production cooperatives, its employees. Concentrating on the first of these for the sake of clarity, it follows that, since the members are the customers, the cooperative must be concerned with promoting not only its own business interest, but that of its members as well. A balance has to be maintained between the two: a cooperative should aim to be a sound business, but not at the expense of its members; and it should promote its members' interest, but not at the expense of its own business.

A cooperative is a business, and the test of success in business is profitability. It is sometimes argued that a cooperative does not make a profit in the usual sense. Whatever sense is used, a cooperative like any other business must make a profit; if it does not, it will not survive—without external support. The difference between a cooperative and other types of business lies in what it does with the profit once it is made. Profit or surplus in a cooperative is plowed back as reserves, paid out as a limited flat rate dividend on share capital, or distributed proportionally to members as a patronage bonus. When operated properly, this system has great economic strength. It pays interest on capital sufficient to attract investment shares; it builds up reserves; and through the patronage bonus, it attracts customers. If the members are encouraged to leave some of the patronage bonus on deposit, this is a further method of building up capital.

To be profitable and to keep a balance between its own interests and that of its members, the cooperative should generally operate at normal market prices. The record of cooperatives in the developing world, however, shows how this basic principle has been disregarded, usually because of the government's instrumentalist approach. Marketing cooperatives have been required to operate within narrow margins laid down by marketing boards and governments, for example, while credit cooperatives have always been required to lend at artificially low rates of interest.

Credit as Business

Much of the discussion heard on the subject of credit gives the impression that it is some kind of charity or system of welfare. But credit is a commercial concept: banks offer credit because they make profits from the interest earned; merchants give credit because it increases the demand for their wares. If there is a case for helping small farmers, over and above what is commercially sensible, it should be done by grants and subsidies and not by credit. Credit belongs to commerce and should be practiced only if it can be made a commercial success. The real question is, then, not whether cooperatives can be used as instruments to get credit to the people, but under what conditions (if any) can cooperatives make credit into successful business.

Single-purpose Credit

The original cooperative introduced into India in 1904 was the Primary Agricultural Credit Society (PACS), whose sole purpose was to make loans. Later, the Cooperative Land Mortgage Banks or, as they are now called, Land Development Banks were introduced to make long-term loans against mortgage security. In many countries, primary cooperatives do nothing else but lend money. The principle behind them is that a group of small farmers, if organized as a cooperative society, can borrow on better terms than the individuals borrowing on their own account.

After nearly a century of experience, it can hardly be denied that single-purpose credit, under *any* institution (not only cooperatives), is not good business. The record of direct government loans as well as loans through development banks, informal groups, commercial banks, and cooperatives all tell the same story of overdues, default, and losses. In fact, the only one who has made a success of rural credit is the much-maligned village moneylender, and even he is usually in other businesses as well.

Some of the reasons small-farm credit is a commercial loser are:

- High administrative costs. The work involved in appraising, supervising, recording, and recovering a small loan is not much less than doing so for a larger one. Proportionate to value, the cost is very much higher.

- High risk. Small farmers are bad risks. They are unused to handling money, do not keep accounts, are under social and family pressures to mix up the farm money with their own, and are prone to crop failures. They have few resources to cushion them and little to offer as collateral security.
- Lack of equity involvement. With single-purpose credit, the borrowers have little or no equity stake in the lending institution and therefore no sense of personal responsibility. In single-purpose credit cooperatives and similar institutions, loans are approved by committees who have no financial stake in what they are doing.
- Low interest rates. Because of political or moral pressure, interest rates are usually below lending cost.

It is hardly surprising that large numbers of single-purpose credit societies have failed. Even in Botswana, where consumers and marketing cooperatives have been conspicuously successful, the experiment in single-purpose agricultural credit societies was a failure. The single-purpose credit society and its variants are consequences of two errors: the first is that cooperatives should be instruments of government policy, and not businesses in their own right; the second, that the simplest form of organization is the easiest to run. In business, diversification (up to the limits of management capacity) produces strength: it spreads costs and it spreads risk.

Savings and Credit Cooperatives (Credit Unions)

Nowadays, the best-known savings-cum-credit cooperatives are the credit unions. Unlike single-purpose credit societies, they are firmly based on regular savings contributions by the members. The collectively owned savings then constitute a fund from which the members can borrow. The security for loans is the savings of the borrower himself plus those of up to two other members whom he can persuade to act as guarantors. Under this system, the credit union is fully covered. Credit unions also use more conventional forms of security including collateral. Interest on loans is traditionally 1 percent a month, a rate which, at least until the recent inflation, was more than adequate to make the union profitable. When a profit is made, it is handled in accordance with cooperative principles.

Credit unions are firmly established in Latin America and the Caribbean, where they are the most conspicuously successful of all cooperatives. They have more recently been introduced into Africa, and in Cameroon and Lesotho, for example, they seem to work. It would be a mistake to claim too much for credit unions; they do have their limitations, and there have been failures. Nevertheless, they make much better commercial sense than the single-purpose credit societies, and in the countries where they have become established they are among the best examples of modern nonstate enterprise by the not-so-well-off section of the population. Although they have received some aid, it has been much less than that for many other less successful organizations. It is significant that they are reasonably well managed without excessive government supervision.

The real debate about credit unions is not whether they work, but whether they are suitable for agricultural credit. The largest and most successful credit unions have been urban, or among rural salary and wage earners. The system of periodic savings works best among regular wage earners, especially where arrangements can be made for savings deposits and loan repayments to be deducted from the payroll. Small farmers do not receive a frequent or regular income, and the organization of regular savings or loan repayments is much more difficult. Nevertheless, there is some evidence that credit unions can be made to work outside plantations in rural areas; the core membership may well be school teachers, civil servants, and the like, but the small farmers are brought in. There are difficulties, too, in making loans for agricultural purposes, since agricultural credit is risky. Committees approving loans know that their own money is at risk. This very self-sufficiency, which is the basis for their success, makes credit unions difficult to use as instruments for government credit policies. If a credit union accepts a large external loan, its self-reliance is undermined.

Multipurpose Cooperatives

A multipurpose cooperative provides two or more different kinds of service to its members. Of the many possible combinations, the most relevant for this discussion is the cooperative for credit, input supply, and marketing. The member is supplied with fertilizer and other inputs on credit before planting; after the harvest he delivers his crop to the cooperative, which deducts the loan from the proceeds before paying him the balance. In the better organized, such as the coffee cooperatives in Kenya, there is also a savings deposit system, so that the member's passbook account is active throughout the year. [See chapter 36 for a review of Kenyan experience.]

Some have argued that the borrower's crop is useful as security only if there is compulsory one-channel marketing. This view is too extreme. The multipurpose cooperatives in Gambia do not have sole purchasing rights over the crop, for example, but do have a consistently high record of loan recovery. Even when there is a single-channel marketing requirement, however, the borrower who is determined to default can find a way to evade payment. The multipurpose system is, on the whole, less insecure than most others, and ought to be continued. Education can help: members can learn that it is not in their long-term interests to dodge loan repayment.

Although the security argument is the one most quoted for the multipurpose system, it should also be recognized that a diversity of operations makes for a much more viable business. The costs of management are spread over a wider range of activities. A full-time bookkeeper can be afforded. There is much more consistent cash flow. If credit is seen, as it should be, as a part of the whole business enterprise, some of the risk can be absorbed as operating costs on the supply and marketing business. If multipurpose cooperatives give credit, they should do so as part of a profit-making business and calculate the risk as a business cost.

Security and Loan Discipline

Frequently, governments enforce some kind of collective responsibility for loan repayment by not allowing a cooperative society to have a new loan until it has paid a stipulated proportion of its previous debts. Although some kind of discipline is necessary, this method has the disadvantage of punishing the good individual payers along with the bad. Overdue debt may be perfectly respectable, provided the cooperative has built up the reserves to carry it and the occurrence is temporary. Persistent arrears, however, are evidence of commercial failure, and such cooperatives are not worth further credit.

Other types of security are land, chattel mortgages, and penal sanctions. Land is normally used as security for long-term loans; with default, the lending institution may become the proprietor of land it cannot sell, or there may be great political difficulties in taking possession. Chattel mortgages could be used for farmers when the loan is paying for something durable, such as a cow or a piece of agricultural machinery. Penal sanctions are not so much a form of security in themselves as a reinforcement of other forms.

Although various potentially effective systems of security exist on paper, there is in fact a widespread reluctance to enforce them. Under Indian cooperative law, a society can take a debt dispute to the registrar of cooperatives and can get an award which has the force of a court judgment. The legal framework is quite comprehensive. The failure to make use of it can only be explained by the fact that the money on loan does not usually belong to the society itself but has come from the government or a government institution, so that the committees and managers do not feel either their own risk or a sense of responsibility.

When a cooperative is run as a proper business, it has a normal business's motivation to collect its debts and improve its cash flow.

Rate of Interest

The Rochdale cooperative principle of trading at current market prices and distributing any resultant profit or surplus as a patronage bonus has hardly ever been applied to agricultural credit. If it had been, the original agricultural credit societies would have charged the same rate as the moneylender and (presumably) made a large profit which would have been refunded after the end of the financial year. This would produce a genuine net going interest rate. It was impossible to do this in most countries because right from the beginning a low rate of interest was part and parcel of the government's scheme. Since the farmers' alternative was to borrow from the moneylender, and borrowers had to go back to him when their cooperative collapsed, the argument against market rates of interest had no ethical basis; but this is not the prevailing view. With short-term credit, the amount of interest is trivial, even if the annual rate is high; if the farmer cannot pay the interest, he cannot pay the principal either.

Artificially low rates of interest have been forced on cooperatives and other credit institutions for political and pseudoethical reasons and have pauperized entire credit systems, with only trivial and transient advantages to the borrowers. The whole credit system is static and dependent on everlasting financial replenishments from government and international aid. The source of payment for credit should be the additional production it ought to produce; if a loan does not result in gains to the borrower more than enough to repay the principal plus the going rate of interest, it should not have been issued in the first place. Artificially low rates of interest are responsible not only for operational losses in the lending institutions, but also for corruption and misuse of loan funds. The richer and socially more powerful members of the community have an incentive to borrow because it is cheaper to do so than use their own funds or go to ordinary commercial channels, and they use their power to manipulate the credit allocation in their own favor.

Conclusion

The purpose here is not to examine the credit performance of noncooperative institutions, but a glance at their record will show that, in the case of unsupported low-cost agricultural credit, it is no better than that of cooperatives. The truth must surely be that this type of credit is unsound business in itself. It mixes the commercial concept of credit with charity and welfare. If governments feel it is necessary for political, social, or macroeconomic reasons, they must be prepared to subsidize it ad infinitum. The best hope of establishing dynamic and self-supporting credit systems in rural areas is through commercially viable organizations such as credit unions, multipurpose cooperatives, and private enterprise.

42. *Agricultural Credit Cooperatives, Rural Development, and Agrarian Politics in Madras, 1893–1937*

Bruce L. Robert, Jr.

[Credit cooperatives were first formed in Madras in the early 1900s under legislation enacted to assist the poor. In spite of these intentions, cooperation developed into a means by which the rural elite secured economic and political power. This occurred first through the recruitment of locally important citizens to organize and administer societies and was furthered by large deposits of government funds at cooperative banks. Cooperation provided a large and lucrative framework for political patronage. Tenants, landless laborers, and small farmers never obtained effective access to cooperatives or participation in their management.]

Agricultural credit cooperatives were launched in India in 1904, and subsequent government support allowed them to play a key role in many development programs. Proponents saw in cooperatives a means of reducing the influence of moneylenders while increasing savings and providing easier credit terms to small farmers. Official assistance enabled the number of credit cooperatives to grow from only 2,000 in 1906 to nearly 100,000 by 1930. These cooperatives, however, failed to make a significant economic impact on rural society. Moneylending continued, the poor were excluded from the movement, and societies captured only a small fraction of the rural credit market. If credit cooperatives were unable to meet their objectives, how were they able to grow at such a rapid rate and maintain official support?

It is argued here that the growth of the cooperative movement was the result of combined economic and political benefits derived by the village elite, Indian politicians, and the British government. Concen-

Adapted from *Indian Economic and Social History Review*, vol. 16, no. 2 (April-June 1979), pp. 163–84, by permission of Vikas Publishing House Pvt Ltd.

trating on the Madras presidency (one of three divisions of British India, originally under a president of the East India Company), I discuss the development of economic and social goals which guided the movement, the reasons for the societies' inability to meet their objectives, and the political dimension of the movement which was a principal reason for its continued growth and official and unofficial support.

The Raiffeisen Model

Frederick Nicholson, a distinguished civil servant with the Madras government, has been described as the father of Indian cooperation. His *Report Regarding the Possibility of Introducing Land and Agricultural Banks into the Madras Presidency* [Bombay, Reserve Bank of India, 1960; 1st ed. 1895] was the product of five years of research and writing and proved to be a comprehensive discourse on the problems of rural finance in Madras and their solution.

Nicholson found that most rural loans were in kind between *ryots* (farmers) for small sums negotiated on a short-term basis (one to two years). These were grain loans, used by farmers for seed or subsistence. Moneylending played a small role in the overall rural credit structure of Madras. Nicholson considered lending by ryots to be a necessary precondition to the establishment of cooperative credit. Ryot lending was based largely upon mutual goodwill and knowledge of character and status, principles congruent with cooperative theory. Undaunted by his own findings, which depicted ryot lenders as keen to obtain local influence and land, Nicholson argued that this source of credit was superior to professional moneylenders since the ryot's "loans are frequently and perfectly friendly." But Nicholson believed that ryot lending was not the best possible system. What was needed was the "promotion of facilities for savings" and "the encouragement of the national virtues of thrift, foresight, and self-help through the institutions organized for those needs." Nicholson viewed rural indebtedness as a problem of character as much as of credit, when a ryot borrows beyond his means for unnecessary or unproductive purposes. To develop thrift, prudence, and self-reliance in the peasantry, Nicholson proposed a credit structure founded on Raiffeisen lines.

This model for credit cooperatives was based on principles developed in mid-nineteenth-century Germany by a village mayor named Raiffeisen. Societies were to be small, located at the village level, and composed of villagers who were allowed to join because of their personal character (creditworthiness). Societies were to be funded primarily by the deposits and share capital of local members. Loans were to be disbursed with interest rates and repayment schedules fixed by the members themselves. Mutual trust in the members' ability to repay was reinforced by the principle of unlimited liability, that is, every member was to be financially obliged to the full extent of his property to make good the debts of the society.

In 1896 Nicholson's lengthy report reached the government of Madras and was greeted with blistering criticism by his colleagues. Members of the agriculture department of the government of India read it, however, and Nicholson was invited to sit as a senior member of the Famine Commission of 1901. One of the commission's main recommendations was to establish a rural credit system on Raiffeisen lines. The government of India enacted the Cooperative Credit Societies Act of 1904, which incorporated, in modified form, the Raiffeisen principles suggested by Nicholson.

Existing Rural Structures

Viewed by the Madras government after 1904 as an inexpensive and politically expedient means of tackling the thorny problem of rural indebtedness, cooperatives were also intended to instill in their membership the principles of thrift, prudence, and self-help. Did the movement in Madras achieve its objectives? Historical evidence in government reports and other sources of data for two "dry" and two "wet" (irrigated) districts were surveyed to answer the question.

In dry districts limited rainfall, poor soil, and volatile commodity prices largely determined that political and economic control was most firmly exercised by large landholders. Throughout the nineteenth century they managed to manipulate revenue, credit, and local political institutions to their advantage. Although the economic component of rural lending is self-evident, the political role was equally important to the rural lender. Because high rates of interest were frequently impossible to collect from the rural poor, the ryot lender was more often interested in gaining a lien on his debtor's crop, a promise of his labor, a pledge of loyalty in case of a faction fight, or perhaps the prestige associated with magnanimity.

In wet districts a similar inegalitarian socioeconomic structure was wedded to a more complex and diffuse credit system. Irrigation canals made the Kistna-Godavari districts lush, prosperous, and heavily populated and attracted a variety of creditors. Prior to the introduction of cooperative societies, cultivators could borrow from three main sources: richer farmers, professional moneylenders, and merchant lenders; unlike their counterparts in dry districts, the delta ryot merchant lenders were forced to share the market with competitors. This militated against the strong credit-dependency relations found in some dry districts, but did not preclude more prosperous ryots from exerting power through different means, which included the cooperative movement.

Cooperatives in the Rural Structure

Although the socioeconomic and credit structures of wet and dry districts differed, there were influential ryots capable of capturing a new government institution in both. The government, which often reminded its subjects that the societies were meant for the poor, nevertheless set about systematically laying the foundation for eventual control by rich ryots.

According to the 1904 act, the primary credit society was the heart of the cooperative financial structure. Primary societies dealt directly with ryots. Societies included a president, secretary, council, and members. The council had the tasks of financing, admitting members, determining who should receive loans, and on what terms they were to be granted.

From the beginning, the government sought wealthy and influential ryots to become leading members of cooperatives. P. Rajagopalachariya, the first Madras registrar of cooperatives, welcomed and encouraged rich ryot control—he considered it a "healthy sign" which inspired public confidence in the movement. Registrar G. R. Hemingway supported the participation of rich ryots because he believed a cooperative's purpose was not to be a "charitable cover." Although the courting of the rich and powerful seems difficult to reconcile with the movement's professed aims of aiding the small farmer, the government was not at a loss for an explanation. One registrar clarified this apparent contradiction by asserting that "poor people unaccustomed to cooperation and banking" would trust a managing body only after the "actual workings" were demonstrated. The poor, however, knew only too well the working of the societies.

Not surprisingly, government's attempts at recruitment were a success. Rich and middle-level ryots controlled the councils of both wet and dry regions of Madras. The All-India Maclagan Committee on Cooperation found similar practices in other presidencies. Comfortably in power, the rural rich could easily operate cooperatives to suit their purposes. Although cooperatives were designed to serve tenants, laborers, and small farmers, on a presidency-wide basis tenants and landless laborers constituted only 21 percent of the societies' membership. Registrar Hemingway, after discussing this problem with representatives of "hundreds of societies," found that a tenant or laborer was able to join societies and borrow money only on the surety of a well-to-do ryot, who usually expected him to be "at his beck and call" for the duration of his debt.

Ultimately the success or failure of the movement depended on the honesty and integrity of the council members. Unfortunately, few cooperative leaders possessed these qualities. Too often loans found their way to friends, loyal minions, or officers themselves. The most popular device used by powerful cooperators to maximize their profit was the *benami* transaction. A society president or secretary would get loan applications approved under the names of dependents; the money then was delivered to the president or secretary. It was estimated that over 30 to 40 percent of all cooperative loans were thus transacted. In other instances many influential council members simply looted the society's coffers.

Although some sources estimate that in wet districts cooperatives captured 30 percent of the credit market, a more reliable appraisal is that the societies in both regions accounted for no more than 7 percent of the rural debt. Societies in both regions incorporated less than 12 percent of rural households in the movement. Complicated loan procedures and rigid repayment schedules convinced many would-be members that it was more convenient to do business with moneylenders. For those who were not the inside manipulators, cooperative societies were poor or nonexistent competitors to established credit sources.

The principle of unlimited liability proved illusory. When the government attempted to liquidate assets of defunct societies, it found that cooperators had alienated (through benami transactions) most of their valued property so that the liquidator had little to sell. If he could find something to auction there were no bidders, "owing to combination amongst the villagers."

Cooperative Superstructure

To support the movement, the government abandoned the goal of local cooperative self-finance and constructed in its place a three-tier financial structure with an "apex" bank in Madras and "central bank" affiliates in the districts over the village-level primary societies. The new structure profoundly influenced the movement's history. By 1920, its peak development, there were thirty-three district central banks which supplied funds to primary societies in long-term loans (ten years) at relatively low interest rates (6 to 7 percent).

Until 1920 the central banks were financed and managed by individual, urban, middle-class depositors, many of whom were government employees, businessmen, or professionals. After World War I a business upturn in Madras caused a flight of capital from the cooperative banks to urban banks paying higher interest. The government assisted the central banks by allowing district boards (units of local government) to invest in the movement. The boards' involvement had an important political and economic influence on the movement; by 1929 board funds made up 32 percent of working capital. The infusion of these funds proceeded more rapidly than the central banks or societies could find ways to utilize them, and many central bank directors began to loan money with an eye to immediate results rather than sound investments.

The investment of local board funds brought a fundamental change in the composition of central bank directorates. Until 1915 district central banks were dominated by urban interests, and members of primary societies had virtually no voice in their management. By 1919, however, primary society member shareholders (rural) exceeded individual shareholders (urban) by two to one in both wet and dry districts. Banks that had been headed by urban men of character and integrity were now in the possession of the suspect rich peasantry. Central bank board meetings were often racked with bitter quarrels between society members and urban interests: rural representatives wanted money as cheaply as possible, while urban investors fought for security and 9 percent interest. Rural society members, being in the majority, frequently won.

The liberal lending policies that ensued brought the cooperative financial structure to the brink of disaster. Central bankers continued to advance money to societies in the face of increased arrears on past loans. On a presidency-wide basis, arrears on principal skyrocketed from 9 percent in 1910 to 63 percent in 1931, threatening the movement.

One solution was greater fiscal discipline in the societies. This posed a serious problem to the government: nothing the administration could conceive of could bring it into greater disrepute than playing the role of bill collector. The government did not want to become the "Great Usurer" in the eyes of the rural masses. The way out, so it seemed, was to have the societies supervise themselves by organizing supervisory unions composed of selected members of society councils. The government was pleased with this idea since it did not involve either its prized revenue apparatus or the cooperative department in the sticky business of collecting overdue loans. Equally attractive, the scheme would not cost the government a penny. Unfortunately, the proposal was tantamount to asking the thief to mind the store.

The development and organization of supervisory unions began in 1915, and throughout the period of study they proved thoroughly useless as a means of controlling arrears. Although unions were formed in almost all locations where societies existed, overdues continued to rise. The council members who composed the ruling bodies of supervisory unions were often principal defaulters themselves and could hardly put pressure on their underlings. Moreover, if a council member decided to collect overdue loans with any rigor he ran the risk of losing his seat and igniting a faction fight for power. By 1931 the situation had deteriorated to such an extent that the registrar recommended dissolving the unions.

Politics, Patronage, and Power

Those who dominated the movement made a mockery of cooperative principles and goals. The poor were excluded, moneylenders thrived in and outside the movement, and the financial structure was nearly brought to ruin. With all of these problems and shortcomings, how did the movement continue to grow and maintain official support?

The Montagu-Chelmsford reforms of 1919 modified the political structure of Madras. The reforms enhanced the powers of local boards, created a legislative council, and placed control of the cooperative department in the hands of Indian politicians. This drew the movement into the vortex of the tumultuous politics of district and province. Furthermore, British rule was coming under increasing attack from nationalist agitators. Under these conditions both the British and collaborating Indian politicians required the support of rural India to maintain themselves in power.

C. J. Baker [*The Politics of South India, 1920–1937*, Cambridge, Eng., Cambridge University Press, 1976, pp. 134–35] has argued that the politics of dyarchy (rule shared by the British with elected Indians) at both provincial and district levels relied heavily on patronage. This is exemplified by the Justice party which controlled the Madras legislative council and ministries until 1936. They maintained power by dispensing patronage, in the form of jobs and contracts, which linked the center (Madras City) with the districts. Party loyalty was often purchased. Under this system cooperatives became a choice plum for local and provincial politicians. By 1920 the movement had a membership of over a million, working capital of nearly Rs2,000 million, and a financial and administrative structure that served as an excellent means by which patronage and political support could be amassed and distributed. Endowed with such assets, it soon became a stepladder for local politicians to ascend to the provincial level and, in turn, for provincial politicians to extend their influence into the countryside.

In both wet and dry villages the cooperative structure proved a useful mechanism for political control. In dry districts, indebted farmers not only had to work gratis in their benefactor's fields, but also were expected to "help in all village politics and factious quarrels and in all kinds of litigation." In wet districts the patron-client bonds based on credit were often weaker, and competition for economic and political power was intense. Although there was a difference of style between regions, participation in the movement offered a good opportunity for select rural elite to improve their positions.

The credit-patronage system extended to supervisory unions and central banks. Since rural society council members held key positions in these institutions, the village became linked with the subdistrict and district structures. The patronage system in the cooperatives became apparent to the government when it attempted to improve the effectiveness of the supervisory unions and was met with intense hostility. This response compelled the registrar to note that union directors feared outside control "as if they sought and retained office merely for the patronage it secured." The "party spirit" of the unions had forced "honest men" to abandon the movement.

What occurred in the supervisory unions was repeated in the central banks. With the source of financing for the central banks shifting away from urban depositors to local board funds, the rural elite and their representatives used their leverage within the cooperative structure to enter into provincial and district politics, and large sums continued to flow into central banks from the local boards. The cooperative structure began to resemble a political machine which could be used by cooperative "bosses" to provide votes for themselves during local board and legislative elections. Strong cooperative ties also proved useful at the provincial level, as members of the Madras Legislative Council discovered.

The British were aware of the political patronage system, which chiefly benefited the collaborationist Justice party. The British also understood the essential role of the village elite in the administration and the maintenance of power in Madras's vast agrarian tracts. The government had consciously vested leadership and responsibility in the influential ryots of the village, at first in the revenue system and later in the cooperative movement. In the operation of cooperative societies, the payoff to the rural elite came in the form of self-supervision, which meant patronage, power, and prestige. In return, the government received the loyalty of village officers. However, the Depression altered this mutually compatible relationship.

The worldwide economic depression of the 1930s struck rural Madras particularly hard. Agricultural prices were halved, so that debts owed by farmers were virtually doubled. Many cooperative societies could no longer advance loans to members since central banks were severely pressed for funds. The Depression significantly reduced revenue, which caused a dramatic fall in local board investment in cooperative banks. Because central banks could no longer depend on this previously steady source of funds, they had to press societies for repayment of past loans. To enable central banks to retrieve the societies' arrears, the government was forced to liquidate a large number of credit cooperatives. Many supervisory unions and village councils were divested of their independence by government agents appointed to manage the societies. To extract overdue loans from cooperators, the long-forgotten principle of unlimited liability was now strictly enforced. As a result, numerous society members had their property attached or auctioned by liquidators, which brought the movement into general disrepute. This sudden reversal of policy would have significant political repercussions.

The efficiency drive brought on by the Depression affected all departments and strata of the bureaucracy. The new policy eliminated many of the patronage opportunities that had been the substance of politics. The result was a serious weakening of the Justice party, as demonstrated by the overwhelming Congress party victory in the elections of 1937. Dissatisfaction created by government intervention in the supervision of societies, coupled with the constriction of credit, spurred many cooperative political leaders to shift their allegiance to Congress (which was working for Indian independence).

Conclusion

In forty-five years (1892–1937) the cooperative movement in Madras evolved from a ridiculed proposal for a technical and moral solution of the problem of rural indebtedness, to a highly politicized credit structure of 1,800 million rupees manipulated by rural elites, local politicians, and government. The small Raiffeisen cooperatives visualized by Nicholson to aid in the revival and maintenance of the alleged cooperative instincts of the rural populace proved illusory. The movement, with government acquiescence, soon became the preserve of the rural elite who used the credit apparatus for their personal ends. The movement also linked the rural elite with the political center at Madras. It was a relationship the various actors cultivated for different reasons. The rural elite saw in the movement the opportunity to enhance their wealth and prestige. The politicians of dyarchy viewed it as a means of extending and strengthening their patronage networks in the countryside. The British found the movement useful since by supporting it they could appear progressive and show critics in India and England that they were taking action to improve the economic condition of the masses.

Ostensibly begun to establish small-scale credit institutions for the poor, these had within a quarter century evolved into a large and powerful bureaucratic structure. This growth was the result not of its economic merits, but of its political influence. The inequities of the rural socioeconomic structure worked to exclude the poor and place the rural rich in a dominant position in the movement, which became a useful "patronage bank" of considerable utility to politicians.

Interest Rates

Interest rate controls are one of the most important types of political involvement in financial markets. The benefits of these controls are widely publicized and frequently cited. Very little is said about their cost. The chapters in this section stress the damage they cause and conclude that the costs generally exceed the benefits. Several essays challenge the assumptions on which low interest rate policies are based and outline how financial reform could be implemented.

Gonzalez-Vega (chapter 43) summarizes many of the new views about rural finance and attacks many of the assumptions used to support low interest rate policies. He argues that interest rates are such an important price in most economies that misguided policies can do great damage. He stresses that low interest rate policies have a very adverse effect on resource allocation and on income distribution. He concludes that interest rates in rural financial markets should be more flexible, and that real rates of interest should be generally positive if the goals of efficiency and equity are to be realized. Sicat (chapter 44) reinforces many of these points and argues that laws imposing interest rate ceilings in the Philippines reduced savings, led to corruption, and supported inefficiency. In many countries, modification of usury laws is one of the first steps required for interest rate reform.

Sayad (chapter 45) reports some of the results of the great growth in formal agricultural credit in Brazil in recent decades. Brazil is a very important case to study because the volume of formal agricultural credit there in the late 1970s and early 1980s was possibly close to half of all the formal agricultural credit available in developing countries. Credit has been used in Brazil as a major policy instrument to promote rural development, and real rates of interest have been consistently negative. The massive increase in credit and the extreme interest rate restrictions have given prominence to the problems associated with these kinds of policies in Brazil. Sayad documents the extent of credit concentration in Brazil and suggests that it has had a very regressive impact on income distribution.

Although the arguments against cheap credit are gaining acceptance, critics of traditional thinking on rural finance have not developed operational guidelines for implementing interest rate reforms. Vogel (chapter 46) suggests one of the first steps in this regard. He stresses that arguments used to sustain existing policies must be understood and countered before reforms are attempted. He reviews four common arguments against interest rate reform and concludes they are all deficient. Political considerations aside, Vogel finds no significant economic barriers to financial market reform.

In chapter 47, Irvine and Emery discuss how interest rate reforms were conducted in Taiwan during the 1950s. Taiwan is a particularly interesting case because it has not followed traditional cheap credit policies in agriculture. Largely to fight inflation, the Taiwan government was very aggressive in adjusting nominal interest rates so that real rates of interest on both credit and savings deposits were generally positive during most of the 1950s and 1960s. These high rates of interest induced households, especially in rural areas, to deposit a large part of their savings with financial institutions, including farmers' associations. These deposits funded loans issued to a large proportion of Taiwan's farmers. Credit and savings activities also provided a financial base for other activities of the associations. Irvine and Emery strongly suggest that rapid and equitable economic growth is possible with higher interest rates.

43. *Arguments for Interest Rate Reform*

Claudio Gonzalez-Vega

[Interest rates held below market levels are common in low-income countries and have a variety of undesirable results: reduction in savings, slower capital formation, and inefficiency in investment. In farm credit programs interest rate ceilings also reduce small producers' access to credit and subsidize a few large producers.]

During the 1950s, lack of economic growth in the low-income countries was explained mainly by a shortage of physical capital and a vicious circle of poverty. It was assumed that a small capacity to save resulted from a low income level, which in turn reflected low resource productivity. Low productivity was seen as a consequence of the lack of capital, which was explained in terms of the limited capacity to save. Many argued that capital formation plays a key role in economic development as the means of breaking out of the circle.

Given the insufficiency of individual savings, credit was seen as an important way to promote capital formation. Shortage of credit was recognized as one aspect of the capital shortage, as well as a consequence of structural deficiencies of the banking system. In particular, according to these views, the established financial intermediaries could not provide agricultural credit because their objectives and institutional organization severely limited their ability to serve the rural sector where productivity, income, and savings were lowest.

The credit problem was perceived as structural, and the solution as institutional: to create special agencies to provide agricultural credit in appropriate forms. Agricultural banks were created and instructed to expand credit at low interest rates. Thus, although the scarcity of capital was amply acknowledged, credit became cheap by decree, while the new financial agencies were given limited powers to stimulate and mobilize savings.

Over the past three decades credit has become one of the main components of strategies for rural development. In most low-income countries the volume of institutional agricultural credit has grown rapidly. It represents an increasing share of total national loan portfolios and absorbs large portions of the external funds channeled by international agencies for their agricultural sectors. Despite this expansion of credit volume, however, only a small fraction of the farmers in low-income countries have received formal loans.

It has been estimated that only about 5 percent of farmers in Africa and perhaps 15 percent of farmers in Asia and Latin America have had access to formal credit. There has been much concentration of these loans in the hands of a few large farmers. Frequently, about 5 percent of the borrowers have received about 80 percent of the amounts disbursed. This means that, in a typical low-income country, less than 1 percent of the farmers have received about 80 percent of the rapidly expanding credit, that about 15 percent have benefited from the remaining 20 percent, while over 80 percent have not shared in this process. In addition, accumulating evidence on the poor results of many rural credit programs has directed increasing attention to the impact of credit on agricultural output and productivity, on the rate of adoption of technological change, and on employment and the distribution of income in rural areas. Special emphasis has recently been placed by researchers on the role of low interest rates. This chapter reexamines the most important arguments on the level of interest rates.

Importance of Interest Rates

Interest rates have received much attention because they are the most important relative price in a market economy; they have been the most frequently controlled price; and interest rate controls have introduced the most widespread distortions in all markets of the economy. Like other prices in a market system, interest rates are signals which influence decisions: interest rates affect more numerous, diverse, and important decisions than any other price.

The Price of the Future

In the most fundamental sense, interest rates are the price of the future in terms of the present. They are a signal influencing the decisions to consume in the present or in the future by saving and capital formation. They also reflect the rate at which the community is willing to postpone consumption for the sake of more in the future, a function of the tastes and needs of the community.

If interest rates below equilibrium are imposed, the terms of trade between present goods and future goods are twisted. The fact of life is scarce capital; but low interest rates tell savers not to bother with saving, that the future is amply provided for, that now is the time to consume. The same low rates tell investors that savings are plentiful, and that high prices can be bid for investment goods to induce a transfer of resources away from the production of consumables. Unfortunately, *there can be no investment without savings.* The conflict between the decisions of savers to save very little and of investors to invest much has to be resolved by administrative rationing, by decisions on some basis other than the willingness of individuals to save and invest. When interest rates are deprived of their role as a price that allocates resource uses, capital remains scarce and resources are misallocated.

In summary, interest rates affect the intertemporal decisions determining savings and investment, and through these they influence the rate of growth of the economy, the levels of activity and employment, as well as the stability of these important economic variables.

The Price of Financial Assets

Interest rates are also the prices relevant in financial markets. As such, they are a signal influencing the composition of assets held by individuals. Savings can be incorporated in gold, jewelry, housing, inventories of goods, and in foreign or domestic financial assets. Wealth holders compare the returns, risk, and liquidity of alternative assets in choosing a portfolio. The interest rates paid on domestic financial assets determine the extent to which these are incorporated into wealth portfolios. Thus, they influence the nature of domestic savings and the proportion of these savings mobilized for use in investment through the domestic financial system.

In high-income economies with relatively integrated capital markets, rates of return on assets are fairly uniform. In the low-income countries characterized by fragmented capital markets, large differences among rates of return reflect a poor correlation between the investment opportunities and the endowment of resources and access to credit of different people. Many producers with good opportunities to make highly productive investments cannot take advantage of them for lack of access to resources; others with surplus resources are forced to devote them to investments with low returns. Given the resulting dispersion of rates of return, one additional unit of savings will have a different impact on growth depending on how it is saved, that is, the type of asset chosen for saving.

The availability of an easily accessible financial asset such as a bank deposit, which earns a sufficiently high interest rate, would induce farmers to revise their portfolio decisions. Investments with low returns could be eliminated in exchange for acquiring this rewarding financial asset. The resources thus liberated would in turn be channeled by the financial intermediary to other farmers who have better investment opportunities and are willing for this reason to pay a sufficiently high interest rate. Obviously, the elimination of projects with low returns and the financing of better ones would improve the allocation of the nation's resources and promote its growth.

In summary, in low-income countries the movement of resources from inferior to better uses is as important as the accumulation of capital. Even those with a pessimistic view about the interest elasticity of aggregate savings—those who doubt that higher interest would bring about much more saving—must recognize the role that interest rates can play in channeling the available savings through the financial system to the best investment opportunities.

The Price of Capital

Interest rates are related to the price of capital. As such, they may influence decisions concerning the choice of techniques, that is, the proportions in which factors of production are combined, as well as the selection of investment projects. This is because capital costs affect total costs in accordance with relative factor intensities. If interest rates are too low, relatively capital-intensive projects may become more profitable, and this will be a signal to reduce costs by diminishing the labor intensity of production. This increases the unemployment and underemployment of labor and tends to concentrate income distribution.

With a given stock of capital for the economy as a whole, the greater capital intensity of the sectors given access to credit at low interest rates reduces the capital available for other sectors. Thus, while the overcapitalized sectors frequently operate below capacity, the undercapitalization of other sectors leads to their low productivity and low incomes and contributes to economic dualism.

Interest Rates Too Low

Most low-income countries have regulated the *nominal* interest rates paid and charged in their banks and the institutions of the formal financial markets. *Real* interest rates, after inflation was discounted, have not been controlled. Even in the presence of substantial inflation, most low-income countries have fixed nominal rates at levels that have frequently been too low.

Interest rates have been too low for several reasons. (1) They have not reflected the true scarcity, opportunity cost, or shadow price of capital. (2) They have not equated the supply and demand for formal credit. Instead, they have created excess demand which has required administrative rationing to clear the market. These rationing processes have not resulted in the selection of the best investment projects because they relied more on noneconomic considerations, such as collateral, than on the profitability of the projects financed; and in any case they have been very vulnerable to the influence of pressure groups and to the abuse of political power. (3) Bank interest rates have been much lower than those prevailing in informal markets. (4) In inflationary economies they have been negative in real terms, erratic, and unpredictable, thus reducing the capacity of banks to mobilize savings.

(5) They have not covered the costs and risks associated with the administration of credit and have thus frequently led to operating losses and eventually to the decapitalization of financial institutions. To remain financially viable, many intermediaries have restricted their operations to the largest and safest borrowers. In particular, since the low lending rates have not covered the higher costs associated with marginal clients, the small, poor, or innovative borrowers have been denied access to credit. (6) Interest rates below cost have transferred a substantial income subsidy to the (not so poor) beneficiaries of institutional loans.

Arguments for Low Interest Rates

A long-standing opposition to usury can be traced from the Babylonian Code of Hammurabi and Deuteronomy in the Old Testament, through Roman law, the rules of the Koran, and a variety of medieval European prohibitions. Even today this tradition strongly influences attitudes and regulations concerning interest rates. But, although marginal rates of return on capital and rates of growth in national economies have risen significantly since medieval times, perceptions about the "correct" level of interest rates have changed little and still influence economic policies in low-income countries.

The interest rate policies of the low-income countries have also been, in part, a consequence of the uncritical acceptance of Keynesian theories about unemployment. However, the controversial Keynesian model, even if appropriate for a mature industrialized economy that has fully used its investment opportunities, is not applicable to most low-income countries. These are characterized, not by excess savings and a lack of investment opportunities, but, on the contrary, by numerous productive opportunities that cannot be taken advantage of because of the insufficiency of savings and the fragmentation of capital markets. Keynesian theories, however, have served as a convenient rationale for finance ministers wishing to attract a larger portion of the scarce savings to the public sector at a low cost.

Reallocation of Resources

Conceived initially to stimulate total investment, the regulation of interest rates has also been used to reallocate resources among sectors. Thus, specific interest rate policies, such as those prevailing for the agricultural sector, have been justified on the grounds of a need to promote particular activities.

It is frequently argued that underequilibrium interest rates are indispensable if certain investments are to occur. Without the subsidy, it is claimed, such activities would not take place. Few inquire why this would be the case. A careful analysis, however, might show that the investments are not profitable enough. Their low profitability may be the result of lack of knowledge of a more productive technology, the unavailability or uncertain supply of a key input, the absence of a road to take the product to the market, or the lack of any market. These constraints and bottlenecks cannot be removed by merely granting cheap credit.

Interest rate subsidies cannot create a nonexistent technology, the unavailable inputs, the missing roads, or the absent market. In such circumstances, issuing credit at underequilibrium interest rates may make the investment opportunity appear to be profitable from the private point of view of the few privileged borrowers who receive the underpriced loans, but it cannot correct the underlying absence of social profitability.

On the one hand, if an activity is sufficiently profitable, its returns will adequately cover the costs of the resources employed. In this case, subsidy is not needed to promote the activity but is merely an arbitrary gift for income redistribution. On the other hand, if the activity is not profitable, the subsidy obscures this fact but does not attack its causes. Many governments in low-income countries lower the price of loans by decree, while avoiding the more complex task of supplying the missing infrastructure, markets, technologies, and inputs. Cheap credit favors particular groups with subsidy, but leaves fundamental problems unsolved. If credit is granted to basically unprofitable activities, defaults and repayment problems begin to affect the financial institution, which finds it increasingly difficult to provide access to the underpriced loans even to the few borrowers favored in the initial stages of the program. Eventually, the program disappears or the loan funds become concentrated in the hands of a few large borrowers.

Sometimes it is argued that underequilibrium interest rates are required to compensate for market imperfections that lower the private returns of certain activities below their social level. Such imperfections do exist in low-income countries, but economic theory shows that when these imperfections are not corrected at their source by appropriate policies, the attempted compensation introduces other distortions, previously absent, which reduce efficiency and welfare. Few of the distortions prevailing in the markets of low-income countries are related to the price of credit; low interest rates, therefore, are very seldom the appropriate policy for correction. They introduce new distortions, particularly in the choice of techniques and the debt-equity ratios of firms, and further fragment capital markets.

Redistribution of Income

It is frequently argued that low interest rates are one of the few politically feasible mechanisms for the redistribution of income in rural areas. Unfortunately, underequilibrium interest rates, as a redistribution tool, are inefficient, since the same distributive goals could be achieved at much lower social costs by other policies. Their effects tend to be perverse because, instead of helping achieve equity goals, low interest rates lead to a greater concentration of income.

Interest rates are a price, and as such they should reflect the true social value of the resources transferred in a loan transaction. To the extent that this is not the case, there is a free transfer of resources, an implicit subsidy. When a rate of 10 percent is charged, for example, instead of a correct rate of 30 percent, which covers the opportunity cost of the funds and the expected rate of inflation, for each dollar lent there is a gift of 20 cents. This subsidy influences income distribution in two ways: directly through the free transfer of resources; indirectly by affecting the access to credit of different borrower classes and, therefore, their income growth potential.

The direct impact of the subsidy is regressive. First, to receive the subsidy, the beneficiary must be one of the small proportion of farmers who have access to institutional credit. Second, the amount of the subsidy is directly proportional to the size of the loan. Since there is a high correlation between loan size, on the one hand, and wealth, social influence, and political power on the other, the large farmers receive large loans accompanied by large subsidies. Medium-size farmers receive smaller loans and smaller subsidies, while the poor farmers get no loans and no subsidies.

The indirect impact of the subsidy may be even more important. In the capital-short low-income countries, access to credit is a key to income growth. Those with access to external funds can move beyond the constraints of self-financing to expand their productive opportunities and adopt new technologies. Access to credit is comparable to access to land.

In the presence of interest rates below equilibrium and of excess demands for loans, access to credit is determined by the rationing mechanisms adopted by financial intermediaries. Most lenders treat loans to different borrower classes as different products and differentiate among them in terms of administrative cost of lending and risk of default. On the basis of risks and costs in relation to potential revenues, most lenders determine the proportion of their portfolios to be lent to different borrower classes and the size of loans to grant in each case. Interest rate policies significantly influence these decisions.

Underequilibrium interest rates tend to separate borrowers into three classes: nonrationed borrowers, usually large and well known, who receive the amount of credit they demand at the going interest rate; rationed borrowers, usually smaller producers, who receive loans of a smaller size than they demand at the low interest rate; and excluded borrowers, who are willing to borrow but are not accepted by the bank. When the interest rate charged covers the marginal costs of lending including a premium for risk, borrowers need not be rationed in the sense of being given loans of a smaller size than they wish. If, however, the interest rate does not cover the average variable costs of lending to a class of borrowers, these borrowers are excluded from the portfolio.

Elsewhere I have called this set of relationships the *iron law of interest rate restrictions*: as a ceiling on interest rates becomes lower and more restrictive because of the increased cost of the subsidy, the size of loans issued to nonrationed borrowers increases, since at the lower rate they demand more; the size of the loans granted to rationed borrowers declines, since the lower rate covers risks and costs to a lesser extent; and more borrowers are excluded altogether from access to credit. As a result, credit portfolios are redistributed in favor of the large borrowers. Thus, the lower the interest rate, the larger the subsidy transferred to a smaller number of producers. The reduced access to credit means fewer resources and lower income for the small producer, who finds little consolation in the lower rates charged.

Except in a few unusual circumstances, the arguments that attempt to justify the low interest rate policies of the low-income countries are not valid. What is important is access to credit. The policies that have kept the price of credit low have modified loan access in undesirable ways and have aggravated distortions that work against efficiency and welfare. These policies, therefore, have reduced the allocative efficiency of affected economies and their rates of growth of savings and investment; they have endangered the financial viability of institutional lenders and contributed to the concentration of income in the rural areas of low-income countries. Revision of these policies is a necessary, although not a sufficient, condition for the progress of the rural poor in many low-income countries.

44. *Toward a Flexible Interest Rate Policy, or Losing Interest in the Usury Law*

Gerardo P. Sicat

[A usury law was passed in 1916 in the Philippines to protect the small borrower. Lenders get around interest rate ceilings through fees and service charges, while interest on deposits is kept artificially low. Low interest rates encourage corruption, capital flight, and unproductive investment, while discouraging saving, employment creation, and export industries. Agriculture suffers extensively. Small borrowers and savers, whom the law was supposed to protect, are burdened by the effects of low interest rate policies. Since this was written, many interest rate restrictions in the Philippines have been abolished.]

Traditional disdain for the usurer dates back to the Middle Ages. In fact, Shakespeare has dramatized it well: Shylock, the merchant of Venice, is internationally known for cleaning people's pockets. The legal response to usury is now well ensconced in the jurisprudence of many countries. Ceilings are set on interest rates, and any rate in excess of these ceilings is called usurious and punishable by law. Throughout succeeding generations, social values have always held usurious practices in contempt. Social morality has largely remained humanitarian in spirit.

Although much of Filipino contemporary thought has diverged from some of the old notions, traditional thinking on the subject of usury has persisted through the ghost of a law passed in 1916. Sad to say, the specter of this law has today become the biggest obstacle to an effective monetary policy. The law was expressly written to protect the small Filipino borrower from the claws of unscrupulous loan vultures. It consequently pegged ceiling rates on what it deemed were the only types of borrowing: secured and unsecured loans. For loans of the former type, the law provided for an interest charge no higher than 12

Adapted from the Philippines Government, *Report of the Inter-Agency Committee on the Study of Interest Rates* (Manila, March 1971).

percent a year. On unsecured loans, the law allowed a higher ceiling of 14 percent to cover possible additional risks inherent in lending.

This law was passed thirty-three years before the economy had evolved central banking. Times have greatly changed since the turn of the century, and the capital market has become more sophisticated and complicated. Credit is now available in different forms and with varying maturities and risks. Lending itself is classified as direct and indirect. Rapid developments over five decades have rendered the usury law not only obsolete but dysfunctional as well. The capital market is literally bursting at the seams, with supply badly dislocated from demand at the prevailing rates.

The General Picture

The overloaded demand for capital may be traced to low interest rates that cling faithfully to the law. On the supply side, the savings response has remained rigidly timid for the same reasons. An uneven strain, therefore, has developed within the capital market. And there is no proof that whatever supply of capital exists is actually being allocated in the most efficient manner.

The usury law covers direct lending only, without regard to maturities and collateral. It thereby discriminates against riskier, longer-term loans which require relatively higher interest rates. Therefore, commercial and rural banks have been known to slap additional charges on loans for handling, appraisal, and notarial and other services. Another circumvention popular among financial institutions is the deduction of the initial year's interest from the total loan amount at the time of release. In practice, effective rates have risen to something like 16.8 percent for commercial banks and 18 percent for rural banks. Development banks and investment banks have caused effective rates to rise to as much as 15 percent. Government-financed institutions have reached effective rates around the level of 16 percent.

This regulation of direct lending has favored credit in the form of bonds, installment purchases, and other commercial paper—in other words, indirect lending has substituted for direct credit. With bond flotations, for example, smart borrowers have attracted resources by intentionally offering issues for less than par value, which gives a higher effective rate than nominally stipulated. In the area of consumer credit, installment schedules have been devised to effect monthly rates of over 4 percent, with annual rates ranging from 51 to 61 percent.

The preceding cases were all observed from actual transactions in the organized money market. The fluctuation in the unorganized markets is much wider, oscillating between 60 and 400 percent. These figures do more than expose the concealed cost of capital; they reflect its acute shortage as well. Of course, within the extended family system there are still noteworthy examples of interest-free lending by close relatives. But these are exceptions, and they cannot hold sway over the most important and prevalent types of ordinary unregulated loan transactions.

In making these observations, I am probably attacking some peoples' long-cherished views. Yet any knowledgeable person would easily be in a position to concur with these statements. After all, the interest rate is simply the price of credit and should be allowed to behave like any other price. From the business community, clamors to keep capital cheap will be strong. Labor has become increasingly expensive, and this came about largely through other protective laws. The widespread fear is that higher interest rates would discourage investments and consequently retard economic progress. This contention is not entirely wrong, but it is not comprehensively right either.

Low Savings: An Important Constraint

High interest rates and progress are neither contradictory nor mutually exclusive. Interest rates are simply the cost of the commodity, credit, and the price of such a commodity has to be reckoned via the market forces for purposes of optimal allocation. Businessmen, familiar with the operation of market forces, know very well that price fluctuations are within the realm of ordinary, day-to-day business risks. Mature business decisions are expected to cope with such risks.

At current interest rates, demand exceeds supply and a few entrepreneurial dreams have to be left unrealized. Yet this need not be the case. Some resources remain dormant and detached from the market because deposit rates are unattractive. In fact, with the inflation rate eating into it, the effective rate becomes very much smaller if not negative. And realistic interest rates should be a basic weapon against inflation. These untapped resources are largely in the form of rural savings, hidden in the proverbial *alkansiya* (piggy bank) or stacked inside bamboo posts and bed mats, and of capital tied up in real estate speculation and stashed away secretly in foreign banks. One way of getting them out into the open is to raise interest rates. Unless a deposit habit is inculcated among the rural folk, more and more resources in the form of hoarded savings will get displaced from the investment stream.

Experience of Neighbors

The experiences of Taiwan and the Republic of Korea in the 1960s give optimistic indications of the positive response of rural savings to increases in interest rates. In 1965 Korea raised its interest rates to a maximum of 34.5 percent a year for deposits and 26 percent for loans, with the government subsidizing commercial bank losses. Within a year, savings were 1.6 times higher than originally. The private sector accounted for 86 percent of the total, and corporations for about 14 percent. Investments increased from 14.7 percent of gross national product to 21.6 percent.

Taiwan, in its attempt to attract more savings in 1958, maintained a high level of interest rates for the next decade—initially 1.6 percent monthly on time deposits with loan agreements, and 1.8 percent for those without loan agreements. Meanwhile, the interest charge on loans reached as high as 1.83 percent monthly. The result of this policy was a thirteenfold increase in savings deposits over the 1958–68 period. Later, monthly charges on loans went down to 1.11 percent and time deposit rates to about 1 percent.

Indonesia, reeling from a decade of stagnation and extreme inflation, also raised interest rates on deposits and loans in accordance with market forces. As bank loan rates approached unregulated market levels, an increasing proportion of total loans went into the organized (regulated) market. Another result was an increasing inflow of repatriated Indonesian funds from overseas deposit accounts when local rates exceeded overseas rates.

In the Philippines, farmers and industrial entrepreneurs are also sensitive to price incentives and inducements. Clearly, there is a case for raising the rates in order to ease the strain on the financial market. Where supply of savings is low, primarily on account of an outmoded legislative regulation, there is danger of corruption.

Corruption: Supporting the Inefficient

Because of the meager supply of loanable funds rationing becomes inevitable, and the temptation to corrupt the lender exerts tremendous pressure on countless borrowers. Ten percenting (or kickbacks) used to be standard operating procedure during the days of import-exchange controls. In lending this is also not unlikely, given conditions of credit rationing. There is a strong suspicion that a number of strange loan transactions may have been decided solely on the merits of collateral, rather than on economic efficiency. This setup leaves ample room for entertaining big but relatively inefficient projects.

Meanwhile, the loan that the small, helpless borrower needed to finance a modest but efficient project is hard to come by. The oligarchs are left to share whatever few spoils there are. Does anybody ever take time to remember for whom the law was tailor-made in the first place? Who is it that in the end is helplessly forced to borrow at the usurious rates of the unorganized money market? That is right, the common man—Juan de la Cruz—and sometimes all this hassle discourages him from borrowing at all.

The Export Drive

A rise in the interest rate ought to do two things for exports: encourage labor-intensive industries, which substantially abound in the Philippines' export sector owing to an international comparative advantage in labor supply; and provide a wider interest rate differential that could be used to promote export priorities, as was done in Taiwan and Korea. The discrimination against labor input (partly owing to low interest rates), together with the undervaluation of foreign exchange and an outmoded tariff system, have been the staunchest barriers to Philippine export diversification.

The increased cost of capital goods purchased with credit, which would result from freeing interest rates, should somewhat offset the artificial advantage that capital inputs have been enjoying over artificially high-priced labor. In large measure, this would help correct the economic distortions that have indirectly stifled export growth. A higher general interest rate would also allow for preferential lower-rate schemes to stimulate labor-intensive export activities. Supported by favorable policies such as a realistic foreign exchange rate, entrepreneurs should receive more export incentives.

Regional Development

A corollary to export promotion is regional development. Where export promotion is being strangled, consciously or unconsciously, the chances are that the program of regional development also gets choked. Does the farmer stand a very good chance of being uplifted when the well-established businessmen in the cities monopolize access to most of the loan funds?

Furthermore, Philippine exports have been primarily rural or agricultural. When capital is made cheap relative to labor and other inputs, capital intensity in new industries is encouraged, and development begins to occur more progressively in urban areas. Meanwhile, exports are discouraged, and agricultural development is made to suffer. What happened is that the Philippines tolerated this state of factor-mispricing too long. Is it any wonder, then, that dreams of regional development commensurate with urban progress have not been satisfactorily realized?

The Urban Game of Speculation

Some urban income earners, who have not had a propensity to invest productively, manage to direct unused resources to less productive and highly speculative assets: real estate, jewelry, and stock market manipulation. Every peso tied up in these assets means an equivalent amount of forgone investment and, correspondingly, much more forgone production. There is reason to believe that resources pumped into these unproductive endeavors are not insubstantial. As more resources revert to these areas, the savings rate suffers, and more output is forgone. With less production, assuming the spending rate is undiminished, there is inflation.

I am citing a host of maladies that are so intertwined I do not know where to stop. The point is that the same old theme of overprotection appears to yield the same old results: misallocation of resources, graft, corruption, and economic distortion. All of these are by now familiar. I only warn that often the wrong means can kill the most righteous goal. To reach the goal of regional industrialization envisioned, unrealistic interest rates are certainly not the most rational means. The reform I seek is intended only to end the protection and to encourage more desirable directions in our development policy.

45. *The Impact of Rural Credit on Production and Income Distribution in Brazil*

João Sayad

[Subsidized interest rates are an important policy tool in Brazil. In 1977 the subsidy given to agriculture through loans at interest rates below the rate of inflation amounted to 25 percent of total expenditures by all levels of government in Brazil. It is doubtful that these subsidies stimulate agricultural production because interest rates alone are an insufficient incentive for farmers to undertake agricultural investment. It also appears that borrowers rechannel their agricultural credit subsidies to other activities. Further, subsidized credit tends to be concentrated among the larger farmers and thus makes the distribution of income and wealth more unequal. Since this was written, Brazil has reduced or eliminated some credit subsidies.]

The objective of this chapter is to analyze the effectiveness of using credit in Brazil as an incentive to promote agricultural investments, and to assess its effect on income distribution. The conclusions are that rural credit programs do not change the share of agriculture in total investments if the returns on these investments are not changed; furthermore, these programs make income distribution less equal.

Brazilian Rural Credit and Its Economic Environment

Brazilian financial markets before the mid-1960s consisted largely of commercial banks extending short-term loans (up to 180 days) and a few new consumer credit companies. The 1966 Capital Markets Reform Law inaugurated a new era. Investment banks, savings and loan associations, development banks, and other financial firms were created, and the National Housing Bank was launched. New types of financial asset were created, including national treasury bonds that earned interest plus a return represented by the indexation of their

Adapted from a paper presented at the Second International Conference on Rural Finance Research Issues in Calgary, Canada, August 1979.

Table 45-1. *Government Expenditures and Annual Flow of Subsidized Credit Programs, Brazil, 1970–77*
(millions of current cruzeiros)

Year	*Government expenditures*			*Rural loans from Banco do Brasil and commercial banks*	*Other subsidized loans*			*Ratio of loans to government expenditures*
	Current (1)	*Capital (2)*	*Total (1 + 2) (3)*	*(4)*	*Federal development banks (5)*	*State development banks (6)*	*Total loans (4 + 5 + 6) (7)*	*(7 ÷ 3) (8)*
1970	20,512	8,273	28,785	2,676	1,262	250	4,188	0.15
1971	26,779	10,596	27,375	3,519	819	492	4,830	0.18
1972	34,688	13,854	48,542	5,985	2,466	1,199	9,650	0.20
1973	46,190	18,061	64,251	13,606	3,907	1,837	19,350	0.30
1974	65,455	28,715	94,169	18,749	12,876	4,023	35,648	0.38
1975	99,345	43,359	142,704	36,211	23,484	6,275	65,970	0.46
1976	157,434	65,643	223,077	42,717	41,423	13,949	98,089	0.44
1977	220,840	90,487	311,327	53,240	59,902	18,584	131,726	0.42

Sources: Centro de Contas Nacionais, *Conjuntura Econômica* (October 1978); and *Boletim do Banco Central*, various issues.

value to a general price level (monetary correction for inflation) and savings accounts that earned 6 percent interest plus monetary correction. Large income tax deductions encouraged the holding of financial assets. The result was a rapid growth in privately held financial assets. High income and output growth rates in 1967–74 provided further incentive for the growth of private financial assets. Nonmonetary financial assets, equal to only 4 percent of the gross domestic product (GDP) in 1966, rose to 40 percent in 1973.

In rural credit, 1965 laws created the National System of Rural Credit, comprising the Banco do Brasil and commercial banks. Banco do Brasil is a government-owned bank which holds 40 percent of the nation's demand deposits and implements many government planning decisions. Its agricultural loans are made in accordance with plans issued by the National Monetary Council. Under the new laws, commercial banks have to lend not less than 15 percent of their demand deposits to farmers. When this amount is not attained by a bank, the difference has to be kept as required reserves in the central bank, which then lends it through the Banco do Brasil or other commercial banks. The rural credit interest rate for working capital was fixed at 17 percent a year, at a time when inflation rates ranged from 20 to 40 percent a year. In 1971, the rural interest rate was lowered to 15 percent a year.

After 1973, Brazilian economic trends shifted drastically. The inflation rate, which had been decreasing, moved rapidly back to the 40 percent level. Annual growth of national product, after averaging 10 percent in the 1968–73 period, began to oscillate, reaching as low as 4 percent in 1978. Balance of payments conditions were tightened by the drastic increases in oil prices and by large debt service payments.

The rural credit system, using heavy foreign borrowings, continued its 15 percent nominal interest rates. Special programs were started to stimulate agricultural expansion in specific regions, including those with poor soil (the *cerrados*) or low incomes (the Northeast), where long-term rural credit was offered at rates as low as 5 percent. Credit for fertilizers was subsidized through zero interest rate loans to compensate for higher fertilizer prices after the oil crisis.

Table 45-1 shows the annual flows of subsidized credit, rural and other types, in 1970–77 and the ratio they represent to total government spending. Rural loans are the most important in terms of subsidy. In 1976 and 1977 the value of total rural loans came to about 90 percent of farm income in Brazil, whereas it had been less than 20 percent in 1960. (This expansion was far more than that in total bank loans as a share of GDP, which had only a minor increase.)

Agriculture is considered a high-priority sector by the administration which took office in early 1979. Improvements in the balance of payments, the urban real wage, and the supply of new energy sources all depend, at least partly, on increased farm production. The economic policies directed to the sector continue to rely on subsidized interest rates. "Planning through credit" remains a preference of Brazilian economic authorities. Food price ceilings and taxes on agricultural exports or lower exchange rates for specific export crops are also widely used policies in Brazil. Agriculture has a weak short-run incentive to increase production at these controlled prices.

Subsidized credit seems to be regarded as a way of increasing agricultural investment and production without having to rely on changes in relative prices. Investment expenditures can start immediately since they do not have to wait for a growth of profits that can be reinvested in the sector. Planners seem to believe that rural credit programs can work magic and change the private sector pattern of investment quickly, without inflationary pressures or uncertainties. When planning decisions are implemented through credit, there is no need for changes in tax laws or legislative approval of new expenditures; these programs are implemented by the efficient centralized bureaucracy of the Banco do Brasil with more than 1,000 branches. The government preference for special credit programs instead of price or fiscal incentives is analogous to the usual explanation of the preference for inflationary financing. Subsidies as high as 20 percent of agricultural production are not visible to noneconomists and make credit programs look even more attractive to political authorities.

The Impact of Rural Credit on the Financing of Agricultural Production

The argument for compensatory low interest rates runs as follows: When price controls or lower exchange rates are imposed, agricultural production and investments become less profitable. When the market rate of interest is unchanged, investments in agriculture decrease. But if the government supplies credit at a lower subsidized interest rate, investments in agriculture increase to the level they would have attained if there were no price controls.

The argument is subject to several criticisms. First, borrowers are private firms trying to allocate their investable funds in the most profitable way. If the rate of return in agriculture is decreased by government policies, subsidized interest rate loans cannot by themselves increase the rate of investment in this sector. Farmers will accept the offer of loans at lower interest rates, and they may even invest these loans in accordance with the loan contract. But they will transfer the maximum amount of their other funds to more profitable activities or assets. The outcome might be more financing of agricultural investments directly by the rural credit system, but this amount would be offset by less internal financing and fewer commercial bank loans going into agriculture. The result would be an unchanging total amount of agricultural investment. [See chapter 8 for an exposition of the effects of the fungibility of credit.]

This result occurs when all investors are rational profit seekers capable of substituting investment funds from one use to another without difficulty. Substitutability is a matter of degree. Within a given market, large firms, firms whose profits grow fast, and firms with more access to financial markets will have larger substitution capabilities and will more easily substitute rural credit for other sources of finance. Therefore, the effectiveness of the rural credit program in increasing agricultural investment as intended depends heavily on the characteristics of its borrowers. Thus loan distribution policies have a very important impact on the amount of the rural credit program that goes into new agricultural investments and the amount that merely generates substitution. Such a rural credit program would be more effective in its allocation objectives where financial markets are segmented and transaction costs very high—factors inhibiting substitution among different sources of finance.

Rural credit is often tied to the purchase of tractors or other particular items. In Brazil, some lines of credit are tied to the purchase of so-called modern inputs, such as fertilizer or special seeds. But if substantial substitution occurs, special credit programs are not likely to change the input mix in farm production for the same reasons they are not likely to change the investment mix between major sectors. That is, there will be no shift unless the modern technology is profitable.

Loan Terms and Wealth Distribution

The interest rate is only one item in a loan contract. A loan contract also specifies maturity, collateral, compensating balance, risk, and liquidity. There is a relation of substitutability between interest rates and other items. For example, lower interest rates are generally accompanied by higher collateral, and borrowers with more liquid assets are charged lower interest rates than less liquid borrowers. Consumer loans, for example, require less collateral than commercial loans and have higher interest rates.

If this kind of substitution is general, commercial banks will prefer to supply a large share of rural credit to large borrowers, to borrowers with more collateral per dollar of loans and more liquid assets, and to borrowers who represent a smaller risk. But these characteristics happen to be also those of borrowers who have lower transaction costs in finance markets and larger possibilities for substituting other sources of finance for rural credit loans. With low interest rates, larger and more liquid borrowers will have the largest share of rural loans.

Table 45-2. *Total Costs of Subsidized Agricultural Credit Programs, Brazil, 1970–77*
(rates in percentages, monetary amounts in millions of current cruzeiros)

Year	*Total subsidized loans outstanding*[a]	*Annual inflation rate*[b]	*Real rate of interest*[c]	*Total subsidy cost*	*Government expenditures*	*Subsidies as percentage of expenditures*
1970	15,041	19.8	−4.2	631	28,785	2
1971	20,872	20.4	−4.7	980	27,375	4
1972	32,038	17.0	−1.7	544	48,542	1
1973	53,649	15.1	0	0	64,251	0
1974	55,790[d]	28.9	−12.1	6,750	94,169	7
1975	97,219[e]	30.1	−13.1	12,735	142,704	9
1976	243,313	41.2	−18.6	45,256	223,077	20
1977	375,039	43.4	−19.8	74,257	311,327	24

a. Includes rural loans and development bank loans.
b. General price index from *Conjuntura Econômica*, various issues.
c. Assuming a 15 percent nominal rate of interest.
d. Excludes Banco Nacional do Desenvolvimento Econômico.
e. Excludes all development banks.

One might argue that Banco do Brasil and the other government-owned banks involved in rural credit are concerned with social objectives of government policy, and that the preceding observation about loan distribution policies does not apply to them. But a bank has characteristics that do not allow this type of behavior. Assume, for example, that Banco do Brasil decides to increase the share of small, less liquid, and riskier loans. Once this decision is made, bank managers know that the percentage allowed for defaulted loans will have to increase. But control of loan operations becomes impossible if managers tell borrowers that a higher percentage of default on rural loans is now allowed. The banking business is subject to a special information problem which does not allow this type of arrangement.

The low interest rate policy of the rural credit system not only increases the share of large farmers' loans in the total, it also affects income distribution. Table 45-2 shows the amount of subsidies implicit in the rural credit program, calculated as the difference between the interest rate in rural loans (estimated as 15 percent a year) and the inflation rate. They come to almost Cr75,000 million in 1977 (equivalent to about US$5,300 million at 1977 exchange rates), which is 25 percent of total spending by federal, state, and municipal governments in Brazil. These subsidies are distributed mostly to the large landowners who constitute the bulk of the rural credit system borrowers. The effects on wealth distribution are easy to understand.

Although it is argued here that higher interest rates would generate a less concentrated distribution of rural credit among different-size borrowers, this does not mean that higher interest rates alone would be capable of doing so. In general, banks discriminate against small borrowers for security reasons, and they distribute new purchasing power and new investments not in proportion to the current wealth distribution, but in a more concentrated way.

Empirical Evidence

The effectiveness of rural credit programs depends on how loans are distributed among different-size farms and borrowers with different degrees of liquidity and profitability. In this section some empirical evidence on the distribution of rural credit in Brazil is presented to test the hypothesis that larger, more liquid, and more profitable farms use loans more efficiently.

A sample of 1,686 farmers answered a questionnaire about sources and uses of funds in 1971. The sample and questionnaire were designed for research on technological innovation. Information for this year understates the seriousness of the subsidy problem because the real interest rate was much less negative than in later years. The inflation rate in 1971 was about 20 percent a year while the rate of interest on rural credit was 17 percent, but after 1973 inflation rates averaged 40 percent a year and interest 15 percent. The data in this sample refer to flows of income—cash income, new loans obtained, and amortization payments during 1971—while the issues of the previous section involve *stocks* of loans, of liquid assets, and of investable funds.

The sample is composed of farms scattered over all Brazilian states except São Paulo. It is composed of farms almost equally distributed among five size classes. Farmers were classified in terms of liquidity (an index using cash income minus cash payments divided by cash payments, called L; and a coverage ratio index labeled C, defined as cash income minus cash expenses over interest rate payments) and in terms of profitability (profits over total value of assets). The sample provided information on the total amount of expenses of each farm per year including investment (plus stock changes), current expenses, and non-cash payments (basically the expenses of subsistence, estimated as the regional wage of the region times the number of family members, counting women as part-time workers). The value of new loans obtained divided by total expenses was called the share of debt in total finance. Long-run credit was estimated as new credit obtained in 1971 minus amortization paid in that year, and short-run credit was estimated as amortization.

Analysis of this data showed that it was not possible to reject the hypothesis that larger farmers use a larger share of debt to finance their expenses. Short-term credit was quite evenly distributed; there was no significant difference for different sizes of farms. But long-term credit was significantly more concentrated among larger farms. Farms classified according to different levels of profitability did not have systematically different shares of debt to finance their expenses. The differences were statistically significant, however, when farms were classified according to liquidity, measured by the coverage ratio.

Thus, there is empirical evidence that low-interest rural credit in Brazil, particularly long-term credit, is concentrated among larger and more liquid farms. The results are limited by the quality of the sample and the estimates used for total and long-term credit.

46. *Implementing Interest Rate Reform*

Robert C. Vogel

[Four arguments are made frequently against the possibility of successfully implementing interest rate reforms: (1) the impact of reforms on financial institutions; (2) the problems arising from other distortions that adversely affect the agricultural sector; (3) the short-run disruptions and losses for borrowers that would be caused by reforms; and (4) the interrelations between financial reforms and international trade policy. The first two arguments should not present serious barriers to reform. The third and fourth arguments could, for reasons that are at least partly political, but there may be scope for compensatory actions to ease the adjustments required by reform.]

Widespread agreement is emerging that financial reform would be beneficial for rural financial markets in developing countries and that a key element in any such reform is higher interest rates that are positive in real terms. The purpose here is not to reiterate arguments in favor of interest rate reform, but rather to examine some of the barriers that seem to have inhibited the reformation of rural financial markets in developing countries. In particular, four arguments have often been made, not against interest rate reforms themselves, but against the possibility of successfully carrying out such reforms. Given the infrequency with which rural financial market reforms have been implemented, these arguments cannot be ignored. For the arguments that appear valid, the costs of implementation must be weighed carefully against the ultimate benefits if interest rate reforms are ever to become widespread in developing countries.

Viability of Financial Institutions

The first argument against the possibility of financial reform is that it will lead to the bankruptcy of many financial intermediaries. Raising interest rates to competitive levels, or at least making them positive in real terms, is likely to entail substantial increases, especially in those countries with substantial inflation. Where the primary function of financial intermediaries is to issue short-term (liquid) liabilities and to hold longer-term (illiquid) assets, these institutions are likely to face serious difficulties when interest rates increase substantially. On the one hand, they must immediately pay higher competitive rates on their short-term liabilities in order to retain deposits and avoid a liquidity crisis. On the other hand, they cannot charge higher rates on their long-term loans until these investments mature and can be replaced. Thus, they face large losses or even bankruptcy, depending on the size of the interest rate increase and the term structure of their assets and liabilities.

A program of government loans to rescue the financial institutions threatened with bankruptcy is one possible solution to this problem. Under certain circumstances, however, this solution could cause the monetary authority to lose control of the money supply; this would generate more inflation and necessitate even higher interest rates. A more attractive alternative is to raise interest rates on outstanding loans. Such a policy would remove not only the threat to financial institutions but also the subsidy still accruing to the recipients of old loans with low interest rates. It might be argued that this would breach the sanctity of contracts, but loan contracts in developing countries often allow for the subsequent adjustment of interest rates. There are also precedents for the *ex post* adjustment of interest rates, especially in situations involving indexation for inflation.

Another reason that the possible bankruptcy of financial institutions should not be a serious barrier to financial reform is that most financial institutions in developing countries simply do not have a substantial portion of their assets committed to long-term loans. In fact, one of the main complaints about finance in developing countries is that it is mainly short term. For agricultural credit in particular, medium- and long-term loans to farmers are typically supported by long-term loans from international lending institutions or the government, and not by short-term deposits.

There is, however, an additional threat that higher interest rates may pose for the viability of financial institutions. In some developing countries borrowers repay promptly in order to maintain continuing access to low-interest loans; higher interest rates might therefore remove an important incentive against delinquency and default. Financial institutions will need to improve other elements of their service to borrowers by eliminating unnecessary paperwork, procedures, and delays that have grown up to ration low-interest loans, and will need to impose stricter measures against delinquent borrowers.

Second Best

The second argument against implementing a program of financial reform is based on the theory of the second best. Given the distortions that are said to pervade developing economies, it is not certain that alleviating distortions in financial markets by raising interest rates, while leaving distortions undisturbed in other markets, will in fact make an economy better off. In particular, it has been argued that preferential low interest rates should be maintained for the agricultural sector to compensate for other distortions that place the agricultural sector at a disadvantage and that cannot easily be removed. An example is government trade policies that turn the terms of trade against agriculture. Prices of food and other primary products are kept low to subsidize the urban-industrial sector, while prices of manufactured inputs for agriculture are kept high to encourage domestic industrial production.

It is unrealistic to think that such distortions can be overcome, or even ameliorated, simply by requiring that loans to the agricultural sector be made at low interest rates without the necessity of confronting each distortion directly. In particular, such a view neglects the fungibility of credit. Because credit is fungible, preferential low interest rates for the agricultural sector will fail to allocate resources to the favored activities in the agricultural sector. Preferential low interest rates do not change the technologies available to farmers or the prices paid by farmers for inputs or received for output. Hence, cheap credit does not alter the relative profitability of agricultural and nonagricultural activities or the relative attractiveness of different activities within the agricultural sector.

Since credit provides general command over resources, it cannot easily be tied to the production of particular goods, the purchase of particular inputs, or the use of particular technologies. Diversion of loans to other than prescribed uses by farmers in developing countries is widespread and has not been overcome by even the most diligent programs of supervision. More subtle and pervasive is the case in which a farmer presents the lender with his most attractive undertaking, one which would have been carried out even if a loan were not received, and then uses the additional resources obtained with the loan for some unspecified activity. Such behavior is particularly likely for large farmers in developing countries who obtain the lion's share of agricultural credit and who most often have a variety of activities outside the agricultural sector.

It is sometimes argued that low incomes in the agricultural sector can be compensated by preferential low interest rates. Although the distribution of income is indeed biased away from the agricultural sector by the distortions mentioned above, it is wealthy farmers who receive most of the benefits from preferential low interest rates. The majority of farmers receive no credit whatsoever at preferential low interest rates, so it is unlikely that the distribution of income is improved according to most notions of equity. In spite of widespread distortions against agriculture, the theory of the second best does not provide a good reason for continuing policies of preferential low interest rates and for failing to implement rural financial market reforms.

Short-run Losses

The third argument against implementing interest rate reform ironically grows out of a forceful argument in favor of reform. It has been convincingly argued that many costs of a traditional stabilization program can be avoided when a program of financial reform is used instead to combat inflation. In traditional programs, monetary expansion, and hence credit, is curtailed. This reduces not only aggregate demand, as intended, but also aggregate supply as the availability of credit for working capital is curtailed. Depending on the reduction in aggregate supply relative to demand, little or no headway will be made against inflation. The major result will be an immediate and sharp reduction in output and jobs, which cannot long be tolerated.

A program of financial reform presents a more attractive approach to combating inflation. Higher interest rates on deposits divert demand away from goods, especially inflation hedges, and thus help alleviate inflationary pressures. The greater demand for financial assets permits an expansion, rather than a contraction, of credit for working capital. At the same time, higher interest rates on loans improve the allocation of resources by diverting credit away from activities with low rates of return and toward those with high returns. Inflation is thus reduced by policies that permit continued economic expansion, and the initial reduction in output that has undermined so many traditional stabilization programs is thereby avoided.

The paradox which may present a serious barrier to implementing such a reform is that the potential benefits from interest rate reform will be greater the more that savings have been flowing into investment projects with low yields. This implies the existence of a substantial stock of fixed capital which will be inappropriate for the postreform economy, but which is currently being made profitable by the subsidy implicit in low-interest loans. Unlike working capital, however, it cannot be reallocated readily to more profitable activities precisely because it is fixed capital. Thus, a significant portion of the capital stock may suddenly, with the advent of reform, be written down substantially in value. Under such circumstances it may be difficult to avoid a short-run loss of output, even though the long-run benefits from improved resource allocation will be greater. In addition, there may be strong political opposition from those who are losing their access to low-interest loans and are having their fixed capital written down substantially in value. Perhaps this group can be compensated into acquiescence in a manner that is less harmful to resource allocation than the current interest rate subsidy. Similar compensation has sometimes been proposed for those who lose the subsidy implicit in tariffs during the process of international trade reform.

Reform of International Trade Policies

The fourth argument against implementing financial reform is that it cannot be separated from other reforms, not in terms of the second-best arguments discussed above, but rather because of a direct link with a reform of international economic policies. Consider a situation in which a developing country has achieved, at least temporarily, a stable exchange rate and a reasonable equilibrium in its balance of payments. The introduction of financial reform with its higher interest rates on deposits will make the return on domestic financial assets higher relative to the return on foreign assets, and this will bring about an inflow of capital as both foreigners and residents shift out of foreign assets and into the country's domestic financial assets. In addition, the higher interest rates on loans will make it more attractive for those who previously had access to low-interest domestic loans to borrow in foreign financial markets.

The resulting inflow of capital is usually viewed as a good thing, at least initially, because it represents a potential increase in foreign exchange reserves. Under a system of fixed exchange rates, which is typical for most developing countries, this potential increase translates into an actual increase not only in foreign exchange reserves but also in the country's monetary base, which permits a multiple increase in the money supply. The monetary authority is thus faced with either restricting domestic credit to offset the increase in foreign exchange reserves or permitting a multiple increase in the money supply. Restricting domestic credit may lead to the reduction in output that the financial reform was seeking to avoid, while permitting the money supply to increase will lead to more inflation and thereby undo the increase in real interest rates that the financial reform was trying to accomplish.

Alternatively, the potential increase in foreign exchange reserves can be offset directly by changing the exchange rate, that is, by increasing the value of domestic currency relative to foreign currencies. (This happens automatically for those countries with floating exchange rates.) Another policy that can produce essentially the same results is a liberalization of imports to offset the potential increase in foreign exchange reserves. Such a liberalization would involve the reduction of tariffs and the elimination of quotas and most other nontariff barriers against imports. However, import liberalization or exchange rate adjustment is likely to be strongly opposed by domestic producers of import substitutes who would be threatened with increased competition.

There is a significant parallel between the gainers and losers from interest rate reform and the gainers and losers from tariff reform. A point frequently made about the politics of international trade reform is that the gainers from reduced protection are a widely dispersed group—consumers—each of whom benefits relatively little from reform, whereas the losers are likely to be a small and cohesive group—producers of import substitutes—each of whom may lose a great deal from reduced protection. The gainers from financial reform are likewise a widely dispersed group—the holders of deposits—each of whom is likely to gain relatively little through higher interest rates, whereas the losers who have been enjoying subsidized low-interest loans are likely to be a relatively small group of important individuals. Although gains outweigh losses in the aggregate, the losers are likely to have the incentive and the position to oppose reform strongly and effectively. Other sources of opposition to financial reform are government officials and loan officers who see the distribution of credit at subsidized low interest rates as a possible source of patronage.

Conclusions

An examination of the first two arguments against implementing interest rate reform suggests that these arguments should not present serious barriers to reform. The last two arguments, however, provide political and economic reasons to be concerned about the possibility of implementing a program of reform. To the extent that financial reform promises significant long-run benefits because of substantial current misallocation of resources, it also promises a disruption of output in the short run, and those who experience substantial capital losses from reform can be expected to present particularly strong opposition. Because of capital flows, it would be difficult to carry out successful financial reform without some accompanying measure of international trade reform. The parallels between financial reform and international trade reform may suggest compensatory devices to minimize the opposition to financial reform.

47. *Interest Rates as an Anti-inflationary Instrument in Taiwan*

Reed J. Irvine and Robert F. Emery

[The government attached great importance to overcoming inflationary psychology and establishing public confidence in Taiwan without impairing political support. Beginning in 1950 rates of interest of more than 100 percent a year were offered on special savings deposits. These deposits rapidly absorbed a large amount of liquidity, diverting funds from consumption into savings, but without creating the antagonism that would have been generated by compulsory measures.]

Rampant inflation was one of the important factors leading to the downfall of the Nationalist government of China in 1949. The problem of rising prices continued to confront the government on Taiwan. The problem was exacerbated in 1949 by the large influx of approximately 0.5 million migrants. It was not easy to see a solution to the problem of supporting this burden from the slender resources of the overcrowded island of Taiwan. Relations between the local population and the immigrants were delicate. The government was acutely conscious that excessive taxation would alienate the local population, so substantial budget deficits were unavoidable.

The dilemma was partially relieved by U.S. grants to pay for imports, which permitted the government to run a current account deficit in its balance of payments of approximately US$100 million a year in the early 1950s. But this was not large enough to absorb all of the inflationary additions to the money supply. In 1950 net money supply more than doubled, and wholesale prices rose by 85 percent.

It was evident that self-help measures to combat the inflationary pressure were required to avoid a repetition of the monetary debacle of China. The Taiwan government endeavored to immobilize, in the form of time deposits, a substantial portion of the money being disbursed to the public. The memory of wartime compulsory saving

Adapted from *National Banking Review*, vol. 4, no. 1 (September 1966), pp. 29–39.

schemes was still fresh in people's minds, and compulsory savings would have been just as unpopular as additional taxation. With prices rising at a rate of 85 percent a year and the position of the government none too secure, there was not much hope of using patriotic motives to persuade the public to put funds into bonds or savings accounts. The one alternative left was to use sufficiently attractive interest rates to induce the public to save voluntarily.

Preferential Interest Deposits

Given the prevailing rate of inflation, an extraordinarily high rate of interest was needed to encourage a large number of people to buy financial claims rather than goods. In March 1950 the government introduced a special system of time deposits, known as preferential interest deposits, paying extraordinarily high nominal rates of interest.

The authorities recognized that under highly inflationary conditions the public could not be expected to accept financial assets having long maturities. They therefore started by offering deposits of one-, two-, and three-month maturities. The rate of interest offered on the one-month certificates in March 1950 was 7 percent a month, which compounded monthly comes to 125 percent a year. This rate was attractive to savers even under the prevailing inflation. Time deposits in the banking system quickly rose from NT$2 million early in 1950 to NT$37 million by August, which was a little less than 5 percent of the net money supply. The price increase was temporarily halted, with the wholesale price index actually declining between May and July of 1950. The government, no doubt encouraged by this success, sharply reduced the rate of interest payable on one-month deposits in July 1950 by half, to 3.5 percent a month. This reduction halted the rapid increase in time deposits and the total fell slightly. In spite of this, the government lowered the interest rate further to 3.0 percent a month on one-month deposits in October. This cut, combined with the sharp rise in prices that had resumed in August, prompted many depositors to withdraw their deposits. Total preferential interest rate deposits fell to only NT$21 million by January 1951. In March 1951 the one-month rate was raised to 4.2 percent a month (64 percent a year) and held at this level for the next thirteen months.

During 1951 the volume of preferential interest rate deposits rose spectacularly to more than NT$160 million by September, or over 17 percent of net money supply. The increase slackened in the final quarter of the year, but resumed momentum in January 1952. By April 1953 the total had increased to NT$350 million, 38 percent of net money supply. At that point, the government believed that public confidence warranted introducing six-month deposit certificates at a rate of 4.2 percent a month. At the same time, it began a series of steady reductions in the deposit rates. The approach was more cautious than in 1950, when large rate reductions had seriously reduced the willingness of savers to renew their certificates. The reductions were made during 1952 by approximately half a percentage point every two months with the exception of one reduction at a one-month interval.

In April 1953 the state of confidence appeared to justify the introduction of one-year deposit certificates at a rate of 3.0 percent a month. The rise in deposits continued, with an especially strong growth in one-month maturities. Total deposits rose to NT$650 million by July 1953, nearly 50 percent of net money supply. At this point, the authorities considered it safe to cut the interest rate again, and rates were reduced twice in the second half of 1953. This led to a sharp switch to the longer maturity deposits, especially the six-month category. In June 1953, 75 percent of deposits were in the one- and three-month categories, but by December of that year the six-month and one-year deposits accounted for nearly half of a somewhat reduced total.

The growth of deposits resumed in 1954, with the six-month category showing the greatest popularity. This result permitted another reduction in interest rates in July 1954, which again slowed down the growth in deposit volume for several months. The growth accelerated in 1955 with total deposits rising to NT$876 million in September, 32 percent of net money supply.

Fears of Excess Liquidity

The growth of deposits was such that in late 1955 and early 1956 the authorities became concerned that they represented a potential source of increased liquidity, even though 58 percent of the December 1955 total carried a maturity of six months or a year. It was thought that even in the case of the long-term deposits, the privilege of borrowing and using the deposit as collateral gave all of the deposits a high potential liquidity. Therefore, in March 1956 rates were adjusted to make the shorter-term deposits relatively less attractive. The rate on one-month deposits was cut by 15 percent, on three-month deposits by 9 percent, and premiums of 15.4 percent and 12.5 percent were offered on the rates for the six-month and one-year deposits if the depositor was willing to forgo the privilege of borrowing against long-term deposits. In June the borrowing option was removed, and all the deposits were declared ineligible for use as collateral for loans.

As a result of this change, a substantial number of depositors switched from the one-month to the higher paying three-month deposits, and from six-month to one-year deposits. By the end of 1956, 26.9 percent of time deposits were for one year. Later however, too many people found the premium inadequate compensation for the loss of liquidity. The number of six-month deposits, formerly the most popular category, dropped sharply, and as a result there was an overall decline in total preferential interest deposits. The fears that prompted this shift do not appear to have been well grounded, however.

Two-year preferential deposits were introduced in July 1957. At the same time, rates on deposits were generally lowered. The same interest rate (1.8 percent monthly) was established for two-year deposits as had previously been paid on one-year deposits, while the rate on one-year deposits became 1.35 percent monthly. Nevertheless, one-year deposits became the most popular category, as one-month deposits were discontinued and three-month deposits paying only 0.85 percent a month lost favor. The volume of one-year deposits more than doubled in 1958. Six-month deposits also increased substantially. By the end of 1958, preferential interest deposits totaled NT$1,508 million, or 29 percent of the net money supply. All preferential interest rate time deposits were terminated at the end of 1958 in favor of regular time deposits.

These results attested to the merits of astute and bold use of interest rate policy. The savers were, at first, induced to put their money into banks at what seemed to be outrageously high interest rates for very short maturities. Actually, the real return on the savings was not outrageous at the time. Given a rate of inflation of 52 percent a year in 1951, the real return on a one-month preferential interest deposit was only 12 percent a year, with the nominal interest rate at 64 percent. As inflation was brought under control, partly by the absorption of liquidity through the preferential interest rate deposits, savers were able to obtain a higher real return even though the nominal rate of interest was lowered. For example, with prices rising only 3 percent, the real return to the saver on a one-year deposit in 1958 was about 17 percent. As depositors became accustomed to the savings habit and learned to appreciate the benefits of compound interest, it was possible to reduce greatly the nominal rates of interest and to stretch out the average maturities of the deposits.

Conclusions

As the Nationalist government consolidated its position on Taiwan, it was able to improve its fiscal performance greatly. This improvement deserves major credit for the degree of stabilization in the 1960s which, in turn, owes much to the tremendous gains in economic productivity. From 1951 to 1964, gross national product per capita rose 57 percent. This growth was accompanied by a large expansion in the country's ability to earn the foreign exchange needed to supply the population with imported goods and services. In 1951 total exports were US$102 million, while in 1965 they totaled US$450 million.

Among the factors responsible for the success of the economic program on Taiwan was the skillful use of realistic interest rates to encourage voluntary saving, especially in the difficult early years. It was essential, at that time, for the government to overcome inflationary psychology and establish public confidence without dangerously impairing political support. The preferential interest deposits rapidly absorbed a large amount of liquidity without creating any of the antagonism that would have been generated by compulsory measures. This voluntary method helped lay the foundation for the subsequent political stability and economic expansion.

The Taiwan experience has relevance for other economies. It demonstrates the feasibility of using interest rates to fight inflation even when the rate of price increase has already got out of hand. Taiwan showed that, even in a hyperinflation, there is some rate of interest that will divert funds from the pursuit of goods into savings. The greatest obstacle to this intelligent use of interest rates is the tendency to focus on the nominal rate of return on money and to ignore the more important real rate of return. The Taiwan government demonstrated that by giving savers a positive real rate of return, even if this necessitated setting the nominal rate at a seemingly outlandish level, it could counteract the inflationary psychosis. Thereafter the authorities were able gradually to lower the nominal rate to what is conventionally regarded as a more reasonable level, as they succeeded in absorbing excess liquidity and avoiding its creation. They wisely focused on the rates paid to savers rather than the rates charged to borrowers, to the extent of having the Bank of Taiwan at times incur losses in supporting the rates paid to savers when the banks had difficulty in finding profitable use for all the funds they were attracting. The emphasis was, therefore, on diverting funds from consumption into savings, rather than on the less popular approach of simply restraining investment. Political unpalatability was, therefore, avoided.

Savings Mobilization

Rural finance includes allocation of credit and mobilization of savings. New views on rural financial markets emphasize extending, strengthening, and promoting voluntary savings mobilization in rural areas. Several benefits are claimed for this. First, it involves voluntary action to mobilize surpluses. Other mobilization techniques, such as taxation and inflation, contain elements of coercion. Second, formal financial institutions can serve more people by mobilizing deposits than by dispensing cheap credit. Third, savings mobilization can strengthen formal financial intermediaries and reduce their dependence on governments and donors for loanable funds. Efforts to obtain loanable funds locally encourage intermediaries to be responsive to the local market. Also, successful savings mobilization can reduce political intrusions into rural financial markets.

Adams (chapter 48) shows that substantial potential exists for mobilizing voluntary savings from rural households in developing countries. Opportunities to save and interest rates giving incentives to save are key factors in developing this potential. He presents information from several Asian countries to show that relatively large savings capacities emerged in rural areas when incentives and opportunities to save were present. Adams argues that potentially large savings propensities exist even among low-income rural households. He implies that many low-income households in many countries do not save because they do not have opportunities or incentives to entrust their savings to financial institutions.

It is difficult to find comprehensive information on rural savings behavior outside Asia. Mauri (chapter 49) draws upon extensive experience in Africa with savings mobilization efforts assisted by a private Italian group. He lists some of the key ingredients in aggressive savings mobilization programs. Von Pischke (chapter 50) develops this theme and argues that much more attention ought to be given to the financial technology required to mobilize voluntary savings in rural areas. He stresses that popular misconceptions about rural savings capacities and behavior impede the development of savings mobilization programs. He demonstrates that from a financial perspective savings occur before consumption rather than being something left over after consumption.

48. *Mobilizing Household Savings through Rural Financial Markets*

Dale W Adams

[Rural household savings have been generally neglected in financial policy making and in discussions of rural development. Reasons for encouraging household savings and ways in which this could be done are outlined.]

There is general agreement that in the early stages of development most low-income countries must rely heavily on agriculture for capital. Much less agreement is found on questions about the magnitudes of agricultural savings capacity and on how surpluses can be mobilized most efficiently. Only a handful of countries have stressed mobilization of voluntary household savings through rural financial markets. Policy makers have assumed that rural households are too poor to save, and that those that do acquire additional income spend it on consumption or ceremonial sprees. It will be argued that these assumptions are incorrect, that rural households have a substantial capacity for voluntary saving, but that household savings are strongly influenced by rural financial markets that have generally tended to discourage savers.

Household Savings Decisions

Relatively little is known about rural household savings in low-income countries. Exacting data requirements, the large number of heterogeneous decision-making units involved, the complexity of the household decision-making process, and inadequate theoretical models of household savings behavior have hindered analysis. In most studies of national savings problems, household savings are ignored and emphasis is placed on government, corporate, and aggregate savings performances. Nevertheless, household savings generally

Adapted from *Economic Development and Cultural Change*, vol. 26, no. 3 (April 1978), pp. 547–60, by permission of The University of Chicago Press. also published in *Development Digest* (April 1979), pp. 12–23.

make up the largest part of aggregate savings in market-oriented economies; the U.N. Economic Commission for Asia and the Far East conducted a study of seven countries in Asia, for example, which showed that household savings made up one-half to two-thirds of total savings. Ronald I. McKinnon [*Money and Capital in Economic Development*, Washington, D.C., Brookings Institution, 1973], Edward S. Shaw [*Financial Deepening in Economic Development*, New York, Oxford University Press, 1973], U Tun Wai [*Financial Intermediaries and National Savings in Developing Countries*, New York, Praeger, 1972], and Hugh T. Patrick ["Financial Development and Economic Growth in Underdeveloped Countries," *Economic Development and Cultural Change*, vol. 14, no. 2, January 1966, pp. 174–89 (chapter 5 above)] have argued that household savings as well as aggregate savings are closely related to financial market policies. They argue that financial markets influence the forms in which savings are expressed, as well as the total amount of potential consumption which is diverted to savings.

Many studies have been done on farmers' production activities and on rural household consumption and household investment-savings activities. In most cases, however, the farm-firm (that is, the farm treated as a business firm of producers) and the consuming household are studied independently. An integrated model must include at least three interrelated sets of activities: production, consumption, and savings-investment. The production activities may be carried out not only within the farm-firm, but also in some nonfarm enterprise owned by the household or within the household itself. A complex set of consumption activities takes place simultaneously. Some of the goods consumed may be drawn directly from the farm's production. Additional goods may be purchased with owned or borrowed money, while still other consumption goods may be received in exchange for products or services. The firm-household's savings-investment activities may be fewer in number, but more complex than either production or consumption activities. The complexity is due to the uncertainties associated with the stream of future income expected from possible activities.

The dimensions of the firm-household decision-making process are easy to specify, but the interactions between the various dimensions over time are difficult to quantify when a number of changes are occurring together. For example, the effects on household decisions of a real increase in interest rates paid on financial savings are hard to sort out when household incomes move up and down, rates of return on various activities may be jumping around, and attractive new consumption goods may become available to the household; in addition, the makeup of the household may be changing.

Role of Rural Financial Markets

Rural financial markets may influence household behavior in several ways. They may augment the household's liquidity pool by providing credit. This additional liquidity allows the firm-household to use more inputs in production and may increase the net income of the household from these activities. Rural financial markets may also stimulate households to save more by offering various types of financial savings instruments; if these instruments provide positive real returns to the household, they may induce the household to convert some of its liquidity into financial savings. The rate of return realized by the household on its savings portfolio may thus induce the household to divert still more of its income to savings.

Evidence on Rural Savings Capacities

At this point, two major questions might be raised. The first is, do rural households in low-income countries have a significant savings capacity? Although sketchy and scattered, some data are available to answer this question. Findings on average propensities to save of rural households in five economies are presented below, and information on rural savings behavior from a few other economies is summarized. The second question is, how strong is the relationship between the rates of return expected on various kinds of savings, especially on financial savings, and the consumption decisions in the household? Unfortunately, little hard evidence is available on these relationships, although some findings are suggestive.

Taiwan

Recently completed studies in Taiwan provide a review of rural savings capacities. From 1953 to 1970, the real rates of interest paid on time deposits in Taiwan were negative in only two years, 1953 and 1960 (that is, the nominal interest rate paid on deposits was less than the rate of inflation). Savers could expect to receive a positive real rate of return on their time deposits of about 5 to 6 percent over most of the 1953–70 period. From 1954 to 1970 the value of financial deposits in farmers' associations increased from the equivalent of less than US$6 million to more than US$124 million. [See chapter 47 on interest rate policies in Taiwan.]

The average propensities to save (APS) shown in table 48-1 are drawn from very reliable data collected by a farm record-keeping project in Taiwan. (The APS is defined as the ratio formed by subtracting the total annual value of household consumption from total net household income, and dividing this savings value by total income.) The house-

Table 48-1. *Average Propensities to Save of Farm Record-keeping Households in Taiwan by Farm Size Group, 1960–74*

Farm size groups in hectares[a]	*1960*	*1962*	*1964*	*1966*	*1968*	*1970*	*1972*	*1974*
0.5 or less	−0.03	0.09	0.09	0.19	0.19	0.15	0.19	0.17
0.5–1.0	0.15	0.17	0.22	0.16	0.23	0.14	0.16	0.26
1.0–1.5	0.14	0.20	0.27	0.25	0.25	0.20	0.16	0.31
2.0 or more	0.27	0.25	0.29	0.38	0.36	0.26	0.32	0.39
Average all households	0.19	0.21	0.23	0.28	0.28	0.20	0.23	0.31
Total number of households	95	233	535	430	416	404	452	461

Note: The average propensity to save is equal to one minus the ratio of total household consumption to total net household income.

a. One hectare equals 2.47 acres.

Source: Provincial Government of Taiwan, Department of Agriculture and Forestry, *Report of Farm Record-keeping Families in Taiwan* (Nantou, various years, 1960–74).

holds included in the project have incomes and farm sizes somewhat larger than average for Taiwan, though they are small farmers by the standards of most other countries. However, all consumer durables and expenditures on health and education were defined as current consumption rather than investment. The APS for all households ranged from 0.19 to 0.31 over the 1960–74 period. The APS among even the smallest farm size groups were large. Additional analysis of these farm records indicated that savings were related to changes in the rates of return on farm assets; households saved more when they had profitable investment possibilities.

Japan

Although no longer a low-income country, Japan's rural household data do provide insights into savings behavior of small-farm households. Since the early 1920s, agricultural cooperatives in Japan have mobilized financial savings well in excess of the amount of agricultural loans extended by the cooperatives. A large part of these excess funds moved out of the rural sector through financial markets. [See chaper 3 for a review of the role of cooperatives in this process.] Postwar data collected annually by the Japanese Farm Household Economy Survey can be used to calculate the APS. The APS for the average household from 1950 to 1973 increased from 0.10 to 0.22. After 1960 the savings of households with very small farms increased even more markedly to reach equivalence with other groups, in part because of their rapid increase in household income from off-farm sources. Because of the survey techniques used, household incomes were probably underreported, and as a result, estimates of actual household savings capacities are conservative. Other household studies of rural consumption and savings in Japan show, without exception, that rural households in Japan have had high average as well as marginal propensities to save, and that incentives played an important role in stimulating these savings.

Republic of Korea

In September 1965 the Korean Monetary Board approximately doubled the rates of interest applied to loans and time deposits. Nominal interest rates on time deposits were raised to 30 percent. As a result, real rates of interest in excess of 8 percent were paid on financial savings from 1965 to 1971. This financial reform resulted in large increases in financial savings; total time and savings deposits in all banks jumped from only W39,000 million in 1964 to W566,000 million in 1968. Financial deposits in agricultural cooperatives increased at about the same rate, and the number of savings accounts also increased sharply during this period. [See chapter 34 on savings and agricultural cooperatives in Korea.]

The data in table 48-2 are drawn from annual farm household surveys carried out by the Ministry of Agriculture and Fisheries. The average APS for all households rose from 0.04 in 1965 to 0.33 in 1974. As in the Taiwan and Japanese data, the APS among households with small farms were surprisingly large. It is particularly noteworthy that the APS increased substantially from 1965 to 1974. Part of this increase was undoubtedly due to expanded incomes and to farm policies that increased the returns to on-farm investments, while part was due to the more attractive incentives provided by financial markets.

Malaysia

A cross-sectional study of household savings activities in the mid-1960s in West Malaysia provides some additional evidence of rural savings capacities. (Lee Hock Lock, "Household Saving in West Malaysia and the Problem of Financing Economic Development," Faculty of Economics and Administration, University of Malaya, Kuala Lumpur, 1971, pp. 54–57.) Approximately 60 percent of the 5,147 households surveyed were in rural areas. Although the survey techniques used probably resulted in underreporting of incomes, the APS calculated suggest that significant savings capacity exists among the surveyed rural households, and that savings rates increase rapidly among farm operators and fishermen as their incomes increase.

Table 48-2. *The Average Propensity to Save in Korean Farm Household Economy Survey by Farm Size Group, 1962–74*

Farm size groups in cheongbo[a]	*1962*	*1965*	*1966*	*1968*	*1970*	*1972*	*1974*
0.5 or less	0.05	−0.05	0.01	0.06	0.03	0.02	0.22
0.5–1.0	0.12	0.01	0.09	0.11	0.13	0.21	0.29
1.0–1.5	0.16	0.06	0.10	0.20	0.16	0.34	0.35
1.5–2.0	0.15	0.12	0.13	0.23	0.26	0.30	0.43
2.0 or more	0.22	0.13	0.23	0.24	0.19	0.30	0.40
Average all households	0.15	0.04	0.11	0.16	0.15	0.24	0.33
Total number of households	1,163	1,172	1,180	1,181	1,180	1,182	2,515

Note: The average propensity to save equals total farm household net surplus/total net disposable income.

a. One cheongbo equals 0.992 hectares or 2.45 acres.

Source: Republic of Korea, Ministry of Agriculture and Fisheries, *Report of the Results of Farm Household Economy Survey* (Seoul, various years, 1962–75).

India

A large number of the studies on rural savings have been done in India. In general, they show smaller savings capacities than noted for Taiwan, Japan, and Korea. This is due, in part, to lower per capita incomes in rural areas of India. One might also argue that rural people in India have fewer incentives to save; on-farm investments in many areas yield low returns, and badly fragmented financial markets may not offer savers attractive rates of return. Nevertheless, a study of 180 farm households in two districts in the Punjab area during 1966–70 show that savings capacities expanded rapidly there in the late 1960s. (A. S. Kahlon and Harbhajan Singh Bal, "Factors Associated with Farm and Farm Family Investment Pattern in Ludhiana [Punjab] and Hissar [Haryana] Districts, 1966–67 through 1969–70," Department of Economics and Sociology, Punjab Agricultural University, Ludhiana, 1971, p. 116.) These are prosperous areas which benefited substantially from changes in agricultural technology during the late 1960s. The average annual household savings ranged from 12 to 37 percent of its income. In some years, savings capacities among even the smallest farm size groups were quite high (over 30 percent on average). On the basis of household-level studies in another state of India, B. M. Desai and D. K. Desai found substantial savings in households experiencing income increases ["Potentialities for Mobilizing Investible Funds in Developing Agriculture," manuscript, Ahmedabad, Centre for Management in Agriculture, Indian Institute of Management, 1971]; they report marginal propensities to save of 0.29 and 0.63 for two groups of rural households.

Advantages from Mobilization of Voluntary Rural Savings

At this point, a skeptic might argue that, even if some voluntary savings potentials do exist in rural areas, they are too costly to mobilize via financial markets and that other resource mobilization techniques are more efficient. There are at least three strong reasons for stressing voluntary rural financial savings. The first reason is that they may be important to the overall strengthening of rural financial markets. Until recently, most economists assumed that financial markets played a neutral or minor role in development, but this view has been strongly challenged.

A second reason is that mobilization of financial savings could play an important part in strengthening local farm credit and service organizations. For years, many developing countries have tried to bridge the "institution gap" in rural areas between national service organizations and the individual farmer by building cooperatives and farmers' associations. Despite some success in a few countries, the experience with building these intermediate credit organizations has been disappointing. Typically, their loans have been offered to members at low rates of interest.

These concessionary interest rates weaken the intermediate organization in several ways. Low interest rates force intermediate organizations to ration their "bargain credit," and these nonmarket rationing decisions are highly vulnerable to various types of personal influence, political persuasion, and outright corruption. In addition, concessionary interest rates on credit almost always force an intermediate organization to concentrate its loans in the hands of relatively few borrowers in order to minimize lending costs. The lament that the large farmers capture most of the concessionally priced cooperative credit can be heard around the world. Further, low interest rates that do not cover the costs of lending make it next to impossible for intermediate organizations to maintain, let alone expand, the real value of their loanable funds. This capital erosion is exacerbated by inflation, which also undermines the ability of credit organizations to offer sufficient interest-rate incentives to induce members to deposit funds voluntarily in their organization. Cooperatives and farmers' associations must therefore live the uncertain life of a beggar, dependent on central banks or foreign aid agencies. Mobilization of voluntary savings, however, could allow these intermediate organizations to develop a much larger degree of independence and self-sufficiency.

A third reason for mobilizing financial savings is the favorable impact it can have in discouraging household consumption. The incentives to save provided by financial markets offering attractive returns on their assets can be strong inducements for households to defer consumption.

A Savings Mobilization Strategy

If financial markets are to play a positive role in countering rural poverty, fundamental changes in policies will be necessary in most low-income countries. Current policies result in badly fragmented financial markets, in the concentration of concessionally priced credit in the hands of relatively few people, in unprofitable financial operations in many rural cooperatives, and in little or no incentive for rural households to defer consumption. Overall, these financial policies are very regressive: the relatively well-off benefit from the concessionally priced credit, and the poor are denied access to production credit as well as remunerative savings instruments. More rational financial market policies, combined with aggressive savings mobilization programs, would eliminate many of these undesirable features.

Some changes must be made at the national level before substantial voluntary savings can be mobilized. In general, these changes include a more flexible interest rate structure. Where inflation is above 20 percent a year, savings instruments might be value-linked to price changes. Legal changes so that cooperatives and other organizations can handle credit and savings activities are often necessary. Nationwide deposit insurance programs can also help assure savers of secure deposits.

At this point, it might be objected that raising interest rates is great in theory but politically impossible to carry out. Some politicians view concessionary credit as a way of buying political support. But cheap credit policies lead to cheap savings policies, and only those who receive cheap credit benefit. More votes could be positively influenced by high rates of return on savings deposits, which will make credit more widely available, than by concessionary credit given to only a few.

The exact makeup of savings mobilization programs will vary from area to area. In some countries new institutions are needed, in others existing ones could expand their clientele. In some cases, various types of nonvoluntary savings programs may be appropriate: requiring share purchases in an organization, compensatory balances, regular contractual savings, or even the deposit of cash receipts in an unblocked savings account might be stressed in the start-up phase of a savings mobilization program. The mobilization effort, however, should begin early to stress voluntary savings incentives; the Taiwan, Korean, and Japanese experiences suggest that voluntary savings should make up the bulk of the savings mobilized. The key element in a voluntary mobilization program is the attractiveness of the reward paid on savings, along with the convenience, liquidity, and security of the savings.

Any savings mobilization effort will work better in conjunction with rapid agricultural growth and increasing rural incomes. A national savings program should, therefore, initially stress savings promotion in areas where agriculture is on the move. Above all, the program should be strongly supported and promoted by government actions.

In general, "development from below" appears to be the only way to reach the rural poor effectively. The savings programs briefly outlined above might be a first step in a bootstrap approach to rural development in low-income countries. It would stimulate the rural poor to increase their own capital base, it would provide a more healthy environment for local organizations to grow, and it would allow local financial institutions to integrate into national financial markets. Current financial market policies in most developing countries are an unmitigated disaster for most rural poor. It is past time for making policy adjustments so that rural poor are more fairly treated by this most important development instrument.

49. *A Policy to Mobilize Rural Savings in Developing Countries*

Arnaldo Mauri

[Mobilization of voluntary personal savings in rural areas permits increased capital accumulation in agriculture and helps develop the spirit of enterprise. Savings mobilization requires a system of financial intermediaries and cooperatives at the grass roots. Savers must have a wide choice of safe financial assets offering attractive returns. Contractual savings arrangements play a role in rural areas and should be considered in the design of new institutional services for small savers. Positive real interest rates can be an important factor in savings mobilization.]

Agricultural development in developing countries involves an increasing use of capital resources that have to come largely from sources within the countries themselves. Domestic savings are classified as public savings, business or corporate savings, and personal or household savings. The formation of public savings falls within the decision-making sphere of central or local government and governmental agencies, while business savings decisions are made by top management and entrepreneurs. In personal savings, only a fraction of what is actually saved derives from a deliberate decision to save; the rest may be considered as residual nonconsumed income.

Too Little Rural Savings and Agricultural Investment

To some extent public and business savings can be channeled into investments for agricultural development. But since these savings are generated by reducing the disposable income of farmers through taxation or by pushing up prices for agricultural inputs and keeping down prices for outputs, the net inflow of capital to rural areas from these sources is probably less than it appears to be in official figures. Furthermore, no substantial flow of personal savings formed in urban

Adapted from *Savings and Development*, no. 1 (1977), pp. 14–25.

areas can be expected to gravitate into investments in farming because more attractive opportunities are offered in other sectors of the economy or in foreign countries. Consequently, agricultural investments have to rely chiefly on what is saved by rural households themselves.

The general view, influenced by official statistics on income per capita in developing countries and by estimates of rural incomes in these countries, is that it is very doubtful whether these households can save. Closer analysis shows, however, that the rural areas of these countries do have substantial savings capacity. Here it is important to note that the use of exchange rates in international comparisons introduces distortions, as do underestimations of the contribution of a subsistence economy to GNP. Furthermore, the savings threshold—that is, the minimum income level above which savings can occur—is generally much lower in developing countries than in industrialized countries, and lower in the countryside than in cities. Factors responsible for this include climatic conditions (which permit less expenditure for housing, heating, clothing, and food), thrifty habits, and the absence of many consumer goods and the demonstration effect of affluent consumption. These conclusions are based on evidence that in rural areas of developing countries part of the disposable income of the household sector is removed from consumption. Hoarding, that is, nonmobilized saving, is very common there. Real assets such as jewelry and precious metals, cattle, and durable goods of various kinds are hoarded. The extent of hoarding is a measure of the gap between what is productively invested and what could be invested without substantially changing consumption patterns.

Where the economy is already monetized to a certain degree and farms produce cash crops in addition to subsistence crops, a surplus in money may emerge. This is not enough to trigger the savings mobilization process, for the simple reason that money itself can be hoarded. Hoarding national currency is less deleterious than hoarding physical assets or foreign currency, since it does not necessarily immobilize real productive resources. Even so, it does not stimulate agricultural development.

Setting up banking facilities to collect savings and, more generally, financial outlets in rural areas will have a significant impact on savings mobilization. It will not only enable savings to be properly invested which would otherwise have been kept idle and sterile, but will also encourage farmers to save or to save more. The presence of branches of financial institutions in rural areas does not, however, guarantee that farmers' savings will be mobilized in favor of agricultural development. Commercial banks are not greatly interested in attracting small savings accounts, because they are troublesome and costly to handle. Even in countries where the bulk of GNP is generated by farming, it is not uncommon to find commercial banks making available only 5 to 10 percent of their total lending to the agricultural sector. Within this small percentage, most of the funds are lent to big farmers, plantations, and agricultural marketing firms. [See chapter 16.]

The behavior of commercial banks can easily be explained: they are traditionally concerned with short-term and low-risk lending transactions based on well-proved "sound banking principles"—quite different from the technical features of agricultural credit in developing countries. By following this lending policy they cause savings to flow from rural to urban areas. Post office savings banks have the same effect, albeit by a different route, when their branches act simply as collecting points for savings, which are legally required to be invested in government securities or deposited with the treasury.

Methods of Mobilizing Rural Savings

Policy makers in developing countries should develop and implement suitable measures to mobilize savings in rural areas. Some measures, such as reforming the land tenure system or setting up proper infrastructure in rural areas, are steps to increase the proportion of cash crops in the small-farm sector. Similarly, governments should supply agricultural inputs on terms that are not too onerous, set up efficient marketing channels for agricultural outputs, and provide extension services to small farmers. They should also create a financial institutional apparatus with a widespread branch network to collect household savings in rural areas and plow back into agriculture the resources raised.

An efficient mechanism for capital mobilization in rural districts of developing countries would assemble savings that would otherwise be fruitlessly hoarded or siphoned off elsewhere, and it would also stimulate new savings. In the short term, it would enhance the propensity to save; in the medium and long term, additional rural investments would generate an increase in income that would provide a further impetus to the accumulation of savings. It should be stressed that financial institutions that collect rural savings must be the same as those that provide small farmers with loans. In theory many types of financial intermediary might undertake these functions. From practical experience, however, only a few types have specific competence in this field. These include savings and credit banks, agricultural banks, credit unions, rural banks, and cooperative bodies for agriculture in general. Savings and credit banks in several European countries were extensively engaged in this field before the beginning of this century.

A special kind of financial apparatus for agriculture should be built in developing countries. This apparatus should take the form of a combination of financial intermediaries, with cooperative bodies representing the base of the pyramid and a savings and credit bank or some other suitable institution representing its apex. Where such an apex institution does not exist, its role could initially be played by an agricultural development department in the central bank.

This kind of financial structure has the advantages of a high degree of flexibility and a widespread branch network for both collecting deposits and granting loans without high administrative costs. Clearly a synergetic effect could be achieved with the adoption of the measures listed above, particularly in bringing innovations into marketing mechanisms for agricultural inputs and outputs and establishing adequate extension services.

Ways and means of promoting and attracting household savings in rural districts of developing countries should be worked out and should take into account the requirements, habits, and motivations of small farmers. Only when detailed information on the particular local situation has been gathered and considerable familiarity with the problems involved has been gained, can a suitable combination of measures be devised. The launching of savings campaigns is likely to include educating the population to save, especially in schools, and testing and applying various kinds of incentives.

On a technical level, a broad variety of financial instruments should be brought into play to attract a wide range of savers and to induce each saver to deposit the maximum amount of money. Terms and conditions of financial assets offered should be suitably diversified. This diversification should be reflected in interest rates and in various monetary as well as nonmonetary returns and rewards. The return on financial instruments should vary inversely with their degree of liquidity.

Interest Rates

The level of interest rates is controversial, since much of the economic literature does not identify any clear and significant causal link between the level of interest rates and accumulation of savings. The monetary and banking authorities and the managements of financial institutions in many developing countries have tended to accept this viewpoint and have subordinated savings mobilization to other considerations. This has led to cheap money policies to keep down the cost of capital for government and private business and thereby provide an incentive for investment. As a result, rural financial savings earn the lowest rates.

Because of widespread inflation, the outcome in many cases has been negative real interest rates on deposits in many organized capital markets. Apart from the ethical and social implications of these policies, which tend to impoverish small savers and cause unfair redistribution of income, there are objections on economic grounds. In practice, these policies inevitably encourage hoarding, lead to suboptimal allocation of resources, and do not contribute to economic growth. Yet recent empirical surveys of rural districts in selected developing countries demonstrate that the level of interest rates has a positive impact on the mobilization of savings. This suggests that conventional views on this matter need to be reconsidered and more realistic policies adopted with regard to the returns available on financial savings.

Security of Savings

The security of savings deposited merits separate consideration. Security is a basic requirement common to all savers. No kind of reward or incentive will be effective unless savers have total confidence in the financial institution in which their money is deposited. Appropriate rules and arrangements must thus be devised to protect depositors against frauds and bankruptcies.

Inflation

The problem of inflation is different, though it sometimes leads to the same consequences for the saver. Inflation causes financial savings to lose their purchasing power. Inflation might have little influence on savers in a peasant community at the initial stage, but once the destructive effects of inflation have been understood, savings that lose value will not remain in an institution. Even if inflation is accepted as an inescapable condition of economic life, positive real rates of interest are needed to promote savings. This could be achieved, for example, by introducing some form of indexation for financial savings.

Contractual Savings

In addition to voluntary savings in rural households already discussed, there are contractual savings, whereby a saver voluntarily enters into a commitment to make a predetermined series of payments at certain dates and on certain terms.

The most common forms of contractual savings are life insurance and savings schemes for housing, but neither are of great significance in rural areas of developing countries. It is improbable that life insurance will catch on outside towns where regular wage earners live, and insurance companies are unlikely to invest in rural areas. Savings schemes for housing might be more successful than life insurance in developing countries, but they too are likely to be more popular in urban areas. It would be advisable to devise other kinds of contractual savings more closely tailored to the needs and habits of peasant societies. For example, it might be possible to link savings to the attainment of specific goals for the farm family. Financial institutions that collect deposits at periodic intervals would be prepared to grant loans on given terms for specific objectives such as the purchase of capital goods. Credit could also be distributed to farmers on the basis of their savings deposit balances.

Contractual savings also include the collection of money by indigenous savings associations in many countries in Africa and Asia. The best-known type is the rotating savings and credit association in which all members make regular payments to a common fund, from which each withdraws money in turn. Members make a free choice when they join the association, and their subsequent payments constitute obligations. [See chapter 30 on these associations.]

Compulsory Savings

Compulsory savings are accumulated irrespective of the saver's will, but more or less to his advantage. The most common kinds of compulsory personal or household savings relate to compulsory life insurance policies and pension schemes, in many cases based on deduction at source from wages and other types of income, or social security schemes in the most general sense. In rural areas compulsory savings may be implemented through the control of crop marketing channels by price manipulation. In some cases even more drastic measures have been used, such as unremunerated forced labor and expropriation of produce. Compulsory savings can sometimes play a useful complementary role, but they can hardly be used as the sole way of generating savings.

Conclusions

The promotion and the mobilization of voluntary household savings in rural areas of developing countries is a crucial issue for two reasons. First, voluntary savings enable more rapid accumulation of real capital in agriculture. Second, the challenge presented by a voluntary decision to save helps engender and develop an entrepreneurial spirit. In effect, voluntary personal savings in themselves constitute a useful educational device to bring farmers more closely into a cash economy and instill sound principles of money management. Much still remains to be done in this field. Positive experience of well-conceived ventures in some developing countries, which lend themselves to adoption elsewhere, holds promise for favorable developments in the future.

50. *Toward an Operational Approach to Savings for Rural Developers*

J. D. Von Pischke

[The poor people who make up the majority of rural inhabitants in developing countries are often viewed as being unable to save because of their poverty. In fact, they can and do save. The task of institutionalizing some of these rural savings is primarily a question of financial technology, that is, of finding ways to provide the financial services that rural savers want and will respond to.]

Saving is necessary to finance; assets accumulated through saving are commonly used to finance future consumption or investment. The relationship between savings and finance is most clearly seen in the function or role of finance. As stated by F. W. Paish [*Business Finance*, London, Pitman, 1957, p. 5]: "Probably the only living creatures which do not require any form of finance are those for whom the enjoyment of the fruits of their efforts to obtain food is simultaneous with the making of the efforts. For all other creatures there is some interval of time between efforts and enjoyment, and it is for the provision of the means of existence during this interval that we need finance." So, finance is necessary for human survival. The existence of intervals between the realization of income and the act of expenditure is normal and virtually universal. Thus, almost everyone saves.

E. L. Furness [*An Introduction to Financial Economics*, London, Heinemann, 1972, p. 9] lists four reasons that flows of receipts and flows of payments may have differing time patterns:

• Payment for a continuous service on a continuous basis is frequently inconvenient for both buyers and sellers. Convenience favors periodic settlement. For example, riders on public transport are charged once for the journey, not once per kilometer or meter

Adapted from *Savings and Development*, vol. 2, no. 1 (1978), pp. 43–55; also published in *Development Digest* (April 1979), pp. 3–11.

traveled, which would be inconvenient to the point of being impractical. Electric bills are sent once a month.

• Many commodities are characterized by indivisibilities. They are costly in relation to income earned over a short period, and their purchase requires a buildup of wealth or payment out of expected future income. To use a rural example, the purchase of a cow or a tractor requires much more funds than do everyday transactions in the rural economy. Large purchases are financed by savings and perhaps by credit.

• Income flows vary over life cycles. For individuals, savings accumulation in the economically most productive years or periods of life is a rational response to the probability of diminished real income in the future because of illness, old age, or uncertainty of employment.

• Time periods required for production may not coincide with the time periods applicable to producers' consumption and other needs. Most methods of production involve long gestation periods between the start of the production process and the sale of the finished goods. These periods must be financed so that shorter consuming cycles may continue. Workers are paid on a weekly or daily basis in industry to accommodate them as consumers, regardless of industry's cycles of production. In an agricultural economy harvests occur once or twice a year, while consumption of agricultural produce occurs continuously.

These examples show that abstention from consumption is a normal characteristic of economic activity; and rather than being something left over after expenditure, saving commonly precedes expenditure. Abstention may be for only a very short period: a worker in the city receives his pay on a Friday afternoon and that evening uses part of his pay to take a bus back to his village—he does not spend the bus fare money the instant it is received. Economists have not specified what the minimum holding period must be for funds not spent to be considered as having been saved. The usual convention in economic analysis is to treat funds carried over from one period to the next as savings, and economists fix the length of time to suit the purposes of their analysis. But in principle any income not disbursed the instant it is received may be regarded as saved until such time as it is disbursed.

The argument presented here is not concerned with the purpose for which funds are eventually spent. The economic definition of saving as abstention from consumption does not specify the reasons for saving. In financial terms, funds saved for the eventual purchase of beer are no different from funds saved for protection against sickness or disability. Money is fungible, which means that one unit of the national currency has the same essential properties as every other unit. It can be misleading to say that money received from a particular source is used for particular expenditures only. [See chapter 8.]

Toward a Concept of Savings Appropriate for Rural Development

The concept of saving outlined here is direct and uncomplicated. It does not get bogged down in disputes over the period of time or the purpose for which funds are held. Its only requirement is that funds be held. It is obvious, however, that funds are held for some reason, and this reason is normally related to the ultimate use of the funds. Saving is, after all, a means to an end, and the ultimate reason for all economic activity is consumption. Consumption usually involves a prior investment of some kind, and investment may be defined for this purpose as behavior in the present (or past) which is (was) designed to increase future production. Only through increased future production can there be sustained increases in future consumption.

The largest share of an individual's monetary income is commonly spent for the purchase of goods and services for consumption. However, a portion of consumers' monetary income is commonly devoted to investment in new real or tangible goods, such as new tractors and houses, or for services leading to future production.

Money may also be used for investment in financial assets. These assets are claims, evidencing debt or ownership. Debt claims include savings accounts, which are a claim by deposit holders on a bank, post office, cooperative, or similar institution. Shares in cooperative societies and company shares or stocks are common forms of ownership claims.

Money is also used for working cash balances, held primarily for convenience. Money is required to pay for daily purchases; many people keep a little additional money on hand to offer some protection in times of hardship or unexpected events. From the standpoint of its owner, some money is temporarily idle or stranded in the flow of economic activity because it is being held for future use. Working balances are clearly savings because they represent abstention from consumption. The "institutionalization" of working balances involves their conversion from cash into debt claims, such as deposits with financial institutions.

Financial Technology Determines the Role of the Financial Sector

The financial sector is composed of institutions which specialize in creating and processing financial assets. The manner in which the financial sector creates and processes money is broadly referred to as financial technology. The provision of the means of payment includes issuing currency and coin, as well as facilitating transactions between buyers and sellers who do not deal face to face but at a distance, through some medium of communication, and who use checks and other transactions on bank accounts as a means of payment. A more interesting function of the financial sector is the manner in which it transforms claims by serving as an intermediary dealing in claims. For example, cash deposited with a credit union is transformed into the depositors' claims on the credit union; the credit union further transforms these resources into loans to its members, into deposits with a commercial bank, or perhaps into government securities.

Financial institutions tend to be somewhat specialized. In financial terms, specialization is reflected in different types of debt claims issued or purchased. Debt claims exhibit a variety of maturities, rates of interest, minimum denominations, and other characteristics such as negotiability which influence their liquidity—that is, the ease and speed with which they can be converted into cash. These differences determine the level of access rural people may have to financial markets. If minimum balance requirements are large in relation to the daily income of agricultural laborers, for example, they commonly exclude agricultural laborers from the ranks of savings account holders, since workers may not wish to tie up several days' wages in this sort of debt claim on a savings institution.

From the perspective of a saver, the attractiveness of debt claims and other institutional alternatives to holding cash depends on the financial technology involved. Little progress can be expected in bringing the savings—that is, working balances—of rural people into the formal financial system as deposits until appropriate financial technologies are devised. The product of any financial technology must also be properly packaged to be acceptable by rural people. The nature of the most appropriate packages of rural financial services would vary from one area to another because of different underlying patterns of cash flow, but some tentative observations may be stated.

The supply side of rural savings rests on the situation of the target group of depositors: under which circumstances are they most likely to entrust their savings to intermediaries in the financial sector? The demand side of rural savings involves the efforts of financial intermediaries to market their services to rural people. What sort of services are likely to appeal to rural people sufficiently to make them institutionalize some portion of their working balances? It appears reasonable to assume that deposit accounts are most likely to be used under the following conditions:

- When cash flows of the target group are growing. Growth may reflect increasing monetization of the rural economy, as well as increasing production by the target group for the market.

• When target group income is "lumpy," not spread evenly over time.

• When intermediaries operate offices that are convenient for rural people—for example, by being near the market and open on market days.

• When deposits can be made with an intermediary that provides other financial services. One such service is the provision of money transfer facilities. Linking credit access to the existence of a deposit relationship with the borrower or prospective borrower is a useful device. It gives the potential borrower greater incentive to accumulate deposit balances, and it reduces the lender's risk because savings accounts may be used to secure loans and because the lender acquires more knowledge of his customers by dealing with them as depositors than he would if they were only borrowers.

• When deposits can be made in connection with nonfinancial services, such as the purchase of cash crops. Payment for crops presents an opportunity for intermediation because the buyer could establish an account payable on his books in favor of the farmer. This account could be transformed into a financial service for the farmer simply by allowing the farmer to withdraw balances in his favor as he wishes, rather than by obliging him to accept the whole of his delivery proceeds in cash.

• When minimum transaction and balance limits are not too large in relation to the size of daily rural financial transactions by the target group.

• When the fees, charges, and other costs of access to savings facilities are reasonable in relation to the amounts of savings involved in the average transaction.

• When the intermediary expands the opportunities available to the target group. A new intermediary is unlikely to be successful in attracting deposits simply by duplicating existing channels or services, especially when the costs of dealing with him are higher than those of dealing with existing intermediaries offering more or less the same financial and other services.

• When deposit services are operated by intermediaries capable of planning, promotion, implementation, and control.

• When the intermediary enjoys the confidence of depositors. Although some government involvement may help create confidence, too much government presence may undermine confidence through fear of tax assessments or loss of confidentiality. Confidence almost always requires voluntary participation on the part of depositors.

Interest Rates and the Mobilization of Small-scale Deposits

In rural areas where most members of the target group do not have deposit accounts, people will initially be more responsive to improved services and access than to higher interest rates alone. The potential advantage for rural people of financial services depends on their safety and liquidity. The alternative to a deposit account may be to keep money in a hole in the ground, the rafters of a house, a tin can, or a mattress. At the early stage of financial development, the marketing challenge consists of providing the target group a better means of handling their working balances and reducing the costs of maintaining liquidity in the form of working balances. These costs tend to overwhelm interest rate considerations in small-scale finance, so that convenience is the paramount issue. Since some working balances are normally held, the question is largely that of designing services which will result in their institutionalization.

Any intermediary that hopes to be competitive in rural areas must be sensitive to the service mix most suitable for stimulating the institutionalization of small balances. In certain situations it might be unwise to appear to be "discriminating" against small savers by offering them different sorts of accounts or lower rates of interest than larger depositors, in spite of the relatively higher overhead costs of servicing small accounts. In most cases, however, many of those currently without access to financial services would probably respond favorably to an innovative savings medium designed specifically to support and facilitate their savings behavior, but with sufficiently low interest payments to be commercially attractive to the intermediary.

This treatment of interest rates is intended only for the narrow context of this discussion. At the national level there is increasing evidence that interest rates play extremely important and usually underestimated roles in resource mobilization, investment decision making, determination of the level of liquidity in the economy, and in the structure and role of the financial sector. Problems of this nature, however, do not commonly occupy the attention of the managers of financial intermediaries who live within financial regulation as they find it. The competitive lender will be conscious of the use of interest rates both to attract rural depositors and to produce revenue. Net earnings from interest and other income can provide resources for reinvestment in the intermediary's business; intermediaries could expand effective rural access to financial services by expanding the range of services available. This means, in effect, expanding the financial choices of the target group.

Perspective and Implications

For rural developers and others concerned with rural welfare in developing countries, perhaps the most important philosophical implication of the argument presented here is that it is not very helpful to view rural people as financial basket cases, as merely "poor." Rather, it is obvious that rural people do save and that the development challenge lies in the design of financial technology to serve the savings needs of rural people. The packages of financial services that will permit more effective rural access to formal institutional financial markets needs to be explored. Rural people and rural savings should be seen as a marketing challenge. Rural developers will have success in institutionalizing rural working balances when they can design financial services that rural people find more beneficial than existing alternatives.

Recommendations for Further Reading

Agrawal, Ramesh Chandra. "An Analysis of the Contribution of Nationalized Banks in Financing Indian Agriculture." *Zeitschrift für Ausländische Landwirtschaft*, vol. 14 (1975), pp. 144–58.

Bangladesh Bank. *Problems and Issues of Agricultural Credit and Rural Finance*. Dhaka, 1979.

Boulding, Kenneth E., and Thomas Frederick Wilson, eds. *Redistribution through the Financial System: The Grants Economics of Money and Credit*. New York: Praeger, 1978.

Desai, B. M. "Rural Banking in India: Its Performance and Problems." *Prajnan*, vol. 8, no. 2 (April/June 1979), pp. 113–34.

Donald, Gordon. *Credit for Small Farmers in Developing Countries*. Boulder, Colo.: Westview, 1976.

Fry, Maxwell J. "The Cost of Financial Repression in Turkey." *Savings and Development*, vol. 3, no. 2 (1979), pp. 127–35.

Galbis, Vicente. "Inflation and Interest Rate Policies in Latin America." *International Monetary Fund Staff Papers*, vol. 26 (1979), pp. 334–66.

Gonzales-Vega, Claudio. "Interest Rate Restrictions and Income Distribution." *American Journal of Agricultural Economics*, vol. 59, no. 5 (December 1977), pp. 973–76.

Hammond, Bray. *Banks and Politics in America: From the Revolution to the Civil War*. Princeton, N. J.: Princeton University Press, 1957.

Homer, Sidney. *History of Interest Rates*. 2nd ed. New Brunswick, N. J.: Rutgers University Press, 1977.

Howell, John, ed. *Borrowers and Lenders: Rural Financial Markets and Institutions in Developing Countries*. London: Overseas Development Institute, 1980.

Kane, Edward J. "Short Changing the Small Saver: Federal Government Discrimination against Small Savers during the Vietnam War." *Journal of Money, Credit, and Banking*, vol. 2 (1970), pp. 513–22.

Kratoska, Paul H. "The Chethar and the Yeoman." Institute of Southeast Asian Studies Occasional Paper no. 2. Singapore, June 1975.

Myint, H. "Financial Dualism and Monetary Dependence and Independence." *The Economics of the Developing Countries*. 3rd ed. London: Hutchinson, 1967.

Reynolds, Clark W., and Jaime I. Corredor. "The Effects of the Financial System on the Distribution of Income and Wealth in Mexico." *Food Research Institute Studies*, vol. 15 (1976), pp. 71–89.

Issues for Discussion

1. How do financial intermediaries evade the intent of credit controls?
2. Do nationalized banks behave differently than private banks?
3. Are the short-run results of credit controls and other regulations on financial intermediaries different from their longer-run impact?
4. Why are agricultural credit projects so popular with donor agencies?
5. Why are agricultural credit projects a popular political tool?
6. Why do the local elite often take over the operations of credit cooperatives?
7. Can interest rates be used as instruments of equity and social justice? Is there evidence of success in this endeavor?
8. What level of interest rate on loans is necessary to ensure survival of unsubsidized institutions lending to small rural borrowers?
9. What are the principal obstacles to interest rate reforms? How can they be most effectively overcome?
10. What are the principal requirements for mobilizing rural savings?
11. Is reliance on contractual or required saving justified to augment voluntary saving? Are there ways of forcing people to save that will strengthen voluntary savings habits?
12. What national policies undermine the performance of rural financial markets?
13. How can a political system use financial markets to reward certain groups?
14. To a banker, there is no such thing as "savings," but only deposit accounts having different rates of turnover. Is this view valid? Does it provide insight into savings behavior and opportunities to assist the development of the rural economy?
15. Is there one ideal form of rural financial intermediary?

PART VII

SUMMARY

Rural financial markets is a term that evolved among those who have developed a new perspective on farm credit and rural finance in low-income countries. The main purpose of this book is to outline this approach and to suggest how it applies to farmers, to those lending to farmers, and to national development policies and how it relates to the overall function of finance in development. While challenging many traditional views and policies, the thrust of the new thinking is toward eliminating barriers and constraints commonly found in rural financial markets so that these markets can function more efficiently and equitably. These concluding comments attempt to summarize the new consensus and discuss the concepts on which it is based.

Financial Behavior of Farm Households and Nonfarm Rural Firms

Most rural credit programs are justified and evaluated on the basis of changes in the operations of borrowers' farms or firms which are attributed to credit use. It is very difficult, however, to know what happens in borrowing households and firms as a result of loans. Formal loans, informal loans, and money in general are fungible; these claims on real resources can be used to buy any good or service available in the market. To identify the impact of a loan requires comprehensive information on all sources and uses of these claims in borrowing households or firms. Estimates of what would have been done without the loan are also required to identify the incremental activity associated with the loan. Even if theoretically possible, this task is time consuming, costly, and in any case virtually never done. Rural credit programs must therefore be evaluated and justified on other bases.

Development economists have learned enough about farmers and entrepreneurs in low-income countries to understand that they generally respond rationally to changes in prices of inputs and outputs, and in investment opportunities. Nevertheless, many policies are still based on the assumption that rural people are foolish or naive when it comes to finance. For example, it is widely assumed that farmers will not save in financial form, that they are not sensitive to the rates of return on financial investments, and that they will not use formal loans for productive purposes unless these loans are provided at low rates of interest and accompanied by close supervision. In effect, these views imply that farmers do not know how much or why they ought to save or borrow, and that these decisions should be made by public officials, development planners, or technicians.

The performance of many credit delivery systems established under the influence of these views is unsatisfactory. It appears that the designers of these systems overlooked the possibility that borrowers are sensitive to the type of treatment they receive from the staff of the credit agency, that they are disturbed by a loan that arrives several weeks or months after the time it was desired to finance planting activities, and that technical packages and supervision are not sufficient to build confidence between borrowers and lenders. Furthermore, certain officials seem to believe that the irrationality of farmers is demonstrated by their willingness to take loans from "evil" informal lenders.

Many authors in this volume, however, assert that farmers in developing countries are rational in their use of financial markets. This conclusion has important implications for the way rural financial market interventions are designed. It strongly suggests that supply-led strategies for rural development ought to be deemphasized. Rather than merely increasing the supply of loanable funds, attention should be directed toward improving the range and quality of rural financial services. In particular, deposit facilities should be provided for small savers. This service is not handled well in informal financial markets and is outside the scope of the typical credit program.

Rural financial market interventions pursued solely on the lending side of that market imply that all farmers need loans every year for the rest of their lives. This is a highly dubious assumption, yet the logical extension of conventional project design would seem to be that every peasant would be indebted to an agency of the state. Experience with institutions that offer both credit and deposit facilities, however, indicates that many more farmers are in a position to use deposit accounts—every year for the rest of their lives—than could ever seek or qualify for institutional credit. Although more rural people will benefit directly from improved savings facilities than from improved lending services, both are important in rural development strategies.

Much more attention ought to be given to the behavior of formal lenders and to how government policies affect their behavior. In turn, less attention should be given to how rural borrowers use their loans. Experience suggests they will generally use credit effectively when lenders deliver it effectively. Effectiveness in credit delivery requires businesslike behavior and proper pricing of financial services. In most cases it is the performance of government lending institutions rather than that of borrowers that is in greatest need of improvement. This is fortunate for planners and project designers because changing the framework of a development project or sector program can more effectively address the performance of lenders than that of farmers. This view is a positive one, reaffirming farmer rationality; its acceptance should reduce the frustrations that arise when using financial markets to promote rural development.

Performance of Rural Financial Intermediaries

Chapters in this volume on the kinds of organizations providing rural credit indicate that considerable emphasis has been given to finding the single institutional arrangement most capable of providing the best in rural financial services. Cooperatives, for example, have been promoted as the ideal form, especially for reaching the rural poor, and government-owned banks or agricultural credit agencies are also offered as a panacea.

A comprehensive reading of these chapters, however, suggests that different institutions have different strengths and shortcomings. Some are very awkward in dealing with small loans and small deposits, while others may display weaknesses as specialized lenders or in dealing with the risks of financial intermediation in rural areas. It is therefore not the form of financial institution but the process of financial intermediation that deserves more attention. Too little effort has been devoted to understanding why existing financial intermediaries of almost any form often fail to provide the services planners and project designers believe they should provide.

Financial intermediation transfers claims on resources from savers to borrowers. Several different types of institution could do this effectively if they have capable staff and if government policies allow them to realize sufficient revenue to cover their costs. This generalization applies to cooperatives, private banks, and government-owned credit agencies. Experience in many countries suggests that governments change their priorities from time to time, and these shifts can have a profound impact on institutions supplying rural loans and other financial services. Foreign assistance may also shift its emphasis. These uncertainties support the case for rural financial institutions capable of generating sufficient surplus to be self-sustaining. Indeed, strong institutions may be able to attract greater and higher quality assistance and support on their own terms than is available to intermediaries wholly dependent on the public purse or donor generosity.

Government policies and regulations greatly affect the performance of financial intermediaries. Intermediaries develop new techniques or services to get around regulations that adversely influence their costs and revenues. While these arrangements may be of private benefit to borrowers and lenders, they are often antidevelopmental because they increase the social costs of financial intermediation.

Several authors in this volume have kind words for informal lenders. Their viewpoint contrasts sharply with the horror stories about "evil" moneylenders. Some stories cite small loans made to poor people at interest rates that exceed 200 percent on an annual basis. Others tell of the distressed circumstances of a son paying off the informal debt of his father long after his father's death, or relate how moneylenders take away the land of farmers who are unable to repay their loans.

The small amount of research on informal lending that is available suggests that the malicious moneylender stereotype is based on unusual cases. Most informal lenders provide a valuable service that formal intermediaries cannot provide effectively. Otherwise, informal lenders would not remain in business; they cannot obtain state subsidies to help them survive, and they are found virtually everywhere, unlike formal institutions. Under many circumstances, informal lending will expand with the growth of economic activity in rural areas, not disappear. With prolonged and sustained development, however, structural changes may occur that make formal finance more accessible and attractive to rural people and reduce the market share of informal finance.

Government Policies and Financial Market Performance

In many low-income countries rural financial markets (RFMS) are highly fragmented, both geographically and institutionally. Fragmentation is seen in different levels of interest rates and borrowing costs for essentially the same types of loans and risk in different areas and even among lenders in the same area. RFMS are generally characterized by what H. Myint ["Dualism and the Internal Integration of the Underdeveloped Economies," *Banca Nazionale del Lavoro Quarterly Review*, vol. 23, no. 93, June 1970, pp. 128–56] calls financial dualism: formal lenders and their borrowers obtain funds on concessional terms, while lenders and borrowers in informal rural financial markets obtain funds on terms that are relatively unfavorable.

The differences between the conditions facing these sides of dualistic financial markets arise from the benefits the formal sector receives from government intervention in the form of preferences, monopolies, and other means of preferred access to resources, all of which are unavailable to the informal sector. Both dualistic and geographic fragmentation in rural financial markets tend to reflect fragmentation in the national economy.

Financial markets cannot make income and asset distributions more nearly equal when the structure of the economy is conducive to greater inequality. When rural financial markets are used as instruments of government policy in efforts to redistribute incomes and assets to the poor, they will not accomplish their intended task of redistribution effectively or function very well in other respects. Well-functioning rural financial markets, as envisaged here, contain intermediaries competing to provide loans to those capable of undertaking attractive investments, whether they be rich or poor.

Clearly, charging low interest rates on formal loans and paying even lower interest rates on savings deposits is the most harmful policy in rural financial markets. Interest rates below the opportunity cost of capital, and even below the rate of inflation, damage the fabric of financial markets and seriously limit the contribution these markets make to rural development.

Low interest rates have two important effects on lenders and borrowers. First, they inflate the demand for loans and increase the tightness with which lenders ration credit; the result is almost always to concentrate cheap loans in the hands of relatively few people. To cover costs, lenders tend to economize by concentrating the bulk of their rationed loans in the hands of large borrowers who have strong collateral, established relationships with the lender, and political influence. Small or new borrowers and those who have weak collateral are rationed out of credit markets under these conditions. The net result of this rationing process is increased concentration of incomes and ownership, and inefficient allocation of real resources.

The second major effect of low interest rates is on household savings, especially among low- and middle-income households. Low interest rates deny these households the alternative of holding their savings in financial form. They continue to hold their liquidity in low-return, nonfinancial forms or simply consume any surpluses that might otherwise be used for investment. Savers who keep their savings in financial form when rates of interest paid on savings are below the rate of inflation are taxed because the purchasing power of their savings falls. As a result, the ability of an economy to encourage financial savings is reduced and capital formation is retarded.

The inability of financial markets to attract savings has implications that extend beyond the household and influence the structure of development. Rural financial intermediaries that cannot offer attractive rates on deposits forgo an opportunity to mobilize funds that could be recycled as loans. Formal lenders without access to rural savings depend on government support and foreign assistance for funds, which are frequently available at lower, subsidized financial costs than the cost of servicing small savers. In a sense, these funds are cheap substitutes for savings deposit balances.

Reliance on government and external funds for lending, moreover, easily establishes patron-client relationships among borrowers, lenders, and suppliers of loanable funds. The results can include political intrusion into the market, corruption, and political intrigue. When financial markets recycle rural resources among rural people, however, such dependency is likely to be less pronounced. An actively competitive RFM creates multiple roles for small farmers and thus diffuses possibilities for dependent relationships. Saving account owners, for example, are normally also borrowers from time to time.

The way financial markets in rural areas are used for political patronage is particularly important where financial markets have a strong influence on changing the distribution of incomes and asset ownership. Income transfers through negative real rates of interest and loan defaults easily become part of a political patronage system. But relatively little attention has been paid to political intrusions into rural financial markets, despite their frequency and their consequences for income distribution.

What Role for Finance in Development?

Several chapters in this volume explain the contributions that effective financial intermediation makes to development. These may be summarized as the social benefits of voluntarism, resource mobilization, efficiency in resource allocation, better management of risk, and, to a very limited extent, social equity.

Voluntary savings create claims in the form of deposits, but if the claims come from government budgets or from the printing of money, the savings may be involuntary. Differences between voluntary and involuntary means of resource mobilization deserve more consideration because of their implications for the quality of development. Although value judgments regarding the merits of these alternatives are of course subjective, there is considerable evidence that the potential for voluntary savings mobilization, for example, has been insufficiently explored. It is too frequently rejected as a viable strategy on the basis of inadequate or misleading information.

Several authors point out that financial services are particularly useful, and may be critical, where there is significant economic growth. Because opportunities for growth do not occur uniformly throughout an economy, some households, firms, and regions have too few attractive investment or consumption alternatives to absorb the resources at their disposal. At the same time, there are other households, firms, or regions that have too few resources to be able to capitalize on the attractive investment and consumption opportunities available to them. Financial intermediation, if it is working properly, will transfer claims voluntarily provided by savers, who are the individuals, firms, and areas with underutilized resources, to borrowers, who are the individuals and firms and areas with underexploited opportunities. It will do this at relatively low cost. Borrowers, in turn, can use their claims to attract real resources. This process of moving real goods and services into economically fruitful uses and areas results in a more efficient overall allocation of resources, a larger output of goods and services, and higher returns to voluntary savers, lenders, and borrowers than would be possible without intermediation. It can also provide borrowers as well as savers more convenient ways to manage their risks.

Financial markets can also affect the distribution of income and asset ownership because borrowers may realize a net gain from the use of their loans by buying assets that yield a return they otherwise would not receive. At the same time, savers who make rewarding investments in financial claims are also gainers. In ill-functioning RFMs this distribution of gains among borrowers and savers becomes distorted. Borrowers, for example, gain in other ways, by receiving loans at negative real rates of interest or by defaulting on their loans. Savers who are unfortunate enough to receive negative real rates of interest on their saving deposits find that they lose a part of the purchasing power of their savings. The net result is to transfer income to those who borrow and away from those who save or who would otherwise save.

Such evidence as is available suggests that financial markets have the potential to contribute to both growth and social equity in economies where privilege is falling because of competition. This can be brought about when structural reforms outside financial markets spread economic opportunities more rapidly than stocks of wealth are redistributed, thus creating greater scope for financial intermediation. In such conditions the windfall gains to the rich from their superior access to credit on easy terms are diminished, and financial integration reduces the fragmentation that protects their privileged position. In this scenario the range of individuals and firms having access to formal credit is extended. Greater integration of the economy also increases the supply of financial capital to the informal sector, with the results that interest rates on informal loans are lower and competition among lenders is stronger.

This volume shows that the developmental role of rural financial markets is not realized by augmenting the supply of concessionally priced agricultural loans. If policy makers and project designers permit and encourage financial intermediaries to perform a broader role, they can improve income distribution, the efficiency of resource allocation, and the overall vitality of financial markets serving rural people. The specific measures required to improve the quality of rural financial markets in different economies will vary. But it appears that most efforts should contribute toward the integration of these markets, emphasize voluntary savings mobilization by formal financial institutions, and allow interest rates to be determined flexibly by market forces.

Index